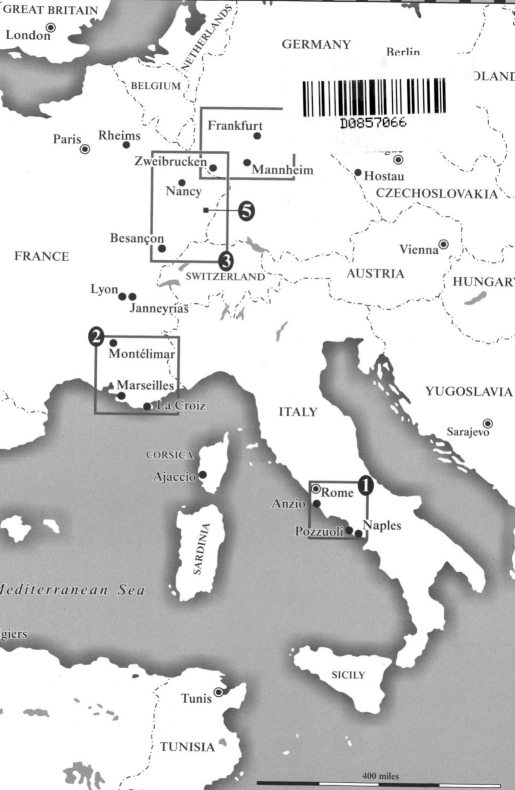

"A great story about a great soldier and leader. Phil Larimore was a Dick Winters from the *Band of Brothers*–type of frontline, small-unit combat leader, the kind who makes all the difference as to who wins or loses and who lives or dies in war. The storyline with the horses and the twists and turns of his love life and military career adds to the compelling narrative. *At First Light* has the makings of a great movie or Ken Burns miniseries. My bet is that Phil's son and the book author, Walt Larimore, will be besieged by offers."

—**Col. Alexander P. Shine, U.S. Army, Infantry (Ret.), Masters in U.S. History from Harvard, Professor of Military Science and National Security Strategy at the Army War College**

"Intelligently written and descriptively rich, *At First Light* is tailor-made for anyone who cherishes powerful World War II stories."

—**Marcus Brotherton, *New York Times* bestselling author of *We Who Are Alive and Remain* and *Blaze of Light***

"Call my agent! *At First Light* needs to be greenlighted for a multi-episodic film series today. I loved reading about Philip Larimore's personal journey before, during, and after World War II. While being a compelling and enjoyable story, the book doesn't hold back on the gruesome realities of war and left me grateful for the young soldiers who sacrificed their lives for our freedom."

—**Gerry Gacek, singer/songwriter and screenwriter**

"Fortitude and sacrifice—that's the story of Phil Larimore. His son, Walt Larimore, has put together a leadership narrative played out by the youngest Army officer in World War II. All Americans need to read this book so they can understand that 'freedom is not free' and was won on countless battlefields throughout our history. *At First Light* will instill in you a commitment to continue the battle by honoring the sacrifices of this great soldier."

—**Lt. General Bruce Fister, U.S. Air Force (Ret.) three-star general, and author of *Growing and Building: Faith, Prayer, and Leadership***

"As an individual who has committed his life to the training and education of our next generation, *At First Light* was a powerful and meaningful reminder of the service and sacrifice that have been made by so few, to enable the freedoms we all enjoy today in this great nation. While reading the pages, I reflected on Phil Larimore's courage in the face of intense combat and was humbled by his willingness to make the ultimate sacrifice."

—**Mark D. Bieger, Vice President of Strategy, Louisiana State University**

"Every generation of warriors stands on the shoulders of those who came before them. Reading about Phil Larimore fills you with an unspeakable sense of admiration for this member of the greatest generation. *At First Light* is much more than a story of combat; it's a story of a young man who achieves greatness in unexpected ways."

—**Col. Lee Van Arsdale, U.S. Army (Ret.), former Special Forces Delta Squadron Commander who led the "Black Hawk Down" Battle of Mogadishu, Somalia in 1993**

"It would be so easy for *At First Light*—a tale with so much true horror and heartbreak—to be a heavy, depressing experience, and to leave your reader saddened. What Walt Larimore has managed to achieve instead is a story that doesn't shy away from the true facts of war but manages to deliver them in such a way that the result is ultimately hopeful, uplifting, and serves as a reminder that soldiers are ultimately people, not numbers. I found myself hurrying onward through the pages whenever Phil was injured, sighing deeply at his setbacks, and tearing up with joy at the end."

—**Mal Windsor, copyeditor of *At First Light***

"A captivating and compelling story of a true American hero. As the son of a World War II veteran, *At First Light* made me reflect on the great dedication and sacrifice embodied in Phil Larimore, who fought to protect everything that is great about America. His courage and leadership in the face of intense combat shows what is deep in the heart of every soldier. Thanks, Walt Larimore, for sharing your amazing father with us!"

—**Lt. General R.L. VanAntwerp, U.S. Army (Ret.) three-star general and former Chief of the U.S. Army Corps of Engineers**

"*At First Light* is an astonishing story. As a former infantry officer, I appreciate the grit, ingenuity, and tenacity of the frontline U.S. Army Lieutenants in World War II. Phil Larimore, as an eighteen-year-old platoon leader and company commander on the front lines, demonstrated remarkable leadership while facing horrifying odds of his own mortality and that of his soldiers. But Phil's story doesn't end there, as what he accomplished after the war is even more compelling. *At First Light* is a superb story of courage, honor, and sacrifice."

—**Lt. Gen. Robert L. Caslen, U.S. Army (Ret.) three-star general, formerly the 29th President of the University of South Carolina and the 59th Superintendent of West Point**

"All wars are full of tragedies, and World War II was no exception. The list of those maimed and killed, and whose lives were interrupted through no fault of their own, was in the millions. Such a magnitude of despair can easily overshadow the good in humans. Phil Larimore made the world a better place, and his son Walt has made World War II literature better as well with his labor of love, *At First Light*."

—**Col. French L. MacLean, U.S. Army (Ret.) and author of *Custer's Best* and *The Fifth Field***

"My husband Troy and I survived the Route 91 mass shooting in Las Vegas in 2017, even though Troy took a bullet to the leg. We were shot at for ten minutes. Phil Larimore was shot at for nearly 400 days. What an incredible story!"

—**Shannon Zeeman, co-author of *Active Shooter: How to Survive the Most Important Four Minutes of Your Life***

"*At First Light* features all the elements of a Hollywood blockbuster. But unlike most books turned into films, *At First Light* isn't based on a fictional character. This is the true-life account of an indomitable Army officer, supported by years of meticulous research, creating an unforgettable masterpiece of military history."

—**Dan Brownell, Marine Corps Infantry and Artillery, 2nd Marine Division, 1981–1985**

"Outstanding personal history of an infantry officer during the Second World War. The book covers the experiences of Phil Larimore from Anzio, to the invasion of southern France, to the invasion of southern Germany. The personal accounts and experiences make this book a valuable addition to military history libraries."

—**Col. Raymond Millen, PhD, U.S. Army (Ret.), professor of Security Sector Reform at the Peacekeeping and Stability Operations Institute, U.S. Army War College**

"As the author of a book on Frances Slanger, the first nurse to die after the landings at Normandy, I was thrilled to read how she inspired Lieutenant Phil Larimore while he was recuperating from his wounds in a French hospital. Better yet, I was deeply moved by the way Walt Larimore and Mike Yorkey crafted Phil Larimore's unbelievable stories into a gripping five-star read!"

—**Bob Welch, award-winning journalist and author of *American Nightingale: The Story of Frances Slanger, Forgotten Heroine of Normandy***

"*At First Light* returned me to my time as a 2nd lieutenant in the 15th Infantry Regiment, 3rd Infantry Division. It made me feel like I was walking side-by-side with Phil Larimore and is an excellent firsthand account of the trials and tribulations of frontline officers in combat."

—Lt. Col. Patrick A. Schado, U.S. Army, Aviation/Infantry (Ret.)

"*At First Light* is not a 'horse story,' but I loved the way horses and horsemanship played starring roles in this fascinating story about a World War II hero."

—Cyndy Feasel, author of *After the Cheering Stops: An NFL Wife's Story of Concussions, Loss, and the Faith That Saw Her Through*

"Just when you think you've read every World War II story there is, along comes 2nd Lieutenant Phil Larimore, a young man—a teenager, actually—from Memphis who participates in one heroic action after another in some of the deadliest fighting in the war."

—SFC Ryan Hendrickson, U.S. Army (Ret.), author of *Tip of the Spear: The Incredible Story of an Injured Green Beret's Return to Battle*

"As someone who's undergone plenty of hardship, I identified with Phil Larimore's story of deprivation and trials. He deserves to be called a hero."

—Elishaba Doerksen, author of *Out of the Wilderness*

"As a veteran of Southeast Asia and a World War II buff, I was excited to read *At First Light*. What I wasn't expecting was the true story that unfolded before me—and what a story it is! *At First Light* is about the life of heavily decorated Philip Larimore Jr., from childhood to commanding men in battle during some of World War II's biggest battles. The story follows him from the day he landed in Naples, Italy, to the south of France, and on to Germany. I'm not sure why we have never heard about this true American hero before, but I won't forget him now."

—Ross Mitchell, U.S. Air Force sergeant (1972–1976)

"The recreation of epic battles that Lieutenant Phil Larimore found himself in—including the hand-to-hand combat—kept me firmly gripped. This is a real war story."

—Casey Diaz, author of *The Shot Caller: A Latino Gangbanger's Miraculous Escape from a Life of Violence to a New Life in Christ*

"Philip Larimore Jr. was born just before the Great Depression. His parents taught him to be independent, hard-working, and self-sufficient. On his trips to a family farm, he learned to swim, shoot, and ride and care for horses. These lessons formed who Larimore was as a soldier and human being, leading to his extraordinary military accomplishments during World War II. Philip Larimore's story is similar to Audie Murphy's as depicted in the movie *To Hell and Back*. Both illustrate how small-unit leadership can make the difference in winning wars. The intertwining of the stories of Larimore's military career, love life, and Lipizzaner horses makes for a great read."

—Maj. Thomas A. Devaney, U.S.M.C. Heavy Helicopter Squadron, 1971–1983

"This is a heckuva story about an incredible hero that reads like a movie. I felt like I was sitting across a table at Starbucks listening to Walt Larimore telling his father's story. As a professional editor, I initially thought *At First Light* should have ended when the wounded hero came home. Boy, was I ever wrong! The stunning last section was a great way to end the book and left me with a lump in my throat."

—Lois Johnson Rew, author of *Editing for Writers*

"In these dark days, we need a hero and Phil Larimore's story certainly provides one. His dedication to those around him while maintaining a steadfast devotion to duty makes him a role model for us all. *At First Light* is a story you enter instead of read. I have two sons who served in Operation Desert Storm and a grandson who is career Army and served in Afghanistan. All of whom will get a copy of *At First Light*."

—**Del Weightman, U.S. Air Force Captain (Ret.) and B-52 Electronics Warfare Officer**

"This fresh story from World War II will appeal to readers everywhere. I was incredibly inspired by Phil Larimore, with his selflessness, struggles, and triumphs, from the very first page. Meticulously researched, *At First Light* is an irresistible, compelling read."

—**Col. Christopher Scharf, U.S. Marine Corps (Ret.), former UH-1N/AH-1W pilot and veteran of operations in Iraq**

"As the author of fifteen novels set in World War II, I'm always drawn to a great story from a fascinating time in history. *At First Light* does not disappoint. The pages turned quickly in this compelling story about a brave man, Philip Larimore."

—**Tricia Goyer, author of *Dawn of a Thousand Nights* and *Songbird Under a German Moon***

at
FIRST
LIGHT

at FIRST LIGHT

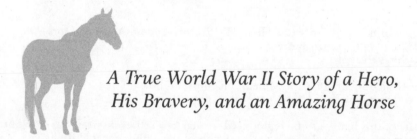

A True World War II Story of a Hero,
His Bravery, and an Amazing Horse

WALT LARIMORE
and Mike Yorkey

A KNOX PRESS BOOK
An Imprint of Permuted Press
ISBN: 978-1-64293-959-0
ISBN (eBook): 978-1-64293-960-6

At First Light:
A True World War II Story of a Hero, His Bravery, and an Amazing Horse
© 2022 by Walter L. Larimore
All Rights Reserved

Cover Design by Emily Muse Morelli, bluemusestudio.com
Interior Design by Yoni Limor, yonilimor.com

Permuted Press, LLC
New York • Nashville
permutedpress.com

Published in the United States of America
2 3 4 5 6 7 8 9 10

The veterans from World War II were so appreciative of us
being there, especially the 30th Infantry veterans.

A few actually cried when they found out
we were portraying them.

I asked an elderly veteran, *"Are you alright?"*

His response was, *"I'm crying because I thought
myself and all the guys I knew along with the regiment
had been forgotten about. It makes me happy to know
I haven't been forgotten."*

He just kind of smiled after that. So did I.

**—Sgt. James Dunigan, III, Able Co.
U.S. 30th Infantry Regiment
3rd Infantry Division (Reenacted)**[1]

To the memory of Philip Bonham Larimore, Jr. and the American soldiers who fought in World War II's "forgotten" southern European front

TABLE OF CONTENTS

PART I:
PREPARING FOR WAR

PART II:
THE ITALIAN CAMPAIGN

PART III:
THE FRENCH CAMPAIGN

PART IV:
THE GERMAN CAMPAIGN

PART V:
AFTERMATH

A NOTE TO THE READER

I've written forty books over the years, and until the publication of *At First Light*, my books almost never included any potentially offensive words, especially the four-letter variety. With this book about my father, Philip B. Larimore, Jr., however, I wanted to re-create as realistic a story as possible, quoting him and his fellow soldiers as accurately as possible.

Thus, *At First Light* contains some profanity, which is used judiciously and in the right context. If you have an aversion to swearing and profanity or believe such language is not suitable, then this book might not be for you. However, there is no sexualized content or descriptions of sexuality in *At First Light*.

A note of clarity: whenever the terms "30th" or "30th Infantry" are used, I'm referring to the 30th Infantry Regiment and not the 30th Infantry Division, which was also called the "Old Hickory Division." Please note that any complete dates with the month, day, and year are as accurate as we can determine and correlate to the events described in this book. In the interest of telling as detailed and full account as possible, scenes and dialogue have been enriched based on reasonable assumptions given time, place, and circumstances—but always within the context of the moment.

—**Walt Larimore**

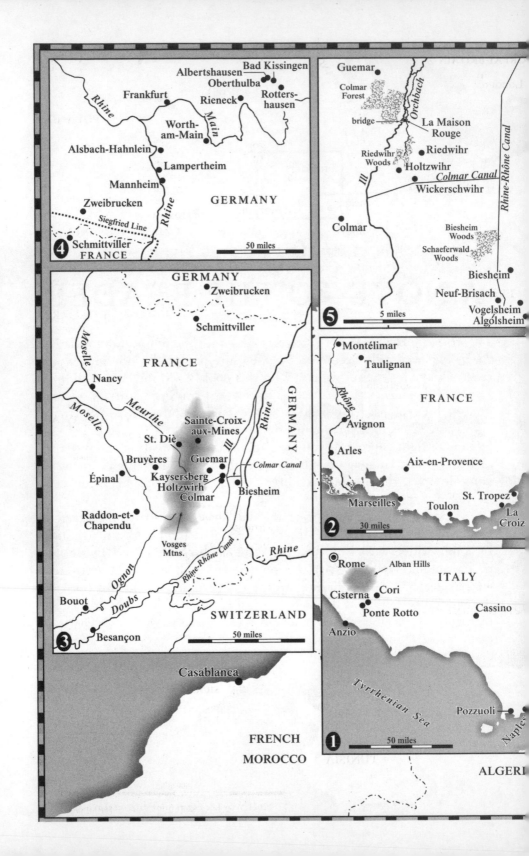

Map 4

Albertshausen
Bad Kissingen
Oberthulba
Frankfurt
Rieneck
Rotters-
hausen
Rhine
Main
Worth-
am-Main
Alsbach-Hahnlein
Lampertheim
Mannheim
GERMANY
Zweibrucken
Rhine
Siegfried Line
Schmittviller
FRANCE
50 miles

Map 5

Guemar
Colmar
Forest
Orchbach
bridge
La Maison
Rouge
Ill
Riedwihr
Woods
Riedwihr
Holtzwihr
Colmar Canal
Wickerschwihr
Rhine-Rhône Canal
Colmar
Biesheim
Woods
Schaeferwald
Woods
Biesheim
Neuf-Brisach
Vogelsheim
Algolsheim
5 miles

Map 3

GERMANY
Zweibrucken
Schmittviller
Moselle
FRANCE
Nancy
Meurthe
Moselle
Sainte-Croix-
aux-Mines
St. Diè
Rhine
Ill
GERMANY
Bruyères
Guemar
Colmar Canal
Épinal
Kaysersberg
Holtzwirh
Colmar
Biesheim
Raddon-et-
Chapendu
Vosges
Mtns.
Rhine-Rhône Canal
Rhine
Ognon
Bouot
Doubs
SWITZERLAND
Besançon
50 miles

Map 2

Montélimar
Taulignan
Rhône
FRANCE
Avignon
Arles
Aix-en-Provence
Marseilles
Toulon
St. Tropez
La
Croix
30 miles

Map 1

Rome
Alban Hills
ITALY
Cisterna
Cori
Ponte Rotto
Cassino
Anzio
Tyrrhenian Sea
Pozzuoli
Naples
50 miles

Casablanca

FRENCH
MOROCCO

ALGERI

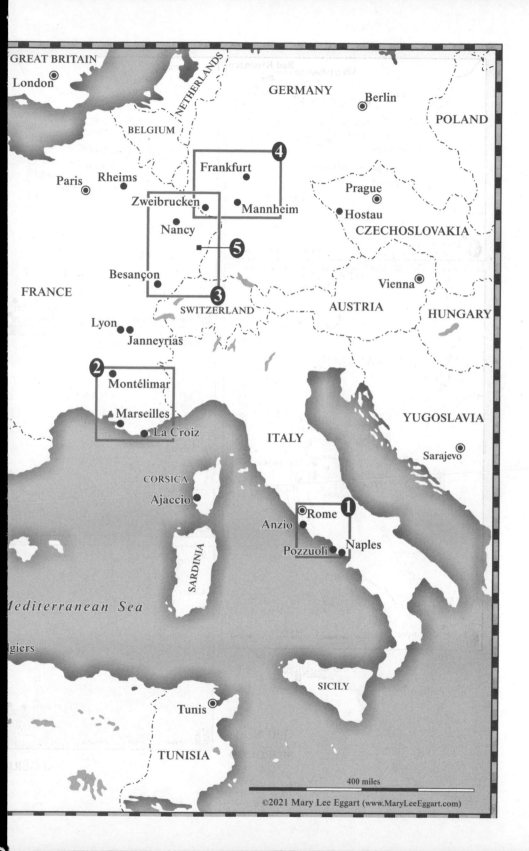

PROLOGUE

"I do feel strongly that the Infantry arm does not receive either the respect or the treatment to which its importance and its exploits entitle it. This may possibly be understandable, though misguided, in peace; it is intolerable in war. So, let us always write Infantry with a capital 'I' and think of them with the deep admiration they deserve."

—British Field Marshal Archibald Wavell, who lived from 1883–1950[2]

As he crept forward inside a cold, dark forest, Lieutenant Philip B. Larimore, Jr. and his men darted from tree to tree, stooping low, fingers poised on their M1 Garand rifles[i] while using their other hands to signal to one another.[3]

Larimore found the unexpected lull unnerving as he peeked around a massive tree trunk for enemy movement. After surviving almost fourteen months of intense combat, the company commander worried continuously that "one lead pill"[4] could explode inside his body at any second and take his life, so close to the end of the war.

With the Russians bearing down on Berlin and the Allies steadily advancing across Germany, the Yank soldiers had heard the scuttlebutt that the German Army could surrender any day. Larimore, filled with cautious optimism, was no longer saying, "If I live," but rather, frequently thinking of home and plans for the future.

---

i   The M1 Garand was a .30-06 caliber semiautomatic rifle that was the standard U.S. service rifle for frontline enlisted men during World War II. The rifle was named after its Canadian-American designer, John Garand, and was the first standard-issue semiautomatic military rifle. General George S. Patton called it "the greatest battle implement ever devised."

But Larimore also heard the rumors that Germany's dictator, Adolf Hitler, had ordered fanatical "last man" stands to give the German forces time to mount final defenses in larger cities so that the High Command could retreat into Austria. The result was stiff resistance from desperate German soldiers, which was turning into a significant military problem.

The latest snag was a firefight in a heavily wooded forest bordering the German village of Rottershausen on this chilly spring evening of April 8, 1945. German snipers nestled in towering firs were picking off his men one at a time. Machine gun nests hidden behind a camouflage of evergreen boughs were keeping the GIs pinned down. Simultaneously, well-disguised artillery was firing projectiles into the canopy of hundred-foot-tall evergreens, timed to burst and rain splintered wood and white-hot shrapnel onto the soldiers below.

Larimore was keenly aware that death lurked in every direction.

Even though he was only twenty years old, Larimore was considered an "old man" on the battlefield because he'd been part of the 30th Infantry Regiment since arriving on the Anzio beachhead in Italy in February 1944, part of the 3rd Infantry Division.

After liberating Rome, taking part in an amphibious landing on southern France's famed Côte d'Azur beaches, fighting his way through France's Provence region into the Vosges Mountains, and now making a final push across Germany, Larimore was well aware that he had been waging war in an active combat zone for over 400 days.

At Officer Candidate School at Fort Benning, Georgia, he'd learned that the typical frontline infantryman typically couldn't take much more than 200 to 240 days of combat before mentally falling apart. He wondered if he was fighting on borrowed time.

Suddenly, the forest ahead erupted in gunfire, and his radioman's SCR-300 backpack walkie-talkie[ii] sizzled with distress. The voice of one of his sergeants came through.

"Love 1[iii], this is point squad alpha."

A squad leader was calling him.

"We've been ambushed in a glade!" the sergeant yelled. "There are nine of us and probably a 150 Krauts[iv] around us. The rest of the platoon behind us is pinned down. We have four wounded. We're low on ammo. We're in a clearing. Help needed now, sir!"

---

ii   The SCR-300, a battery-powered, backpack-mounted radio transceiver, was primarily used by combat troops as they moved forward, which is how the term "walkie-talkie" came into use.
iii "Six" was reserved as the call sign of the unit (platoon, company, battalion) commander. The other subunits used one through five and when they called the company commander if the radio operator answered, he would answer "Love Six;" however, if the unit commander was reached directly, he would say "Love Six Actual."
iv   "Krauts" was a derogatory term for Germans and German soldiers during World War II.

German potato masher grenades[v] joined the cacophony, answered by American grenades and machine gun fire. Projecting a calmness he didn't feel, Larimore called orders to each of his platoons and radioed back to armor. "I need a medium can now!" he yelled into the radio handset, requesting a Sherman tank.

Then he spread a field map on the ground and studied it with his Executive Officer (XO), Lieutenant Abraham Fitterman, and a field artillery Forward Observer (FO)[vi] who'd just come up to the front.

"Our trapped squad must be here." Larimore pointed to the northwest edge of the only nearby clearing. Turning to the FO, he said, "I need fire massed on the other side of the clearing."

He ran his finger along what appeared to be a forest lane on the map. "Abe, you take over the CP[vii] staff. When the first tank gets here, I'll take it to the clearing to get to our guys."

Within a matter of seconds, all three men heard rumbling. Larimore looked up and was delighted to see three Sherman tanks advancing in their direction instead of one.

"Abe, I'm hopping a ride on the lead can." Larimore's experience had taught him that when officers or NCOs[viii] didn't accompany the tanks, they frequently got lost, which often resulted in more guys dying.

Before his XO could object, Larimore and his radioman leaped onto the back of the vehicle and squatted behind the massive tank's turret. The radioman found the intercom handset that would allow him communication with the tank commander inside. As they approached the clearing, green tracer rounds[ix] from enemy machine guns laced the air from directly ahead.

"Our guys are fifty yards ahead! Friendly platoons are coming up from behind on our left and right!" Larimore called to the tank commander. Speaking into the radio, he said, "Second Platoon, send up all three of your squads, pronto! One behind each can as we move up!"

---

v   The *Stielhandgranate* (German for "stick hand grenade") was widely used by the German armed forces, or Wehrmacht, during World War II. The baton-like hand grenades were called "potato mashers" by Allied soldiers because they resembled a kitchen tool used to mash potatoes.

vi   An XO or executive officer was the second-in-command, reporting to the commanding officer, and typically responsible for the management of day-to-day activities, freeing the commander to concentrate on strategy and planning the unit's next move. An FO or forward observer was an artilleryman embedded on the frontline as a liaison observer who directed the artillery fire via phone line or radio communication.

vii   CP stands for Command Post.

viii An NCO or non-commissioned officer is a military officer who usually obtains his position by promotion through the enlisted ranks. Non-officers, which includes most or all enlisted personnel, are of lower rank than any officer.

ix   Tracer ammunition (tracers) are projectiles built with a small pyrotechnic charge in their base, which burns brightly, allowing its trajectory to be visible to the naked eye, day or night. Tracers allow the shooter to visually trace the flight path and make ballistic corrections without having to see an impact or even use the weapon's sight. American and German tracers were generally different colors: red for the U.S. and green for Germany.

His men sprinted from the forest to the shelter of the tanks. "Shermans, move into the clearing!" Larimore commanded as the two trailing tanks fanned out along the clearing's western edge, one on his left flank and the other to his right.

Enemy fire poured in, churning up dirt all around them. Larimore quickly identified at least three machine gun nests on the other side of the clearing. He ducked as the slugs of multiple snipers came from at least two directions, missing him by inches. Larimore ordered the gunners inside the tanks to use their 76-mm cannons and .30-caliber machine guns to lay down suppressing fire as he manned the turret-mounted .50-caliber Browning heavy machine gun, firing and taking fire across the clearing. Spotting his besieged squad, he shouted into the radio, "I see our guys! Twenty yards ahead. Let's get 'em outta here!"

The men behind the tank's protection now emerged, running up and evacuating the wounded. Enemy fire erupted again, and Larimore fired his remaining ammunition, killing several Germans and drawing more hostile fire as his patrols used the diversion to withdraw. His machine gun now empty, Larimore jumped off the back of the tank to direct his men as another hail of German bullets came in his direction. Suddenly the back of his head took a jolt as a sniper's bullet blew the helmet off his head and knocked him off the tank.

He landed on his butt, stunned and seeing stars.

His radioman jumped off and carefully ran his fingers through Larimore's hair. "Just nicked your scalp, Lieutenant, but it's bleeding like hell." He reached into his overcoat and pulled out a gauze bandage, tearing the wrapper off to press against it against the wound and carefully tying off the cloth as bullets ricocheted off the tank.

"You okay, sir?" the radioman asked.

Larimore refocused his eyes as he became more alert. "Yeah," he said. "Just a scratch."

"It's more than that, sir, but we gotta get out of this hellhole!" the radioman exclaimed.

As Larimore and the radioman moved back between the tanks and retreating men, laying down suppressing fire, enemy fire from the far side of the clearing intensified, coming from three directions. The other men started running as fast as they could for the protection of the trees. Larimore was beside the last tank backing out of the clearing, rapidly firing his M1 Garand as bullets shredded the earth around him.

Suddenly, an excruciating jolt of searing agony shot up his right leg. He hit the ground, groaning. Despite unbearable pain, Larimore managed to roll himself away from the tank's treads and into a shallow ditch.

From the safety of cover, he peeked over the edge. The three Sherman tanks were rapidly pulling away from him, and scores of Germans, firing as fast as they could while screaming at the top of their lungs, were giving chase. When the Krauts were only twenty to thirty yards from him and closing fast, Larimore lowered his head and played dead. Within seconds, the enemy soldiers leaped over the ditch and kept running.

Not daring to move, Larimore thought, *They didn't see me. Maybe I'll make it.*

The violent blasts of the raging battle around him strangely began to wane. His vision dimmed. Even the overwhelming discomfort began to melt away.

Larimore understood what was happening: he was bleeding out, and he didn't have the strength to pull off his belt and apply a tourniquet. Soon the world around him was silent, and his body completely numb.

So, this is what it feels like to die. Not as bad as I imagined.

Tired beyond measure, he closed his eyes.

He felt his breathing slow. Maybe, just maybe, his long, grueling war was finally over.

PART I:
PREPARING FOR WAR

"Build me a son whose heart will be clear, whose goal will be high; a son who will master himself before he seeks to master other men; one who will reach into the future, yet never forget the past. And after all these things are his, add, I pray, enough of a sense of humor so that he may always be serious yet never take himself too seriously."

—General Douglas MacArthur, five-star general, and Supreme Commander for the Allied Powers at the end of World War II [5]

1

THE LITTLE STINK

"In your pursuit of your passions, always be young."

—Tom Brokaw, author of *The Greatest Generation*[6]

Philip Bonham Larimore, Jr., born January 4, 1925, was about two weeks old when the first letter about his birth arrived at his parents' home at 565 South Holmes Street in Memphis, Tennessee. The note from his mother's childhood friend, who lived deep in the backwoods hill country of north Arkansas, said:[7]

> *Dearest Ethyl and Philip,*
>
> *There is nothing that brings the happiness and joy of a little babe. You can never realize just what they mean to you until you keep them awhile and feel your very life bound up in them. I wish I could see the little rascal. Of course, he had to be a Jr. It is almost always that way with the first one. Kiss that little stink for me.*
>
> *Ever fondly,*
> *Alta*[8]

After little Philip began walking and talking precociously early, he never slowed down and quickly became the prophesied little stink. His tendency toward delinquency happened because he was a latchkey child: his father was a Pullman conductor gone for days at a time, and his mother was a legal secretary.[i] A succession of Negro nannies tried to keep him in rein but to no avail. Even two years at Miss Lee's School of Childhood did not tame him.

During the annual Chi Omega May Festival for Children pageant, four-year-old Philip joined the other pupils of Miss Lee's for the *Alice in Wonderland* segment. He was given the part of a bumblebee, along with one of his best friends, Luke McLaurine. Unfortunately, Philip was too hyperactive to remain in the flower he and Luke were assigned to. Master McLaurine screamed at Philip to return to their blossom, which did nothing to affect Philip's improvised role as a young bee freely buzzing around the stage. The audience chuckled as his mother sat mortified.

One year later, Philip was no more successful as an elf in *Hallowe'en* when he couldn't resist the temptation to trip a witch running across the stage on her broomstick. The young girl picked herself up and then began beating Philip with her broom as they ran off the stage to the amusement and laughter of parents in the audience.

Seeking to instill some values into her child, Ethyl tried religious education, but Philip couldn't sit still during the services or children's Sunday school at St. Luke's United Methodist Church. He did somewhat better at Vacation Bible School, but he was still considered a "rascal" by his teachers. His mother tried evening prayers and reading Christian storybooks, as well as a book of her grandfather's sermons, *The Story of a Happy Life*, but the lessons failed to stick.

On trips to the family farms of relatives, the youngster found great joy in hunting, fishing, and most of all, caring for and riding horses. His father taught him how to shoot guns, and by his sixth birthday, Philip could knock kernels of corn off a fence post with a .22-caliber rifle at twenty-five yards while standing, kneeling, or lying prone. His other great skill was getting a running start and mounting a horse and riding bareback.

Because his father was a conductor, the boy could ride the Cotton Belt train to Pine Bluff for free, and did so every weekend so that he could pal around with cousins and friends while hunting, camping, and taking long rides in the woods. Too bad he didn't cotton as well to schoolwork.

---

i   Philip Larimore Sr. was a sergeant in a machine gun company during World War I. After returning from the war, he took a job with the Illinois Central Railroad. He met Sara Ethyl McClanahan in Little Rock, Arkansas, and after a whirlwind romance, they married in 1922. He was twenty-five, and she was twenty-eight. Philip was soon promoted to Pullman conductor on the *Panama Limited*, a first-class-only train, and the *City of New Orleans*. The trains traveled from Memphis to New Orleans or Chicago and back. As a result, the couple moved to Memphis, where Ethyl, who could type upwards of ninety words a minute flawlessly, took a job as the executive assistant for Walter P. Armstrong, the senior partner of an influential Memphis law firm. Having only one sibling each, the couple desired to have as many children as possible, but Philip Larimore Jr. was their first and only child.

Following his first six-week grading period at his local public school, the first-grader received "unsatisfactory" marks in all his subjects. After significant and painful discipline, as well as parental threats that he would never return to his relatives' farms in northeast Arkansas or ever ride a horse again, Philip buckled down. He improved his marks to "acceptable" in all disciplines—both academic and behavioral. Throughout his elementary school years, his mother wondered if academic accomplishment prompted his promotion to the next grade, or whether his teachers were just anxious to see him move on.

On Saturdays, when his father was out of town on train trips or his mother was involved in trial preparation, he was forced to attend Miss Lee's or the Free Art School. He loathed both and did not succeed at either. He often played hooky to spend time at a nearby stable where he could hang around the massive workhorses that pulled carriages or trolleys throughout the city. It was there Philip learned the rudiments of caring for these gigantic yet gentle creatures. He found out that he could innately communicate with them, so much so that one of the grooms told his mother that her son was a natural when it came to horses.

On his ninth birthday, his mother hosted a "duck" birthday party at the Peabody Hotel,[ii] known for the Mallard ducks that spent their nights in a "rooftop palace" and then marched down a red carpet from the main elevator to a marble fountain in the hotel lobby each morning. After enjoying the day frolicking in the fountain, the ducks would march out in the evening. Both marches were accompanied by a recorded version of John Philip Sousa's "King Cotton March," and their "rooftop palace" was an elaborately decorated doghouse.

Philip and his friends were overjoyed to see and play with the Peabody ducks on his birthday. The boys all laughed when, on a dare, Philip sat down on the floor and began calling the ducks. Before long, the drake and his four ladies were camped on Philip's lap and between his legs.

By fifth grade, he earned the highest marks in physical education and geography, so his mother relented to her son's pleas to take him out of Miss Lee's and the Art School and let him spend his Saturdays and Sunday afternoons under the capable supervision of the stable hands.

Philip also became involved with Scouting and joined the local Boy Scout troop, where he found immediate success in Troop 40 of the Chickasaw Council in Memphis and received his Tenderfoot badge in the sixth grade. A Scout Master gave him a copy of Horace Kephart's 1906 masterpiece, *The*

ii   The Peabody is probably the grandest, most historic hotel in downtown Memphis, dating back to 1869 when the original Peabody Hotel opened. The resplendent hotel became the social and business hub of Memphis, building its legacy as the "South's Grand Hotel." During the Depression in 1933, ducks were placed in the hotel's lobby fountain, setting in motion a tradition that continues today with the March of the Peabody Ducks.

Book of Camping and Woodcraft: A Guidebook for Those Who Travel in the Wilderness, which he devoured. The lessons he learned about how to read a map and use a compass were put to good use at Scout camps, where Philip traversed the wildest swamps and the most desolate canyons.

Throughout his adolescent years, wearing camouflage, pathfinding, stalking and trapping game, and identifying every sort of edible plant all became second nature to him. He could dress wild game, catch fish, cook over campfires in the worst weather, and create comfortable camp bedding while setting up a safe camp in any wilderness environment (known as bivouacking). He learned first aid skills and imagined becoming a physician for wilderness expeditions.

His greatest love, though, was being around and riding horses. As a young equestrian, his skills grew. During his summers and holiday breaks, he rode the horses of friends and family, winning various competitions across western Tennessee and northern Arkansas. Rows of blue, red, yellow, and white ribbons covered the movie posters in his bedroom. His equestrian trophies filled several shelves.

Philip often took a trolley to attend horse shows at the Mid-South Fairgrounds a few miles from his home. Other times, he snuck out after bedtime to visit nearby stables. He could not seem to keep away from horses—nor they from him.

ᕦᕤ

A wise trainer taught Philip the three most important virtues he needed when around a horse: patience, observation, and humility.

Even the hot-blooded and high-strung Thoroughbreds acted calm around him, and Philip developed an uncanny way to speak to them with finger and hand commands or with an almost inaudible whisper and very low-pitched squeaking sounds. He came to believe the adage that a good rider can hear his horse speak, but a great rider can hear his horse whisper.

"He's incredible with horses," one of the grooms told his mom. "He can speak to them *and* hear them."

"How does he do it?" his mother asked. "What's his trick?"

"There's no magic. No mysticism. He's curious about them. He seems to recognize that they are his kin. He gives them gentle love and genuine respect. They pick up on it pretty quick."

The young boy spent his hard-earned yet meager allowance on every Western movie that played downtown. One of the posters in his bedroom pictured the movie cowboy, Tom Mix, and his trusty steed, Tony, the first horse to bear the name "The Wonder Horse."

Phil was mesmerized by reading books about the Wild West. He would sit on the front porch for hours reading Zane Grey novels and imagining himself as the hero. He'd look up when the freight trains passed by, their beckoning whistles sounding like summoning sirens. The boy would break out in goose bumps, knowing for sure he was being called to some mysterious land, to some great battle—on his favorite horse, of course.

During the first light of each new day, he would imagine the adventures he would experience and the stallion that might take him there.

Philip Larimore Jr. had no idea that many of these dreams would come true.

2

THE BIG MUDDY

"The spirit is there in every boy; it has to be discovered
and brought to light."

**—Robert Baden-Powell, 19ᵗʰ century
British Army officer and founder of the
worldwide Scouting movement[9]**

Since his earliest days, Philip had been an excellent swimmer. During
the summer of 1936 when he was eleven years old, he took a junior
lifeguard course with his pals, Luke McLaurine and Billy O'Bannon, at
Camp Currier, a 300-acre Boy Scout camp located just south of Memphis
near Eudora, Mississippi.[10]

Late that summer, they convinced their moms to allow them to swim the
Mississippi River as part of an annual race sponsored by the Memphis Chicks
semi-professional baseball team. Their competitors, all of them teenage boys,
boarded a rented paddle steamer and were taken about fifteen miles upriver.

Once at the starting point, the boat turned sideways. On the steam whistle
signal, all the boys leaped off the top deck of the paddle steamer and into the
river. The current moved steadily at ten miles an hour, and the smooth water
was the color of milk chocolate; thus, the river's nickname, "The Big Muddy."

While the older boys swam for a trophy, the younger boys just paddled
down the river accompanied by a small armada of sixty motorboats, each

equipped with a pile of swim vests in case anyone encountered trouble. When Philip, Luke, and Billy successfully swam to the pull-out on the southern point of Mud Island, a peninsula on the east side of the river that connected to downtown Memphis, they ran out of the water screaming in joy, hugging and swatting each other's backs, and feeling exceptionally manly and heroic.

This only emboldened them the following year when, on an unusually warm, seventy-six-degree day in March, Philip and Billy decided to swim *across* the mighty Mississippi, unaware that the fast-moving river was carrying the largest volume of water since the historic flood of 1927. The ordinarily tranquil waterway, now the color of intensely dark chocolate, was a frothing, pulsating monster that roiled and rampaged downstream, throbbing with the unrestrained power of one million gallons of water per second rushing south. The newspapers further downstream were calling it the "Great Flood of '37."[i]

After placing towels and their clothes into small waterproof backpacks, the boys dove into the raging current just south of where the Loosahatchie River drained into the Mississippi River, about four miles north of the Mississippi River bridge crossing from Memphis to Arkansas. They stroked across a three-quarter-mile section of the bone-chilling, raging torrent, dodging trees and barrel-sized litter to the large and mostly wooded Loosahatchie sandbar near the west bank.

Philip thought they were far enough upriver that their swim would put them safely on the sandbar, but the current swept them downstream three miles so fast that they were barely able to make it to shore in a small bay on the southern section of the sandbar. Although exhausted and shivering from their ordeal, they each pulled out a towel from their backpacks, dried off, and briefly warmed themselves in the midday sun. They considered the option of hiking a half-mile across the island, swimming a half-mile channel, and then walking almost two miles to the bridge and hitchhiking back to Memphis. After thinking things through, they decided that they had no choice but to swim back to Memphis from the uninhabited island.

Philip, who had meticulously studied maps of the area in planning their escapade, reasoned they should aim for Mud Island. Given the incredible speed of the water, he calculated that they'd need to walk at least a mile up the Loosahatchie sandbar before taking off, which would give them a greater margin of safety, as well as more time to warm up from the cold water.

Philip spied a small herd of Shetland ponies grazing on the south end of the island. He and Billy walked up to them, and finding them tame, chose two to mount bareback. Grabbing the ponies' manes, the two boys whooped and hollered as they rode their steeds back up the island. After dismounting,

i   "The Great Flood of '37" occurred in January and February, when the Ohio and Mississippi Rivers experienced floods that exceeded all previously recorded stages. When measured by the loss of life and property, these floods constituted a major catastrophe.

saying a brief prayer, and encouraging each other with an Indian chant they learned as Scouts, they slowly waded back into the frigid water and began their swim to the distant shore. Fortunately, Philip's calculations were correct, and it became clear they were going to make it to the safety of Mud Island.

Near the end of their swim, however, Billy ran out of steam and began to go under. He screamed out, yelling for help. When Philip saw his buddy panicking and fighting to keep his head above water, he used powerful strokes to bridge the distance quickly. Calling upon his lifeguard skills, Philip dove just below the surface and grabbed Billy by the waist. Then he promptly turned his buddy, surfaced, put him in a cross-chest lock, and hauled him to shore at Joe Curtis Point on Mud Island's southernmost section. Upon reaching dry land, Billy dissolved into tears, embracing Philip, and thanking him repeatedly for saving his life. After a time to rest and warm up, they dressed and hitched a ride back home.

Although Billy wanted to nominate him for a Red Cross or Boy Scout medal for bravery, Philip begged him not to. He didn't want to get into more trouble because he was sure his father, upon learning of another one of his harebrained escapades, would reward him with yet another trip to the back-yard toolshed for a whipping. This time Philip was lucky to escape punishment since he'd saved his friend's life, but he realized how close he had come to losing his buddy to the heartless river.

$$\wp$$

Philip's twelfth birthday was his most memorable. At the stables, he learned that the world-famous Lipizzaners from the Spanish Riding School in Vienna, Austria,[ii] would be performing at the fairgrounds the same weekend as his birthday. On a Saturday morning, Philip rode the trolley to the fairgrounds and watched the horses and their trainers practice the choreographed steps they would execute at their evening performance. He spent most of the day with the riders and grooms, asking endless questions. Best of all, they allowed him to brush and groom some of the magnificent stallions.

While brushing and talking to one of the Lipizzaners during the early afternoon, an observant stableman from Austria leaned toward him.

"A stallion like Gustav here may be perfectly schooled after about six years, but an apprentice rider—what we call an *Élève*—needs a full ten to twelve years of training to earn the right to show these magnificent horses," the stableman said. "They first have to spend years feeding, grooming, and leading the horses around before they are allowed actually to ride a Lipizzaner. After

---

ii   The Spanish Riding School is an Austrian institution dedicated to the preservation of classical dressage and the training of Lipizzaner horses. The school was first commissioned in 1565 and named for the Spanish horses that formed one of the bases of the Lipizzan breed, which is used exclusively at the school.

that, they graduate to the rank of *Assistant Reiter*, or assistant equestrian. Few outsiders—maybe a royal here or there—have ever been granted permission to ride one of our Lipizzaners. But I can tell that Gustav here has taken a shine to you and that you have the makings of a master equestrian. Would you like to mount him?"

Philip's eyes widened in wonder as a smile spread ear to ear. "Are you kidding me? I'd *love* to!"

The man smiled and looked around to be sure they were alone. He nodded and indicated to Philip that he would lift him onto the back of the massive stallion. Philip could feel the steed's muscles quiver between his legs. He instinctively leaned forward to stroke the horse's neck and whispered into his ears. Gustav immediately calmed down, shook his head, and continued to feed.

"He likes you," the man whispered. "But let's get you off before I get into big trouble."

In the late afternoon, Philip's mother hosted his birthday party, with cake and ice cream, and then took him and several of his friends to the arena for the evening show. They were mesmerized by the gala performance as they watched the expert riders and their Lipizzaners demonstrate the most demanding movements, all accompanied by classical Austrian music.

At one point, a stallion was led into the ring on a long rein without a rider. Philip recognized Gustav and leaned forward as the stallion was led to the center of the ring. The announcer described each increasingly tricky jump. "We call these 'the airs above the ground' or 'school jumps.' Only certain breeds have the strength and intelligence to perform these difficult airs today." The crowd applauded after each incredible movement.

"To complete this amazing performance, Gustav will demonstrate the *capriole*, a word which means the 'leap of a goat.' On command, he will jump straight up into the air, kicking out with his powerful hind legs, and then land on all four legs at the same time. It is considered the most difficult of all the airs above the ground."

The crowd burst into raucous applause after Gustav completed the arduous maneuver flawlessly, while Philip sat captivated. Then the boy's heart skipped a beat when the horseman led the stallion toward him. He recognized the "stableman" who had put him on the same Lipizzaner that morning. The man spoke to the horse, which then bowed by kneeling on one leg, extending the other leg in front, and lowering his head to the ground. The horseman smiled, tipped his black riding hat toward Philip, and mouthed, "Happy Birthday."

The crowd erupted in applause again as all attention fell on Philip. He felt exceptionally proud and would never forget that day or Gustav's *capriole* and bow. The boy vowed to himself that he'd one day travel to Europe to see these magnificent horses in person again.

Little did he know that would happen in an unimaginable way.

೧

The school years became more challenging for young Philip as he continued to do poorly in academics. His mother found it increasingly difficult to discipline him, mostly since his father was away from home on railroad trips so often. Finally, at her husband's insistence and the encouragement of Philip's scout-master, Ethyl applied for her son to attend the Gulf Coast Military Academy (GCMA) in Gulfport, Mississippi,[iii] a distance of 360 miles. GCMA's motto was, "Send us the boy, and we will return you the man." She could only pray that this would be the case for a fun-loving son not inclined to academics.

His four years at GCMA were a success by every measure and among the best in his life. The structured and regimented environment proved to be a stimulating learning atmosphere for the easily distracted teenager. Although Philip struggled with some of the mundane academic subjects, military topics became his forte—military history, strategy, operations, tactics, and weapons. He turned out to be a quick learner when motivated, and he became adept at competitive shooting, compass work, navigation, wilderness skills, sailing, and close combat. Philip also learned to fly a Piper Cub at a nearby airbase and became certified as a glider pilot. He enjoyed his time in the air, but the two areas in which he experienced even more joy were equitation—the art of horsemanship—and romance.

His happiness as an equestrian was primarily due to a feisty, chestnut Thoroughbred stallion nicknamed Moose. A trainer tried to steer Philip to a gentler horse, explaining, "Thoroughbreds are known for their agility, speed, and spirit, but they are also hot-blooded horses."[iv] But when Moose lowered his nose and relaxed as Philip spoke to him and stroked him, their partnership was sealed.

Moose was large by Thoroughbred standards, standing seventeen hands and weighing just under 1,200 pounds. Moose's rich mahogany coat made him look—except for the absence of antlers—like one of his namesakes. On Moose's back, Philip not only excelled in showing, jumping, and steeplechase competitions, but he also won more show ribbons than he could count.

As for the romance side, that excitement started in his senior year of high school with a blind date. Marilyn Fountain was a beautiful brunette with a

---

iii   GCMA was a military preparatory school for boys founded in 1912.
iv   The Thoroughbred breed is said to have been developed in 17th- and 18th-century England, where native mares were crossbred with imported Oriental stallions of Arabian, Berber, and the now-extinct Turkoman breeds. All modern Thoroughbreds trace their pedigrees to these three stallions. The breed was imported into America starting in 1730.

thin face, high cheekbones, and a radiant smile. She was from Des Moines, Iowa, and had just begun her freshman year at Gulf Park College in Gulf-port, a junior college for girls close to the Gulf Coast Military Academy, even though she and Philip were born weeks apart.

They met because Philip's roommate at GCMA, Billy "Tex" Metts, began dating one of Marilyn's suitemates. After Billy found out that Marilyn's father was an Army officer and that she had a fondness for horses, being the newest member of her college's Bit and Spur Club, he deduced she and Philip might be a match made in heaven.

Billy arranged for them to meet under the Friendship Oak located on the campus of Gulf Park College. This massive Southern oak stood over five stories tall and spread its immense fingers of foliage over 150 feet in each direction, providing over 16,000 square feet of cool, moist shade. The Friendship Oak was also the center of a legend: those who entered the shadow of her branches would remain friends for all their lives.

Under this magnificent tree, Philip and Marilyn first met, and then not too many days later, they first held hands and kissed. In the fall of 1941, the young couple could not have been happier, but they had no idea how their lives were suddenly going to be altered forever.

3

A DAY OF INFAMY

"Great crises in human affairs call out the great in men.
They call for great men."

**—Brevet Major General Joshua L. Chamberlain, Union
Civil War general and Medal of Honor recipient after
the Battle of Gettysburg**[11]

On Saturday evening, December 6, 1941, "Phil," as Marilyn called him and as he now liked to be called, took her out for dinner at the Bungalow, a popular seafood restaurant in Biloxi, Mississippi that overlooked the calm, brown waters of the Mississippi Sound.[i] The menu had something for every taste: fresh seafood, choice steaks, Southern fried chicken, Cajun specials, and even Chinese dishes. After enjoying the surf-and-turf special, the young couple decided to go to the cinema.[12]

Marilyn had wanted to see the romance, *Johnny Eager*, starring Lana Turner and Robert Taylor. In contrast, Phil had a yearning to watch *Tarzan's Secret Treasure*, starring Maureen O'Sullivan alongside his favorite movie star, Johnny Weissmuller, one of the world's fastest swimmers. They compromised with *Ball of Fire*, starring Gary Cooper and Barbara Stanwyck.

---

i   The Mississippi Sound is a massive estuary—a body of water where fresh river water meets a salty sea— that runs east-west along the southern coasts of Mississippi and Alabama. The water is brown, brackish, and shallow due to several rivers that drain into it.

The next morning dawned clear with unlimited visibility and an unseasonably warm fifty-nine degrees predicted as the high. Rather than attending church together, which was their habit, Phil and Marilyn decided to play hooky. He picked her up early, and they trailered their horses to the nearby De Soto National Forest, where they rode through the gently rolling terrain. When they located Black Creek, Mississippi's only National Scenic River, they followed the meandering ribbon of water until they found a wide white sandbar. There they set out a picnic lunch and talked for hours in the warm sunshine about their hopes and dreams—and, for the first time, about the prospects of a life together.

Late in the afternoon, they returned to the stable and found a group of people gathered around a radio. "Whatcha listening to?" Phil asked. The men shushed him as he and Marilyn leaned closer to listen.

The announcer blurted, "This is KTU in Honolulu, Hawaii. I am speaking from the roof of the Advertiser Publishing Company Building. We have witnessed this morning the severe bombing of Pearl Harbor by enemy planes, undoubtedly Japanese.... This is no joke. It is a real war... There has been serious fighting going on in the air and on the sea."[13]

Phil and Marilyn's eyes met, and he pulled her close. There was another second or two of static. Then the announcer continued, "We cannot estimate just how much damage has been done, but it has been a very severe attack."[14]

The sound of rustling papers came through the small radio as the announcer took a deep breath. "Oh, this is much worse than we've heard up to now. The BBC is now reporting, and I quote, 'At oh seven fifty-five local time, the first wave of between fifty and one-hundred-fifty planes struck the naval base for thirty-five minutes, causing several fires and untold damage to the Pacific Fleet. The Japanese squadrons dropped high explosive and incendiary bombs. A second strike followed at about oh nine hundred when a force of at least one hundred planes pounded the base for an hour,' end quote."[15]

Phil looked at his watch. This meant the attack had started just before 1 p.m. in Gulfport, located in the Central Time Zone.

The broadcaster continued, "The BBC also says, and I quote, 'The *Times* newspaper's Washington correspondent says the U.S. government expects Germany and Italy to declare war on the U.S. within hours. Although the attack has shocked the American people, there is little doubt that it has been brewing for some years,' end quote."[16]

Marilyn began to cry; Phil pulled out his handkerchief and handed it to her. "Oh, Phil," she muttered, "This can't be happening, can it?" He could only hold her close as a zillion thoughts raced through his mind. Their shared disbelief mirrored their astonishment.

The announcer paused a moment, and the clacking of a teletype machine could be heard. "This just in. This just in. Japan declares war! Japan declares war!"

Someone whispered to the man. The pitch of his voice increased as he announced, "This wire is just in from Hirohito, the Emperor of Japan. Here are his words, and I quote, 'We,[ii] the Emperor, hereby proclaim unto our loyal and valorous subjects that we have now declared war upon the United States of America and Great Britain,' end quote."[17]

Phil's mind swirled. He thought, *So, this is it. This is really it. Soon, I'll be off to war. I'll be going into battle.* He couldn't have imagined such a confluence of excitement and horror occurring in one moment. Marilyn continued to weep in his arms.

"I have to get back to GCMA. Now!" he said.

She nodded. They ran to the car and sped away.

ᔕᓄ

The next morning, Monday, December 8, the nation awoke to even more bad news: the extent of the damage from the surprise attack on Hawaii. At that point, no one knew that the Japanese attack had killed 2,403 U.S. personnel, including sixty-eight civilians, and destroyed or damaged nineteen U.S. Navy ships, including eight battleships, and destroyed or damaged 328 aircraft.[18]

Not even the U.S. government was aware that the ship with the most lives lost, the battleship *USS Arizona*, would report 1,177 dead—meaning that about one half of those who perished at Pearl Harbor were on the *Arizona*. What everyone *did* know was that Japan also attacked the Philippines, Wake Island, and Midway on the morning of December 7. The only good news was that the three aircraft carriers of the U.S. Pacific Fleet had been out to sea on maneuvers.

After a hastily arranged Protestant church service at GCMA, Phil received a call from his father. He had been working on the train running between New Orleans and Memphis. At a stop in Water Valley, Mississippi, Phil Sr. had been given a handwritten note:

Do not permit any Japanese to ride your train. Orders of the Federal Bureau of Investigation.[19]

Then Phil and his fellow cadets attended a solemn assembly at 11:30 a.m., during which they listened intently to the nationwide radio broadcast

---

ii The "we" used by the Emperor is called "the royal we," or "the majestic plural," and refers to a single person who is a monarch.

of President Franklin D. Roosevelt's address to a joint session of Congress inside the U.S. Capitol. The President started his speech with these memorable words:

> *Mr. Vice President, Mr. Speaker, Members of the Senate and the House of Representatives. Yesterday, December 7, 1941, a date which will live in infamy, the United States of America was suddenly and deliberately attacked by naval and air forces of the Empire of Japan.*[20]

After recounting details of the aerial assault, the President concluded his speech with this:

> *No matter how long it may take us to overcome this premeditated invasion, the American people in their righteous might will win through to absolute victory. I believe that I interpret the will of the Congress and of the people when I assert that we will not only defend ourselves to the uttermost but will make it very certain that this form of treachery shall never again endanger us.*
>
> *With confidence in our armed forces, with the unbounding determination of our people, we will gain the inevitable triumph—so help us God. I ask that the Congress declare that since the unprovoked and dastardly attack by Japan on Sunday, December 7, 1941, a state of war has existed between the United States and the Japanese empire.*[21]

The roars of approval and tsunami of applause from the members of Congress could be heard over the speakers, and was joined by the young GCMA cadets as they bounded to their feet, throwing their caps toward the ceiling, and hugging and swatting one another on the back. As the cheers faded, though, they became aware that America was about to face an extraordinary test—one that would potentially threaten her very being. The young men at GCMA knew that their training put them in a position to quickly make a difference and play a significant role in the days ahead.[iii]

The next five months flew by, and on a beautiful, cloudless, and calm seventy-degree Saturday, May 16, 1942, Phil graduated with honors from GCMA and the Reserve Officers Training Corps, or ROTC.

---

iii   On December 8, the Declaration of War against Japan passed with just one dissenting vote. Three days later, Germany and Italy, allied with Japan, declared war on the United States. America was now drawn into a global war and became part of the Allies—most importantly, Great Britain and the Soviet Union.

Before Pearl Harbor, he had planned to begin pre-med studies that fall, but with America in the midst of a global conflict against the Axis powers,[iv] he realized that he would not be studying medicine anytime soon.

Philip Larimore Jr. understood that he was destined for war.

---

iv   The major Axis powers were Germany, Italy, and Japan. The military alliance began to form in 1936 and was called the "Rome–Berlin–Tokyo Axis."

4

ON TO BENNING

"Now to the Infantry…the mud-rain-frost-and-wind boys. They have no comforts, and they even learn to live without the necessities. And in the end, they are the guys that wars can't be won without."

—Ernie Pyle, American journalist and war correspondent[22]

On September 10, 1942, instead of heading to college, Phil told his parents goodbye in Memphis and traveled back to Gulfport to spend a few days with Marilyn. His girlfriend was continuing her education at Gulf Park College. Before they knew it, their time together raced to an end. They embraced for one long hug and a kiss under the Friendship Oak before he boarded a Greyhound bus heading to Infantry Officer Candidate School (OCS)[i] at Fort Benning, Georgia.[23]

Upon arrival, he and 199 other candidates formed four platoons of fifty men each, and each platoon was assigned to one of four two-story barracks.

---

i   During World War II, OCS became the leading source of new Army officers with candidates commissioning as 2nd lieutenants upon graduation. From 1941 to 1947, over 100,000 were enrolled in 448 Infantry OCS classes with 67 percent graduating. Most of the candidates came from the enlisted ranks and college ROTC programs. In Phil's case, it was almost unheard of to go directly from high school to OCS, but because of the urgency of World War II, the Army broke normal protocol as Phil's military school record and ROTC experience made him a top candidate.

All four platoons had a Tactical Officer (TO), also known as the platoon's TAC (Teach, Access, and Counsel) Officer. In Phil's case, the TAC was a 1st lieutenant who was not only in charge of the platoon's training, but he would be able to choose which of the men would be commissioned as officers. As Russell Cloer, another OCS candidate from Jersey City, New Jersey, said, "In other words, he was God for the duration of our stay!"[24]

The TOs' pith-style helmets had an Infantry School insignia front and center that read *Follow Me*, the motto of the Infantry School, which was also nicknamed "Benning's School for Boys." At their first formation, Phil's platoon was told that fewer than half would graduate while the rest would "wash out." He had no way of knowing that this was an exaggeration intended to motivate the men, but it worked: Phil determined that failure was not an option. He was also aware that he was the youngest in his class.

A typical day involved the men being awakened before sunrise, usually at either 4 a.m. or, more commonly, 5 a.m., by a bugler playing "Reveille."[ii] The recruits were given enough time to "shit, shower, and shave" and wolf down a quick breakfast before falling into formation and being trucked to the day's training area. The officer candidates had to perform no mundane duties—just training, training, training.

For most men, their OCS physical and mental exercises were grueling, but Phil found the drilling and physical workouts to be surprisingly gratifying. He was in much better shape than most of his classmates, and although a fair share had more intellectual prowess, few could match how quickly he learned, how expertly he handled small arms, rifles, and marksmanship, or how skillfully he could lead men when called upon to do so.

The officer candidates had free time every Saturday afternoon and all day Sunday. Many of the guys would put on their uniforms, with the required OCS patch sewed to their shirt pocket, and take a bus six miles into the nearest town, Columbus. Phil, however, occupied his free time either studying or writing home to his parents and Marilyn. On Saturday and Sunday evenings, he would treat himself to a movie at the theater on the post.

But once Phil learned about the Fort Benning Hunt Club,[iii] an on-base stable, he could be found there on most weekends. The first time he walked through the barn, he carefully looked at each mount. A bay-colored Thoroughbred mare seemed to respond to him. As he approached her, she whinnied, shook her head in approval, and walked across the stall to let him gently rub her nose.

---

ii   "Reveille" is a bugle call used to awaken military personnel at sunrise and comes from the French word for "wake up." This bugle call is also used when the flag is raised in the morning and honors are paid to it.
iii   Before World War II, almost every major post in the Army operated its own foxhunt. Besides the Infantry Hunt at Fort Benning, other major hunts were the Cavalry Hunt at Fort Riley, Kansas, the Artillery Hunt at Fort Sill, Oklahoma, and the 1st Cavalry Division Hunt at Fort Bliss, Texas.

"She's a beaut," one of the passing grooms commented. "Rita Hayworth she's called, after the movie star. Lotta the guys like riding Rita, or at least writing home and saying they did," the groom chuckled.

For the weekends that followed, Phil and Rita were inseparable. Phil believed, as did British Prime Minister Winston Churchill, that "No hour of life is wasted that is spent in the saddle."[25] He and Rita not only swept nearly all the on-base equestrian events, but it was at Fort Benning that Phil experienced his first foxhunt.

The hunt used a pack of American Foxhounds maintained with the assistance of the Army MWR (Morale, Welfare and Recreation) Division. A retired colonel who served as the Master of the Foxhounds invited Phil to his first hunt and introduced him to the most recognized tradition of foxhunting—the distinctive attire.

Working out of a closet owned by the club, the distinguished gentleman had Phil try on several outfits until he had the perfect fit for a scarlet jacket, beige jodhpurs (or riding pants), tall black boots, and the traditional black top hat. The brightly colored coat's primary purpose was to ensure that riders were not mistaken for prey and shot as they chased their quarry through the woods, the colonel explained.

As the colonel helped Phil into his overcoat, he said, "Traditionally, only the Hunt Club members get to wear the red coat, which is called a *pink*, but in your case, the Master of the Foxhunt gives permission."

Phil smiled. "Thanks, Colonel."

"You've earned it, son. I've seen you ride and jump. As for these tight-fitting britches, they reduce the chance of getting caught up in branches or brambles, and the tall boots protect your legs from scratches and scrapes."

"Thanks for the explanation. What game do you chase?"

"The game for our hunts is usually a coyote. The hunt area here at the post is so large and rugged that the game rarely has any trouble eluding the hounds and the hunt field. It's not considered sporting to kill the game. What we love are the pure joy and sport of the hunt—and the chase. And," he added, "the social time after the hunt is a wonderful time to meet folks from all around the post and the surrounding area."

Phil and Rita both loved the hunts—the galloping and jumping. Although many of the less-experienced riders fell during jumps over creeks, logs, or narrow ravines, Phil and Rita were both expert jumpers and nearly always at the front of the pack. The colonel often told him, "Horses lend us the wings we lack."[26] And, as the colonel had predicted, the social hours after the hunt were always an enjoyable time to share drinks and stories.

Having spent four years in military school, Phil did not wrestle with homesickness as some of the men did, but he desperately missed Marilyn.

Fortunately, the Southern Bell Telephone Company's phone room allowed the men to call home and their gals once a week for no charge. Of course, he wrote her as often as he could.

For Phil, the exhilaration of riding on weekends and the military instruction during the week combined to make the time fly.

5

CAPTURE THE FLAG

"I remember OCS as being one of the most intense episodes of my life, aside from Infantry combat, which, of course, was what it prepared us for. Our determination to successfully complete the program was the primary goal of our young lives."

—Russell W. Cloer, an Officer Candidate School graduate[27]

At Fort Benning, there was never any hazing or what the OCS candidates called "chickenshit" from the TOs. But one thing the men all grew to hate was what was called the "Fuck Your Buddy Sheet."[28]

During the last half of their training, the men were required to rank the other men in their platoon in order of officer suitability. For the first five and last five men on their list, each candidate had to write a sentence explaining his justification for the ranking. As one candidate, Russell Cloer, wrote, "There could be no hedging because someone had to be first and someone had to be last. And showing favoritism didn't pay because we were each rated by the TO on our ability to evaluate others effectively."[29]

Toward the end of OCS, the officer candidates had to rotate as first-time instructors in subjects they had completed. Their TO and the other students graded them on the quality of their performance. It was during this phase that Phil learned he was a natural teacher. He was primarily encouraged by one of his instructors, 2nd Lieutenant Ross H. Calvert, Jr., from Nashville, Tennessee, who had graduated from OCS a few months earlier and had done so well that he had been invited to stay on the teaching staff.

Although relationships between candidates and staff were discouraged, the two men quickly became fast friends, given their Tennessee roots and mutual love of bourbon, horses, and outdoor sports. Phil and Ross shared meals and drinks at the Officer's Club during their free time and learned to play contract bridge—a trick-taking card game played by four players, with partners sitting opposite each other. They quickly became one of the best competitive teams on the base, pocketing a fair amount of spending money in winnings. On weekends, they also loved riding together.

At the end of supper one day, Phil's platoon was unexpectedly ordered to double-time to the barracks. Once there, platoon members were handed field coveralls, a small backpack, a loaded carbine,[i] and a sidearm. Then they were marched in the dark and placed in a large windowless box truck. After being driven around in disorienting circles for about thirty minutes, the truck stopped, and the back gate was slung open.

The TO jumped in. "Gentlemen, I'm going to have you leave the truck in groups of four. As you get off the truck, I'll assign a squad leader and give you a compass bearing. Follow that bearing to the first road you find, which will be between two and three miles away. You'll be traversing forests, fields, ravines, and, if you're unlucky, an alligator-infested swamp with mosquitos and snakes. We have men posing as the enemy scattered between the roads. Some of them are hunting for you, while others are hunkered down in machine gun nests, waiting to kill as many of you as they can. Your weapons and their weapons have been preloaded with blanks. Feel free to fire at will at the enemy. If you don't kill him, rest assured he will kill you. There are to be *no* prisoners in this exercise."

The TO paused and looked over the men. "Each of the enemy will have a small flag attached to their belt by a rubber band. When you exit the truck, one flag will be attached to your belt. When a man is killed, the killer pulls the band to prove his kill. If you're killed, your night—and perhaps your training—will be over. But if you either kill or avoid the enemy and achieve your objective, then when you get to the road, I want you to find the nearest stake, pull it up, and write your arrival time on it.

"Each stake is numbered, and your performance will be judged on how close you come to the proper stake and how long it takes you to get there. Bonus points will be awarded for any kills you make. Then stay by the road.

---

i   A carbine is a shortened version of a full-length rifle. The M1 carbine was significantly shorter and lighter than the M1 Garand rifle and was intended for rear-area troops who couldn't be hindered with full-sized rifles but needed something more powerful and accurate than a pistol. The M1 carbine was not a shorter version of the M1 Garand, but a wholly different design, firing a smaller, less-powerful cartridge.

You may sleep if you have any time left, but expect to be picked up at zero six hundred hours sharp. And if you're not at your pickup point at zero six hundred, you will have a long, long walk back to the barracks. Good luck."

The exercise reminded Phil of a traditional game played at Boy Scout camp after dark, where two teams each had a flag in their home camp. The objective was to capture the other team's flag and bring it back to your base without getting "killed." Players were eliminated from the game when a piece of cloth attached to their belts by rubber bands was pulled loose by an enemy combatant.

As Phil and his three teammates exited the truck, the TO assigned him to be the squad leader. Phil felt his stomach tighten and his pulse quicken. One of his squad mates was a Lumbee Indian from Lumberton, North Carolina, whom Phil swore could hear a mouse walking on a carpet of grass at fifty yards. For the two of them, it was a marriage made in heaven.

Other than a minor stumble into an unrecognized but shallow ravine, the group was able to thread its way through the forest quickly and quietly. Fortunately, a Southern forest at night is alive with the booming sounds of tree frogs, pond frogs, bullfrogs, crickets, cicadas, katydids, and even whip-poor-will birds chanting their name, along with any number of other critters.

Phil was glad it was fall so that the echoing chatter could conceal any inadvertent sound he or one of his men might make by stepping on a small twig. A snapping stick could sound like a gun going off in a quiet forest, and point the enemy directly toward them.

While making their way through the woods, the Indian suddenly hand-signaled that they should crouch and be quiet. He listened for a minute and pointed ahead, indicating one hundred yards with hand signals.

Looking across the darkened field, Phil nodded as he saw the red glow of two cigarettes. Using hand signals, he broke the group in two, and they circled the enemy ambush. Approaching from opposite sides, Phil and his men snuck up to within yards of the four men who were in hushed conversation while smoking in a small depression that they had made into a machine gun nest.

Apparently, "the enemy" had not expected the trainees to arrive so quickly. On Phil's signal, they swarmed over the edge of the nest, gripping sheathed knives. Before the unsuspecting enemy could react, they pretended to cut their throats. To make an even bigger statement, the Lumbee Indian shoved his shocked victim to the ground, placed his knee on the man's chest, pulled off the man's cap, and pretended to scalp him. The soldier looked terrified as Phil's buddy stood over him, softly chanting in his native language as he held the imaginary scalp to the stars.

Phil's other two men got into the act, whooping and hollering as they "scalped" their victims, but Phil quickly shushed them. They each collected a flag from the men they had "killed" and stuck them in their pockets. As Phil bent over his man, he was startled to see that he had subdued his good friend Ross Calvert.

"Good job!" Calvert whispered through a smile that spread from ear to ear.

Phil grinned and turned to his men. "We need to move quickly!" he said with urgency in his voice. They resumed their speed hike silently through the forest in single file. The Indian led the way, and as he darted from tree to tree, each man would quietly follow in succession. They would stop every five minutes for Phil to pull out his compass and take a reading by moonlight.

The sharp snap of a breaking twig about seventy yards in front of them brought them to a crouch. The three crept up to the Indian. They heard another snap and muffled voices in the distance.

"There's a patrol just ahead of us," Phil whispered. "Gents, it's time to set up an ambush." He looked at the Indian. "Can you tell the direction they're walking?"

The man nodded and swept his arm from side to side to show the direction they were traveling.

"Okay, boys," Phil quietly directed, "on my hand signal, let's separate. We'll form a ten-by-twenty-yard perimeter, and when they walk into it, I'll whistle, and we can all open up with our weapons."

Then he smiled. "We'll mow 'em down before they know what hit 'em."

The ambush went off without a hitch, other than being roundly cursed out by the eight enemy combatants, all of whom were enlisted men out to earn rewards and bragging rights for "killing" the candidates. One of them exclaimed, "You boys literally scared the shit outta us!"

Following their capture, Phil and his men pulled off their flags, pocketed them, and melted into the woods. In short order, they found the right road and the nearest stake. It had taken them only three hours to traverse the course. As much as they could determine, they were the first group out of the woods.

"Time to take a nap," the Indian said.

But Phil was suspicious that there could still be a trap. "Let's pull up our stake and move back into the woods a bit. We'll still be near enough to the road to hear the trucks when they come. We'll rotate watch every hour. Two men up; two asleep. Just to be safe."

Phil sensed the men's dissatisfaction with his decision, but they quickly pulled off their field packs and used them for pillows, and the first two men immediately fell asleep. Phil and the Indian took the first watch.

Slowly, other men came out of the woods, pulled up their stakes, and lay down to sleep. After his first watch, it was Phil's turn to nap.

Just before dawn, one of the men shook Phil from his sleep. He pointed across the road. They could see "the enemy" exiting the woods, one man every ten yards. They all moved into the ditch across the pavement from the sleeping trainees. Then one blew a whistle, and the enemy charged across the road, their guns blasting away. All of the asleep men were "killed." Cries of cursing erupted up and down the road as the candidates realized the tables had been turned, and they had been caught in an ambush of their own.

The enlisted men laughed and hooted—that is, until Phil and his men, who had spread out twenty to thirty yards apart, came running out of the woods on his whistle with their rifles and pistols erupting in a cacophony of fire. The "dead" OCS candidates began cheering as they realized one of their teams had the final hurrah.

The victorious outcome energized Phil and gave him confidence that he could successfully lead men and hopefully survive the many battles that lay ahead.

6
THE SCHOOL SOLUTION

"I am the Infantry—Queen of Battle! For over two centuries, I have kept the nation safe. Purchasing freedom with my blood. To tyrants, I am the day of reckoning. To the oppressed, the hope for the future. Where the fighting is thick, there am I. I am the Infantry. Follow me!"

**—Creed of the U.S. Army Infantry Center,
Fort Benning, Georgia**[30]

As the men entered the last week of OCS just before Christmas in 1942, Phil sensed an increase in morale. No one had been dismissed from OCS for a couple of weeks. They now knew they could be almost certain that they would make it and would soon be inducted into the rarified club of being an officer and a gentleman.[31]

Up to that time, the training had been grueling but interspersed with light moments, like the time when Phil's platoon received covert permission from other training officers to play a trick on their TO. Three of the men snuck into their TO's sleeping room in the wee hours. One man held a turned-off flashlight a foot or so from his face. Another man gripped a fluffy pillow above the TO's head. The third began to shake him gently, softly calling his last name.

When the groggy TO stirred, someone shouted, "Look out for the truck!" This was followed by the simultaneous clicking on of the flashlight, temporarily blinding him, while the pillow crashed onto his head.

The TO screamed in fright, and the three men sprinted outside and back to their barracks. The next morning, the men were awakened an hour early and taken on a long morning run by their TO, who rode in a Jeep beside them and never mentioned the reason for the early morning run.

ᏦᎧ

Just before graduation, Phil's Tactical Officer marched his men to a mock cemetery on base. He ordered them to be at ease, and then read the following epitaph to them:

> *"Here lie the bones of Lieutenant Jones,*
> *A graduate of this institution,*
> *He died on the night of his very first fight,*
> *While using the "School Solution."*[32]

"Smoke break," the TO ordered as he joined his men in lighting up. "Gentlemen, what's the OCS motto?"

The men, in unison, sang out, "Follow Me!"

"If you graduate, you'll get a book commemorating your time here. Included in it is a poem called 'The Benning School for Boys.'[33] It begins:

> *High above the Chattahoochee, near the Upatoi,*
> *Stands our noble Alma Mater, Benning's School for Boys."*

He took a drag and continued. "I'm not much for poetry, but the final verses contain what I consider to be fatal advice. See if you can figure it out.

> *Hail to Benning, Hail to Benning, 'Follow Me' is the cry,*
> *You must use the School Solution, 'Follow Me,' or die.*
> *Plenty of action, lots of noise, that's the Benning School for Boys."*

He looked around at the men and then straight at Phil. "Larimore, what's the mistake?"

Phil's mind spun. He thought he knew the answer but wasn't sure. He could feel every eye on him as beads of sweat popped out on his forehead. He gulped and blurted, "The 'School Solution' sucks. 'Follow Me' can be fucking fatal." A beat later, he exclaimed, "Sir!"

The TO walked over to him, positioned himself nearly nose to nose, and glared at Phil for a moment. A smile slowly spread across the TO's face. Then he backed away as he began laughing.

"That's brilliant, Larimore. Fuckin' brilliant!"

The TO's demeanor changed on a dime. He looked at each of his men, meeting their eyes for a moment as he walked in front of them. "And, I might add," he growled, "you can thank your lucky stars you're even being allowed to graduate after that asinine stunt you clowns played on me."

The men stiffened, not sure how to react. The TO, however, was unable to maintain his scowl. A grin returned to his face. "Gotta admit, it's the best one I've ever experienced. You sonsabitches scared the shit outta me—almost literally."

Phil and the men looked at each other, holding back chuckles.

"I cannot wait to pull this prank off on the next new TO," he said, but then his smile evaporated again.

"I want you to hear something from my heart," he continued. "I want you to listen. If you do, it may well save your life and the lives of your men."

Phil could see the men quietly shifting their feet. All eyes were fixed on their Tactical Officer.

"Wise frontline officers on the battlefield have learned the hard way *not* to accept at face value the simplistic battlefield leadership style implied in the cry 'Follow Me!' Indeed, they have to lead by example, as you will, but they also must exercise common sense and judgment in determining successful tactical situations.

"Officers who lead from the front with reckless disregard for their safety quickly become casualties. Companies and battalions that lose their leaders in the early stages of battle became bogged down and confused. In this war, captains and lieutenants have grabbed their carbines and led the way against Japanese or German defenses. Some survive, but *most* do not."

He was quiet to let his words sink in. "Wise and skillful officers in the field quickly come to understand their troops *do not want* or *expect* them to lead from the front. In fact, most frontline soldiers feel better knowing their officers are alive and doing all they can to control the fight and bring the other combat arms to bear. In other words, men, your soldiers know they are more likely to live if you live."

He took another drag. "Company grade officers at the very forefront of attacks invariably suffer high casualty rates, and their loss seriously affects unit efficiency and morale. Gentlemen, when the circumstances require it, I know you will each take bold steps to get attacks moving. But you don't have to prove how brave you are by rushing to the front and getting your ass shot up—it's too hard on you and your men. Are you listening?"

The men answered, "Yes, sir!"

"If your troops do not expect you to lead them from the front, then what do they want?" the Tactical Officer asked rhetorically. He looked over his men. None spoke, so he continued.

"Soldiers believe officers should fight alongside them and share all of their hazards. Good officers do not order or ask men to expose themselves needlessly, or attack in the face of overwhelming odds. Troops desire self-control and emotional stability in their captains and lieutenants. An excitable officer is ineffective. Officers learn that speaking in a calm, firm voice during tense situations is the best way to reassure soldiers. I can only hope I've set this example for you and that you will set it for your men."

He walked over to Phil. "This young man is the youngest OCS student in the history of Fort Benning, which is worth noting. He said something I want you to remember. The "School Solution" sucks and "Follow Me" can be fucking fatal.'"

The TO was silent for a moment and then gave one final nod. In a whisper, his voice choking with emotion, he said, "Gentlemen, you are among the best trained and most prepared officers in this man's Army. I've taught you how to follow and how to lead. How to kill and how not to be killed, and how to bring as many of your boys home with you as possible. My job is done, but yours is just beginning."

The TO took a final drag off his cigarette. Phil was sure he saw the mist in the man's eyes. He turned his back and faced the tombstone, fieldstripping[i] his cigarette before sticking the butt in his pocket.

"You are dismissed."

⁂

On graduation day, 140 of the original 200 men in Phil's class received their Certificate of Completion, which simply stated:

---

i   Soldiers were taught to "fieldstrip" cigarette butts and not toss them away carelessly since littering left a trail in a combat zone. Fieldstripping often involved rolling and pinching the butt firmly backward and forward between two fingers until the remaining tobacco fell out, extinguishing it.

The Infantry School
United States Army

*This is to certify that Cadet Philip Bonham Lari-
more has successfully completed the Rifle and Heavy
Weapons Company Officers Course given during the period
September 21, 1942, to December 17, 1942.*

Philip H. Kron, Colonel of Infantry[34]

They then swore the oath together, Phil exclaiming with the others:

*I, Philip B. Larimore Junior, having been appointed
temporarily a Second Lieutenant in the Army of the United
States, do solemnly swear that I will support and defend
the Constitution of the United States against all enemies,
foreign and domestic; that I will bear true faith and allegiance to the same; that I take this obligation freely, without
any mental reservations or purpose of evasion; and that
I will well and faithfully discharge the duties of the office
upon which I am about to enter.*[35]

The men then shouted in unison: "So help me God!"

Less than three weeks before his eighteenth birthday, Phil was not only
the youngest member of his class, but also the youngest candidate to ever graduate from Fort Benning's Infantry School. After the oath, Phil's TO pinned
the cherished gold bars on his shoulders, whispering, "I still think that pillow
stunt was fucking brilliant, Larimore."

"I'm told that the man in charge of that raid learned it at a Scout camp.
Of course, I can't confirm that, sir," Phil replied in all earnestness.

"I wouldn't think so. But you got me good."

Phil watched as the TO finished pinning the rest of his platoon before they
were dismissed. The men hugged, danced, sang, and shook hands, knowing
that most of them would never see each other ever again.

And many of them would never see the war's end—much less old age.

7

FLYING COFFINS

"It is possible to fly without motors but not without knowledge and skill."

—Wilbur Wright, inventor of the world's first successful airplane with his younger brother, Orville Wright[36]

The Christmas and New Year's season of 1942–1943 was one of joy and celebration for Phil. He spent time with Marilyn and her family in Des Moines, and then he took her to meet his mother's family at a reunion in northern Arkansas.[37]

On January 4, they celebrated his eighteenth birthday with friends in Memphis. Though Phil had been provisionally sworn in and assigned a temporary rank at his OCS graduation, he was officially commissioned a 2nd Lieutenant on January 20, the lowest rank of a commissioned officer. Two days later, he was sworn into the Army, and three days after that, he began his official entry into extended active duty. At eighteen years and twenty-one days of age, Phil officially became the youngest officer in the U.S. Army. In mid-January, he received his first orders: Report to Camp Wheeler, Georgia, an infantry replacement center.

Phil left Memphis, traveling to Gulfport to visit Marilyn for a few days. While there, he was honored in absentia at the annual Boy Scout Chickasaw Council Dinner with the Eagle Scout award, the highest achievement attainable, with only 4 percent of Boy Scouts earning the rank. His mother tearfully accepted for him.

The next week, the Memphis newspaper reported, "Just two weeks ago, he was commissioned a second lieutenant in the Army. Last week, he was made an Eagle Scout, and at eighteen, is the youngest commissioned officer in the Army."

When Phil arrived on February 5, Camp Wheeler was at the height of its training effort, containing 17,000 trainees and 3,000 cadre personnel. His first assignment was a bit of a shock to him.

He wrote this to his mother:

> *I was given command of a Negro platoon.[i] We have to treat them a little bit differently than white troops. They have to be watched all the time.*[38]

Phil, growing up in segregated Memphis during the Jim Crow era, carried with him the bigotry reflected in the Army in general, which at that time considered blacks unfit for combat duty. After a few days of commanding the "Negro men," though, Phil's view began to change. He wrote:

> *The corporals and sergeants are plenty tough and work the boys hard. That's the main reason we have the best Company on the post. They're good men with good hearts. They love their families, their church, their God, and their country as much or more as I do. I'd be honored to lead them into battle anywhere, anytime.*[39]

Phil was impressed with the remarkable variety of men he encountered at Camp Wheeler—men from every corner of the country, including farm boys and factory hands, multigenerational Americans and new immigrants, rich and poor, as well as Protestants, Catholics, and Jews. Phil and almost every other soldier were exposed to more social, ethnic, economic, and religious diversity in the Army than they had ever met.

---

i   The U.S. Army was officially segregated at the time, so regiments were either all-white or all-black. Ignoring the superior performance of black troops in battles during the Civil War and World War I, when American black soldiers were allowed to fight only alongside French troops, during World War II, the U.S. Army assigned the great majority of black soldiers to non-combat service units such as supply, maintenance, transportation, smoke-screen generation, and anti-aircraft barrage balloon battalions. Due to the severe shortage of Infantry in late 1944, General Dwight Eisenhower allowed volunteer black troops to serve in combat units. While President Harry Truman ordered desegregation in 1948, it did not really happen until the Korean War.

After one week, however, Phil was transferred to Fort Bragg, North Carolina, as a platoon leader for Charlie Company[ii] of the 326th Glider Infantry, one of two glider units assigned to the 82nd Airborne Division.

Soon after Phil's arrival, the Army brass decided to change the composition of the 82nd from a two-glider-and-one-parachute-regiment Division to a two-jump-and-one-glider regiment Division. A flip of the coin decided the question of which glider outfit, the 325th or the 326th, would remain. The 325th won, and on February 10, 1943, the 326th began shipping out to Alliance, Nebraska, instead of off to the war.

∽

Before moving to Nebraska, Phil completed three weeks of glider training and earned his Glider Pilot wings training in the motorless, fabric-covered Waco CG-4A[iii] glider behind C-47[iv] tow planes. The glider was constructed of steel tubing covered with a thin canvas skin, giving the craft a forty-eight-foot-long fuselage and a wingspan of eighty-four feet. A honeycombed plywood floor could support more than 4,000 pounds, meaning two pilots and up to thirteen soldiers and their packs, or a combination of heavy equipment and a small crew to operate the equipment once unloaded.

The nose section, which included the pilots' seats, swung up to create a five-by-six-foot exit door for rapid loading and unloading of a Jeep, a 75-mm howitzer,[v] or similarly sized vehicle or armament. Phil quickly learned there were only four basic instruments on the control panel: an altimeter, an airspeed gauge, a rate-of-climb indicator, and a bank-and-turn indicator. The pilots learned to mistrust all four of them, which is why they called the gliders "flying coffins."

Phil's most frightening experience in the "Fat Goose," as he called his glider, occurred during an early training flight. While tethered to the C-47, he and the left-seat pilot were transporting a Jeep and two infantrymen when they hit a severe crosswind and bucked up and down in the turbulence. The pilot cursed as he struggled to keep the heavy glider horizontal, and then a loud thud was followed by the pilot's windshield and its support rails crashing against the pilot's face and upper body. The pilot, who never let go of his control wheel, immediately slumped forward, bleeding and unconscious.

ii   To avoid confusion from letters which sound alike, the military introduced a phonetic alphabet in World War II where letters were pronounced as distinctive words. A = able, B = baker, C = charlie, D = dog, E = easy, F = fox, G = george, H = how, I = item, J = jig, K = king, L = love, M = mike, etc.

iii   The Waco CG-4 was the most widely used American troop/cargo military glider of World War II, with nearly 14,000 delivered. It was usually towed by a C-47.

iv   The Douglas C-47 Skytrain or Dakota was a military transport aircraft developed from the civilian Douglas DC-3 airliner. The aircraft earned the informal nickname "gooney bird" in the European theatre of operations, where the plane towed gliders and dropped paratroops.

v   A howitzer is a medium-sized artillery piece smaller than a cannon and larger than a mortar. Howitzers, like other artillery equipment, were organized in groups called "batteries."

Fortunately, Phil's windshield was still intact, but the glider's position behind the C-47 was increasingly difficult to maintain. The instruments indicated a flight speed of 150 miles per hour, the maximum safe speed for the glider, and an altitude of 1,500 feet. There was no way for Phil to communicate with the tow pilot or the ground since the gliders could not carry the weight of a radio or communication equipment.

Phil yelled to the men in the back. "Get up here!" When they came up front, straining against the headwinds howling through the broken windshield, he had them unbuckle the pilot and take him to the back. "Bandage his wounds!" Phil commanded as he struggled with the glider's suddenly sluggish controls.

As the C-47 began to bank to head back to the airfield, Phil felt a surge of relief. The turn meant there were only ten minutes of flying time to the airfield. Just then, a loud crack sounded from the back of the fuselage, and the entire glider began to shake violently.

What the hell? Phil thought. The control column began jerking back and forth, and he grabbed the wheel as hard as he could with both hands. Another crack ricocheted throughout the cabin. Instinctively, Phil reached up and pulled the lever to release the tow rope. They would never make it to the runway, so their best chance of survival was slowing down and looking for a place to make a crash landing.

The glider's shaking immediately decreased as Phil pulled up on the control column to slow the glider—dropping the glider's speed quickly to 120, then 100, then 80 mph. At 60 mph, the quivering vibrations finally stopped. He realized, however, that he had to balance going too slow and stalling versus gliding too fast and tearing or cracking an even more vital part of the glider. Too slow or too fast could result in a fatal spin to the ground below.

Either way, Phil knew death was on his doorstep. He wasn't sure if the tremors in his hands were from the fear he felt or the vibrations from the shivering aircraft. He continued to move the control wheel forward slowly, but the glider didn't respond immediately. Instead, the glider continued to slow. Finally, the lumbering box began to respond.

As Phil gently dropped the nose, the airspeed increased ever so slowly—up to 70, then 80, and finally up to 90 mph. As the speed increased, so did the quaking and quivering. Additional creaks and cracks echoed throughout the glider.

Phil wiped the sweat running down his face and decided to aim for an airspeed of 70 to 75 mph. He could see the ground—flat farmlands—rapidly growing closer. The altimeter registered 500 feet. During the time he had been riding this bucking bronco, she had dropped over a thousand feet. Phil decided he'd have to bring the old girl into a dive and nose her up to a near stall just before landing. With her lethargic responses to his commands seemingly getting slower, an unstoppable and fatal dive seemed likely.

Phil could see a field planted with winter wheat beside an old farm road stretching out in front of him. The farmland seemed a safe place to put down. He yelled back to the men behind him. "Buckle up! The landing's gonna be pretty rough!"

He pushed the control wheel, once again slowly taking her into a dive. He pulled the control wheel back as far and as hard as he could at about a hundred feet of altitude. For what seemed an eternity, she continued her dive. The ground was rushing up to meet him when the glider miraculously began to nose up slowly.

Phil continued to pull the control wheel back as hard as possible, afraid that something would break off when the glider slowed to 60 and then 50 mph. He then yelled, "Prepare for a crash landing!"

Fortunately, they were only a few feet above the field. Then the glider dipped and skidded across the wheat field until she came to a halt, still in one piece—a miracle landing.

"Thank you, Lord," he whispered. For a moment, he could not pry his trembling hands from the control wheel.

"Crap, Lieutenant," he heard a voice say as he felt a hand grasp his shoulder. "Couldn't have done better myself."

He turned to see the pilot, bloody bandages circling his head, smiling at him. "Well done." Turning his head to the back, he commanded, "Men, let's unlatch the front and get out of this coffin."

Phil's hands loosened from the wheel, and he unbuckled from his seat. He helped the two infantrymen unhook the latches that secured the glider's nose and then unloaded the Jeep. As the three men and the injured pilot stood around the vehicle, they heard a roar and looked up to see their C-47 tow plane flying low and directly in front of them. Phil gave the pilot a thumbs-up and a wave. The pilot rocked his wings in response.

Pride filled Phil's heart—as well as relief.

That night in the Officer's Club, after the doctor had cleared the pilot, he bought Phil several drinks. But Phil had to sip slowly and deliberately so his buddies wouldn't see the tremors in his hands.

Before the playing of "Taps,"[vi] Phil had a long phone conversation with Marilyn. He didn't tell her what had happened. But her soft, dreamy voice and expressions of love, followed by his bedtime prayers, did more to calm him than anything else. He fell asleep quickly, but he had recurrent night terrors in which he and the screaming men crashed and burned. The dreams did not go away for several weeks.

He'd survived his first brush with death, but those nightmares would not be his last.

---

vi   The bugle call of "Taps," a military signal for soldiers to turn out the lights and go to bed at 2100 hours, was also played during flag ceremonies and at military funerals by a single bugle or trumpet.

8

PLATFORM GIRLS

"The poor bloody Infantry…even though we are unskilled, uneducated, and unimportant, we are indispensable. Without us, the ground will not be taken or held; the battle will not be won."

—Staff Sergeant Earl Ravenscroft, 3rd Infantry Division and Silver Star recipient[40]

A couple of weeks after the glider's emergency landing, a long train carrying the 326th Regiment pulled out of Fort Bragg as scheduled, precisely at 1530 hours on March 1, 1943, for a four-day cross-country trip. On the second day, the officers were called into the commander's conference car. Once they settled into their chairs, forty-seven-year-old Colonel Stuart Cutler, who had commanded the 326th since it had been reactivated for World War II, entered the car. They all snapped to attention.[41]

"At ease!" he commanded. After a moment, he began explaining their orders. "We have been assigned to participate in a prolonged mobilization training plan. For the first seventeen weeks, the entire regiment will train together in basic and advanced individual techniques. For many of you, this will be a duplication of your previous training. But I want us all on the same page. Understood?"

There were nods all around.

The colonel continued. "We'll have a cadre of 1,500 experienced, top-notch regulars who have themselves trained together in various higher-level schools. They will be our coaches and provide our training." The colonel added he was expecting a washout rate of about 20 percent in the first four months.

"During the next thirteen weeks of unit training, through the regimental level to the battalions, companies, platoons, and squads, teamwork will be built in both dry-fire and live-fire training exercises. After that, we'll have fourteen weeks of combined-arms exercises, in which our entire division will be thoroughly, tactically, and endlessly drilled in the field."

The colonel paused a moment to let the impact of months of intense training sink in. "When we're finished, our final phase will be eight weeks of training in coordinated air, mechanized, and anti-mechanized warfare techniques."

Colonel Cutler allowed the news to settle in, then finished with a flurry. "Any division worth a crap has to be a well-oiled machine. We have to live, eat, sleep, fight, drink, and play as a team. There is no individuality bullshit in this division. After the successful completion of this fifty-two-week training program, the 326th will be the best team available for deployment to the combat theater."

Damn, Phil thought. *I've got a lot more training ahead of me.*

The colonel took one more look around the car. "Gentlemen, one year from now, I expect us to be the toughest and best-trained Infantry Division in this country's Army. And I'll tell you the truth: I pity the poor Kraut sonsabitches who are going to have to face us. I do. Because we're going to kill as many damn Germans as we can. How you men train yourselves and the men in this Regiment will determine how quickly we do that and how many heroes we bring home alive. So, rest up as you can because when we arrive, we're kicking butt. You hear?"

The men rose to their feet in a unanimous cheer. Colonel Cutler nodded his approval and briskly turned to leave. As he reached the door, he turned around. "Oh, and by the way, when we arrive, it won't quite be springtime. They tell me that three feet of snow and thirty-below-zero temperatures await us in those Nebraska sandhills. But not to worry, they also tell me the sandstorms in summer are so bad that we may have to issue the men dust respirators, and the mosquitoes are big enough to saddle. Should be a ton of fun. Plan to make a million memories. Like I say, get ready or get out," he growled. "That's for you *and* your men!"

With that, the colonel spun on his heels and left.

℘

The most memorable part of the cross-country trip was a predawn stop in North Platte, Nebraska, just a few hours before they arrived in Alliance. It seems that Nebraskans from hundreds of miles around had started a canteen[i] with a mission to greet every troop train and shower the soldiers with sandwiches, hard-boiled eggs, cookies, doughnuts, and countless loaves of bread and cakes. Pretty teenage girls, known as "platform girls," walked past the railway cars carrying baskets of fruit, cigarettes, candy, and popcorn balls—sundries that were free for the asking.[42]

One of the most extensive volunteer efforts of the entire war—feeding hungry soldiers during their train's brief refueling stop in North Platte—was the brainchild of Rae Wilson, a local volunteer who figured if the North Platte Red Cross ladies could run a canteen during the Great War, then it could be done again. Little did she know how big the effort would become. She named it the North Platte Canteen.[ii]

Volunteers baked various goods and tasty treats, using donated ration books to buy enough flour, sugar, butter, and chocolate. Children even gave up their birthday cakes so the sugar could be used to make cakes for the soldiers. Gas rations were pooled so groups of women could drive in with their baked goods from distant towns or farms. Extra farm produce was saved for the canteen by farm families instead of selling it.

Up to twenty-four troop trains *a day* stopped at North Platte, day and night. Every soldier was greeted, no matter the hour, and every soldier received something to eat. In a typical month, volunteers prepared and gave away over 40,000 cookies, 30,000 hard-boiled eggs, 6,000 doughnuts, countless loaves of bread and cakes, and 3,000 pounds of sandwich meat.

Phil watched in amazement as the platform girls handed popcorn balls to excited soldiers hanging out the window. A conductor named Webb leaned over to Phil, and in a hushed voice, said, "A lot of these girls put their names and addresses in the popcorn balls. The folks that run the canteen don't approve, but I hear it's still happening. Seems like we have pen pals galore around here. Post offices in central Nebraska are receiving hundreds of letters every day from places like Alliance. And at least one marriage has occurred because of this."

---

i   A canteen is a small cafeteria or snack bar where free food is provided for military personnel.

ii   The North Platte Canteen began December 17, 1941, ten days after Pearl Harbor. Men from the Nebraska National Guard were scheduled to stop at 11 a.m., but a train did not arrive until 4:30 p.m. By this time, at least 500 relatives and friends of local servicemen had shown up at the depot. The crowd cheered, but the soldiers weren't from Nebraska. The crowd gave them the gifts and food that were originally meant for their own sons and wished them off anyway. At the end of the war, the canteen continued to operate as men returned until its closure on April 1, 1946. During its time of operation, 55,000 volunteers from 125 different towns, some 200 miles away, served over six million servicemen and women. The volunteers at the train depot would work from five in the morning until midnight because they didn't know when the troop trains would come through since their movements were secret.

"Well," Phil confided, "my gal's in Gulfport, Mississippi, and I suspect her letters will be catching up with me in Alliance. She'll be writing all the time, so I don't suspect I'll be needing any other pen pals."

The conductor smiled. "Good for you, soldier. Good for you."

ॐ

The day after arriving at Alliance Air Base, Phil wrote home:

> Dearest Mom,
>
> Look where your wandering boy is now. Yes, and it's cold. The morning we got here, Friday, March 5th, it was around twenty degrees below, and we had about a foot of snow on the ground, and gosh, it was cold. They have us here so we can get final training with gliders.... Everyone seems to think this outfit is a sure way of getting killed quick. But I don't; in fact, I think it's lots of fun.
>
> With all love, Phil
>
> P.S. Mom, will you have a will drawn up for me? Send it to me to sign, and I'll mail it back. We have to have one just in case.[43]

Phil and the officers gathered to meet with the airbase's commander, forty-five-year-old Lieutenant Colonel D. Arthur Walker. As he entered the room, the men snapped to attention. He was a short, stocky man with a rounded, almost pudgy face, with small eyes that appeared to be squinting at whomever he glared at, and a tiny, pointed nose.

"At ease," he began. "And I might add, this is the last time you'll be at ease during your training here. I say that because we're going to put you and your men through hell. No fake bullets here, gentlemen. Shooting at the students is the best way to cure buck fever before meeting the enemy's bullets. You need to know that we have lost men in this manner. But neither the men nor their families have objected because they know this type of training is the real stuff. They also know it's the best way to teach self-reliance and self-confidence."[44]

He paused, his voice softening a bit. "During the Allied occupation of French North Africa, soldiers who were not previously trained under battle conditions were frightened by their first exposure to enemy fire. The men graduating from here will not be known for that fear. They will be known for their skill and daring, and for the way they attack and kill the enemy. To be in *this* Army takes expertise and guts on both ends of a bayonet. It's not a game! And it's not rough, inhuman treatment of our soldiers. We're teaching them to kill so they won't be killed—that's what it takes to win battles."

Lt. Colonel Walker's voice increased in volume. "Among the tricks you and your men will be taught will be gouging out eyes, tearing noses from the face, crushing facial bones so the fragments will pierce the brain, strangling and snapping the neck, and smashing bones in the feet. The dirtier, the better. You will become specialists in ruthless, dirty fighting. Do you hear me?"

"Yes, sir!" the men shouted.

He was quiet another moment as he looked sternly around the room. "Dismissed!" he barked before marching out.

Phil sat in his chair, contemplating what it would be like to engage in hand-to-hand combat. He wondered how he would react when confronting the enemy, up close and personal, in a kill-or-be-killed moment.

Would he act bravely and show courage?

He believed he would, but as his instructors said, that's when you find out what you're made of.

9

DRAFTS AND SCOTCH

"This one isn't just any old horse. There's a nobility in his eye, a regal serenity about him. Does he not personify all that men try to be and never can be? I tell you, my friend, there's divinity in a horse, and 'specially in a horse like this. God got it right the day He created them."

—Sir Michael Morpurgo, British author and playwright[45]

The men were put through extensive physical testing and conditioning,[i] as well as schools in demolition, artillery, camouflage, hand-to-hand fighting, attack of fortified positions, and the detection of mines.[46]

Fortunately, by late March, the weather warmed enough so that Phil could start flying again. Outdoor drilling exercises continued throughout "mud season," as Nebraskans called it, until the arrival of May and warmer temperatures. On Mother's Day, Phil wrote this:

---

i   In the 1940s, men were generally in excellent physical condition. An average male could either immediately or fairly quickly pass the Army Fitness Test. The man's performance was graded on a scale that ranged from poor to excellent. To score above poor, a man would need to do seven pull-ups, 31 jump squats, 27 push-ups, 52 sit-ups in two minutes, and run a 300-yard sprint in 52.5 seconds. Almost all the men received the highest score. Phil did 20 pull-ups, 75 jump squats, 54 push-ups, 79 sit-ups in two minutes, and ran 300 yards in 44 seconds.

May 9, 1943

To My Mother on Her Day:

This is the hardest letter I have ever had to write. I know what I want to say, but I have so few words to say it with.

Now in the position I am, I can look back on my eighteen years and see how my own sweet Mother has made all this possible for me. How you worked your fingers to the bone, how you have done without so that I might have. I see all that now, and I seem only to be able to say, "Mother, I thank you." But I do want you to know I am proud of you. I burst with pride when I can point you out to people and say, "That's my Mother." And then to know of all the mothers, mine is the best of them all.

There are so many things I want to say, but I just can't make the words. The thing that makes me proudest is to sign my letters,

Your forever loving son,
Philip[47]

Although the training weeks were difficult, weekends were another story. The nearby town of Alliance, a farming community of 6,000 with streets paved in red brick, became known as a "soldier's paradise" with plenty of pretty girls, good laughs, and strong whiskey. At first, Phil avoided the bawdy trips to town by wrangling a weekend pass and hopping on military aircraft to Des Moines to meet Marilyn.

Marilyn's father was an officer with the National Guard, so she could fly military transport and talked Phil into meeting her at a more exciting venue. She chose San Francisco, where they stayed in the Presidio officer quarters, one of the most romantic locations the Army could offer. Phil bunked in the bachelor officer quarters, and Marilyn stayed in the officer guest quarters. For two memorable days, the happy couple walked all over San Francisco, from Fisherman's Wharf to the Embarcadero to Union Square to exotic Chinatown.

A couple of weeks later, their rendezvous was in New York City, where they stayed with his father's only sibling, Aunt Leota, and her husband, Walter Owens,[ii] in their Park Avenue brownstone. After visiting the typical tourist sites, Phil and Marilyn dined in the finest restaurants and danced their nights away at the hottest nightclubs in Manhattan—all costs covered by Uncle Walter, who also introduced Phil to Cuban cigars and taught him to appreciate Scotch whiskey.

Another weekend, Phil and Marilyn met at Fort Meade, halfway between Baltimore and Washington, where Phil was assigned to a special two-week school to learn how to cook with dehydrated foods, which proved to be interesting. Phil thought the powdered milk tasted like chalk.

The United States Army Quartermaster Corps taught the course at its school for Bakers and Cooks. Phil received a Certificate of Proficiency for "satisfactorily completing" the "Cold Weather Cooking Course" as well as the "Theory and Practice of Cold Weather Cooking."

During one of his weekends with Marilyn, though, their relationship hit its first rocky patch. Afterward, Phil began spending more weekends in Nebraska and eventually met the pretty daughter of a local rancher. Her friends called her Sunny because of her bright disposition, effervescent personality, and cheerful smile. Phil enjoyed his time with her and her entire family at their ranch, not far from town. He went to church with them on Sundays and found his quiescent spiritual faith stirred. But truth be told, he was mesmerized with her father's horses: a herd of Percherons, Thoroughbreds, and American Quarter Horses.

Phil wrote this to his parents:

> *Alliance does have some nice women. I know cause I'm*
> *going with a nice, sweet kid now. Didn't go out much when*
> *I first got here, but I do now!*[48]

Sunny had personally named each of her dad's Percheron draft horses, which were exported in the late 19th century from France to the United States about the time folks were homesteading the Midwest. That's when Sunny's grandfather started buying them for the family farm. Percherons were known for their ability to haul bulky goods and harvested crops from the fields. Their Percherons were enormous, standing about seventeen to eighteen hands and weighing just over 2,000 pounds. Sunny mentioned that Percherons accounted for over 70 percent of the purebred draft horses in the United States. "Even though they are massive, they're known to travel more than thirty miles a day—and at a trot no less. Amazing!"

---

ii   Leota Larimore was married to Walter Owens, the president of the United States Casualty Company. Author Walt Larimore is named after him.

In early June, Phil accompanied Sunny and her father as they drove a trailer containing several of their Percherons to the Box Butte County Fair. Phil helped them put on their very best harnesses made from beautifully hand-worked leather with brass hitchings buffed to a high shine.[iii] Their Percherons were going to take part in a draft pull competition in which the fully harnessed draft horses pulled a metal sled loaded with concrete blocks.

The draft horse competition was popular with the locals interested in seeing the gorgeous horses perform at their peak. That day, the stands were packed with an enthusiastic crowd that understood and appreciated the big horses and how they helped build this country. Even the barns housing the animals were full of visitors from early morning until well after dinner.

Phil watched as the family's draft horses were placed in front of the sled, accompanied by her father, who was acting as the "teamster" or leader. Two side men, called "eveners," attached the horses to the load. A whistle was blown, and the Percherons were off and charging, throwing their massive frames into the pull. The leather harnesses and chains pulled taut as the mighty Percherons strained every muscle under the encouragement of the teamster.

The crowd remained quiet, as teams would quit early if they heard a cheer, thinking their draw was done. In no time at all, the horses pulled the cart the required distance until the judge's whistle blew again, signaling a completed pull. Then other teams were given a chance to pull the same load. Those that couldn't were eliminated from the competition.

After each round, the sled's weight increased by a half-ton or 1,000 pounds. The last team able to complete a pull would be declared the winner. After numerous pulls, Sunny's father won the competition with a load of more than 12,000 pounds. Phil was impressed. That night, after watering, feeding, and brushing the horses, Phil and Sunny's family sat next to the trailer and shared a picnic dinner and talked. After a dessert of homemade apple pie, he and Sunny's father smoked a cigar and sipped an aged single-malt scotch.

During his stay in Alliance, Phil enjoyed riding and caring for the mammoth draft horses with Sunny and loved the thrill of his new relationship with her.

The summer of '43 was proving to be a time when Phil spread his wings and realized his world was expanding.

---

iii   The most critical part of the harness were the hames—metal or wooden bars on either side that supported the horse's collar and transferred the massive pulling power of the horse to the equipment in tow via heavy leather traces.

10
FÜHRERVILLE

"When all is said and done, the brunt of the war is carried by the Infantry.... Final victory is won by the Infantry, and final occupation of a country must be made by the Infantry."

—Eleanor Roosevelt, First Lady from 1933–1945[49]

O ne of Phil's favorite training exercises was leading his men into a mock-up German town built by the regiment at the site of an abandoned ranch.[50]

The battalion command called it the "German Village Assault Course," but the men called it "Führerville." The simulated village was overseen by forty-one-year-old Lieutenant Colonel William C. "Wild Bill" Saffarans,[i] who trained soldiers extensively and exhaustingly in house-to-house and street fighting, all under live explosions and the fearsome hail of live shooting aimed at their feet, beside them, and just over their heads. "The darn thing will kill a good man,"[51] Phil said in a letter to his parents.

Führerville caught the attention of a local newspaperman, Jim McKee, with the *Lincoln Journal Star*, who wrote:

---

i   Lt. Col. Saffarans was a former Georgetown Hoyas football hero and rifle team marksman, who had previously been the commandant of the Second Army Ranger School.

> *Their skill and daring were shown by the way*
> *they attacked through mud, barbed wire, and whizzing*
> *bullets to take and occupy Führerville over and over*
> *again. Exercises were held during the day, in the middle*
> *of the night, and during rainstorms and sandstorms.*
> *The fame of the 326ᵗʰ's close-combat course became so*
> *legendary that Yank, the Army Weekly called it "the*
> *toughest in the country."⁵²*

Throughout the intense training at Führerville and elsewhere, Phil saw his men grow and mature into a vicious fighting machine. They were light, fast, agile, smart, and strong, and he expected they'd be hell in battle.

Phil was promoted to Executive Officer (XO), or the second in command, for Company C of the 326ᵗʰ Glider Infantry. He was putting in long days, sometimes from 5 a.m. until ten at night. Still, he took great pride in the success he and his men enjoyed. After they completed the Close Combat Course on June 8, 1943, the battalion was notified they'd start field exercises the next day.

As summer began, the battalion commander observed Phil's leadership qualities and quickly promoted him to the battalion staff as the S-2 intelligence officer.[ii] The S-2 collected intelligence on the enemy and studied enemy tactics to discern how to conduct an attack or defend against one. The S-2 also researched enemy weapons and equipment, comparing them with his company's to determine both strengths and weaknesses.

For the final exam of their Infiltration Course training, Phil took his platoon to the small town of Hyannis, Nebraska.[iii] Here's how he described the mission in a letter to his mother:

> *Our mission will be to go into an enemy town ahead*
> *of the troops and get all the information we can without*
> *being seen. Information such as where the powerhouse*
> *is, where the telephone office and telegraph offices are*
> *at, what times trains run through the town, who the*
> *leading men of the town are, etc. Then we make up a*
> *map of the town. All this has to be done without anyone*
> *knowing we are there.*

---

ii   World War II U.S. Army staff sections were indicated by a letter prefix reflecting their responsibilities. The letter "G" indicates division level and above. "S" refers to divisional brigades and lower (regiments, companies, etc.) Personnel staff were G-1 or S-1, intelligence G-2 or S-2, operations and training G-3 or S-3, and logistics G-4 or S-4.

iii   Hyannis, Nebraska, population 500, was about 60 miles due east of Alliance.

*To make it seem like Hyannis is an enemy town, before
we leave camp, I'll call up the police in the town and the
state police and tell them to be on the lookout for eleven men
who had run away from camp. This is to make our task
harder. Of course, we won't have any place to sleep except
under haystacks.*

*We'll be traveling light: our weapon, helmet, two days
of food, and half a pup tent that we'll use as a blanket. We
will be walking well over 150 miles on this five-day trip and
with only two days of food. The boys will have it rough,
walking about thirty miles each day, mostly at night,
including scouting around the town, but still, I love it.[53]*

On the third night of the exercise, after scouting around Hyannis all
night in a constant rainstorm, he and his men snuck into a barn just outside
of town and snuggled up in the back of the hayloft. They planned to stay in
the barn, get dry, and remain out of sight during daylight. The men quickly
went to sleep, but Phil couldn't stop himself from climbing down to admire
the draft horses. With their chestnut coats, blonde manes and tails, white
stripes on their faces, and four white socks, they were easy for him to recognize
as Belgians.

As dawn approached, he quickly climbed up to the hayloft and covered
himself. He heard the barn door slowly creak open. Instinctively, he drew his
.45 pistol and softly shushed the men. He peered from the loft to see a man
in overalls partially close the door behind him. After brushing each horse, he
gave them fresh water and grain and then picked up a pail and went into one
of the cows' stalls. He pulled a small stool off the wall, sat down, and began
milking the cow. The man's border collie ran into the barn and sat down by
him, his tail vigorously wagging.

One of Phil's men must have rolled over because the board under him
squeaked. The collie whipped around and looked up at the barn loft. He
cocked his head and sniffed the air.

The farmer looked and said to his collie, "It's probably just one of those
big ol' barn rats I've seen up there that's 'bout as big as you." Then he laughed.
"Buddy, they'll eat any varmints that get into our barn."

The grizzled man stood and went to the second pen, quickly feeding and
then milking the cow. When he was finished, he spoke to his dog again. "Let's
get these milk pails into Ma and her cats." He put up the stool, closed the stall
door, and secured the barn door as he and his dog left.

"Whew," whispered one of the men. "That was close."

"Let's wait a bit before we get outta here," Phil warned. "Once the rain slows down, I think we need to find another place to hole up."

Phil heard the dog barking again, and the barking grew closer.

"Be quiet!" he whispered to his men as the barn door hinges squeaked again. This time, the farmer and his collie entered the barn, followed by a stocky woman carrying a large tray covered by a red-and-white checkerboard cloth. She set down the tray. "Let's see what we have here."

Phil could smell wonderful aromas exploding inside the barn. Suddenly, he was famished.

"Well, there's flapjacks and maple syrup," said the farm wife. "Bacon and sausage. Scrambled eggs, fresh-made biscuits, and sausage gravy too."

"'Nuff to feed a small army, I'd say," her husband added, chuckling. "Sheriff said some men might have escaped from the air base down in Alliance. Said they might be up here Hyannis way. No way they'd march this far. Ain't nuthin' up this way anyway. I bet they're just doin' a field exercise like we did before the Great War, and their commander's trying to get them caught. But either way, I remember from my days in training that a man could get right hungry in the field."

The man smiled, bent over, and scratched Buddy's head.

The woman covered the food and backed away from it. Her husband put his arm around her as they walked out of the barn. Turning to close the door, he called the dog, who was still staring up at the hayloft.

"Come on, Buddy!" The dog turned and sprinted through the door. The farmer looked up at the hayloft. "God bless you, men."

Then the door creaked and closed.

Phil told his buddies that he had never eaten a better breakfast—ever.

⁓

After successfully completing their mission, Phil's performance rating was graded as "excellent," and he was promoted to his battalion's S-1 Officer position. The S-1 was the administrative and personnel officer. He managed promotions, evaluation reports, awards, punishments, and gains and losses of personnel.[54]

Phil wrote his mother, saying:

> Oh, yes, did I tell you about my new job? Now I am
> Battalion Adjutant. That's almost assistant to the Colonel.
> Gosh, does he keep me on the hop.[55]

Although delighted with the promotion, Phil was somewhat disappointed to be pulled away from the men he had been training. There was also disappointment on the love front: after additional visits with Sunny and her family, Phil reluctantly recognized that although he loved the camaraderie he had with her, her father, and their drafts, that was all it was. He realized he didn't love Sunny. His heart was still reserved for Marilyn.

In late June, Phil wrote his dad:

> *Yes, Marilyn and I are still going together. After seeing her for the last two years, I still think that I will marry that gal. But not for a while. Hope to fly over and see her soon.*[56]

The following weekend, he hopped on a flight to Des Moines, where he and Marilyn caught a late Saturday afternoon movie, *Random Harvest*, starring Ronald Colman and Greer Garson at the Strand Theater Uptown. This was followed by a candlelight dinner and an evening of slowly sipping drinks and treasuring slow dances played by George West and his band at the Pastime Club.

Phil enjoyed tenderly holding Marilyn's hands and relishing long, passionate embraces punctuated with soft kisses. Their reunion was a joyful combination of long walks and longer talks. The only slight pall of sadness that weekend was saying goodbye to her father, who was being shipped out to Europe to serve on General Patton's staff.

Phil suspected his orders would be coming any day.

11
FINAL PREPARATIONS

"Infantrymen—we signed up to spit in the face of danger, to walk the line between life and death, and live to do it again—or not."

—Unknown[57]

Training continued for a sweltering, dusty summer. By September, the heat began to remit.[58] Phil wrote:

> It's starting to get cold now, and come next Monday, we are going back into the wools. Glad to get back into them again. I like to be in them. But when it starts getting cold, it means most of our glider flying is over.[59]

Phil heard talk that he and his men would be going back to Fort Bragg, but that's all it was—talk. Meanwhile, there was already a skim of ice on nearby ponds by mid-October, and locals were predicting snow before Halloween. What he knew for sure was that he didn't want to go through another severely cold Nebraska winter. He wrote this to his mother:

> Well, I put in for my leave here a few days ago. I asked for fifteen days, starting on December 20. That would mean that I can be home for both Christmas and New Year's.

*Wouldn't that be swell? Yes, Mother darling, it would be
swell except for one little thing. All leaves and furloughs
are canceled until further notice. We are moving out of
here sometime this month or next month and are going on
a two-month maneuver. And we don't know where we are
going till after the maneuvers are over, so for all I know, we
might go straight overseas. There is no telling.*[60]

☙

Plans changed. On October 27, 1943, Phil was suddenly transferred from
battalion headquarters and ordered to return to Fort Benning for specialized
training. He arrived on October 29 and was immediately enrolled in the
Airborne Command Parachute School Demolition course. [61]

Since this was Phil's second time to train at Fort Benning, the post felt
strangely familiar as he was trucked past the manicured lawns, brick buildings,
swimming pools, and base chapel. After his first day at parachute demolition
school, he wrote, "This place is just like all the rest of Benning. Lots of hard
work and very little time to play. But that's what makes time pass by."[62]

He took to the demo training like a duck to water. Phil found out that he
enjoyed explosive work and blowing up steel, wood, and concrete with TNT,
nitrostarch, and so on. The chance to destroy bridges and hydroelectric plants
excited him, as did working on booby traps. He wrote this to his parents:

*This course is lots of fun. They teach us almost every-
thing there is to know about explosives. When we get
finished here and with a bit of extra study, we should be a
darn good bunch. But it's just something to learn that will
come in handy later on.*

During training, Phil was pleasantly surprised to run into Ross Calvert,
who was still on the training staff and proudly wearing his First Lieutenant's
bar. They gave each other a warm hug and agreed to get together for drinks, to
play bridge, and to take weekend rides as often as possible. They also entered
a bridge competition and won the base championship.

"Rumors are I'm shipping out soon," Ross told Phil one evening at the
Officer's Club.

"Where to?"

"Not sure, but there's talk of the 3rd Division having another D-Day[i] in
Italy. You know, they've already had five."

---

i   "D-Day" was an Army designation to indicate the day when a specific field operation began.

"*Five?* I had no idea!"

"Yup. Three division-wide amphibious assaults:[ii] Fedala in French Morocco, then Sicily, and finally Salerno, on the mainland of Italy. Also, two battalion-wide amphibious D-Days, both of which were flanking moves in Northern Sicily. As you've no doubt heard, the fighting in the mountains of Italy is a vicious slugfest. Lots of guys lost—especially junior officers. They say the mortality for our lot is through the roof. So lots of lieutenants are needed. My bet is I'm heading there. What about you, Daddy-O?"

Phil took a sip of his drink. "No idea. But the rumors have been Europe. Wouldn't it be swell if we were in the same unit?"

ↄ

Phil was given a well-deserved furlough to see his parents for a few days and then returned to Fort Benning on November 25, Thanksgiving Day.[63]

A week later, on Thursday, December 2, buses were organized to take the men to Kirven's Department Store in nearby Columbus, where twenty-four hostesses had volunteered to assist the GIs with their Christmas shopping. Other girls—scantily dressed—served candy, cigarettes, and conversation.

It turned out that black nightgowns and negligees were Fort Benning soldiers' favorite gifts to send home since lingerie was in short supply due to the war and not available at the Post Exchange. The newly redecorated Southern Bell Telephone Company's phone booth room was packed with GIs calling their gals. Phil talked as long as he could with Marilyn.

While shopping at Kirven's, he heard Bing Crosby singing "White Christmas" on the phonograph. The song hit Phil with an emotional wallop since he couldn't secure holiday leave and could only be home for Christmas in his dreams. With sadness, he shared this with his parents:

> *This Christmas and New Year's have been the quietest that I have ever spent. On New Year's Eve, I went to bed about 2130, and that was all. I slept the New Year in and think it did me a lot better than if I went out anywhere.*[64]

At the end of his training, Phil was awarded a certificate in Military Specialties as a Demolition Officer. His leave finally came through after New Year's Day. There wasn't enough time to make one last visit to his parents *and* see Marilyn, however. He agonized over the decision of where to go in this letter home:

---

ii An amphibious assault is an offensive military operation that uses naval ships to project ground and air power onto a hostile designated landing beach, followed by the landing of troops on hostile shores.

> *Got a letter from Marilyn today. Mom, I don't know*
> *where to spend my next leave. I want to be with her so bad I*
> *can taste it, and at the same time, I want to be with you just*
> *as bad. Oh, poor me. Why can't I pick a girl from Memphis?*
> *But, oh well. I love Marilyn, and Mom, in my mind, there is*
> *no doubt about it. If I could, I would marry her in a minute,*
> *but at least one of us must finish college, and since it looks*
> *like I'm not ever going to get the chance to go back, I guess*
> *it's up to her to get the schooling.*[65]

In the end, Phil decided to see Marilyn instead of visiting his parents in Memphis. He left Fort Bragg for Des Moines on January 3 for a week-long furlough with his girlfriend. After arriving by military air transport, he celebrated his nineteenth birthday with her on January 4.

While thoroughly enjoying a delightful time with Marilyn, a telegram arrived at her parents' home that shocked Phil. After a year of training with the 326th, he was ordered to report to Fort Meade, Maryland, on January 10, 1944.

What the hell are they doing with me now? he thought. *Guess I won't know until I get there.*

After a couple of calls, he learned Fort Meade was the largest of the Army Ground Forces Replacement Depots—with a capacity for 18,000 replacements. There was a special need for men with his training as a demolition officer. He now knew he was shipping out to the European Theater of Operations.

At the Des Moines Union Station, 2nd Lieutenant Philip Larimore swept Marilyn Fountain into his arms for a final goodbye kiss.

He wondered if he would ever see her again.

જી

Phil arrived at the Fort Meade Replacement Depot, where the staff on base certified that all overseas replacements met medical requirements, had done qualification firing of their primary weapons, and were otherwise qualified for overseas duty.[66]

The depot also issued clothing and equipment, gave inoculations, took blood types, and processed the men. A training program was instituted to prevent deterioration in discipline, morale, and physical condition, as well as to prepare men psychologically for overseas duty. But the training had to be flexible since men remained in the depots for variable, unpredictable lengths of time, subject to shipment on seventy-two hours' notice.

Although Phil had signed a legal and valid will, he was required to do another. And he had enough time to write Marilyn every day and phone her every few days. After a week at Fort Meade, Phil received orders to take a train 200 miles to Camp Patrick Henry[iii] in Warwick County, Virginia. With the usual amount of starting, stopping, switching, and uncoupling, the trip took about ten hours.

Phil was fortunate to learn from another officer in the Officer's Club about the Coast Guard Beach Patrol. That weekend he got a pass and hitched a ride to their station and stables in nearby Virginia Beach, about an hour away. Phil was delighted to be invited to go on a horseback patrol.

The shorter of his two riding partners explained, "We work in pairs, riding about one hundred feet apart, usually covering a two-mile stretch of the beach. We're armed with portable radio-receiver transmitters, compasses, whistles, pistols, and rifles, and we can cover difficult terrain pretty quickly and efficiently. That's why they call us the 'Sand Pounders.'"

"I prefer the term 'Coast Guard Cavalryman,'" the taller guardsman said, laughing. "Or 'Sailors on Horseback.' Anyway, our job is to report offshore enemy vessels and to prevent people onshore from communicating with the enemy at sea."

"When did you all begin using the horses for beach patrols?" Phil asked.

"Just five months ago, in September 1942," one of the men told him. "Within one month, our mounted portion soon became the largest segment of the patrol."

"Where do your horses come from?"

"All from the Army. The Army Remount Service provided all the riding gear required, while the Coast Guard provides our uniforms."

The other man added, "When the mounted program began, a call went out for personnel. A mixed bag of people responded—polo players, cowboys, former sheriffs, horse trainers, Army Reserve cavalrymen, jockeys, farm boys, rodeo riders, and stuntmen. Most of our boys trained on Hilton Head, one of the sites of the dog training schools."

"Enough chitchat!" one of the men yelled. "Let's patrol." He spurred his horse to a gallop, and the others followed. Phil was exhilarated by the salty wind in his hair. The power of the horse underneath him reminded him of an adage he learned at Fort Benning: *Horses lend us the wings we lack.*

The jaunt allowed him to borrow a feeling of freedom, even if only for a few moments, mixed with delight, exhilaration, and true happiness, which would vanish as quickly as it occurred.

iii   Camp Patrick Henry, named after one of the Founding Fathers of the United States, was founded in late 1942 and was a 1,700-acre complex built in a large virgin forest interspersed with impenetrable swamps, leading soldiers to call it "Swamp Patrick Henry." The camp also had a Norfolk & Western train system to transport soldiers to shipside at Chesapeake Bay.

PART II:
THE ITALIAN CAMPAIGN

"We must be ready to dare all for our country. For history does not long entrust the care of freedom to the weak or the timid. We must be willing, individually and as a Nation, to accept whatever sacrifices may be required of us. A people that values its privileges above its principles soon loses both."

—Dwight D. Eisenhower, Supreme Commander of the Allied Expeditionary Force in Europe and 34th President of the United States[67]

12
SHIPPING OUT

"No soldier in any of our theaters of operations is better acquainted with this war than is the Infantryman, and no Infantryman knows war more intimately than does the front-line rifleman."

—Lieutenant General Ben Lear, Commanding General of the U.S. Second Army from 1940–1943[68]

On January 30, 1944, Phil boarded a train at Camp Patrick Henry that would transport the men to Norfolk, Virginia, on the Chesapeake Bay. His eyes focused on three war posters plastered on the front wall of their carriage.[69]

The first said, "Americans Will Always Fight for Liberty." He had seen this depiction of three modern American riflemen marching in front of their military ancestors—three infantrymen from the Continental Army of 1778—many times before.

The second poster made him smile. The graphic pictured an oversized caricature of Hitler falling backward, having been tripped by an Army truck. At the top, a headline said, "Knock the 'Heil' Out of Hitler," and across the bottom, it read, "Let's Keep 'Em Pulling for Victory."

Liberty and victory. A nice series of encouragements, Phil thought, *for guys like me who are getting ready to go overseas and fight.*

Then his eyes fixed on the last poster, a colorful illustration of a young woman who looked a bit like his Marilyn. She wore a red-and-white polka-dot bandana around her head and was flexing her right bicep, which was visible since she had rolled up the sleeve of her blue blouse.

Across the top, a headline announced, "We Can Do It!" Phil knew he would. Well, at least he *hoped* he would, as the train entered the shipyard. He knew that it was up to him to fight to get back to her, and he would.

As the railway cars drew closer to the docks, Phil spotted ships of all sizes as far as the eye could see. As the train pulled into a platform under protective roofing, literally stopping next to their Liberty ship, Phil put on his overloaded backpack and grabbed his duffel-like barracks bag. As he stepped off the railroad car, he was checked off a list and marched toward the waiting ship.

Young female Red Cross workers handed out cups of coffee from fifty-gallon stainless steel containers to each of the boys who wanted them. Then each soldier was checked off another list as he boarded the gangplank onto the ship under the watchful eyes of Army military police and Navy shore patrol. Each man struggled to carry his load up a steep and narrow ramp.

Phil was directed below decks to officer's quarters, where eight officers were assigned to cabins with two-tier bunks with springs and mattresses. In comparison, the enlisted soldiers were shoehorned into tighter quarters with four to five tiers of bunk beds that nearly touched the ceiling. The space between bunks was so narrow that one had to walk sideways to get through, and there was no place to store a barracks bag except on the bunk.

There was considerably more room inside the officer's quarters. While Phil knew he wasn't staying in first-class accommodations, he realized that he had it better than most. Maybe the long trip wouldn't be so bad after all.

ভ৩

Phil stood on the deck and watched his homeland disappear over the horizon. It wasn't long before many of the men got seasick. Even though the soldiers weren't able to smoke below deck or get any exercise, they took the sketchy meals, lack of privacy, and relaxed hygiene standards in stride. They managed to laugh and poke fun at it all, and at themselves, cursing Hitler roundly at all times.[70]

Nine days later, the Liberty ship docked at Casablanca in the North African country of French Morocco on Tuesday, February 8, 1944. Phil and his men knew this wasn't their final destination. By now, even the naivest soldier had figured out that they were going to Italy, where the Allies were being clobbered at Cassino and the 3rd Infantry Division had just landed at Anzio during their fourth amphibious landing on a foreign shore. The 3rd Battalion had also had two additional amphibious landings in Sicily.

While waiting for their duty orders in French Morocco, Phil toured the nearby sights, which he described in this letter home:

I have seen quite a large amount of the mountains here, and they are nice. We have a lot of trouble with the native kids, though. They are always trying to bum a smoke or candy off of you and will steal your eye teeth if you don't keep an eye on them. I let a cute girl that I met near camp teach me French. She said if I would teach her to jitterbug and how to use English slang, she would teach me French. That sounds like a good deal, doesn't it?[71]

He also learned from her about a Moroccan tradition called *lab al baroud* or the "gunpowder game" in which horsemen wearing traditional garb charge in a single line at the same speed firing their *moukhalas*, or muskets, into the air in unison. She said soldiers could participate on a nearby beach where some nomadic horsemen had set up camp. Phil was able to obtain a pass and a Jeep for the short drive. At the encampment, she introduced Phil to an English-speaking Arab who would serve as his guide. The young man first took him to meet the horses.

"Arabian horses," he explained, "are a breed that began here over a thousand years ago. What you are seeing is the result—a bold, fearless horse that is as comfortable in the desert as in the mountains, an incredibly strong and versatile animal."

Looking across the herd, all contentedly eating hay, Phil noted, "They seem to come in many colors."

"Yes, all colors, and as you can see, with a gorgeous metallic sheen to their coat."

"Your English is excellent," Phil commented.

"My parents sent me to London for my education. But my love of Morocco and these horses brought me back."

Phil ran his hand along a magnificent stallion. Its neck was long and muscular, and its chest was wide. He then ran his hand along its high withers, noting the short but muscular back. The horse shook its head, and Phil ran his hand through the plush mane.

"See how long and thick the mane and tail are? Helps protect him from the desert flies, which can be fierce."

Two men dressed in flowing white garments trotted by on their Arabian horses. Phil turned to his guide. "I expected a clunky gait. But they're quite graceful."

The man smiled. "You know your horses, sir. They have an exceptionally smooth trot, which makes them incredibly comfortable to ride. The breed is so characterized by its flowing gait that they are highly valued by the Moroccan royal family. Of course, it seems royal families in every country have their preferred breed. In Europe, they are the Arabian, Andalusian, Friesian, and Lipizzaner breeds. But for us Moroccans, it's this one, which is why we have a saying about the Arabians: 'Nobility without arrogance, loyalty without jealousy, splendor without pride—a faithful servant but never a slave.'"

Phil smiled. "When I was growing up," he said wistfully, "an Austrian with the world-famous Lipizzaners told me that among equestrians from around the world, 'Our hoofbeats were many, but our hearts beat as one.'"

The Moroccan guide nodded. "It's true, my friend. But let's get you dressed and ready for the charge."

The young man took Phil to a tent and outfitted him with a long flowing white gown and a turban. A quick lesson on loading and firing a native musket was followed by a brief demonstration of the foot and knee movements required to guide his horse. The young man explained that the musket had to be held with both hands above shoulder level when fired during the charge. In no time, Phil mastered the technique, much to the delight of his guide.

The riders lined up on the beach, and at a pistol-shot signal, raced together in a single line at the same speed and then raised and fired their moukhalas in unison, the sounds of the shots blending into a single, overpowering burst of sound and gunpowder.

After several reloads and repeat charges, the men trotted back to the makeshift stable to feed and brush the horses, followed by the drinking of traditional mint tea and snacking on Moroccan almond cookies and sweets.

Phil's guide explained more about *lab al baroud*. "This reenactment is practiced all across North Africa and dates back to the eighth century. The cavalry charge began during what we call the 'Islamic Golden Age,' when cavalry maneuvers were performed as displays of power to intimidate enemy armies. The custom of firing the muskets was added after gunpowder and guns arrived in the region in the early 13th century. Since then, it's been popular with tribesmen as well as tourists."

"Tourists?"

"Of course. The most famous perhaps was the French painter Delacroix. Do you know of him?"

Phil nodded.

"Delacroix[i] visited Morocco in 1832, participated in *lab al baroud* and did a series of sketches and paintings of our people and our horses. He introduced Europeans to our traditions, and we've hosted tourist caravans ever since. And now, we have you American and British soldiers to help us carry the tradition back to your homes."

Phil lifted his teacup to his new friend. "May I make it home."

---

i   Ferdinand Victor Eugène Delacroix (1798–1863), son of a noble family from Paris and called the "greatest French Romantic painter," visited Morocco in 1832 as part of a French diplomatic mission. His many drawings and annotations were made in seven sketchbooks during the trip.

"From your lips to the ears of Allah," the man replied solemnly as their teacups clinked together.

Phil soaked in every minute of the exotic experience, pinching himself the entire time.

છ૭

After another eight days, orders were issued for 1,000 men to board narrow-gauge railroad cars for a three-day train ride across Morocco and Algeria to Oran, a major city and port on Algeria's northwestern Mediterranean coast. Thirty men stuffed into each railroad car made for tight quarters.[72]

In Oran, Phil was among 200 infantry lieutenants who boarded the *Highland Queen*, a small British steamer bound for Naples, Italy. He was part of a priority shipment of replacement infantry lieutenants urgently needed in Italy.

The young lieutenants were shipped to Naples in smaller groups for two reasons: there was no ship in the Mediterranean at the time large enough to take them all, and crossing the Mediterranean was extremely hazardous with the threat of German air, U-boat, and E-boat attacks.[ii] The men jokingly said it was the only time junior officers had priority in anything.

Just before daybreak, the *Highland Queen* arrived safely in Naples, but the harbor's condition shocked the men. Sunken ships were everywhere, three-deep around the docks, some capsized, others resting on the bottom.

The *Highland Queen* was tied to the outer ring of wrecks, where army engineers had welded angle iron framework up from the holds of the sunken ships and built a six-foot-wide boardwalk to get to the pier.

As the men stumbled to shore in the predawn light, a deep sonorous rumble penetrated the atmosphere. The sound seemed to emanate from a large thunderhead on the shoreline to the southeast of the city. Phil could see massive lightning bolts flashing, one after the other, from the cloud to the ground while the entire cloud seemed illuminated from behind by a Halloween-orange florescence.

As the sun began to rise, he realized the cloud was actually a massive plume of steam and smoke over the cone of Mount Vesuvius. Phil didn't know it at the time, but he and his fellow soldiers were witnessing the birth pangs of the first major eruption of Vesuvius since 1872.

The volcano's rim lit up the waning darkness with bright orange lava flowing down a portion of the mountain. Gazing at the fiery tableau, Phil wondered if that was what hell would look like.

But as he would find out in due time, hell was located about eighty nautical miles to their northwest.

---

ii   U-boat was an anglicized and shortened version of the German word *Unterseeboot*. E-boat was the Allies' term for a fast-attack craft, similar to the U.S. Navy's PT boat.

13

MEETING MAGELLAN

"At its finest, rider and horse are joined not by
tack but by trust."

—Anonymous Italian Dressage Master

After arriving on the docks at Naples, the ever-present Army 6x6 trucks[i] were waiting to take Phil and the other second lieutenants to the Replacement Depot, which occupied a horse racetrack known as Italian Prime Minister Benito Mussolini's favorite.[73]

By early February, the German Fourteenth Army surrounding Anzio numbered around 100,000 troops, while the Allied Forces totaled a fourth less at 76,400. Both sides had suffered 20,000 casualties since the Allied landing on January 22, 1944, each loss needing at least one replacement. Pulitzer Prize-winning historian and journalist Lawrence Rush "Rick" Atkinson wrote, "Casualties had become so corrosive that each U.S. infantry division in Italy could expect to lose its entire allotment of 132 2nd lieutenants in less than three months of combat."[74]

On average, 500 men were shipped from Naples *each day* to reinforce the so-called "Beachhead Army" of the U.S. VI Corps, led by Major General

---

i   The five-ton 6x6 truck was a class of heavy-duty six-wheel drive trucks used by the U.S. Army. The basic cargo version was designed to transport five-ton loads (or 10,000 pounds) over all types of roads and cross-country terrain in all weather.

Lucian K. Truscott, previously the commander of the 3rd Infantry Division and one of the youngest division commanders in the U.S. Army at the time.

The first day or two after arriving, many of the officers took passes to go into Naples. But Phil had heard about some special horses being kept at the stables near the racetrack. He and another officer, an equestrian who spoke fluent Italian, decided to explore the stables. Suspicious of criminals being present, they drew their sidearms and slowly moved from the door of one ornate stall to another. At one stall, as Phil peered around the door, and a sudden short snort and sharp rap caused him to instinctively drop to one knee and aim his pistol at the potential enemy, using a two-handed combat pistol grip—ready to fire in an instant.

Standing in the stall was one of the most beautiful horses Phil had ever seen, prompting him to lower his gun. The horse's head was small and a bit square, but his neck was elegant, long, crested, and high set. The stallion's body was deep, his back short, and his powerful hindquarters round and wide.

A deep voice from behind surprised the men. "*Cosa stai facendo qui? Tu chi sei?*" A thin old man rapidly approached them, holding a riding whip menacingly, pointing it at them.

"He wants to know what we are doing here and who we are," Phil's companion quickly translated.

"Well, hell!" Phil exclaimed, "Tell him we're just looking around before he beats the tar out of us!"

A hasty conversation reassured the old stablemaster that the men were soldiers and equestrians. He put his whip down.

"Magellan," the old man said in heavily accented English, "is his name."

"I've never seen so magnificent a horse since I saw the Lipizzaners when I was a boy," Phil replied.

"You were in Vienna?"

"No, sir. They were visiting in Tennessee where I grew up."

The old man warmed to these comments. "Can you translate for me?" he asked Phil's buddy, who nodded.

The old man began in Italian. "Magellan is one of the best examples of a rare breed—a Lipizzaner of the Neapolitan bloodline. We call them Neapolitans. They came from Spanish stallions bred with local mares of Etruscan and Berber ancestry back in Roman times. They became very popular in the old kingdom of Naples, but they almost became extinct until dressage changed everything."

"Dressage?"

"It's from an old French word that means *training*. It's a way to teach a horse and rider to communicate and cooperate, an art in which the horse and rider work together to become two hearts with one mind. We who love dressage have a saying: 'Ask me to show you poetry in motion, and I will show you dressage.' It was during the Renaissance that it became an art, when the very first riding school in history was set up right here in Naples."

"Here?"

"*Si!*" the old man emphasized. "In the sixteenth century. From this school came the world-famous Spanish riding school in Vienna 200 years later."

"So that's where the Lipizzaners I saw as a kid came from."

"And that's where most of the Lipizzaner breed is now housed—well, there and their stud farms. Hopefully, they will stay safe as I fear the war is heading toward them."

Phil's fellow officer asked, "Wasn't there a dressage competition in the Olympics?"

The old man smiled. "Here in Italy, competitive dressage began at the beginning of the 20th century and was first included at the 1912 Olympic Games in Stockholm."

Phil remembered reading about the Stockholm Games. "That's the same Olympics where one of our generals, a hell-of-a-horseman named George Patton, competed in the first modern pentathlon."

"Correct. In the 1912 Olympics, dressage was more of an obedience test derived from military tests and not well known," the old man added, "but, by the 1936 Olympics in Berlin, the standard had risen dramatically. The sport is so refined now that a spectator cannot even see how the rider commands the horse."

"So how do they communicate?" Phil's friend asked.

"It's very difficult to learn," was all the old man would say.

Phil wondered if it was an insider's secret. "I'd like to try. Is it possible?"

The man nodded. "Perhaps, but you must come back tomorrow."

ço

Phil returned the next day and began instruction with the master and one of his apprentices, Antonio, who was bilingual.[75]

"He wants you to mount one of his younger horses and watch you," Antonio explained.

As Phil rode in the enclosed ring, the master observed him and seemed pleased as the American advanced through a variety of gaits and movements.

"He wants to tell you about several difficult stances and jumps above the ground," Antonio said. "But not to worry. You won't be doing these today. They take years to master."

"Ah," Phil said. "I remember the Lipizzaner riders calling them 'airs above the ground.'"

The old man nodded his head, smiling. "*Si. Bene.*"

The apprentice translated as rapidly as he could. "The *levade* is where the horse stands up on its hind legs with all its weight on the hindquarters. The hind legs are bent under the belly, and forelegs are bent close to the chest. The body is at an angle of about forty-five degrees to the ground, and the horse remains motionless in this position for a few seconds."

The old man continued. "Then, on command, the horse makes several jumps, without the forelegs touching the ground. That's called a *courbette*. But the most famous, and the most difficult to learn and perform, is the *capriole*. With this movement, the horse leaps high into the air with its body horizontal. At the full height of the jump, the horse kicks out violently with both hind legs."

Phil nodded as the warm memories of witnessing these movements flooded back from his childhood birthday party.

"There are other dressage tricks, but those are the most famous movements. And very few breeds can do them well." The old man took a deep breath as he turned his gaze on his horse. "The Lipizzaner is one of them."

"Might I ride Magellan? Not to do airs, just to ride?" Phil asked.

The old man looked at him suspiciously. He thought a moment before saying, "Why don't you let me think about it? You come back tomorrow, and we'll see."

The next evening, Phil and his friend returned. The old man let Phil brush and bridle Magellan, who not only immediately accepted Phil, but at the end of a walk inside an outdoor arena, nudged him.

"He seems to like you!" the old man exclaimed. "Perhaps he might even trust you."

"I'm honored," Phil whispered.

"In dressage," the old man said, "your horse must know, trust, and like you. And you must understand and love your horse. A true horseman does not regard his horse with the eyes, but he perceives his horse with his heart. It's why I believe that, at their very best, an equestrian and his horse are not joined by tack but by trust."

After mounting Magellan, the old man made sure that Phil could perform the basic gaits: walking, trotting, and the canter. Only when convinced that Phil was indeed an excellent rider, and certain Magellan would respect and obey him, did they move to the next step—working on advanced transitions, such as a collected trot and extended walk.

The old man carefully watched Phil, occasionally barking commands to "Change gait," "Maintain balance," or "Don't pull against the rein."

"When you hold your reins still, you should be able to feel Magellan's mouth without him hanging on your reins," he said. "If you soften your reins forward, he should follow the contact down, neither pulling against the reins nor dropping the contact."

Phil smiled and nodded. He knew this technique from years of riding. He just didn't understand these particular terms.

The old man continued to coach, cajole, and command Phil. "Work on your position in the saddle, Lieutenant. Keep your heels down at all times. Keep your knees at an eighty-degree angle. The balls of your feet must rest on the stirrup irons. Sit tall in the saddle, Lieutenant, without bracing your back. Improve your balance. If you can, you need to whisper very softly to Magellan with no lip movement. It's very difficult. Give it a try."

Phil smiled, thinking, *This will be the easiest of all*. A series of soft sounds emanated from Phil's throat. Magellan's ears tilted forward, and he softly nickered.

The old man smiled. "*Siete pronti, Tenente*," he softly said.

"You are ready, Lieutenant," translated his friend.

Yes, I'm ready, Phil thought.

Ready for a lot of things.

14
GETTING PREPPED FOR HELL

"Praise be to God for this captured sod,
that rich with blood does seep;

With yours and mine, like butchered swine's,
and hell is six feet deep.

That death awaits, there's no debate;
no triumph will we reap.

The crosses grow on Anzio,
where hell is six feet deep."

**—Audie Murphy, World War II Medal of Honor
recipient who fought at Anzio**[76]

On February 19, 1944, Phil received his orders to report to the 30th Infantry Regiment on the Anzio Beachhead. Late that afternoon, he hopped aboard a truck and was driven to the Naples harbor.[77]

When he arrived, Phil saw a hundred or more LSTs[i] in the process of loading. A fellow officer, Russell Cloer, wrote, "I vividly remember trudging up the ramp and seeing large white letters over the gaping entry maw, which read, 'Gateway to Glory.' A patriotic gesture? Or a swabbie's gallows humor? It didn't do much to raise my morale."[78]

Nor did the Italian boys swarming around the gangplank queues hawking an English-language newspaper with the headline, "Anzio Worse Than Salerno," referring to the bloody Allied invasion of Italy on September 3, 1943.

The flotilla of LSTs sailed out of Naples Harbor as the sun set, with Phil aboard one of them in full combat gear. This was it—he was entering a war zone.

In an earlier briefing, he had been told that the trip up the coast to Anzio happened only at night because of German aircraft, E-boat, and U-boat threats. The distance was not far, around 120 miles, but the LSTs did not move very fast, leading some to call them "Large Slow Targets."

Phil was grateful that it was a very dark night as the convoy of LSTs made their way up the coast, staying only a couple of miles offshore. As they approached Anzio, the men could clearly see the shell bursts and machine gun ricochets, as well as an occasional flare, from the inland battle lines. Not a single man could sleep.

At first light on February 20, Phil's LST was about 3,000 yards offshore from Anzio. In the sky above the besieged beachhead, Phil and his companions, who were crowding the deck, gazed at over two dozen sixty-foot long, hydrogen-filled barrage balloons floating in the sky. Also called blimps, they were tethered with metal cables that could be winched up or down to vary their height over the harbor. Their purpose was ingenious: to deny low-level airspace to Luftwaffe dive-bombers, as well as strafing fire from enemy fighters.

Out of the corner of his eye, Phil saw a massive projectile moving faster than a dive-bomber coming in their direction. The shell—which looked larger than a refrigerator—came from a Krupp K5 railway gun,[ii] capable of sending 543-pound shells nearly forty miles. As the shrill whistle of the projectile grew louder, the men instinctively ducked. But Phil kept his eyes just above the gunwale and saw the gigantic projectile slam into an LST next to theirs, which instantly exploded into a mushroom cloud of flames and smoke. He ducked as water and debris rained down on their deck.

---

i   An LST, or Landing Ship, Tank, was a ship developed during World War II to support amphibious operations by carrying tanks, vehicles, cargo, and landing troops directly onto shore with no docks or piers. Its highly specialized design allowed ocean crossings as well as shore groundings. The bow had a large door that could open, deploy a ramp, and unload vehicles due to a special flat keel that allowed the ship to be beached and stay upright.

ii   The Krupp K5 was a heavy railway gun used by Nazi Germany throughout World War II. These 280-mm railroad guns were known by the Americans as "Anzio Annie," "Anzio Express," or "Whistling Pete" due to the express train-like sound the shells generated. The railway gun had a 71-foot long, 11-inch bore barrel that fired shells weighing nearly 600 pounds. The shells traveled as far as 38 miles, and even duds could crater fifty feet into the earth.

It was an awful moment, and if there was any consolation, it was that this particular LST was carrying only ammunition and supplies and no men other than her doomed crew. Because of the desperate need for ammo on the beachhead, some LSTs sailing from Naples carried a hundred tons of ammunition, triple the prudent load.

Then the signal came. Phil's LST lurched forward, rapidly coming to full speed, and made its run for the beach. He was fully aware that the LST's clear mission was to get in, unload, and back out as quickly as possible.

When his LST hit the beach, the clamshell doors flew open, the ramp quickly dropped, and fifty fully supplied 6x6 trucks unloaded in less than four minutes. The 6x6s raced down the ramp and headed toward their predetermined destinations—widely scattered supply dumps one or two miles inland. Between the trucks, Phil and the other soldiers dashed down the ramp.

As the last vehicle was gunning down the ramp, the LST signaled, and a stream of 6x6s carrying hundreds of casualties—the toll of the previous day's battle—lined up to board for the return trip. Phil got a glimpse of wounded men on litters clutching their X-rays in big brown envelopes. Those in casts wore medical descriptions of their injuries scribbled on the plaster. As soon as the injured aboard the trucks were loaded, the ramp went up, the clamshell doors slammed shut, and the LST headed back out to sea.

Phil and his fellow replacements moved forward at a trot in two columns. When they had gone about half a mile, they came to a large open field, where they stood in line to receive their assignments. When Phil got to the front, a seasoned officer handed him a paper notifying him of his assignment: Platoon Leader, Ammunition Pioneer Platoon,[iii] Headquarters Company, 3rd Battalion, 30th Infantry Regiment, 3rd Infantry Division, VI Corps. The officer commented, "Welcome to the Rock of the Marne,[iv] son. You're a Dogface Soldier[v] now."

Phil was one of 182 men (17 officers and 165 enlisted men, including men returning from the hospital) who received slips indicating they would be replacements for the 3rd Battalion, which normally contained at least 800 men. It didn't take a genius to realize his new battalion had taken quite a licking.

---

iii   An Ammunition & Pioneer Platoon, or A&P Platoon, was typically one junior officer (a 2nd lieutenant), a sergeant to assist him, and a driver for the Platoon Jeep, which mounted a .50-caliber heavy machine gun. Each of its three eight-man squads was led by a sergeant. The platoon was also equipped with two bazookas for antitank defense. They carried ammunition to the riflemen on the front line, set and cleared mines and booby traps, rolled out concertina wire, and did small engineering projects such as marking, building, or repairing paths or trails.

iv   "Rock of the Marne" was a nickname the 3rd Infantry Division earned in World War I when the division was outnumbered and fought with primarily inexperienced young men against hardened veterans. Their heroic actions proved to be a turning point during the last German offensive as they stopped three German divisions from crossing the Marne River.

v   "Dogface" generally refers to a U.S. Army foot soldier serving in the Infantry, especially in World War II. The term was adopted from a song, "The Dogface Soldier," written in 1942 by two GIs and widely played and sung during the war.

The men were re-packed into the trucks. During daylight hours, anything moving could be subjected to accurate shell fire, so caution was vital. If a vehicle moved too fast along a road in daylight, it left behind a trail of dust similar to an airplane contrail and was sure to be fired upon.

After a couple of miles along a rutted road, the trucks turned off into a field with a large patch of scrub oak, where Phil and the men unloaded. He learned that this was the regimental service company and rear command post area. When the regimental commander arrived in his Jeep, he didn't waste any words.

"Close in so you can hear me," barked Lieutenant Colonel Lionel C. McGarr,[vi] the 30th Infantry Regiment commander. "You're now part of the 30th Infantry, and you're going in as replacements to the best damn regiment in the United States Army. You're joining the best unit in a crack division and will be expected to live up to the traditions of this regiment and this division."[79]

McGarr took a deep breath and looked at each of the men. His voice softened, and Phil thought he sounded almost like his father.

"You're going to suffer. You came here to suffer. You're going to suffer everything that the Boche can throw at you," he said, using the French slang word for German soldiers. "You're going to suffer everything that goes with a miserable damn climate. But you're going to take it like men."

McGarr paused, his face tightening. "Everyone is scared in his first battle. If he says he is not, he is a liar. The real hero is the one who fights even though he is scared."

The colonel then took a deep breath and let the air out slowly. "We've quit playing games. This is serious business. The Boche is sitting out there with at least seven divisions, and he's trying to shove us into the ocean. Upon you, men, depends the future of every living soul on this beachhead. Don't make any mistake about it. It's men like you going into frontline foxholes and stopping the attack that the Boche is going to throw at us. And you're going to get up there with the idea that you will kill as many of them as possible. The only thing that's going to keep us from being shoved into the sea is killing Boche."

Then the colonel saluted and got into his Jeep and drove off.

Hot damn, Phil thought. *That's a man I'll go to hell with!*

He smiled, thinking of a little poem he heard while at Fort Benning:

> *When an Infantryman gets to heaven,*
> *to Saint Peter, he will tell,*
> *"Just another soldier reporting, sir.*
> *I've served my time in hell."*[80]

---

vi   Colonel Lionel C. McGarr (1904–1988) graduated from the United States Military Academy in 1928 and served in command and staff positions of increasing rank and responsibility. He saw extensive combat in North Africa and Europe as commander of the 30th Infantry Regiment, beginning in October 1943.

15

INTO NO MAN'S LAND

"The first time a man goes into battle is strangely like the first time a man makes love to a woman. The anticipation is overpowering; the ignorance is obstructive; the fear of disgrace is consuming; and survival is triumphant."

—Ben Bradlee, World War II veteran and executive editor of *The Washington Post* from 1965–1991[81]

In the middle of February, the weather turned rainy, and the wind was sharp and ice-cold. Phil and the other men were a miserable bunch, and they hadn't even reached the front yet. The incessant shelling and artillery only compounded the men's misery.[82]

When Phil and the other replacements arrived at their battalion command post, a small stone farmhouse in the Italian countryside, the only thing colder than the weather were the looks cast at them by the enlisted men surrounding the building. One of the replacements observed, "They didn't say much when we came in, clean and shiny with our new overcoats, packs, and helmets. They just looked at us."

The enlisted men were led off, and seventeen new officers were invited inside a small barn on the property attached to the main house. The windows were blacked out with army blankets, and a Coleman lantern[i] lit the barn.

---

i   Small, portable lanterns made by the Coleman company were declared an "essential item" for troops serving in World War II. Nearly 70,000 lanterns were distributed for use by the GIs fighting in Europe.

Captain Robert M. Boddy, the battalion S-3 who was the officer in charge of operations, training, and various other responsibilities, walked into the barn and introduced himself. No sooner had he shaken a few hands than a medic arrived and started dispensing morphine syrettes to each of the men with an explanation on how to use them.

"You may get to your casualties before we do," the medic began. "It's like a syringe, except it has a squishable, collapsible container, kinda like tooth-paste. After the injection, pin the used tube to the soldier's collar to inform others of the dose administered. Don't be afraid to use them. We've got plenty more where these came from."

At that moment, 3rd Battalion Commander Major Allen F. Bacon, who had taken over command on February 20, strode in. The men all popped to attention. He had them sit while he pulled up a chair.

"Men, we've been assigned to what the brass is calling an 'aggres-sive defensive strategy.' We're to hold our sector of the beachhead against a relentless and determined enemy. We'll be continually patrolling and raiding, all the while expecting persistent strong enemy armor-supported attacks. We expect enemy air activity to be intense—heavy bombing and occasional strafing. At night, we won't rest. We'll have reconnaissance and combat patrols probing the enemy positions, and we'll be ordered into sporadic attacks involving artillery and tank destroyer[ii] fire support. This will be made all the more difficult as the Germans are well dug in and camouflaged, defending the key positions in their outer defense line with deadly automatic weapons fire."[iii]

He let his difficult words sink in and then continued. "Let me be clear. We're fighting for our lives on this flat, shell-swept beachhead. Ten battal-ions from seven German divisions occupy an iron ring on our perimeter and hammer us relentlessly. Many of our men are in water-filled foxholes for days on end, afraid to let the tops of their helmets show at all. Casualties have been dangerously high."

Major Bacon leaned back in his chair, then leaned forward. "But know this. This battalion will *not* stay bogged down. We're in Corps Reserve right now, but I'm expecting to be placed on alert status at any moment. And then, when the time comes, we'll break out. And we'll kick butt. And each of you"— he slowly looked at each officer—"will make that happen. I look forward to serving with you."

---

ii   A tank destroyer (TD), a highly mobile lightly armored tank-type vehicle used to fight tanks in World War II, had thick front armor, relatively thin armor on the sides and in the rear, and a long-barreled, high-velocity gun capable of outranging enemy tanks.

iii   An automatic firearm is a firearm capable of automatically cycling the shooting process without needing any more manual operation from the user than simply keeping a trigger depressed. Examples include machine pistols, submachine guns, and machine guns.

After the major left, Captain Boddy handed out the assignments, saying that guides would take them up to their companies. He looked at Russell Cloer. "Your assignment is platoon leader of the I&R Platoon."[iv]

Then he turned to Phil. "Your assignment is platoon leader for the A&P Platoon.[v] Across the road is another house. Your non-coms are over there. Walk across the road, and they'll tell you what you're supposed to do."

That was it. The captain then pronounced, "Dismissed."

Phil blinked as he walked out into the bright daylight. It took a few seconds for his eyes to adjust. Then he received a welcome surprise.

"Son of a bitch!" was all he could gasp as he recognized the man waiting for him with an East Tennessee smile spreading from ear-to-ear.

"Welcome to Anzio, you son of a bitch, you!" exclaimed Ross Calvert, his good buddy from OCS training. The two men embraced, laughing and slapping each other's backs. "We can catch up later, Phil. Let me get you to your men because you've got one hell of an assignment. Mind if I give you some advice?"

"Not at all."

Ross took out a pack of cigarettes and offered one to Phil. They lit up, and after a puff, Ross said, "You've got some amazing guys serving under you. They'll be the warhorses you and I have talked so much about. A lot of them are what we call 'old men,' meaning they've been with the unit since French Morocco. Their last 2nd lieutenant was a ninety-day-wonder[vi] who was an obnoxious, self-centered, know-it-all asshole. Hadn't been in the company two or three days when he got his head blown off 'cause he didn't listen to his men. He was a dumbass. I know you won't be. But you need to know these good men need—no—*deserve* a hell of a leader."

"Thanks, Ross. I really appreciate the head's up."

Ross walked him into the building, where Phil's men rose to attention.

"At ease!" Ross ordered. He introduced Phil and added, "I trained this man myself. He's the youngest ever to enter and survive OCS, and he did so with honors. Lieutenant Larimore was one of my best students. He's a good leader and a better learner. Also, my friend." Ross looked around at the men. "I need y'all to take care of him, ya hear?"

"Yes, sir!" responded the soldiers in unison.

---

iv An I&R or Intelligence and Reconnaissance Platoon was typically led by a junior officer (a 1st lieutenant), a sergeant to assist him, and a driver for the Platoon Jeep. There were another eighteen Infantrymen. They collected, evaluated, and disseminated information under the supervision of the regimental intelligence officer (S-2). The platoon also carried out counterintelligence measures and surveillance.

v The Ammunition and Pioneer Platoon and its men, called "sappers," had to transport ammunition from the rear to the frontline soldiers. The A&P platoon also had frontline pioneer or combat engineer duties, such as preparing and strengthening field defenses and fortifications by laying defensive wire and mines, as well as clearing enemy minefields.

vi A "ninety-day wonder" was a derogatory term for recently commissioned graduates of the three-month-long Officer Candidate School at Fort Benning, Georgia.

One of the sergeants looked at Phil, then Ross. "As long as he ain't a numskull like the last one, sir."

"He ain't," Ross said, laughing and patting Phil on the shoulder before leaving.

Phil sat down with the men, and as he looked in their eyes and heard their stories, he realized that Ross was right: he had a cracker jack unit under his command.[vii] Of the twenty-six men in his platoon, fifteen of them were "old men" who had hit the beaches in North Africa.

Phil knew that the mission of an Ammunition and Pioneer platoon, or A&P platoon, was to undertake a wide variety of manual tasks, including the extremely risky job of hauling ammunition to forward positions, often under enemy fire.

Each of his three Pioneer squads was led by a sergeant with seven to ten riflemen. Phil also had at his disposal a driver for the platoon's Jeep, which was armed with a mounted .50-caliber heavy machine gun. He also had two additional Jeeps capable of pulling quarter-ton trailers loaded to the brim with ammunition, mines, mine-defusing equipment, and necessary tools like wire cutters.

One of Phil's sergeants explained what they were up against.

"I have to be honest," the sergeant said. "Life here on the Anzio Beachhead isn't beer and skittles. Each day is muddy, dirty, dangerous work. We have to stay in our foxholes from first light until night and keep our heads down because the battlefield is on flat ground."

The sergeant waved a hand toward the Lepini mountains ringing the beachhead. From their perches, the German artillery platoons had a perfect view of the entire beachhead, which was ten miles wide and eight miles deep.

"The Krauts look right down our throats. Every time someone moves, they throw all kinds of artillery at us. But as soon as it gets dark, that's when we start moving up to the front lines, bringing more ammo and supplies. Sometimes we have to deliver TNT. Carrying an eighteen-pound pack of explosives on your back isn't for the faint of heart since an enemy bullet can blow you to smithereens."

Phil knew this, but he still shuddered.

The sergeant continued. "We've been going into 'no man's land' because a lot of our work, from laying down concertina wire[viii] to planting mines, has to be done in front of the lines. If a Kraut patrol catches us, we beat the hell out of them. Then we leave just before dawn so that we're back in our foxholes before sunup."

---

vii The slang term "cracker jack" or "crack" refers to a person, a group of people, or something of marked excellence.

viii Concertina wire was a type of barbed wire or razor wire that could be expanded like a concertina, a small handheld, bellows-type instrument similar to an accordion. It packed flat for ease of transport and could be deployed as an obstacle much more quickly than ordinary barbed wire.

❧

The following night in shivering rain, Phil accompanied his men on his first mission: laying down a series of booby traps and mines in "no man's land" just a few hundred feet from German machine guns.[83]

Phil couldn't believe that this was the way he'd start fighting a war, but those were the cards he'd been dealt. After pushing forward, the Germans started firing magnesium flares into the pitch-black sky, where they hung for a long time while floating down on a small parachute and lighting up a large area. Each time the Krauts shot up a massive flare, he and his men dropped to the ground and sought to maintain a low profile.

Sometimes the Germans opened up with their machine guns at the same time they launched flares. The enemy machine gun tracers were only a few feet above the ground, and in between each tracer were about a half dozen slugs. Phil quickly learned that he could determine how close he was to the Kraut gun barrels by the tracer's trajectory. When tracer rounds came in on a flat trajectory, he knew that he and his men were within a couple of hundred feet of a machine gun nest. Phil also quickly learned it wasn't wise to answer their fire and give away their position. Instead, their job was to lay down mines as swiftly and efficiently as possible.

Late that first night, Private Winfield A. Doner of New York was arming a mine. The procedure involved burying the mine up to the primer, pulling the safety, and carefully sprinkling dirt or leaves over the primer. When the primer was stepped on or otherwise compressed, the mine did its dirty work. When Private Doner pulled the safety pin, the detonator was either faulty, or Doner was careless in the excitement of the night's mission. The mine exploded in his face, instantly killing him.

After dragging Doner's body back to be collected and buried by the GR[ix] men, the first rays of dawn began to stretch across the eastern sky. For Phil, the morning calm became a mourning calm. He crawled into his tent to get some sleep but could not find rest. No matter how much he thought he'd be prepared for war, seeing up close the first of his men killed instantly changed the way he would look at things in the future. He knew he couldn't dwell on the loss right then, but he could not shake the memory.

Echoing in his mind were these unanswerable questions:

Why did he get killed and not me?
Why him?
Why not me?

Private Doner was the first man Phil lost, but he would not be his last— not by a long shot.

---

ix   GR stands for the Graves Registration company.

16
OPENING SALVO

"As we entered combat, I had a strange feeling. All my life, I felt secure, knowing the United States would protect me, but now it was reversed. The country was now depending on me to protect them. It was an awesome feeling, but I was not sure I could bear so much weight."

—Anonymous Veteran, 351st Regiment, 88th Division in Italy[84]

Although Phil was younger than any of his men, he was pleased with how they welcomed him. Like most rookie soldiers, he wasn't sure how he'd respond to active combat. When he entered the Anzio war zone, though, he was gratified to discover that he wasn't a coward and didn't run away or collapse into a pathetic mass of quivering Jell-O.[85]

He remembered his training—that fear was inevitable but could be managed. At the same time, Phil understood there was no way training could have prepared him for the reality of combat. He, along with his men, had to learn how to survive a live battlefield.

One example was the "three-second rule" that one of Phil's sergeants taught him. If an enemy soldier drew a bead on you during a firefight, he was told back in Alliance, Nebraska, it took him three-fourths of a second to locate you. Then it took him another second and a half to raise his weapon and another half a second to put you in his sights. Three seconds was all you had, so that's why, when you came under fire, you had to hit the ground and roll and not get up in the same spot because there might be a bullet waiting for you.

On February 29, 1944, well before the first streaks of light glinted on the snow-covered peaks of the Lepini mountains ringing the beachhead, regimental command had Phil and most of his platoon head toward the division's left sector. This was where the 3rd Battalion expected to receive a major attack by at least one enemy battalion.

They got busy placing wire and mines in front of the American troops and mining and cratering the roads leading into enemy territory. They also became a vital part of the supply chain. After less than two weeks on the job, Phil had instilled into his men the determination to get the ammo, grenades, and mortar shells[i] to the combat men without delay *and* fight with the frontline men when necessary. In other words, whenever one of his squads delivered ammunition into a dangerous area and a small arms engagement erupted, they joined in the battle.

When the anticipated assault came at 0530 hours, Company I[ii] was hit by at least two enemy infantry companies in the first wave of the attack. The Germans poured intense machine gun and rifle fire on the American soldiers. Phil's men kept the ammunition supply line fed up to the Main Line of Resistance (MLR), which was extremely dangerous because of the machine gun, rifle, and small arms fire, along with an increasing barrage with mortar and artillery shells, some landing as close as twenty yards.

The frontline soldiers continued to hold off all enemy advances with continuous small arms and automatic weapons fire. They provided enfilade fire[iii] against the enemy units that had penetrated the battalion lines as heavy fighting continued in the 3rd's sector throughout the day. Although heavy clouds and squalls nullified the Allied air support in the morning, the skies cleared by the afternoon. Allied bombers appeared to the cheers of the men up and down the front as they watched their planes pummel the enemy attackers. They witnessed quite a demonstration of American air power as 247 fighter bombers, along with twenty-four light bombers, bombed and strafed enemy armor and infantry close to the lines.

---

i   The M2 mortar was a 60-mm smooth-bore, muzzle-loading, high-angle-of-fire weapon used by the GIs in World War II for company-level fire support. The firing pin was fixed in the base cap of the tube, and the bomb was fired automatically when it dropped down the barrel. Depending upon the shell, the mortar had a range of 200 to 2,000 yards.

ii   During World War II, most infantry regiments consisted of three battalions (1st, 2nd, and 3rd) with each battalion consisting of three rifle companies and a heavy weapons company. Rifle companies A, B, C, and heavy weapons Company D were part of the 1st Battalion. Rifle companies E, F, G, and heavy weapons Company H constituted the 2nd Battalion. Rifle companies I, K, L, and heavy weapons Company M were in the 3rd Battalion. There was no J Company as the letter *J* because in 18th and 19th century old-style type, the capital letters I and J looked alike, and were therefore easily confused with one another.

iii   Enfilade fire is when weapons are aimed across the longest part of an enemy formation.

The German shelling finally stopped. Phil had a bit of time to clean his weapons while reflecting on surviving his first couple of weeks on the battle lines. He felt he had proven himself and now had a good idea of what to expect and what was expected of him. He and his men were no longer strangers thrown together randomly by war. Now they were veterans of combat together.

More importantly, Phil had lived to fight another day.

෬෭

On March 3, Phil received his first battlefield evaluation, handed to him directly by Major Bacon. The key finding: "Manner of Performance: Superior."[86]

As the major smiled, the command staff applauded, with Ross Calvert leading the cheers. "Phil," he said, "I could not have been more pleased or proud of my former student's first performance in battle, and the performance of your brave men."

That afternoon the men were read a copy of a telegram that President Roosevelt had received from Winston Churchill, the Prime Minister of Great Britain: "I must send you my warmest congratulations on the grand fighting of your troops, particularly the United States 3rd Division in the Anzio Beachhead."[iv87]

A series of newspaper stories stressed that the 3rd Division, dubbed the "Rock of the Marne" in July 1918, had become the "Rock of Anzio" in 1944, when the better part of seven German divisions was unable to drive the American and British forces into the sea despite three significant attempts. The enemy abandoned daylight air raids, leading the men to tell rookies, "Look up. If you see silver airplanes, they're American. If you see camouflaged airplanes, they're British. If you don't see any airplanes, it's the Luftwaffe."[88]

Nevertheless, anywhere from one to half a dozen attacks were made every night, and the enemy shelling substantially increased after dark. Every day at dusk, the feeling of tension only grew and dispelled any illusions of security. The battle of the Anzio Beachhead remained a grim and deadly struggle.

Of course, Marilyn remained on Phil's mind. He wrote to his mother:

> By the time you get this, it will be April, only a month
> until you go to Gulfport for Marilyn's graduation. Boy, how
> I would like to be there. Wish you would buy her something
> very nice for me and give it to her.[89]

---

iv   The GIs appreciated the sentiment, but they had little respect for British cigarettes or soldiers, whom they called tea- and warm-beer drinkers. The Brits quipped that the Yanks were "overpaid, oversexed, and over here." Not to be outdone, the GIs snipped back laughingly that the English were "underpaid, undersexed, and under Eisenhower." General Truscott himself grew increasingly impatient with the British Army's ability or desire to provide sufficient replacements, leading him to depend far more on his American divisions.

Because the Germans were bombarding the beachhead day and night, he couldn't think about Marilyn very often, however. There was only one practical answer to the constant pounding: go down into or under the ground. As a result, the Anzio Beachhead became a honeycomb of wet and muddy foxholes, dugouts, long slit trenches—even underground rooms. The ghastly battlefield was appallingly reminiscent of World War I trench warfare.

By mid-March, the Anzio Beachhead quieted down and took on the characteristics of garrison life. Because Phil and his men spent a lot of time in wet trenches, many came down with severe colds, including Phil. He wrote to his parents:

> *I have been sick the last day or so, not able to hold my food down, but last night the Major [Battalion Commander] made me go to bed right after supper, and the doctor came up to see me. He made me drink brandy and suck on some homemade candy.*[90]

The next day Phil's condition worsened, and he developed a high fever with chills and sweats, a severe headache, and crippling fatigue, all accompanied by worsening nausea and vomiting. One of the frontline medics quickly sent him to a field hospital.

He arrived with a boiling temperature of 105 degrees and in delirium. With a rapid treatment of aspirin, intravenous (IV) fluids, and cold packs, his temperature finally subsided. He awoke, groggy, to see a nurse from the Army Nurse Corps (ANC).[v] She looked exhausted in her fatigues but took his hand in hers. Phil thought she was heaven sent.

"You're on the mend, soldier," she said softly, with a marvelous smile and a reassuring attitude. "Just a bad case of malaria."[vi]

The nurse continued her rounds as one of the Red Cross volunteers—women who helped the nurses meet the soldier's basic needs for comfort by washing faces, giving drinks of water, lending a listening ear, and assisting soldiers when writing letters home. She picked up a chart hanging on the foot of the cot next to Phil's.

The chart listed the patient's name and where and how the patient was wounded. Phil noticed her eyes widen.

"How on earth did you ever get shot with two arrows?" she blurted to the soldier.

---

v   At the start of World War II, there were fewer than a thousand nurses in the Army Nurse Corps. Initially, the ANC took only unmarried women between the ages of twenty-two and thirty who had their RN training from civilian schools. By the end of the war, the ANC had 54,000 nurses—all women.

vi   Prior to the war, Mussolini had dug canals and installed pumps to drain the marshes on the Anzio plain to create farms. Before the invasion, the Germans reversed the pumps, flooding the canals and low-lying fields. This became a perfect breeding ground for malaria-carrying mosquitoes. Historians debate whether this was a case of biological warfare or not.

Phil looked at the man, obviously from some Indian tribe because of his complexion and straight black hair.

"That's my name, not my injury!" he replied with consternation.

❦

After dinner that evening, Phil felt well enough to walk to the stove at the end of the officer's ward tent to have a smoke. He pushed the pole holding the IV flowing into his arm.[91]

"Can I sit with you?" one of the nurses asked.

"I'd be crazy to refuse an offer like that." Phil clicked his Zippo[vii] to light her cigarette. "You look tired. Long day, eh?"

The nurse blew out her first puff. "Every day's long here on the 'Bitch-head.' But we sure had a strange encounter in the OR this morning. Received two frontline men who'd been shot last night while patrolling behind enemy lines. When the surgeons went in to clean out the wounds, which were not fatal, they found wooden bullets."

Phil thought he hadn't heard right. "Wooden bullets?"

"Yes, sir," she replied. "It's happened a few times before. The bullet is made in the pattern of a regulation .30-caliber cartridge with a brass casing and hardwood-like mahogany pressed inside. The Krauts use them at night, especially when they send a patrol behind our lines. That's when they open up on our boys with these wooden things. Their range is short. That way, their bullets don't go past our men and back into their lines."

Phil laughed. "I hadn't heard about that."

The nurse inhaled another draw. "Who's waiting for you back home, soldier?" she asked.

"A special gal."

Phil reached into his vest pocket and took out a picture of Marilyn. "She says she wants to marry a doctor. Maybe I'll go into medicine when I get back to the States. So, tell me: What's the most stressful part of your work here on the beachhead?"

She thought a moment. "There are two things. The first is the fact that we nurses are often the last person a soldier sees or touches or talks to before he dies. It's hard to see so many die so horribly. You don't forget something like that. Not ever." Her eyes misted as she solemnly flicked ash into an ashtray.

"The OR is the second big stress," she continued. "If we're in the wards or our sleeping quarters and the shelling begins, we can duck into the bomb shelters dug into the berms surrounding each tent. But if we're in the OR in

---

vii   The most common Zippo lighter used by the GIs was the Black Crackle Zippo, which was covered with a special black crackle paint that would not reflect light, thereby avoiding the attention of enemy snipers.

the middle of surgery, we can't stop unless absolutely necessary. A corpsman will go by each OR table and place a helmet on the head of each doctor and nurse and one over the patient's face. Even then, we might have to hit the ground when shrapnel comes through the tents, but we get up immediately and continue once the danger has passed."

She took a long draw on her cigarette and flicked off more ash. "For us nurses, just like for you boys, everything is based on trust. We're in a war zone, and we nurses trust each other to a tee. But we never talk about what we see or what we do each day. I don't think we can. We all know that we could get killed, but none of us dwell on the fact. We just do what we need to do. If we get hit, that's just the way it is."

Phil felt his head nod in agreement as he watched her stub out her cigarette and stand up.

"Back to work for me, Lieutenant. Thanks for letting me unload. I think that most any sorrow can be borne if we're able to share our story with someone."

"Think nothing of it."

She smiled. "It's hard, but I think once we share them, it softens the pain."

Phil made eye contact with this angel in white, who leaned over and kissed him on the forehead. "Thanks for listening," she whispered. "Break a leg."

❧

In his next letter home, Phil wrote:

> *I'm sorry, honest I am, that I have not written in so long, but for the last few days I have been in the hospital.... Just a case of malaria, but I will be out in a few days and back with the outfit.*[92]

Then he shared his tremendous admiration for the nurses and Red Cross volunteers with his mother:

> *Boy, you sure have to take your hats off to those gals. They come up here on the beach with their hospitals. They treat all of the boys in the hospitals well. They are supposed to get in their foxholes during air raids, but they don't. They stay in the wards where the boys are. There have been some of them killed when the shells came in. When a hospital gets ready to move, they all help tear the tents down and load*

the trucks. When they set up, all the gals work putting the
tents up, digging ditches around them, digging foxholes, etc.
They sure are a swell bunch.[93]

As Phil began to feel better, he didn't feel right occupying a bed that only a genuinely wounded man should have. Bronchitis, influenza, malaria, dysentery, and trench foot—all common maladies among the frontline men— seemed too easy a way out. He was among the new-to-the-line, incredibly young soldiers trying to prove themselves as heroes, but they didn't yet understand that a sick soldier was a danger to his buddies.

By his third hospital day, Phil felt much better—hydrated, nourished, rested, and ready to get back to his men. Although his eyes carried the telltale yellow caused by the medication Atabrine, he talked a surgeon into releasing him.

"You either discharge me or report me missing," he told his doctor. "Either way, I need to get back to my men."

In many ways, Phil believed the war was just starting for him.

17

BAPTISM BY FIRE

"In every battle, the last one hundred yards of the fight belongs to the Infantry. Armed with rifle and bayonet, Infantrymen must face and defeat the enemies of our nation."

—National Infantry Museum, Fort Benning, Georgia[94]

The night of March 15, 1944, found Phil and one of his squads attached to Company L under Captain Robert B. Pridgen, a twenty-eight-year-old officer from Henderson, North Carolina, who had joined the regiment only a few days before. Ross Calvert was serving as his executive officer.[95]

Throughout this period, there were nightly actions around the scattered homes that had housed farm families using Mussolini's fascist farm model. The Italian dictator had built hundreds of modern (in the Italian manner) thick-walled stone farmhouses that were spread across the landscape and were all alike, except for color. Each house was given a number—1, 2, 3, and so on—by the Allies on neatly marked air photos and maps.

The Germans had converted these stone houses into fortified strong-points. Bunkers were dug into the floors, so if a house was destroyed by tanks, tank destroyers (TDs),[i] artillery, or mortar fire, the debris fell on top of the bunkers. This strategy increased camouflage and significantly strengthened the German defense.

Phil's company received orders to take over Houses 5 and 6 in the middle of the night, relieving the 509th Parachute Infantry Regiment, which had captured them at the cost of fifty-three casualties, effectively advancing the front by 500 yards. Unfortunately, the decision was also made to have the 509th abandon the houses and *then* have Company L move in.

Captain Pridgen vehemently disagreed with the tactic because he didn't think it would be wise to leave the houses vacated for even one moment. Orders were orders, however. As the last man from the 509th crossed the main line of resistance (MLR), Captain Pridgen looked at his radio operator, PFC Adam Malinowski.

"Ready?" he asked. "We need to get up to those stone houses pronto."

The two men dashed across a hundred yards of no man's land, under continuing mortar and small arms fire, determined to get into the pair of homes as soon as possible. They covered the distance in less than thirty seconds and took possession of House 6.

At the MLR, Phil lay beside Calvert. Staff Sergeant James A. Light, Calvert's communications sergeant, on the other side, listened to the transmission from the house. "Lieutenant," he said to Phil, "Captain wants four of us up with him immediately."

"I'm in," Phil said. First Lieutenant Boris A. Hicks, one of Pridgen's platoon leaders, nodded his assent as well.

"Phil, you don't need to go up," Ross said, "Just make sure we have the ammo we need. I'll go."

A wry smile etched Phil's face. "What? And let you have all the fun?"

"Okay, you win," Ross replied. Then, turning to Sergeant Light, he issued an order: "Tell the men to provide cover fire and fill in the ditches behind us."

The three men then followed Calvert as they sprinted in a hunched-over position toward House 6, following a canal. The company provided intense protective fire, which afforded barely enough light for the men to see their way forward.

As the rest of Company L moved up behind them, the Germans fired illuminating flares, followed by relentless mortar fire. When a second wave of American firepower gave them an opening, Phil and the three men sprinted into House 6 and took cover.

---

i   A tank destroyer is an armored fighting vehicle armed with a direct-fire artillery gun designed specifically to engage and destroy enemy tanks. For the U.S. in World War II, the M18 Hellcat was the fastest and most effective fighting vehicle, having a higher kill-to-loss ratio than any other tank or tank destroyer.

Then the Germans counterattacked, supported by machine gun, mortar, tank, and artillery fire. Phil peeked around a windowsill and saw a dozen German soldiers swarm and enter House 5, which was empty.

"The Krauts took 5 again," Phil announced.

"Damn!" Captain Pridgen yelled above the din of gunfire. "Why'd the sonsabitches have the five-oh-nine withdraw? Now we've gotta retake 5."

Pridgen called attack instructions to the platoons coming up the canal. Then he, Phil, and their fellow soldiers at House 6 each took a window and began firing at the enemy.

Phil caught glimpses of Germans crawling toward House 6. They couldn't have been more than twenty-five yards away.

"Damn! They're moving up quickly!" he barked. Just then, several Kraut soldiers rolled on their backs, pulled the pins on their potato-masher hand grenades in unison, and began lofting them at the house.

"Grenades!" Phil shouted as the men ducked. The explosions shook the ground. The fight had just ramped up several notches.

Twice the attackers were repulsed as Captain Pridgen, Phil, Ross, and radioman Adam Malinowski engaged the enemy from the windows of House 6 with Garands, carbines, and grenades, supported by mortars and small arms fire from the company. During their third attack, German soldiers gained positions near a corner of the house and began throwing potato mashers in even greater numbers.

"Cover me!" Pridgen shouted.

"What the hell are you planning?" Phil hollered.

"We need to shut these assholes up!" Pridgen shouted.

Under suppressive fire from Phil and the other men in the house, Pridgen jumped out of a lower window to the ground and crawled around the house to within ten yards of the enemy. He tossed several grenades and employed carbine fire, killing three Germans and wounding several others. When the remaining soldiers ran for their lives, Phil and Ross took a bead on the fleeing men. Even in the darkness, they picked them off one at a time like they were shooting moving targets at the county fair when they were kids.

The air grew strangely quiet. Phil heard Pridgen's footsteps as he ran back to the house and leaped through the window. The captain spoke into the radio, "Company L has House 6 conclusively. Now we're going after 5."

Fortunately, the Germans didn't have time to get established defensively. After a vicious fight in which grenades and close-in fighting were required, the resolute Company L regained House 5. By 0320 hours on March 16, both houses were in American control, but the gains had been costly, as Company L had sustained eighteen casualties, including two officers wounded.

Captain Pridgen, Ross, and Phil immediately began working together to outpost the houses, placing men and guns at strategic points to defend against another counterattack. They set their defensive positions so that their fields of fire would crisscross to the front to prevent further enemy infiltration.

As Phil's men transported ammunition, wire, and mines to the front, the rears of the houses were demolished by tanks in order for them to take up a safer position inside. A tank firing through a window in a stone house provided significant protection from most enemy anti-tank fire.

Meanwhile, Phil's platoon was assigned the additional responsibility of improving the positions with barbed wire and hastily laid minefields. Just before dawn, Phil and his A&P Platoon laid fifty-four AP mines[ii] in front of Houses 5 and 6, as well as AT mines across the road at the bridge near House 6.

The men accomplished this extensive amount of work in the two hours before dawn, knowing that at the first light of sunrise, any exposed men would be an easy target for German snipers located in well-fortified houses only 100 to 150 yards away. The fact the enemy-held houses were on higher ground made daylight movements even more dangerous due to the enemy's superior vantage point.

As the sun rose on the cold, crisp morning, Major Bacon and an aide evaded detection and showed up to inspect the houses and congratulate the men on their exceptional work. The major detected a potential problem while looking over the landscape, however. He called Phil to the table where they were meeting. As they sipped their hot coffee, the men looked over a map of the surrounding battlefield.

Phil described what happened next in a letter home to his father:

> *When the major that commands my battalion was briefing me, he talked to me just like a father. He said he needed an anti-tank minefield in the road. He was afraid the Germans would try to take the houses with tanks. You see, anyone that moves around during daylight hours on the front lines, they shell the heck out of that area instantly.*
>
> *Well, the major knew I would have to crawl out on the flat open road and would be in plain view of the Jerries only 100 yards away. I said, 'Yes, sir.' It was the only thing I could say. A couple of my men and I had to crawl 500 or 600 yards to get additional mines, then crawl back, and then I went out on the road. I laid my field and crawled back in the ditch. About that time, all hell broke loose, but I was on my way back.*[96]

---

ii   Anti-personnel (AP) mines were designed for use against humans, as opposed to anti-tank (AT) mines, which were designed for use against vehicles. Mines were often designed to injure and not kill their victims, in order to increase the medical support required by keep them alive.

German machine gunners and a Panzer IV tank[iii] had started shooting at Phil, but he somehow managed to crawl back hurriedly despite shells and machine gun fire shredding the ground around him. Covering fire from the Americans allowed him to stand up and sprint to the safety of House 6. As he dashed back, the men in the foxholes all cheered and whooped for him. Inside the house, Major Bacon and Captain Pridgen gave him congratulatory slaps on his back. "You ought to get a medal!" Pridgen exclaimed.

Ross Calvert hugged him and then poured a healthy swig of scotch that they shared. Phil tried to calm his trembling hands. "When you left," Ross said, "all I could think was, 'He's gonna die!' Kinda glad you didn't."

Phil was unable to quell his still-shaking body. "Me too."

Ross put his arm around his friend. "Well done, Phil," he said. "Well done, indeed."

Phil and the Dogfaces of the 30th did not intend to lose the two houses—and they didn't. The strong defenses Phil and his men set up around Houses 5 and 6 demonstrated the value of ground on the beachhead. Colonel William P. Yarborough told his troops, "The price of ground here is skyrocketing, just like the price of Scotch whiskey—high as hell and just as hard to get."[97]

The men of the 30th Infantry learned that to seize beachhead property was one thing—but to hold it was another thing entirely.

ဢ

During another mid-March night, while Phil was supervising his men as they ran ammunition to the front lines, an orange light brightened the horizon to the southeast. The variation in the light's intensity—alternately orange, red, and yellow—left the men wondering, *What the hell is that?* [98]

The men guessed it might be an ammunition dump blowing up near Naples—or perhaps a massive gas or oil depot on fire. Whatever it was, the conflagration continued to burn the entire night. The next morning, the men learned that Mount Vesuvius had experienced its first major eruption since 1631,[iv] killing twenty-six civilians, displacing 12,000 persons, and destroying eighty-eight American B-25 Mitchell medium bombers—$25 million worth of aircraft.

On April 5, at a battalion ceremony in the Pine Grove, Phil was surprised to be awarded his first battle medal, the Silver Star—the third-highest military combat decoration awarded for bravery in action beyond the call of duty. The Silver Star was presented to him by Brigadier General John Wilson "Iron

---

iii   The Panzerkampfwagen IV, commonly known as the Panzer IV, was Germany's most abundant tank and the second-most common German armored fighting vehicle of World War II.

iv   Various sources disagree on whether the eruption was on March 17 or March 18, 1944. Mount Vesuvius has not had a major eruption since then.

Mike" O'Daniel,[v] the 3rd Division commander, with the 30th Regiment Commander, Colonel Lionel C. McGarr, standing by his side.

"How old are you, Lieutenant?" O'Daniel asked while pinning Phil's medal on him.

"Nineteen years and ninety-one days, sir!" Phil responded.

O'Daniel chuckled as he looked at McGarr. "I'm not sure I can remember being that young."

"He's young, but he's one hell of a fighting man," McGarr commented, smiling, as he shook Phil's hand and then saluted him.

On April 7, Phil attended Good Friday services held in a picturesque grove graced by a large white wooden cross, which reminded him of the outdoor services he had enjoyed at the Boy Scout camps of his youth. Then on April 9, Catholics and Protestants massed side by side for an Easter service under a special dispensation from Lieutenant General Lucian K. Truscott, Jr. The commander of the VI Corps had previously issued orders to prevent large gatherings since they made good military targets.

As the Easter service was conducted, the enemy threw in a few artillery concentrations, which gave those assembled a sharp reminder that they were still on Anzio. Throughout Holy Week, chaplains recorded a dramatic increase in confessions, conversions, and ceremonial baptisms. All had been baptized by fire, and now some were christened by water.

As warmer weather approached, Phil knew that defeating the Germans and the Allied generals' salvation at Anzio rested on the infantrymen like him at the front. They were the valorous men who knew that "this pestilential plot, this woe, this kettle of grief,"[99] as author Rick Atkinson[vi] would later describe it, could not go on forever. They were spurred on by snowballing rumors that a breakout was coming any day.

Even though the Anzio Beachhead had been a dreary and dismal death trap for almost three months, Phil and his men had a sense that if they could break out of the hell that was Anzio, then the rest of Italy was ripe for the taking.

---

v   General O'Daniel was nicknamed "Iron Mike" during World War I after being hit in the face by a German machine gun bullet and becoming severely wounded, yet he kept on fighting. He was awarded the Distinguished Service Cross, the nation's second-highest award for valor, as well as a Purple Heart.
vi   Rick Atkinson is the Pulitzer Prize-winning author of the "Liberation Trilogy," about the southern and "forgotten" front of the European Theater of Operations.

18

MULES TO THE RESCUE

"The Infantryman, the soldier whose greatest armor is his courage; whose most dependable vehicle are his own two feet; whose weapons are those only which he can carry and use with his hands."

—Robert Vermillion, United Press war correspondent during World War II[100]

In early April 1944, during a two-week training layoff from combat, Phil longed desperately to see Marilyn. He fell asleep and woke up gazing at her picture, which he carried in a pocket next to his heart. He was growing more concerned about not receiving any letters from her, but mail delivery was spotty.[101]

On April 11, the 3rd Infantry Division moved into position to relieve the 45th Division. By 0600 hours on April 16, the 3rd was in command with a mission to straighten out its lines, alleviate enemy pressure on vital strong points, and improve its defensive positions. The regiment spent its first day locating sniper posts, improving their defensive works, and establishing outposts and listening posts.

The men and their commanders were convinced that the Allied positions on the Anzio Beachhead were more robust than ever after eighty-four days of reinforcing and digging in. They believed the Germans, now on the defensive, didn't have the faintest chance to drive them back into the sea. The Allies were finally showing superiority in every department—artillery, air support, and troops.

In the previous month, the situation on the beachhead had transformed a bitter holding battle to bustling preparations for a massive offensive. Patrols were sent out at night for the sole purpose of giving them combat experience and to test the leadership and initiative of younger officers like Phil.

Thanks to increasing air supremacy, the Americans flew single-seat Piper Cubs over the beachhead as artillery and combat aircraft spotters. Initially, the Germans fired at them, but that quickly changed when the Nazis realized that they were giving their positions away. The Cub spotters—known as Grasshoppers—would call in their locations. Within minutes, those positions received an avalanche of artillery fire with devastating results. This was why German fighter pilots received twice as many points toward an air medal for shooting down a Grasshopper rather than a fighter plane.

For three weeks, Phil's command post or CP was on the ground floor of a two-story stone farmhouse with an attached barn. Artillery observers occupied the home's upper story, while the owners lived in the top of the barn. The older Italian couple cooked for Phil and his men and washed their clothes to earn money.

A barn-like smell permeated everywhere. Just outside the home, in an "L" created by the junction of the house and the barn, was an area the men thought was hidden from the German observers. Phil parked a half-track[i] with a large antenna and radio system inside the "L" to serve the A&P Platoon and the artillerymen. They were spotting targets and using the radio to call back German artillery positions.

Phil befriended the Italian farmer, who had a small pack of mules, which he called a "barren." That was a word Phil had never heard used for mules. The farmer employed the mules for transporting supplies to other farmers.

The farmer, whose English was impeccable, explained that when a male donkey breeds with a female horse, the offspring is called a "mule." All mules are sterile and incapable of reproducing themselves, the farmer explained. Now everything made sense to Phil about why a group of mules was called a "barren." The farmer was quite proud of his barren and declared, without equivocation, that mules were smarter than donkeys, which were much more intelligent than horses.

"Do you really think a mule is smarter than a horse?" Phil inquired.

The man nodded. "In almost every way. Mules endure heat better than horses, they have fewer feeding problems, and they eat less. Mules rarely have hoof problems, excel in physical soundness, and are far more sure-footed and careful than horses."

---

i   A half-track was a heavy-duty vehicle with regular wheels at the front for steering and continuous tracks at the back to propel the vehicle and carry most of the load.

Phil cocked his head. He had never heard such things. "Really? More sure-footed?"

"*Si,*" the old man replied. "On the physical side, the mule has a narrower body than a horse of the same height and weight. He gets this from the ass side of the family. His legs are strong, and his feet are small with a narrow structure. The small hoof configuration enables him to place his feet carefully. On the psychological side, mules tend to assess situations and act according to their views, most of which have to do with self-preservation. When I take my mules into the mountains, I usually let my mule pick the safest way down a bad path."

Phil and one of his men, a private from Missouri experienced in handling and training mules, came up with an idea: *Why not train the mules to carry ammo to the front lines at night?* As the private told Phil, "Mules have much better night vision than we do." When they ran their idea by the farmer, his enthusiasm to say yes was fueled when Phil said he could get him paid for allowing his mules to work for the Army.

Phil's superiors quickly approved his request for mules for several reasons. Off the roads in the mountains of Sicily and on the Italian mainland, weapons and supplies had been carried by mules where motorized or tracked vehicles could not navigate. Also, the U.S. Army had a fond affection for mules. Most of Phil's commanders were West Point graduates, and the Academy's mascot was a mule that attended all Army home football games.

Each morning, Phil and several of his men worked with the farmer to train the mules. The farmer emphasized to the men, "In trying to communicate with mules, the first thing to understand is that they want to please you. Underneath what may appear to be an unsympathetic character is a willing and intelligent creature." Phil quickly found that mules—after communication and trust had been established—were some of the hardest working and most devoted animals that he'd ever dealt with.

Within days, the remarkably intelligent beasts were carrying cases of ammunition and other supplies to the front lines and the outposts each night. The A&P Platoon was able to carry out its work far more quickly and efficiently, whether under fire or not.

The men even trained the mules to lie down instantaneously when a flare exploded in the night sky, making them less visible and less likely to be shot by the Germans. Finally, the mules also gave the lead soldier a barrier to get behind when an attack started.

At the company CP during breakfast, Ross commented with a wry smile, "Phil, I think the reason you get along so well with the mules is because you're a jackass too. Doesn't like attract like?"

Phil chuckled. "Well, Ross, you certainly get along well with horses. Does that make you a horse's ass?"

The two friends shared a much-needed laugh.

❧

Starting on April 29, the 3rd Battalion was relieved to prepare for an offensive that they hoped would break the beachhead stalemate. At first light, Phil and his men presented gifts to the family that had shared their farmhouse with them for the previous month. This earned Phil a kiss on both cheeks by every member of the family.[102]

As the men began to depart, a disaster unfolded. Suddenly, a shell zipped in, sailed over the farmhouse, and exploded. Then another arrived short of the barn. A third blew up in front of them, too close for comfort. As they raced to take cover behind stone walls, Phil instantly knew what was happening. German artillery was bracketing[ii] the house.

"Move out!" Phil yelled. He turned to the farmer. "Get your family into the drainage ditch! Now!"

The family quickly sprinted across a narrow blacktop road and leaped into a drainage ditch about ten feet deep. As the Jeeps and half-track filled up with American soldiers, Phil screamed to the stragglers, "Double-time! Move it!"

Phil knew there was very little time. "Run, damn it!" he cried out.

Then he saw a huge cloud of colored dust rise from the barn, followed by another as the concussion of the blasts hit him.

Lord Almighty! Direct hits! Phil thought, realizing he still had men inside. When the artillery barrage ended, he counted eight dead and eleven wounded men, a near wipeout of his platoon.

Fortunately, Phil's rapid action saved most of his men, but there was no time to grieve the losses or say goodbye. He needed to get his men to safety and leave the dead behind to be picked up and buried by the GR men.

Phil prayed they would never have to come for him.

❧

For the 30th, the first three weeks of May were devoted to preparation for a giant all-out attack to smash out of the beachhead and carry the Fifth Army to Rome. The new offensive was code-named Operation Buffalo. The mission called for the VI Corps, now bolstered with 14,000 replacements—up to a fighting strength of 90,000 in seven fully equipped and manned divisions—to break out of the beachhead toward the mountain village of Cisterna, located in a mountain gap and leading down to Highway 6 directly to Rome.[103]

During this time, Phil wrote his mother:[104]

---

ii   Bracketing is a method of adjusting fire in which a bracket is established by obtaining a spot over and a spot short of a target along the spotting line, and then successively splitting the bracket in half until the target is hit.

We are out of the front lines now and back in a rest camp where we are training. We have to get the new men that have joined us in the last two months all trained. But we are eating swell and can move around a lot.

During all my spare time around here, I have to spend it studying, writing lectures, and censoring mail, and this platoon of mine sure can write a heck of a lot of mail. But I don't mind sitting around late at night censoring mail because the sooner I get it out, the sooner it will get to their homes.

As he reviewed his men's letters to their moms and girlfriends, he missed his mother and Marilyn even more and wrote them two to three times a week. But there was still no mail from Marilyn.

❧

The physical and mental training was purely offensive, emphasizing storming pillboxes and other infantry emplacements, use of battle sleds, street fighting, coordination of the infantry-tank teams, defense against tanks, attack over open country, and attack against protected riverbeds. Overall cooperation of infantry and tanks was stressed.[105]

The men heard on May 11 that their Fifth Army colleagues had launched their spring offensive, Operation Diadem, against the Gustav Line in the south. After only three days of stubborn fighting, two of the Fifth Army's corps broke through the Gustav Line positions and started a rapid drive northward toward Rome.

By then, every man at Anzio knew it. They could feel it in their bones—they were next to break out. Everyone was preparing—studying area maps and working on tactics in sandbox models. The men cleaned their weapons and made certain they were ready for action. Sergeants made sure everyone had bayonets, knives, hand grenades, and plenty of ammo. This was going to be a do-or-die operation. Phil and his men were anxious to get going and get the thing over with, and yet fearful of what might happen.

❧

Starting May 17, the 30th Infantry Regiment had several award ceremonies in the Pine Grove Corps Reserve Area. At the age of nineteen, Phil was promoted to 1st Lieutenant, receiving his silver bar from Colonel Lionel McGarr, commander of the 30th Regiment, during the ceremonies. McGarr had just been promoted to full colonel himself.[106]

And to the surprise of the men, over 2,000 of them were awarded the Combat Infantryman Badge (CIB),[iii] with Colonel McGarr presenting the badges to each of his men. This award was restricted to officers, colonel or below, and enlisted men assigned to an infantry unit that had been actively engaged in ground combat and had participated actively and satisfactorily in that combat.

Near the end of May, the 30th Infantry was ready. The command team studied every detail of the terrain, noting where the enemy strongpoints were. The minefields were mapped out, and gun positions were plotted. When Phil saw the plans, he realized that they had the enemy completely cased, almost down to each machine gun nest and fire pit. This information came from long and careful interrogation of prisoners, detailed study of air photos, and constant patrol activity.

This would be the final attack from Anzio Beachhead, and military planners made every effort to ensure its success because enemy opposition was expected to be severe. To that end, over 10,000 soldiers had secretly arrived by sea over the previous four days. Not since Sicily had the men been better prepared physically, or better conditioned mentally, to enter brutal action.

As the commanders at the beachhead were making their final preparations, they were determined to inculcate an offensive spirit in soldiers who had long been on the defensive. This may have been their easiest job, as the men were more than ready. They had been cooped up for so long that they felt like coiled rattlesnakes waiting to strike a venomous, fatal blow. When released, they would immediately attack.

As for Phil and his men, they were ready and poised to kill a lot of Germans and escape the "bitchhead." Now was the time to put their extensive training and experience to work—to practice their ruthless and merciless art and take a big step toward winning the war.

As Phil wrote to his father:

> *I'd fight with these men anytime and anywhere, but I wouldn't fight against them on any day. Pity the SOBs who have to.*[107]

---

iii   Most Infantrymen consider the CIB to be their most treasured award because it reflects the privilege of serving in active ground combat with other brave, tough, and selfless Infantry soldiers.

19

BREAKING OUT

"We who are living know the success of the Division, and our own very existence is due mainly to those who unselfishly gave their lives in battle. That realization will be with us always."

—Major General John W. "Iron Mike" O'Daniel of the 3rd Infantry Division during the Battle of Anzio[108]

In the early evening of May 22, 1944, Phil and his men were on the move, which felt good. After months of rain, wind, and even snow, the weather had turned noticeably warmer. The crippling hot summer months were just around the corner.[109]

Phil and Ross were part of the 30th Infantry Regiment's march toward the front on a balmy evening, where spikes of twilight glistened through a pine forest. When the men exited the grove, the 3rd Division Band played "Dogface Soldier," the famous marching song of the Marne division. The men sang along, lustily: "I'm just a Dogface soldier with a rifle on my shoulder, and I eat a Kraut for breakfast every day."[110]

"Judging from the remarks of the guys to bystanders and the way they're razzing each other, I'd say morale is higher than ever," Ross observed.

"They're singing and whistling. Some are almost skipping," Phil responded. "Look how high they're holding their heads. I'd say you're spot on, partner. Their attitude's the best I've seen in my three months in this slugfest."

"For me, it's been like this since Sicily," Ross said. "I don't think our men could have been better prepared physically or better conditioned mentally to enter a difficult action. At dawn, we'll bust through those Kraut bastards and begin the race for Rome. Hopefully, we'll beat the damn Brits there."

"You know what I think?" Phil asked.

Ross shook his head.

"Once the capital city falls, Italy is ours!" Phil exclaimed.

"You got that right, Daddy-O!" Ross replied, slapping Phil on the back.

The men looked up. In front of them, thick clouds of man-made smoke produced a low-hanging curtain that concealed the telltale dust of hundreds of moving troop columns.[i] As dusk descended, the artillery commenced what appeared at first to be another of its irritating nightly serenades, and the gun flashes merged like chain lightning. In addition, Phil could hear the distant artillery explosions to the south, where the Fifth Army was pushing north from Cassino after smashing through parts of the Gustav Line, the German's main defensive boundary.

A short distance ahead, beyond the woods, were the front lines that had been braced and fortified by the Germans to a point almost unparalleled in the war. In the previous months, three massive German offensives had not only failed to push the Allies into the sea, but they had made no progress at all in reducing the size of the beachhead.

The exhausted enemy reverted to strengthening their defensive fortifications, bringing additional troops to the front, and placing untold thousands of anti-tank and anti-personnel mines. The enemy had also placed weapons on tactically key terrain to cover nearly all routes of approach. The Allied soldiers would be exposed because much of the ground was flat with few folds, ditches, ravines, or brush.

As darkness fell and gathering clouds dropped a bit of rain, dampening the American GIs' uniforms, Phil issued a quick thank-you prayer. He and his men were now guaranteed that their movements would stay relatively secret with a combination of man- and Mother Nature-created cloud cover. They settled in for the night, catching catnaps while knowing that just before dawn, the big push would start.

At daybreak on the morning of May 23, at 0538, the front remained quiet. The enemy, huddled in their dugouts, was no doubt catching up on their sleep after another vigilant night. Phil was wide awake, though, thinking about his

---

i   The Chemical Corps troops utilized the same smoke generators used to maintain a sixteen-mile "light haze" around the harbor throughout daylight hours. The density of the smokescreen was adjusted to prevent monitoring by German forward observers in the surrounding hills, but not so thick as to not inhibit port operations. Every hour, the smoke generators consumed 100 gallons of fog oil, a petroleum distillate that produced an exceptionally long-lasting smoke similar to natural fog.

parents and Marilyn—and contemplating how much his life revolved around first light, meaning the end of a difficult night's work or, as it would be today, the beginning of another arduous battle.

At 0545, more than a thousand guns, mortars, tanks, and tank destroyers began a deadly bombardment of the German lines and rear-area positions. Ten battalions of light, medium, and heavy artillery poured high explosives into enemy fortifications and gun positions while Phil and his men covered their ears. Adding to the cacophony were 500 large-bore howitzers[ii] that sent high explosives into the air and shredded steel into the enemy's territory for forty-five minutes.

Simultaneously, 300 .50-caliber machine guns and 400 mortars pumped out round after round into the German fortifications. Both the duration and intensity were far greater than anything Phil had ever experienced before. The barrage was so intense that he wondered how anything could be left of the German lines and their soldiers.

One of his soldiers grinned while listening to the thundering explosions and sarcastically said, "Hitler, count your children, you bastard!" The smoke, artillery, and gloomy weather assured that the Germans were both blind and hunkered down.

Then the weather suddenly changed in a way that was almost too good to be true. Clearing skies allowed Allied fighter bombers to pummel the Germans massed behind the Cisterna-Rome railroad that served as the enemy's final line of defense, as well as an assembly area from which to launch attacks. With the Germans appropriately softened up, the artillery bombardment dropped off so that Sherman tanks could start advancing at 0630 hours along the white-taped tracks marked by Phil, his men, and other A&P platoons and mine squads.

When the attack order was finally transmitted to the front, Phil yelled to his platoon, "Come on, boys!" as he and thousands of other Dogfaces charged. Many had their webbed belts heavily hung with pear-sized grenades. Riflemen ran with bayonets fixed. Heavy weapon squads—machine guns and mortars—kept close on their heels. Directly overhead, the .50-caliber machine guns behind them lay down a thick cover of bullets that sounded like an endless high-pitched *thud-thud-thud*. Phil and his men sensed this was a day of destiny for the beachhead.

The main effort of the 3rd Division was made by the 30th Infantry on a 2,500-yard front, but the enemy recovered. Resolutely stiffened, buttressed by well-prepared, camouflaged anti-tank gun positions and extensive minefields, pillboxes, anti-personnel minefields, and barbed wire, the Germans were intent on carrying out Hitler's command to repel any

---

ii   The 240-mm "large-bore" howitzer M1 saw considerable action during World War II, starting at Anzio, where it proved its effectiveness against difficult targets. Army ordnance officers bragged of the devastating firepower and incredible accuracy of the MI howitzer in playing a decisive role in the Italian Campaign, not only in knocking out enemy artillery, but also destroying targets as small as German heavy tanks at long range.

and all efforts of the Allies to affect a breakthrough. The enemy garrison held out stubbornly, but it could not prevent the 30th Infantry on the north and the 15th Infantry on the south from closing in.

The primary attack began with the 2nd and 3rd Battalions of the 30th abreast, under the continuing cover of smoke and tank and M-18 Hellcat[iii] TD fire. Phil and his men, tasked with resupplying forward units with more ammunition, moved forward but came under withering artillery and mortar fire, causing them to join the fight.

One well-placed heavy-caliber mortar shell landed in the middle of the spearhead platoon, wounding or killing all but four of the men. The dead and wounded could not be immediately evacuated, meaning the entire battalion, including Phil and his men, was forced to file through and around the casualties littering a narrow ravine. Some of the men were screaming in agony, which twisted Phil's guts.

He did not stop, nor did his men, because infantrymen were trained not to render first aid to the wounded while attacking since this would slow down the assault's momentum. Phil was comforted that medics would quickly attend to the wounded, and the GR men would come behind to pick up the dead. But the carnage served to embolden Phil as well as the men of the 30th.

Then the German line—comprised of two German divisions or six regiments—stiffened. By 0800 hours, the Allies had hardly gained a quarter of a mile.

Phil's radioman handed him the receiver. "You may want to listen to this, Lieutenant."

Phil recognized the voice of General O'Daniel, the division commander. "It's going too slow!" the general complained. "Throw everything you have at them!"[111]

A staff officer responded that the two lead companies were pinned down. Phil smiled as O'Daniel shouted, "We have no such words in our vocabulary now!"[112]

Phil and his platoon were attached to Company L, led by Captain Pridgen, with Ross Calvert by his side. While moving up a large gorge with more ammunition to deliver, they came to a sharp bend in the ravine where the enemy had installed a company strongpoint. Phil spotted machine gun nests dug into the shoulders of the ravine, outlying rifle pits, concertina and double-apron wire,[iv] and similar positions stretching northwest across the road. He and his men immediately went to work,

---

iii   The M18 Hellcat was an American tank destroyer that was the fastest US armored fighting vehicle on the road, having a higher kill-to-loss ratio than any other US tank or TD. The M18 was not primarily used for tank fighting, however, but for direct fire support for Infantry.

iv   The standard double-apron fence is one of the best obstacles that can be made with barbed wire or razor wire. The effectiveness is increased by raising the top wire to prevent crossing by stepping over and placing low wires just above the ground to prevent crawling under.

carving paths through the minefields and wire barriers. A half dozen soldiers cleared the way, while others covered them, using suppressive fire to reduce the Germans' continuous barrage.

Through these safe alleyways that Phil's guys marked with tape, the men rushed up the stream. When they reached a bend, enemy weapons laid down withering fire, wounding and killing dozens of American soldiers who didn't have the support of the three tanks assigned to the company— one light and two medium Shermans. The tanks couldn't follow them up the ravine.

To make matters worse, the cloud cover had reaccumulated and was a huge negative, eliminating any air support and dramatically reducing artillery's support behind them. They were literally on their own. By 0835, the company, which had fought its way to within fifty yards of the German line, was furiously counterattacked. After another hour of intense fighting, the enemy was beaten off, but at the cost of forty-five more casualties. The remnants of the company intrepidly continued their advance.

During the morning battles, Phil and his men were constantly bringing up ammunition as fast as possible. At one point, Phil and two of his men took a wrong turn in some brush and got into close combat with a German squad. During a brief skirmish, one of his men was shot, and another was captured.

Two Germans stood with their rifles aimed at him. Instinctively, Phil dropped to one knee and shot both men with his Garand before they could get off a round. Both men fell backward, one dying instantly, the other wounded and cursing. Phil laid down more fire, which allowed his men to escape. Then he backed up, continuing to fire at the German squad until he and his men were safely back.

This was the first time Phil killed another human at point-blank range, face-to-face, which weighed on him. All his previous killings had come from downrange shooting and his superior marksmanship.

Any remorse he felt, however, evaporated when he witnessed a German soldier yelling, "*Kamerad!*"[v] He stood with his hands over his head, indicating he had no weapons and was surrendering. As two new replacements stood to take him prisoner, Phil screamed, "No!" But he was too late: the two GIs were mowed down by German small arms fire, and the German faking surrender dropped back to the ground.

Phil reminded himself for the hundredth time that it was kill or be killed. That was the hell he had entered.

---

v "Kamerad," meaning "comrade," was the word that a surrendering German soldier would call out.

ᴄᴏ

Phil and his remaining men joined what was left of Companies A, G, and L in three additional attacks on new objectives throughout the afternoon. Stubborn enemy defenders resisted those attacks in Ponte Rotto, a stronghold about a mile and a half from the village of Cisterna. By day's end, beneath sputtering rain, the men continued to advance, feeling like they were literally inching their way to Rome.[113]

During the painfully slow advance, the 30th Infantry Regiment took the brunt in casualties, which numbered 432, or almost half of the losses suffered that day by the entire 3rd Infantry Division. The regiment lost five company commanders among the twenty-one officers and scores of non-commissioned officers who could not be easily or quickly replaced.

As the first twenty-four hours' fighting drew to a close, the shape of victory was beginning to appear. The German's iron ring around the Anzio Beachhead had finally been breached, and the enemy had suffered staggering losses of men, equipment, and prestige after four months of defensive build-up. In the hard-hitting attack, the 30th Infantry had driven almost two miles, far outdistancing its sister regiments.

By the afternoon of May 24, the resistance continued to crumble. Cisterna was surrounded, and news reports teletyped around the world were declaring, along with the divisional historian, "The steady marching men of the 3rd Infantry Division fought one of the bloodiest single encounters fought by any division in one day in World War II and what might well be classed as the greatest victory of its total combat career."[114] One newsman wrote, "The Germans are receiving one of the greatest thrashings in their history."[115]

Late that afternoon, the Anzio breakout was considered complete. Or, as one of Phil's men said, "The bitch is dead!" After 125 grueling days, Anzio's isolation was over. The beachhead had dissolved and become the left flank of the main fighting front.

Now Phil and his men could set their sights on the Eternal City.

20

ALL ROADS LEAD TO ROME

"Incentive is not ordinarily a part of an Infantryman's life. For him there are no twenty-five or fifty missions to be completed for a ticket home. Instead, the rifleman trudges into battle knowing that statistics are stacked against his survival. He fights without promise of either reward or relief. Behind every river, there's another hill—and behind that hill, another river.

—General Omar N. Bradley, Commander of the Twelfth Army Group[116]

The 30th Infantry had no time to rest and lick its wounds. Phil and his men pressed their advantage and continued to move toward Rome. The Germans were clearing a path for them because they were packing up and running fast, leaving behind tanks, howitzers, and even fully equipped field hospitals.[117]

Nevertheless, as the Americans approached Rome, the Germans stiffened their defenses—likely to give their troops time to escape the city. The further the Allied soldiers advanced, the more unforgiving the firefights and ambushes that marked their route.

One horrific event involved a captured U.S. Army lieutenant and a sergeant who the Germans forced, at gunpoint, to sit on the front of a tank sent down a one-lane mountain road toward oncoming GIs. The Kraut leader thought this would protect the Panzer from tank destroyer or TD fire. This was a fatal miscalculation.

The battle-hardened NCO leading the spearhead platoon made a split-second decision and ordered the tank to be destroyed. When his men began to blast away, the sergeant leaped from the tank, saving himself. The lieutenant, however, froze and was killed by a TD shell that stopped the tank, killed its occupants, and saved quite a few American lives.

Despite the never-ending firefights and the tremendous loss of life on both sides, a spirit of triumph filled Phil and his men. Their morale was heightened by the warm weather, sunshine, gentle breezes, and a cornucopia of blooming wildflowers across the Italian foothills, including bright-red poppies in full bloom in the flowerboxes of villages the men liberated. Phil's upbeat attitude was tempered by the adage, "Where a poppy blooms, a soldier has fallen." It was certainly true for this fight.

He wrote his mother and asked her to send the news clippings of the Battle of Anzio and their march on Rome, adding this thought:

> *I want to see what the U.S. thinks of what we are doing*
> *over here. Boy, I do know that we are happy about it.*[118]

On May 28, 1944, the regiment received 525 enlisted replacements and twelve new officers, each battalion getting 150 to 200 new men. More savage fighting ensued, but on the night of June 2 and into the early morning hours of June 3, the main enemy forces hurriedly withdrew and headed northward, leaving only scattered rear guards to impede the Allied advance into Rome.

Fortunately, the Führer had decided not to draw a line in the sand at the outskirts of the Eternal City, declaring Rome to be an open city. Even though no resistance was encountered, liberating one of the world's greatest cities was a prestigious achievement after many months of struggle on the Anzio Beachhead.

By late Sunday, June 4, American soldiers were streaming through Rome's outer precincts. As the sun set, the first major European capital of an Axis nation was firmly in Allied hands. The following day, Phil and the entire 3rd Division either drove or marched into the Eternal City. Phil and his pal, Ross Calvert, rode together in Phil's Jeep behind the frontline troops. They were overwhelmed by the joyous reception from the citizens of Rome.

Their eyes were drawn to a massive banner on the Pantheon[i] that read, in English: *Welcome to the Liberators*. The delirious crowds decorated the Jeep and both men with flowers. They offered them swigs of Tuscan wine until

---

i   The Pantheon is a former Roman temple that is now a Catholic church (Basilica di Santa Maria ad Martyres or Basilica of St. Mary and the Martyrs).

they arrived at the Piazza Venezia, the central hub of Rome, where Cardinal Venezia had ordered the construction of his own palace, the Palazzo Venezia, in 1455. During an afternoon ceremony, both the U.S. flag and a Union Jack were raised on staffs above the Palazzo.

In the eleven days of battles leading up to Rome's liberation, an offensive of unparalleled fury had shattered a series of powerful German defensive lines that opened the road to Rome. The 30th Infantry paid the enormous cost of 952 casualties, almost one-third of the effective regimental combat strength. Despite these grievous losses, the regiment accomplished its mission with flying colors and was recommended for a Distinguished Unit Citation by President Roosevelt. Furthermore, six Medals of Honor were awarded. But the excitement of the fall of Rome would be quickly forgotten in less than twenty-four hours.

At 0600 hours on Tuesday, June 6, 1944, an aide woke Lieutenant General Mark W. Clark, the commander of the Fifth Army and the youngest three-star general in the U.S. Army, in the Excelsior Hotel suite in Rome with news that German radio had announced the Allied invasion of Normandy.

At the Albergo Città, a BBC correspondent burst into the Allied press headquarters with this breathless announcement: "Boys, we're on the back page now. They've landed in Normandy."[119]

CBS newsman Eric Sevareid was among the war correspondents in the room who, upon hearing the news bulletin, pulled out a cigarette, lit it up, and dropped his half-written story about the liberation of Rome on the floor. He understood that he and his fellow reporters were like a troupe of actors who, at the climax of their play, had looked up only to realize that all the spectators had all fled out the door.

From that day forward, Operation Overlord, forever to be known as *the* D-Day, would overshadow the Fifth Army's remarkable achievement on the Italian boot. The Southern Front would soon fade into the dustbin of history as the "Forgotten Front." While the hardships and victories may have been overlooked back home, none of those who scrapped, sacrificed, and suffered would ever forget what they experienced in the crucible of war. They did themselves and our country proud.

For Phil, despite all he had accomplished in over one hundred days on the battlefield, his war, in many ways, was just beginning.

21

A ROMAN HOLIDAY

"I have arrived in the First City of the World!…
All the dreams of my youth have come to life."

—Johann Wolfgang von Goethe, German poet[120]

The stunning beauty of Rome provided some R&R[i] for Phil and the exhausted, sweat-and-blood-soaked, sore-footed infantrymen. There was a lot to see in Rome, and Phil and Ross took advantage of the respite from the war. An English-speaking monk offered to take them around the popular tourist sites for a couple of days.[121]

Phil wrote about his experiences to one of his best friends in Memphis, Bill O'Bannon:

> *Bill, I have seen all of the things that we studied in our Latin class. It has in many ways been much fun, and it has been all free for me, but it has cost the other men much in ways that can't be repaid in money. Bill, don't feel bad about not being over here. In the first place, it's hell. And in the second place, you are getting far ahead of us guys here. We still have to go back to school and resettle ourselves again from a life of hell and death and being killers, back to just being the kids we were before I left.*

---

i   R&R is a military abbreviation for "rest and recuperation" or "rest and relaxation."

But when I get back, we will do just the same things.
We'll go on double dates and go out to the Rainbow and
dance a while. Then we'll go out to the southern part of
Highland for a little while to look at the moon, then on
the way home stop at the Pig 'n Whistle for a couple of
hamburgers and a malt. Or maybe Kane's. Boy, that's all
to come.

Well, Bill, I will sign off for now. Write me when you
can cause I miss you fellow, bad.

Just a guy.
Phil[122]

Their stay in Rome was short, less than ten days. Now Phil and his men were being told to gird themselves for their next operation. Although they did not know it at the time, they were being sent to train for Operation Dragoon, the amphibious assault on southern France. The first step of their next journey began on June 16, 1944, when the 30th Infantry Regiment took trains heading south to Pozzuoli, situated about twelve miles inland from the bay at Naples.

Why south instead of north, toward Germany? Because Phil and his men needed intensive training for the large-scale amphibious operations that were surely in their future. The beaches and terrain in that area most closely resembled where they were to land in southern France.

The VI Corps commander, Major General Lucian Truscott, the second youngest corps commander in the U.S. Army, reinitiated an extremely strenuous training regimen he had used when commanding the 3rd Division invasion of Sicily. The program was designed to make the men the fastest, toughest marchers in the U.S. Army. Instead of the standard infantry marching rate of 2½ mph, Truscott trained his division to march 5 mph for the first hour, 4 mph each of the next two hours, and then 3½ mph for up to thirty miles. Phil's 3rd Battalion bragged of holding the all-time record for a march of fifty-four miles in thirty-three hours.[ii] The men grudgingly called these hikes the "Truscott Trots."

They trained like dogs, starting at six in the morning with a five-mile, one-hour trot or speed hike, and then going hard until three in the afternoon on a nearby beach, practicing dangerous amphibious landings and other tasks that could save their lives. Nighttime brought no rest for their weary bodies as they would run through close-order drills three times a week before returning to their headquarters and racking out.

Although the men were soon in peak physical condition, those newer to the force grew increasingly anxious. Phil noticed the chaplains were kept busy leading these men in prayer, and the attendance at services grew as the date

---

ii   The record still stands today.

of departure approached. Personally, he thought church services gave both he and his men optimism for the future. As a young lieutenant, he was learning the value of hope in the ranks.

The final rehearsal for the upcoming landing operation was conducted toward the end of July in a training area that had been directly behind the German lines during the previous winter's campaign. German engineers had mined everything so completely that it was one of the most fortified areas in all of Italy.

The major headache of clearing the beaches and shoreline of the dreaded anti-personnel S-mines[iii]—nicknamed "Bouncing Betties" by the GIs—fell to the 10th Engineer Combat Battalion. The nasty mines were planted beneath the ground in metal containers that held hundreds of steel balls and shrapnel pieces.

When triggered, they launched about three feet into the air and then detonated, projecting a maiming spray of red-hot metal in all directions. The intention was to mutilate soldiers rather than kill them. In particular, legs and genitalia were the most vulnerable—the latter being the wound that terrified the soldiers the most.

Phil told his men with great emphasis *not* to take even one step outside of the taped-off area that had been combed for mines by the engineers. Like most of his fellow soldiers, he took that instruction to heart. Some did not, however. One morning, Phil and his men were following another platoon up a taped-off trail toward a railroad. As the men turned onto the tracks, their fresh-faced, brand-new-to-the-field 2nd lieutenant yelled at the top of his voice, "Get the hell off the damn railroad tracks! You wouldn't do that in combat!"

Before Phil could react, the men reluctantly did as instructed. The lead man immediately stepped on a mine. He was blown to bits with parts of his body sticking to the men behind him. Phil sprinted to the spot of the blast, where he found the soldier—barely alive on the side of a still-smoldering hole about four feet across.

He quickly examined what remained: the soldier's legs had been disintegrated to mid-thigh, and his forearm bones had been broken and stripped of flesh. The soldier made gruesome sucking noises. The young lieutenant stood by in shock, so Phil hollered for a medic and began injecting the man with shots of morphine. As a medic ran up, the man gave out one last hideous groan and blew out his last breath.

Phil felt his chest tighten in fury. He took a deep breath to maintain control in front of the men. He slowly stood and faced the rookie 2nd lieutenant, whose face was drained of color. He appeared older than Phil, and was shaking.

---

iii   The S-mine (*Schrapnellmine, Springmine,* or *Splittermine* in German) was also called an "invention of the devil" by American soldiers.

Phil leaned in until their noses nearly touched and whispered so only the officer and the men closest to him could hear him. "Your order just killed one of your men. Now you know what the stakes are. You need to get your shit together if you're going to lead. You get back to the beach, pronto, and report to your company commander. Let him know I have your men. I will keep them safe, and I will bring them *all* back. You understand?"

The 2nd lieutenant nodded.

"Then git!" Phil cried as the officer slipped away.

"Double-time!" Phil barked.

As the officer started running, he turned to the men. "Gather around me but stay on the tracks."

When the men from his and the novice's squads were close, he said, "Men, you need to learn from today. You're going to have buddies, good friends, that'll die right by you in battle when you're attacking the enemy. Some will get shot. Some will be blown to smithereens by artillery, cut to ribbons right before your eyes. You have to remember that you don't stop. You don't *ever* stop. You do, and you'll get killed. You can avenge your loss. Kill the Germans, and we'll win this war. You understand?"

"Yes, sir!" the men cried out.

He looked at one of his men. "You take point."

"Yes, sir!" the private responded. Phil then turned to the men and barked, "Let's move out!"

As the soldiers silently passed, Phil looked at the bottom of the still-smoldering crater. He saw a crisp, brand-new one-thousand lira bill—a so-called "AM-lira," a currency put in circulation by the American military the previous year. At an exchange rate of one hundred AM-lira per U.S. dollar, the bill was worth ten bucks.

It must had blown out of his pocket, Phil thought, as he blinked back tears. *The cost of war...the horrible cost of war.*

From that point on, Phil would preach to his men what was called the "Murphy's Law for GIs," which went like this:

"If the path is easy, it'll be mined."[123]

❧

VI Corps was moved from Clark's Fifth Army to Lieutenant General Alexander "Sandy" Patch's Seventh Army, which was to lead the upcoming amphibious operation in southern France.[124]

For Phil's 3rd Battalion, this would be their *seventh* amphibious assault, but their first D-Day to be carried out during daylight hours. This time the target area was the French Riviera. Further north in the Normandy region, the American and British forces were encountering stiff resistance during the Battle of the Falaise Pocket.

According to military planners, the invasion of southern France would clear out the enemy forces guarding the approaches into France from the south. Once their invasion succeeded, they would push northward and link up with the Allied troops coming out of Normandy. Together, they would form one combined "broad front" and drive the Nazi forces back toward and across the German border.

By August 8, the 30th Infantry finished loading at Pozzuoli and embarked aboard LCTs,[iv] LCIs,[v] and LSTs for their destination somewhere on the French coastline.

After two days of sailing, on August 10, Phil and Ross Calvert were sharing a smoke on their ship's afterdeck when they noticed a speck in the distance, distinguishable as some sort of craft, rapidly approaching. When the speedy launch drew closer, and the men could make out a boat with British markings and a Union Jack approaching their landing vessel, Phil and Ross stared unbelievingly.

The short, stubby figure of Winston Churchill[vi] stood on the deck. Doffing his famous black bowler caused his thinning white hair to be blown askew by the wind. They couldn't believe their eyes. As the launch drew abreast, Churchill waved. Then the doughty little warrior flashed his equally famous V-for-Victory sign—the symbol of hope and determination—with two fingers on his right hand. The American soldiers cheered and waved back.

Phil could barely contain his excitement. "That's Winston Churchill!" he exclaimed. "Wait until I write home 'bout this!"

"Remember, you can't," his buddy reminded him. "Not just yet."

Phil shrugged. "I suppose you're right."

But now, he had another vivid memory to file away and tell his kids someday. That's if he lived to have children.

On that score, Phil knew there was a lot more war left to fight.

---

iv   Landing Craft, Tank (LCTs), much smaller than an LSI, was an amphibious assault ship for landing tanks on beachheads. During Operation Dragoon, however, three-quarters of the supplies on the LCTs were ammunition and gasoline.

v   Landing Craft, Infantry (LCI) were several classes of seagoing amphibious assault ships used to land large numbers of Infantry directly onto beaches. During World War II, these small steel ships could land 200 men at a speed of up to 15 knots.

vi   Prime Minister Winston Churchill was traveling under the name of Colonel Kent, ostensibly on a fortnight's bathing holiday in southern Italy. He had come to keep an eye on an enterprise he bitterly opposed, preferring to reinforce British and American forces in Italy and make amphibious assaults on the oil-producing regions in the Balkans. The decision to invade southern France churned up as much enmity within the Anglo-American alliance as any episode of the war. Nevertheless, Churchill was unable to resist seeing off the invasion convoy, and to wish Godspeed and a quick, successful victory to the United States troops. His visit was a favorable omen. He later wrote, "They did not know that if I had had my way, they would be sailing in a different direction. However, I was proud to wave at these gallant soldiers."

PART III:
THE FRENCH CAMPAIGN

"We have faith that future generations will know...
there came a time when men of goodwill found a way
to unite and produce and fight to destroy the forces
of ignorance and intolerance and slavery and war."

—U.S. President Franklin Delano Roosevelt[125]

22
CÔTE D'AZUR'S D-DAY

"The Infantryman…the man who has, in the final analysis, been winning the wars ever since men first were organized into groups when they went to the fighting. Yet from the standpoint of public appreciation, he has been the Army's most neglected and underrated soldier."

—Robert Vermillion, United Press war correspondent during World War II [126]

There were ships as far as the eye could see.[i] Onboard an LST in the Mediterranean Sea, Phil and Ross Calvert observed the smoke belching from stacks of the great American Naval fleet and could feel not only a steady calm among their men, but also feelings of rock-solid confidence. After winning the Battle of Anzio and liberating Rome, their guys were self-assured, self-confident, and self-reliant veterans. Phil was honored to fight with them—and glad he didn't have to fight *against* them.[127]

---

i   Nearly 900 U.S. naval vessels plied ten routes of the Mediterranean, converging within striking distance of southern France. The great fleet, made up of nine aircraft carriers, eighty-seven destroyers, and 370 large landing ships, were all committed to safely landing some 150,000 troops, including 41,000 French soldiers. Everything each GI owned was in their packs, which brought the average rifleman's combat load to over 68 pounds, far beyond the 43 pounds recommended for assault troops. Each soldier received an American flag armband and two packs of Lucky Strike cigarettes.

A cool breeze coming off the Mediterranean Sea tempered the warm August day. Troops sat beneath tarpaulins on the transport decks, sewing shoulder flashes to uniform sleeves or thumbing through *A Pocket Guide to France*.

It hardly seems that an invasion is on, Phil thought. *Things are so quiet.*

He looked at Ross, and he could tell that his buddy was thinking the same thing. They both retained a small bit of fear because those who didn't have a healthy respect for combat were often as good as dead. In the final pre-invasion briefing, the officers made sure their men maintained the right balance of confidence and humility.

In the earliest hours of August 15, 1944, the massive Allied force crept toward sixteen narrow beaches along the Côte d'Azur, known for its glamorous beach resorts at Nice, Saint-Tropez, and Cannes, as well as the independent principality of Monaco. The 3rd Infantry Division was slated to hit three of the sixteen beaches to the west of these posh resorts. American soldiers were poised to land between Saint Raphael and Toulon, France's largest naval port. This was known as France's Provence region.

With the arrival of daylight, wave after wave of bombers began hammering their targets on and behind the beaches at 0550 hours. Not one German anti-aircraft battery responded. Instead, the defenders crouched in their bunkers and trembled as giant shockwaves ripped through the earth. At 0730 hours, the massive air onslaught waned because it was the U.S. Navy's turn to unleash a deafening, destructive, devastating, and demoralizing naval bombardment from over 400 guns. A deluge of steel ripped through the beaches, the coastal highways, and the hills beyond.

Phil, Ross, and their men, watching from a ship railing, had front-row seats to an awe-inspiring spectacle of naval gunfire and air sorties on an unimaginable scale.

While the shelling continued, LCVPs[ii] were released. But these were not the personnel-carrying Higgins boats, but rather drones laden with high explosives and radio-controlled from other specially designed landing craft. This was a new technique in the annals of warfare, seeing its first use in combat. The Apex craft, as they were called, were radio-steered toward the smoldering coastline, where they successfully cleared lanes up to the deserted beaches.

As the Navy's shelling began to fade at 0755 hours, over forty rocket ships, each armed with 700 rocket-launching tubes, swarmed toward the beaches through the open lanes, unleashing 30,000 flaming missiles. Fired in batches, these missiles hissed through the air like turbo-charged snakes. Once they hit the earth, the missiles detonated mines, blasted barbed-wire entanglements, and unnerved the waiting, cowering enemy.

---

ii   LCVPs stands for landing craft, vehicle, personnel, but they were more commonly referred to as "Higgins boats." Made of reinforced plywood with a thick metal ramp on the flat bow that could be lowered, each thirty-six-foot-long boat could carry thirty-six men and their gear, or one Jeep and twelve men, or two Jeeps and drivers. The Higgins boats could speed toward the shore at 12 knots.

Over a mile offshore, tens of thousands of infantrymen were unloading from hundreds of LCIs and LCTs onto LCVPs manned by naval personnel. Phil and his platoon climbed down a rope cargo net on the side of their ship and stepped into a waiting Higgins boat. There were two Jeeps secured in Phil's landing craft, each with a small trailer attached and loaded with ammunition and engineering supplies.

As the men followed him down the rope ladders into other Higgins boats, Phil yelled to them, "Hold the verticals, or your hands will be stepped on!" He and one of his sergeants rapidly inspected the equipment to be sure everything was in order. Once the men were on board their craft, the coxswain gunned the boat away from the ship. They were on their way with a motto on their minds: "No more Anzios."

Despite the earlier bombardment, there was still incoming enemy mortar, artillery, and rocket fire that caused waterspouts. Small arms fire crackled overhead. Phil and his men couldn't see the beach because the front and sides of the LCVP were too high. The coxswain waited until 0850 hours, when a violet smoke signal informed them and the rest of the invasion force that the beach defenses had been neutralized. They could land, which they did beginning at 0920 hours.

Phil was startled when they hit the coastline because their LCVP ran right up on the beach, dropped its ramp, and deposited them on dry sand. Phil was in the lead Jeep with his driver and radioman, and after their wheels hit the sandy beach, they drove quickly toward the cover of the trees with a second Jeep and his platoon following rapidly behind. Not one of them so much as got their boots wet.

The opposition was negligible. The rest of the 30th hit Red Beach running at H-plus 80 minutes and didn't stop—striking rapidly inland. By 1015 hours, the entire regiment and most of its artillery were safely ashore. Their first destination on Phil's assault path was the village of La Croix, about a mile and a half inland. They encountered no resistance and were entering the town cautiously when suddenly the joyous French people living there were standing on the main boulevard, waiting to welcome them. They poured out of buildings and cheered the Americans with bottles of wine and champagne held aloft, which they shared, while young women and teen girls—dressed in flowing summer dresses that displayed plenty of leg—hugged and kissed the GIs as they marched in.

Phil found himself wishing that he and his men could stick around and enjoy the celebration and hospitality, but they had to keep moving inland because they had the enemy on the run.

As they pressed forward, the men sweltered in the heat. Many hitched rides on the Jeep trailers or the four tanks of the 756th Tank Battalion and the two TDs of the 601ˢᵗ Tank Destroyer Battalion. Phil, in his Jeep, smiled when he heard his men singing. Morale was sky-high. By noon, they were twenty miles inland.

Phil thought, *What a contrast to Anzio!*

Hitler would later declare August 15, 1944, as "the worst day of my life."[128] The German dictator had good reason to be glum: Operation Dragoon cracked the enemy coastal defenses in southern France in a matter of hours and prompted a massive German retreat.

The vast operation successfully opened another front for Germany to defend. The German Army began to flee southern France for its survival. As Phil would learn from briefings held in the coming days, a significant portion of the best German units escaped.

What Phil didn't know was that they would regroup and be waiting in the Vosges mountains along the Franco-German border, which meant the road to victory was still far, far away.

23
HEROES AND LIBERATORS

"Our secret weapon is the Infantry—the weapon about which we have talked the least and upon which we depend the most. The Infantry closes with the enemy, meets him in hand-to-hand conflict, kills him or drives him backward, and seizes the ground…which only he can take and hold."

—Steve Early, press secretary for President Franklin D. Roosevelt[129]

With the German Army in panicked retreat, Phil and his battalion moved almost continuously. They were spurred on by Major General Lucian K. Truscott, who commanded the U.S. Army's VI Corps and told his troops, "If you run out of gas, park your vehicles and move on foot."[130] It was as if Phil and his warhorses were in a horse race, relentlessly overrunning German roadblocks and defensive stands designed to give the Nazi soldiers some breathing room.[131]

The tables had been turned. Whenever the Americans climbed a hill and found a column of German vehicles in retreat passing by below them, someone would yell out, "Remember Anzio!" and open fire. One time, a 3rd Division artillery battery wiped out 222 German vehicles during a three-hour barrage.

After their slow battering for months in Italy, Phil and his men experienced great exhilaration as they advanced through the Provence region. *There's nothing better than progress for a foot soldier*, he thought, because each mile they liberated was another mile closer to going home. What Phil couldn't understand was the enemy's varied reactions when the Americans arrived. In one town, a thousand German soldiers would surrender, while in another, handfuls of holdouts would fight like wildcats to slow the offensive.

Then on the night of August 18, 1944, while working with his platoon to keep ammunition flowing to the rifle squads, a bullet struck Phil in his left arm.

"Medic! Medic!" his radioman called as he reached for gauze, which he unwrapped and pushed against the wound.

The medic ran up. Pulling off the gauze, he inspected the wound. "Looks like a 'through and through,' Lieutenant. No muscle or nerve involvement."

The medic sprinkled the wound with sulfa powder and re-dressed the area. "Let's get you a shot of morphine, and I'll take you back to the hospital."

"Hospital?" Phil said.

"Yup. Three 400-bed evacuation hospitals are being erected, one supporting each of our divisions. Lucky you. The first U.S. Army nurses are arriving here in good ol' southern France tomorrow. You'll get great care."

"Bullshit!" Phil exclaimed. "It's a flesh wound. I'll be fine."

"As you wish, sir. But I'm putting you in for a Purple Heart for this one."

Just over the hill, they heard small arms fire and another scream of "Medic! Medic!"

The medic handed Phil a small bottle of sulfa tablets. "Starting tomorrow, take two twice a day until gone. Gotta go!" the soldier shouted as he sprinted in the direction of the shooting.

"Those guys deserve the Infantry Combat Badge just like infantrymen, don't you think, Lieutenant?" the radioman asked.

Phil nodded. "Damn right!" He respected and admired the medics for how they saved lives. Every frontline soldier felt the same way.[i]

☙

The 30th Regiment continued to break the enemy's resistance, liberating dozens of towns during the next two days. Overjoyed French people,

---

i   Phil was saddened when he learned that the medic who treated him was killed in action later that night. Most field medics were popular, highly respected, and called "Doc" by the frontline men who bitterly resented the War Department refusal—based on the need to maintain the medics' Geneva Convention noncombatant status—to grant eligible enlisted medics the Combat Infantry Badge and the ten dollars a month extra pay that went with it. In some ETO divisions riflemen collected money from their own wages to give their medics their combat bonus. Five enlisted medics in Europe received the Medal of Honor; hundreds of others won Silver or Bronze Star medals for valor. Finally, the Army instituted the Combat Medical Badge in January 1945 in recognition of medics' role in combat.

unaccustomed to freedom after four years of cruel Nazi oppression, jubilantly threw flowers, bestowed kisses, handed out cups of water, and freely gave swigs of their precious wine and potent liqueurs such as Calvados, Chartreuse, and Cognac.[132]

Driving into these picturesque villages didn't get old for Phil. Being greeted so warmly made it difficult for him to hold back tears of emotion. He and his men felt like heroes and conquerors. These were days of happiness. Up to this point, Phil's war had been filthy, fearsome, and unfashionable. Now, in an instant, it was glorious.

An embedded reporter with Phil's 3rd Battalion wrote an article titled, "Daring Tennesseans Give Germans Fright." He filed this report:

> *Nazis in the southern France area rapidly learned to fear the daring antics of two Army officers from the Volunteer State. Lieut. Ross W. Calvert of Nashville and Lieut. Philip B. Larimore of Memphis both are noted for their wild stunts. For example, their battalion was approaching a small French Riviera town recently when Lieutenant Calvert dashed into town, mowed down three Germans with a brand-new Tommy gun,[ii] and ran after another to take him prisoner. He chased the Jerry three blocks while GIs wildly cheered the race. Friends report a grin as long as Tennessee broke across his face as he paraded back with his prisoner.*

> *Lieutenant Larimore, meanwhile, was driving down the road when he discovered old dirt piles. A few jabs with a knife proved they were mines. He defused and picked out twenty of the traps and had the roadway cleared before his buddy returned with the prisoner.[133]*

There was also the dark side of liberation. Phil couldn't help but notice how Nazi soldiers had ransacked cities and towns during their retreats. French women who had consorted with German soldiers—known as "horizontal collaborators"—were paraded into town squares, sometimes naked, and shorn of their hair and then beaten. Some were lined up against a stone wall and summarily executed.

The GIs were learning that the German military utterly devastated or obliterated hundreds of European cities, villages, and farming communities as

---

ii   The "Tommy gun" was the common name for the Thompson submachine gun, which were favored by soldiers for their large .45 caliber cartridge, accuracy, and high volume of fully automatic fire while still being relatively lightweight, portable, and easy to use.

well as transportation infrastructure during their retreats. For Phil, the sight of ruined farms, razed hamlets, and buzz-cut women lying on the ground with a bullet in their heads was too gruesome to write about in letters home.

Instead, on August 22, 1944, Phil penned these words to his mother:

> *Just a short note to let you know I arrived in France in*
> *good condition. "Having a fine time, wish you were here,"*
> *as they say. But as you can see in the newspapers, we*
> *are doing quite well. We caught them where they weren't*
> *expecting us and have kept them on the run. As long as we*
> *keep pressing them, they don't have time to dig in, and we*
> *can make a good show. This, compared to Anzio, is the way*
> *to fight a war.*[134]

The men of the 30th Infantry Regiment advanced over 160 miles in nine fairly uneventful days, except for a nearly disastrous friendly fire incident when ten of their P-47 Thunderbolts strafed and bombed them. Fortunately, only a few men were wounded and nobody was killed, but the friendly fire attack "scared the shit" out of Phil and his men.

On the morning of August 27, Phil was attached to a reconnaissance patrol with his good friend Ross Calvert, who was then the 3rd Battalion S-2. The men were heading toward the village of Taulignan, about twenty miles north of Vaison-la-Romaine and eighty-five miles north of Marseille, in the Provence region, when they spotted a German roadblock. They immediately engaged the enemy, killing nine Germans and capturing three more using their powerful Tommy guns.

The men then rejoined Company L to continue the attack on Taulignan, the two buddies deciding to lead the company as first scouts. They encountered another roadblock, killing twelve and capturing eight. Phil and Ross came across one of their men who'd been wounded by enemy shell fragments and rendered first aid. Ross carried the man fifty yards to the safety of a ditch, while Phil provided suppressing fire with his Tommy gun. Moving another 300 yards, they selected an outpost from which Ross directed artillery, tank, and TD fire on the principal German position north of Taulignan for thirty minutes, killing ten more Germans.

At this point, in the late afternoon, Ross and Phil led the company through Taulignan while the rest of the regiment quickly cleared the town and began to reconnoiter the route to La Bégude-de-Mazenc, about five miles north. Phil's guidebook told him the word *bégu* was derived from the Provençal verb "to drink," and *bégude* meant "drinking place." So, it was no surprise when the men approached the hamlet's edge and spotted thirty bicycles in front of a hotel and tavern. The American pair slowly moved in, hearing boisterous German voices inside the bar. Apparently, they hadn't heard the orders to retreat—or had had one too many for the road.

Two Kraut soldiers were walking up the street in semi-darkness, smoking cigarettes and laughing. Ross and Phil snuck up behind them, stuck their Tommy guns in the men's backs, softly ordered them to halt, and disarmed them. As they were taking them prisoner, one of the men yelled out to warn his fellow soldiers having a drink in the tavern. Phil jammed the butt of his Tommy gun into the man's forehead, knocking him unconscious. The other patrol members placed heavy fire on the building.

After a brief firefight, the Germans inside the tavern surrendered. One of those waving a white handkerchief was a German heavy-weapons company commander who insisted that Phil and Ross join him in the tavern to light up a cigar, sip on a Courvoisier cognac, and comfortably discuss the terms of his complete surrender.

Phil and Ross looked at each other, grinned, and said, "Why the hell not?" After a "strenuous" one hour of negotiations, which required quite a few refills and fine cigars, the unconditional surrender was accepted.

At 0200 hours on August 28, the 3rd Battalion entered Taulignan. The officers enjoyed hot showers, a few hours of sleep in comfortable beds, and a delicious breakfast of croissants and jam at the Hôtel Bitsch.

While enjoying their *petit dejeuner*, Phil had a thought.

"Ross," he began, "when we were fighting yesterday, I realized that we were communicating without words. We were working together just by watching each other and knowing what the other was thinking and doing and going to do."

Ross nodded as he contemplated Phil's observation. "You know, you're right, Daddy-O. Never thought of it, but that's pretty cool."

"My platoon and I are the same way now. It reminds me of what an old horseman in Naples taught me about the word *dressage*, how with training and practice, a horse and rider communicate and cooperate and work together in perfect harmony—like they're two hearts but one mind. We've done that playing bridge together. Now we're doing it in war."

Ross smiled and raised his mug of coffee. "Am I the horse or the rider?"

Phil laughed. "I guess we're both just old warhorses."

"Here's to us and those like us. Damn few, and they're probably dead!"

"Here, here!" Phil exclaimed. Then he offered an early morning toast. "To our coffins," he began. "May they be made from a hundred-year-old oak tree that is planted tomorrow! To us warhorses, forever!"

When Phil learned that Ross would be awarded the Distinguished Service Cross for his heroism and leadership, he was happy for his friend.

But neither one had any idea about the horrors in store for both of them in the next few days.

24
THE HORROR OF MONTÉLIMAR

"There's nothing I don't know about war.
The stench of it.... War is a terrible thing."

—Don McCullin, award-winning war photographer[135]

The next major engagement of the invasion of southern France would become known as the "Battle of the Montélimar Square," an area one hundred miles north of the coastal city of Marseille and along the German route of withdrawal.[136]

Before the war, Montélimar's claim to fame was its reputation as the center of production for nougat, a sticky, tooth-breaking confection popular with French children. But as Allied forces advanced quickly, the German Nineteenth Army had no choice but to pass through Montélimar and continue in a northerly direction through a steep gorge where the Rhône River, railroad tracks, and the Route Nationale 7 highway barely had room to squeeze through together—a fact not lost on General Truscott and his military planners. Units from the 3rd and 36th Divisions raced ahead to strategically occupy the dominating heights on both sides of the gorge just north of Montélimar.

At first light, the American forces on the gorge's east ridge were gripped by the scene below them. Within easy 60-mm mortar range was a German convoy with more than 2,000 vehicles—heavy cargo trucks, half-tracks, numerous requisitioned French sedans—jammed bumper-to-bumper and joined by 1,000 horses pulling carts or trailing behind motor vehicles, most of them stolen from the French. Scattered among them were several thousand German soldiers, including over a thousand on foot—all in frantic retreat from the 3rd Division rapidly approaching from the south.

As the German convoy's lead elements passed through the narrow canyon at 0630 hours, American artillery unleashed a furious barrage. This was like shooting fish in a barrel. Thirty-three ammunition trucks blew up, setting the rest of the convoy on fire, since many of the trucks had been topped off with fuel. A ten-mile stretch of the valley was quickly obscured by the smoking hulks of burning vehicles, dead men, and horse carcasses, not to mention hundreds of artillery pieces and masses of small arms, automatic weapons, ammunition, and other equipment, which created a massive roadblock of wrecked enemy vehicles. The surviving drivers and personnel abandoned their vehicles and raced for the relative safety of the Rhône River.

Then the first of three German trains raced up the valley. The 133rd Field Artillery Battalion scored two direct hits on the lead train of fifty-five cars. Two following trains—blocked by the wreckage—were also hit, including six massive railroad guns. Four were the dreaded "Anzio Annies." To the men's disbelief, they discovered two even larger railway guns that were, until then, unknown to the Allies. These were "Annie's Big Sisters."[i]

After sunrise, Allied fighter bombers poured in at treetop level, inflicting massive damage with their cannons, rockets, and 500- and 1,000-pound bombs on the already hard-pressed enemy. When General Truscott was flown over the valley in a Piper Cub to examine the battlefield, he told others that the "sight and smell of this section is an experience I have no wish to repeat."

ॐ

On the afternoon of August 28, 1944, on the outskirts of Montélimar, Phil was called over to Colonel McGarr's Jeep.[137]

"Lieutenant," the colonel barked, pointing at a map of the area, "I have an assignment for you and a few of your men."

He pointed on the map to the gorge just north of Montélimar. "Along the N-7 here, I'm told the devastation to the enemy is spectacular. A lot of horses were killed and wounded, while many others escaped."

The colonel looked up at him. "You're a horseman, Lieutenant. I want you to handpick a squad of other horsemen, establish a corral, and round up as many of the healthy ones as possible. Put down the others."

---

i   "Annie's Big Sisters" were 131-foot-long cannons with a bore of 4.6 inches, and could fire shells up to 35 miles.

Phil chose a few men from his battalion—all farm boys—and they drove up the N-7 in Jeeps. His buddy Ross Calvert joined them. Just north of the city, they ran into prisoners belonging to the German Nineteenth Army, accompanied by GIs with Tommy guns. Lines of German soldiers, their eyes glazed over and their heads hanging low, streamed by as they headed toward the prisoner cages being set up in Montélimar.

Then Phil and his men passed a small farmhouse with a sizeable courtyard surrounded by a stone fence. Inside the yard were a horse trough and a hand pump. Phil turned to two of the privates.

"You men secure this home. Get any hay or feed you can from the barn or neighbors, fill the water trough, and then wait here at the gate. We'll send back any horses we can."

As Phil and Ross moved further up the road in their Jeep, they encountered overwhelming carnage. Charred tanks and myriad burning vehicles were scattered bumper-to-bumper and side by side in long, disorganized columns. Besides the crackling sound of fires, the air was hushed, except for the buzzing of countless feasting flies. The vultures not already feasting on flesh circled overhead and cast shadows on the corpses. The men were silent in their thoughts about the horror they saw.

They came upon American soldiers from other units walking up the roadway of ruin, the avenue of annihilation. As he tried to take in the degree of devastation, Phil said to Ross, "This looks like a highway to hell."

Along the road and in the fields, they passed the bodies of hundreds of dead Germans, most of them fire-blackened, who had been cut down while trying to escape. The bodies of dead soldiers who hadn't been burned to a crisp were starting to swell in the hot August sun, their mouths agape, filled with flies.

Phil and Ross covered their faces with bandanas because of the horrible, fetid smells. The entire length of the panorama of destruction was worsened by the outrageous odor of bloated horses, burning wood, scorched metal, and roasted flesh assailing the men's nostrils. They quickly named the road the "Avenue of Stenches."

Phil couldn't help noticing how other soldiers were taking advantage of the spoils of war. This was Phil's first experience with widespread looting. Scores of American soldiers stopped to grab Lugers, watches, knives, Nazi patches, and jewelry from the dead bodies. Any pockets containing money and liquor were a bonus.

Also astounding was the number of dead horses littering the roads and shoulders. Phil could tell that most had been stolen from the French farmers because the tack was simple, and the horses were untrimmed. On the other hand, German horses had been groomed with hooves and tails trimmed, as though for a parade, and had impressive tack with highly polished leather and brass rivets that shone brightly.

He was surprised the German Army relied on so many horses to pull, and his men were astonished to learn the German Army was still a horse-drawn military force in many ways, having more horses in an infantry division than they had men for pulling carts, wagons, and artillery pieces.[ii]

It wasn't too long before Phil and his men ran into scared and injured horses that had survived the devastating bombardment that nearly wiped out the convoy. These skittish and traumatized horses needed attention, which he and his fellow warhorsemen were willing to provide.

Phil had been at war about six months, and he was now well acquainted with the sight and sounds of horribly wounded soldiers, as well as the smell and spectacle of dead men. Still, the sight of these shocked and damaged animals affected him more profoundly than he expected.

He was reminded that the butchery and bloodbath of war inadvertently swept over far too many innocents.

---

ii   Horse-drawn transportation was important for Germany as the country was relatively lacking in natural oil resources. Infantry and horse-drawn artillery formed the bulk of the German Army throughout the war. Only one-fifth of the Army belonged to mobile Panzer and mechanized divisions. Each German Infantry division employed thousands of horses and thousands of men taking care of them. The German Army entered WWII with 514,000 horses, and over the course of the war, employed 2.75 million horses and mules in total, averaging 1.1 million horses at any time. Most were used by foot Infantry and horse-drawn artillery troops.

25
A THRILLING ROUNDUP

"Rider and horse…each is totally reliant upon the other.
Each is the selfless guardian of the other's very well-being."

—Author Unknown[138]

While looking for horses under Colonel McGarr's order, Phil and his team found six hitched to a large artillery piece. Four horses were dead, and two were still alive. The driver had been killed, but he still had the reins in his hands. Phil approached the two draft horses at the front. They were dehydrated. Their tongues were dry and cracked, and their breathing was rapid and shallow. Phil gently rubbed the horses' noses and then poured water from his canteen into his hand, letting each horse thirstily slurp the refreshing fluid.[139]

Phil could see the suspicion in their eyes diminish. When he walked around the pair, however, his spirit sank as he inspected their hindquarters. Each horse was severely wounded from shrapnel. Upon closer examination, Phil was horrified to see fly-covered intestines hanging out of their abdomens. The wounds sealed the horses' fate. No wonder their haunch and back muscles were quivering.

Ross walked up to Phil. "These two need relief?"

Phil nodded. His lips pursed, his eyes misted. "Gorgeous drafts, Ross," he said softly as he wrapped his bandana around the eyes of one of the horses. Ross did the same with the other mount.

Phil looked over his shoulder to his men. "Come on up, guys. Given the number of wounded horses we're likely to see, I want you to know how to do this."

As the men walked up behind him, Phil reached into his pocket and pulled out some bullets. "These are soft-nosed.[i] You want to use them instead of one encased in a full metal jacket."

Phil knew from his days on the farm that if done correctly, a shot to the horse's brain was a reliable, instantaneous, externally bloodless, and humane way to put a horse out of untreatable misery and suffering.

"Why use a dumdum?" Ross asked.

"There's a decreased risk that the bullet will pass through the horse's skull and ricochet in such a way as to injure one of our buddies or us."

Phil stroked the nose of one of the horses. "Ross, let's shoot at the same time. It'll keep the other from panicking."

"Behind the ear?"

"Nope. The safest is the exact midline of the forehead. With these big boys, you want to aim about five finger-widths down from the base of the forelock.[ii] For an average horse, it's four finger-widths. My dad told me to draw an X from the base of the ears to the inside corner of the opposite eye and put the shot just a half-inch above there, straight in through the forehead. Either way, just be sure to hold your pistol perpendicular to the skull—aimed directly down the neck. One shot should do it because the bullet rattles around inside the skull and instantly scrambles their brain but doesn't come out."

They both reached for their pistols. "Keep the gun's muzzle at least an inch or two away from the head, men," Phil continued. "It reduces the risk of backfire and lets the bullet gain more velocity. And as soon as you shoot, back up. Sometimes they won't fall straight down but will lurch forward."

Phil continued to tenderly massage the horse behind its ear as he soothingly clucked and gently pushed the horse's nose down. He put his pistol up to the forehead of his horse, as did Ross.

"On three." Phil took a deep breath. "Your pain's over, big fellow," he whispered. "One, two, three."

With twin explosions, both horses collapsed.

Phil, Ross, and their men turned and continued up the road, passing GIs sweeping the entire area. They would take an additional 2,000 prisoners on top of the 2,000 already in hand. In addition, the 15th Infantry Regiment

---

i   A soft-nosed bullet, also known as a soft-point bullet, is intended to expand upon striking flesh, causing a wound diameter greater than the bullet diameter. Expanding bullets became known colloquially as dumdum bullets due the derivation from the Dumdum Arsenal near Calcutta, India, where they were invented in the 1890s.

ii   The forelock or foretop is a part of a horse's mane that grows from the animal's poll (the part of the head immediately behind or right between the ears) and falls forward between the ears and onto the forehead.

collected all the intact abandoned enemy equipment and began clearing the debris along Route Nationale 7 with bulldozers.

Working the entire afternoon, Phil and his men put down over a hundred severely wounded horses. Each mercy killing got harder for them. Their only solace was to see the horrible suffering instantly end. They also had the consolation of finding over three dozen drafts and many mixed-breed horses that had not been wounded. Some were so wild with anxiety that they would rear and kick at the men.

But to his men's amazement, Phil would wave them away from the horses in distress. He then would squat down several yards away from a panicked, pawing, neighing horse and gently cluck. Within a few minutes, the horse would quiet down. Phil would then whisper to the horse and slowly walk on his knees toward it. He would gradually stand, holding a hand out. Each time Phil did this, the horse would calm down. At the right moment, he would reach out and stroke the horse, speaking softly to it as he slowly took cloth strips recovered from vehicles or the dead to blindfold each horse.

The men fashioned halters out of pieces of rope and led their expanding string[iii] forward. After capturing several, Phil and his men would rope them together like a pack train, and then he would send them back to the makeshift corral with a private. For the men who knew how to ride bareback, he would pick a horse with a bridle or fashion a rope harness, and the soldier would ride back to the rear with the blindfolded and calmed horse behind him.

"Take it slow and easy," Phil cautioned each man. "Be sure they get watered, and don't let 'em eat too much until they're calm."

Late in the afternoon, Ross walked up to Phil. "Look over there," he pointed.

They gazed at the edge of the forest about one hundred yards off the road. Through the wafting smoke, Phil saw at least three dozen draft horses nervously gathered in a bunch. They were snorting and pawing. Other than their evident anxiety, they seemed unhurt.

"Okay, Ross," Phil said. "We've both got some cowboy in us. How 'bout we round 'em up and string 'em back?"

"How 'bout I ride with you?" one of his men yelled out. "I grew up with horses."

Phil nodded and picked up a coil of rope from a partially burned truck. He cut it in thirds, handing one each to Ross and the volunteer. They walked over to one of the men holding five beautiful drafts. They each picked one to ride.

iii   A group of horses is called a team, a harass, or a string, but is not called a herd.

"Boys, help us up!"

Three of his men volunteered, each holding their hands in front of their groins, joined palms up, to serve as stirrups to hoist each man onto the back of the drafts. The volunteer's draft began to buck like crazy. The soldier, obviously an experienced horseman, leaned back and reined his horse until he calmed down.

"Good job!" Phil yelled. As the sun was setting, he turned to his men. "We'll meet you at the corral."

As they rode closer to the jittery string, they pulled their horses to a slow walk. Phil knew that horses instinctively wanted to be together. This is why these horses, even with the horrible trauma they had experienced, had readily gathered. Their natural desire for contact with each other was a characteristic that Phil and his men could harness.

As the men drew near, Phil began his soft clucking. The horses were alert; their ears pointed anxiously forward. He knew he would rather walk them back than panic them. Phil dismounted and handed his horse's reins to Calvert. "Wait here," he said.

Phil squatted down, pulling a clump of fresh green grass. He stood and walked away from his friends and toward the string. He quickly was able to identify the alpha mare[iv] that had assumed leadership of the makeshift team. He slowly walked toward the anxious horse, getting to within ten yards before the horse panicked and ran. As the horses sprinted away from him, Phil held his hand up, signaling to the men to wait.

Fortunately, the string stopped after about fifty yards. Phil slowly followed the horses. This time, when he got close, he simply squatted down, gently singing a whispered song as he picked fresh grass.

The alpha mare watched him, initially with alarm, but then the steed seemed to calm to Phil's whispered sounds. Phil continued to cluck, click, and sing, holding up the fresh clump of fragrant field grass. She began walking toward him, stopping every few steps to snort and paw. A couple of times, the horse turned and retreated a few steps. As dusk descended, Phil didn't move. The horse became calmer, more trusting. Slowly, she began working her way to Phil.

When the horse was only a few feet from him, Phil began speaking softly to the mare and held up the grass. The horse snorted and cautiously took a step forward, leaning as far ahead as she could. Then she nibbled on the grass and backed up. Phil reached for his canteen, poured some water into a palm, and held it out as he slowly caressed the horse's nose.

The mare nickered, initially looking at Phil almost disbelievingly. Then her dark eyes and body softened in a sign of trust. The large horse stepped

---

iv   At the top of the hierarchy of horses is an alpha mare. She is the leader, not a stallion, who comes and goes. All the other horses look to her to know what to do and how to feel.

forward and drank from his palm as Phil poured more water from the canteen. He then put the canteen back on his belt as he talked soothingly and stroked the horse.

"We've both been through a lot, big girl. How about we take you to a nice home?"

The horse nodded, as if in understanding. Phil took a loop of rope from his belt and gently passed it over the horse's head. Stroking the mare, he softly said, "Come on. Let me and my buddies take you to safety. How about it?"

Phil led his new friend back to the horse Ross was holding for him. Letting Ross hold the captured horse, Phil took a few steps of a running start, grabbed the mane, and leaped up, kicking his right leg over the mare and pulling himself up.

"I'll lead this big girl up front. You two drive the rest behind," Phil said.

Ross and the other man nodded and rode their horses around and behind the string as Phil and his mount moved from a walk to a controlled trot as the horses fell in behind them. Phil looked back and smiled to see his friends laughing and whooping, swinging their ropes in obvious delight.

For a few moments, they were all transported a very long distance from the horror of war. When they were in sight of the commandeered corral, Phil's mare began to pull up, like she was aware of what was coming. He nudged his heels into his horse, and she resumed a nice, controlled trot.

The entire string followed them into the corral. Phil let the mare have her head and reined his horse around and back where he could join his friends in hooting and hollering as they trotted into the corral. As the horses and the men rode in, his men closed the gate behind them.

Phil and Ross jumped off their mounts and embraced each other, laughing. They knew they had "done good." They felt deep in their hearts a joy and bliss they hadn't experienced in some time. They knew that even amid horrifying wickedness, something noble and good and honorable—even gallant and virtuous—had come from that day's slaughter.

For the first time in months, Phil felt hope—and thankfulness—all brought to his heart by a few dozen magnificent horses. He looked up and muttered a quick prayer, "Thank you, Lord," as he remembered a stableman once saying, "There is nothing better for the inside of a man than the outside of a horse."[140]

What happened that day was more than "something good" for the inside of Phil and his men—instead, it was a blessing in the midst of battle.

He wished his girl back home, Marilyn, had been there to witness the rescue of the horses—but what fun he'd have telling her all about it in his next letter.

26
THE CHAMPAGNE CAMPAIGN

"Relatively few soldiers actually experience the unglam-
orous, unenviable, unique life of a combat Infantrymen.
I can't credit the saying that it took nine men in rear
areas to keep one man fighting. I'll swear it took 900."

—Warren P. Munsell, Jr., author of *The Story of a Regiment*[141]

With the Germans in full retreat, the 3rd Division, as part of the VI Corps, was given the objective to move northward as rapidly as possible and join up with General Patton's Third Army, which was advancing toward Germany in a dash across northern France.[142]

The Mediterranean stage of their operations drew to a close as the European phase opened significantly sooner than planned. As a result, from the last days of August to mid-September in 1944, the two opposing armies in southern France raced up the Rhône Valley like two Thoroughbreds, one on the tail of the other. For the Allies, the drive up the Rhône Valley against scattered opposition became known as the "Champagne Campaign."

On September 1, Phil and his platoon were attached to a platoon from Company L to attack the small village of Janneyrias, about 200 miles north of Marseille. But the race up the Rhône was straining the supply routes from the storage depots just north of Marseille. Every supply vehicle in the Corps was fully engaged day and night, hauling gasoline, ammunition, and rations from the distant dumps[i] to the troops. As a result, the rate of advance depended entirely upon the delivery of desperately needed supplies.

---

i   A military dump is where military supplies are stored.

Not knowing the issues behind them, the frontline GIs fought on. Once in Janneyrias, the men were pinned down by suppressing German fire from houses up and down the street. As soon as the soldiers made a move to advance, the bullets would rain down again. Since artillery wasn't set up to help them, Phil recalled an idea from his training. He called up two bazookas and broke his men into two house-fighting teams.

"Here's the plan," he told the men gathered around him. "We're going to go through the town, staying inside the houses."

Several of the men looked at him incredulously. "How we gonna do that, Lieutenant?" one asked.

"We'll use the bazookas[ii] to knock holes in the dividing walls as we go," Phil instructed. "Toss a grenade or two through the hole before the Krauts have a moment to respond. Then we'll clear that house and repeat it again and again."

"And if we come to a street?" another soldier asked.

"If we have to cross the street to the next block, then we'll throw out a couple of smoke grenades and cross under cover of that."

He pointed to four men. "I want you guys to split up. Two of you work your way down the rear of the houses as we move forward. If any Krauts try to escape, let 'em have it."

The GIs nodded.

"The most important thing in street fighting is to stay off the streets," Phil asserted. "We'll disperse, move fast, and continually move no matter what happens. Keep your head up, your eyes open, and your legs moving, and at all costs, stay apart."

"Yes, sir!" the men answered in unison.

"Smoke grenades on my command. Then put a bazooka hole in that house right over there!" Phil commanded. "Ready? Go!"

Phil was pleasantly surprised by how well this tactic worked. The men advanced from house to house on both sides of the street. In most of the French homes, the stunned German soldiers immediately yelled "Kamerad" and surrendered.

In one house, though, the GIs found a French family hiding behind their overturned kitchen table. The father pointed to the second floor and held up four fingers. The floorboard above them creaked. The Americans opened up with a BAR[iii] and a Tommy gun and heard several thuds. Looking up, the soldiers noticed spots of ceiling plaster turn pink and then red until drops of blood dripped onto the floor.

---

ii   The bazooka was a World War II weapon simple enough for use by rifle squads, yet powerful enough to shoot high-explosive rounds into bunkers and pillboxes. General Dwight Eisenhower ranked the humble bazooka—along with the atom bomb, the Jeep, and the C-47 transport aircraft—as one of the four "Tools of Victory" that allowed the Allies to prevail over Nazi Germany and Imperial Japan.

iii   A BAR, or Browning Automatic Rifle, was capable of semi-automatic or fully automatic operation at a rate of more than 600 rounds per minute. This light machine gun, weighing nearly twenty pounds, was heavy to carry around.

During the four-hour fight that afternoon, a total of 117 prisoners were taken. Toward the end of the battle, Colonel McGarr arrived and found the situation well in hand.

"Excellent work, Lieutenant." The colonel shook Phil's hand and patted his shoulder. "Yet again!" he quickly added.

℘

Allied intelligence suspected that the Germans' next major military move would be a defensive stand at Besançon, around 330 miles north of Marseille. Besançon was a key communication and road transportation center, as well as an important industrial city. Besançon's industrial section was situated in an oxbow loop of the Doubs River with a bottleneck opening solidly guarded by a massive fort called "La Citadelle."[iv] This fort was, in turn, supported by four minor forts. Manning the entire defensive system were an estimated 4,200 well-equipped German troops.[143]

On the morning of September 6, 1944, Colonel McGarr joined a point squad to which Phil and Ross were attached. Although this was considered highly unusual—and even extraordinary—for the typical regimental commander, McGarr's men were never surprised when he visited them on the front line as often as he did.

When they came under intense machine gun fire, Colonel McGarr quickly ran from man to man to direct fire and urge the men forward in an aggressive attack. As the firefight progressed, two 20-mm Flak guns[v] opened fire on the colonel. Yet he refused to take cover, electing to continue fighting beside his men as they painstakingly advanced toward the enemy. Because of light rain, Colonel McGarr was wearing a poncho, which may have prevented him from being recognized as their commander by the enemy.

"Colonel!" Phil yelled. When the colonel turned, Phil pointed to a frightful sight 200 yards down the road. The Germans were ripping camouflage netting off a pair of 88-mm guns.[vi]

"Get the men in safe positions!" McGarr ordered. "I'll call in some tanks."

Phil carried out his orders and pressed himself into a ditch as the German guns lowered their barrels and fired. The German 20s were firing at over one hundred rounds per minute while the 88s began their

---

iv   The Citadel of Besançon is a 17th-century fortress considered to be one of the finest masterpieces of military architecture, occupying twenty-seven acres on Mount Saint-Etienne, one of the seven hills that protect Besançon. Julius Caesar recognized the site's strategic importance back in 58 BC.

v   Flak is a contraction of the German word *Flugabwehrkanone*, meaning "aircraft-defense cannon," the original purpose of the weapon. In English, "flak" became a generic term for ground anti-aircraft fire. The Flak 30 was a 20-mm light anti-aircraft gun and Germany's primary anti-aircraft gun. When shot horizontally at troops, its fire rate of about 120 rounds per minute was deadly.

vi   The 8.8 cm Flak was a German 88-mm anti-aircraft and anti-tank artillery gun and one of the most recognized and feared German weapons of World War II. In Army slang they were known as *acht-acht* (German for eight-eight) by the Germans and the "eighty-eight" by the Allies. The versatile carriage allowed the 8.8 cm flak to be fired in a limited anti-tank or anti-personnel mode when still on its wheels.

murderous fifteen- to twenty-round-per-minute onslaught. The large shells were crashing into the trees and churning up the ground around them. The men's rifles and sidearms were useless against the attack.

As Phil and Ross were considering ordering a charge, they heard the clattering of Sherman tanks moving in behind them. Phil couldn't remember a time he felt so relieved. The Sherman's 76-mm cannons and machine guns began battering the Germans. In rapid order, the 88s, followed by the Flak guns, were blown out of commission. As the tanks moved up, Phil could see Colonel McGarr riding on the back of one, just behind the turret, leading the support tanks.

"Get your asses out of the mud!" he ordered. "Let's kick some Kraut butt!"

The men began to advance with Colonel McGarr and soon took the high ground overlooking Besançon. At 1830 hours on September 7, the white flag of surrender went up. The city fell to the 3rd Division, making Besançon the first large, fortified city in France to fall to the Allies.[vii]

❧

The next day, the 3rd Division continued to chase retreating Germans, encountering heavy resistance by an enemy desperate to escape. The Allied forces were hampered, though, because every time American GIs entered a town, the French locals would ring their church bells, which told the retreating Germans how far away their adversaries were. The French people didn't *want* to give away positions; they were just so happy to see American troops liberating their towns. The GIs were showered with milk, bread, apples, and bottles of wine from dusty cellars.[144]

That afternoon, Phil and the men of the 3rd Battalion were moving forward to cross the Ognon River in the vicinity of Boulot. The battalion met and overcame scattered resistance, knocking out machine gun emplacements to reach the river at 1600 hours. Phil and a scout team came to a bridge destroyed by Germans attempting to halt the push of the 30th Regiment.

They found an abandoned barge and discussed how they could cross the broad river and continue taking the fight to the enemy. The barge was stuck on a sandbar, however, which meant they weren't going anywhere. Suddenly, a pair of machine gun nests and a Tiger tank[viii] on a hill across the river unleashed a torrent of firepower. Phil and his men managed to take cover as hundreds of bullets passed overhead. Phil called in artillery, which quickly destroyed the tank and the two machine gun nests. With the enemy neutralized, Phil could

---

vii   It was no surprise to Phil and Ross that the colonel was later awarded the Distinguished Service Cross for his extraordinary heroism and "outstanding leadership, personal bravery, and zealous devotion to duty."
viii The Tiger was a German heavy tank officially called *Panzerkampfwagen Tiger*. The Tiger is one of the most revered tanks of the war, if not in the entirety of tank history, due to being able to destroy enemy tanks at long range while shrugging off hits from lesser Allied anti-tank guns.

devote his energy toward getting his men to the other side of the river.

He regarded the abandoned barge and sent a private to find a truck with a winch—any winch. When he returned, they attached the winch to the barge and started to free the vessel. As they were making progress, Phil saw flashes of light from the opposite side of the river as two rifle shots rang out. Snipers! Two of his men fell to the ground, dead, their heads blown apart.

In an instant, Phil swung his rifle to his shoulder and fell to one knee. He curled the rifle's sling around his arm from a kneeling position and quickly spotted his target across the river through the specially designed peep sight of his M1 Garand. He took a deep breath and slowly let it out.

The sniper saw him and began to swing his rifle barrel at Phil. Before the shooter could complete his aim, Phil quickly squeezed off two shots. The German's head exploded, and he collapsed. Two other Germans began to run, and Phil expertly cut them down with equally well-placed shots, blowing a hole in their backs and through the chests of each soldier. Satisfied no other Kraut soldiers were in the vicinity, he called out, "All clear!"

"Damn, Lieutenant, what great shots!" exclaimed one of his privates. "I'm glad you're on our side!"

The private slapped Phil on the back. "I'm gonna put you in for a medal for that, and then have Colonel Neddersen[ix] transfer you to the snipers."

Phil smiled. "Just doing my job, private. And I'd a whole lot rather stay here with you guys."

The next order of business was to get a ferry going, using the barge. Lumber was found in a nearby railyard, which allowed the soldiers to push their way across the river and then be winched back. Throughout the night, a nearly continuous operation by "hand power" one way and then the power of a truck's winch the other way took soldiers to the other side, forty at a time, without wetting their feet. By morning, an engineer's bridge had been erected to allow vehicles to cross the river.

In the early hours of that afternoon, Colonel McGarr, while visiting the battalion command post, heard about the improvised ferry. He was intrigued and left his outpost to spend the next several hours with Phil and his men, looking over the situation.

"Damn nice job!" he told Phil. The following day, Colonel McGarr nominated him for a Bronze Star for "valor" and "meritorious achievement."

In seven months of fighting, Phil had been awarded a hat trick of medals—a Purple Heart, a Silver Star, and now a Bronze Star.

And he wasn't even twenty years old.

---

ix   Lieutenant Colonel Richard H. Neddersen was the battalion commander.

As the drive advanced, the 30th Infantry continued moving to the north and northeast, fighting through and liberating village after village as the season turned to fall. The weather was beginning to get colder.[145]

Phil wrote this to his mother:

> *We are still moving along over here, but we are getting an early fall, and I need a pair of leather gloves bad. Will you send them to me? I don't need good ones, but heavy ones, please. France is a beautiful country. So much nicer than Italy. I don't ever want to go back to that country if I don't have to.*
>
> *I write Marilyn, but I don't hear from her very much! Can you call or write her for me? Still have been doing a lot of thinking about what I want to do after all this is over, and still can't make up my mind as to what to do. But I hope soon to have made it up enough.*
>
> *P.S. We've just learned that all of us who were in the D-Day convoy for the southern France landing have earned the Bronze Arrowhead.[x],[146]*

In October 1944, the Vosges Mountains—a range of extremely rugged mountains in eastern France near the German border—lay ahead. The U.S. Seventh Army[xi] was being asked to do what no army in the history of modern warfare had ever done before—conquer an enemy defending the Vosges Mountains.

The French Revolutionary armies gave it a try in the late 18th century, as did the Germans during the Franco-Prussian War from 1870–1871. The French and German troops resorted to trench fighting in the Vosges during the first and last days of World War I, and again in 1940. Now it was America's turn to give it a go against a dug-in foe that dramatically outnumbered them and was much more familiar with the terrain. In many ways, the Vosges Mountains was a make-or-break battlefield for the GIs. Phil and his men would have to prove their mettle here.

---

x   The Bronze Arrowhead denoted participation in an amphibious assault landing, combat parachute jump, helicopter assault landing, or combat glider landing by a service member of the United States Army. This was the last time this award was given to amphibious troops in Europe in World War II.

xi   The U.S. Seventh Army included VI Corps (with three American divisions: the 3rd, 36th, and 45th), five French divisions, and the 1st Airborne Task Force. The 3rd Infantry Division included three Infantry Regiments: the 7th, 15th, and 30th.

In less than two months, allies had raced nearly 400 miles, taken 89,000 German prisoners, and linked up with elements of Patton's Third Army to finally complete the continuous line that Supreme Allied Commander Dwight Eisenhower called his "broad-front strategy"[xii] that he believed was essential for the invasion of Germany.

Standing in the way were uncounted tens of thousands of German soldiers who'd retreated and dug into the Vosges, where they were ordered to halt the Allied advance into Germany at all costs.

Phil sensed that this would be his most important test yet.

---

xii   The "broad-front strategy" was based upon a September 1944 decision by General Eisenhower to build up Allied forces along the Rhine throughout the whole length of the Western Front, from the North Sea to Switzerland, before launching a final drive into the heart of Germany.

27

CRUEL COMBAT

"All battles and all wars are won in the end by the Infantryman. The Infantryman has to use initiative and intelligence in almost every step he moves, every action he takes on the battlefield. The Infantryman always bears the brunt. His casualties are heavier; he suffers greater extremes of discomfort and fatigue than the other arms."

—British Field Marshal Archibald Wavell [147]

As Phil and his men approached France's Vosges Mountains in the middle of September 1944, topo maps showed a granite massif rising steeply from the plains of Alsace, presenting a nearly impenetrable geographic blockade to entering the Rhine River Valley from the west.[148]

Autumn was definitely in the air as cold winds and heavy rains commenced in northeast France, much earlier than usual. Driving sheets of rainfall, as well as veils of fog, reduced visibility to ground level. At the same time, thick clouds drastically curtailed life-saving Allied air support, as well as preventing observation of German activities.

Phil knew full well that the rain and mud would give way to snow and ice once winter arrived, along with continuing overcast skies. This meant the on-the-ground advantage would go to the German Army, which could hide their military actions from Allied air reconnaissance missions and not be subjected to bombing and strafing attacks.

Making winter fighting even worse for Phil and his men was that the valley bottoms within the Vosges drained poorly and contained long, narrow lakes and swampland. The craggy terrain dramatically constricted the road network. Even the main routes were quite curvy and commonly had sharp turns and steep gradients, only to bottleneck in narrow village streets. Secondary and local roads were far worse—extremely narrow, often muddy, full of potholes, and bordered by deep ditches or steep embankments. Phil agreed with the intelligence estimate that virtually every road was unsuited for military traffic. On top of that, the heavily mined thoroughfares were infested with German roadblocks every few hundred yards.

As a result, the enemy occupied a definite, decisive line of resistance and could dig in, hold on tenaciously, and aggressively counterattack when overrun. The German infantrymen could also call upon forest and mountain combat tactics by infiltrating American lines and killing unsuspecting frontline troops from behind. They could also easily ambush supply lines and artillery units.

Furthermore, German snipers had a field day picking off troops and officers, which often resulted in chaos on the battlefield. The life expectancy of the men on the front line fell to just twenty-one days.

The heady days of the so-called "Champagne Campaign" were over.

୧୬

On September 16, the 3rd Battalion, commanded by Lieutenant Colonel Richard H. Neddersen, was assigned the objective of liberating the small village of Raddon-et-Chapendu.[149]

Phil and a platoon of his men—attached to Company L or "Love Company" under Captain Robert B. Pridgen—received orders to help out with clearing the thickly wooded ridge overlooking the village. Narrow passages and soft ground ruled out any use of armor. In the midmorning, the men reached the ridge and began combat preparations along a low rock wall overlooking the village, all the while expecting extensive enemy action.

Shortly after noon, the Germans below spotted their movements. They sent heavy tank and 20-mm fire over the ridge, followed by raking the American company with another Panzer IV tank, a Flakwagen, a self-propelled (SP) StuG gun,[i] and a 150-mm artillery piece, along with heavy fire from machine guns. This concentration was immediately followed by several assaults of fifty to sixty German soldiers, attacking with automatic weapons

---

i   Sturmgeschütz (abbreviated into StuG), meaning "assault gun," were a series of self-propelled (SP) armored vehicles used by the German Wehrmacht.

and grenades. These small onslaughts were followed by an assault from 200 frenzied, screaming Germans, armed with machine guns, machine pistols, rifles, and grenades.

Phil and 1st Lieutenant Glenn Shuler, a Company L platoon leader, assisted Captain Pridgen and his men in fighting off the enemy for several hours, including a second vicious counterattack. They poured deadly concentrations of machine gun, rifle, and sidearm fire at ranges of ten to fifteen yards, wounding and killing many enemy soldiers while taking on increasing barrages of machine gun and machine pistol fire.

And still, Phil and the courageous men stood their ground.

Unbelievably, a third counterattack followed, lasting a half hour. This time German infantrymen, backed up by tanks, Flak guns, an anti-tank gun, and a 150-mm gun, threw everything they had into the attack. Fortunately for Phil and his men, American artillery finally moved up into position and destroyed much of the German armor while causing the remaining tanks to withdraw. Without the tanks, enemy infantrymen fled the area in personnel carriers, the latter taking on heavy fire from the Americans, who inflicted many casualties.

Despite the setback, the Germans regrouped again, this time for a *fourth* attack on Company L led by a German Panzer IV tank followed by an enemy force of forty soldiers laying down blistering suppressing fire. Once again, the tank was destroyed with well-placed artillery, and the enemy was dispersed by machine gun and rifle fire.

After the bitter action seemingly ended, Captain Pridgen called Lieutenant Colonel Neddersen via SCR-300 radio to inform him of the situation. American casualties were mounting, and ammunition was running low. Then Pridgen learned that the members of Phil's A&P Platoon behind the frontline wouldn't be able to get more ammunition up to him since they were out of ammo too.

Nonetheless, Neddersen's orders were "to push forward at all costs." Pridgen responded that he and his men, which included Phil and his platoon, didn't have enough ammo to push forward but would hold out despite the odds and whatever the cost. As it was growing dark, a fifth German attack approached but was again repelled by machine gun fire after the Germans got within twenty yards of Company L's position.

The Germans did not withdraw but remained undercover and continued spraying the Company L men with machine-pistol and small arms fire from close range along the entire company front. At 1730 hours, they began an unprecedented sixth assault. Several Germans made it to the Company's line of resistance, resulting in vicious and bloody hand-to-hand fighting since most American soldiers were out of ammunition. In face-to-face fights, the

Yanks killed Germans with their rifle butts, bayonets, knives, and hands. The remaining Germans finally retreated.

As their two remaining medics tended to wounds, Pridgen and Phil took a quick inventory and determined that all of the company's machine gun and rifle ammunition, as well as all grenades, were expended. All that was left was a handful of rounds of pistol and carbine ammunition. Less than half of their men had survived the flood of attacks, and the remaining men, many of whom were wounded, hunkered down behind rocks, tree trunks, or any cover they could find.

The situation was desperate for the company, which was down to the equivalent of four rifle squads. With their company's strength severely reduced and more counterattacks feared, Pridgen radioed their plight to Lieutenant Colonel Neddersen at 1800 hours.

While waiting for a response, Bob looked at Phil. "You've memorized all the rules of war, Phil. Got one for this type of situation?"

Phil smiled. "Absolutely. It's Rule of War No. 1."

"Which is?"

"It says that there are combat situations that cannot be solved by a rule."

Captain Pridgen laughed. "So, Lieutenant, do you have another option?"

Phil thought a second. "I'd suggest Rule of War No. 16, which says that fire without movement is indecisive, and exposed movement without fire is disastrous. In other words, there must be effective fire combined with skillful movement. In our case, 'fire' will have to be what remaining ammo we have and our ability to shriek like German fanatics. Give the bastards a taste of their own damn medicine."

The captain pursed his lips, looked over the rock wall, and nodded again.

"I'd say let's use what ammo we have for marching fire[ii] and rush the bastards with our bayonets up, screaming our heads off. Since it's getting dark, that'll be an advantage for us."

Pridgen smiled and slapped Phil on the back. "Let's do it. On my command."

They fanned out to prepare their men for the assault and breakthrough—not knowing if what they were planning to do was courageous or suicidal. They had to prepare the men for what was likely going to be a vicious hand-to-hand battle to the death—making sure their bayonets were properly snapped onto their rifles and their knives were ready. Those with remaining ammo would spearhead the attack.

---

ii   "Marching fire" was the technique of advancing on the enemy with all guns blazing—for soldiers to keep pressing forward while throwing a wall of lead before them. This kept the Germans' heads down. This technique, however, was never taught in their initial training, as the soldiers had been coached to fire at specific targets. Early in the European campaign, however, the Army adopted the marching-fire technique to increase Infantry firepower and aggressiveness.

But before Pridgen ordered the attack, the Germans preempted them at 1830 hours when they heard the ominous rumble of an enemy tank moving in. Simultaneously, the Germans began a heavy fusillade from machine guns, rifles, and bazookas that came from at least five different points along the company front. Just as the murderous barrage began to abate, Pridgen and Phil were ready to order their attack.

When the sun set precisely at 1900 hours, a miracle occurred: reinforcements from Company I rushed in. Each man was carrying bandoliers[iii] of ammo and grenades, all of which were quickly distributed.

Phil and his two remaining A&P men rushed back to the rear and began transporting in more ammunition, food, water, and supplies to their front line. After a brief respite, the two companies attacked forward and were pleasantly surprised to find no resistance. The Germans had skedaddled back into the town, presumably to set another line of resistance. When it turned dark, the Americans regrouped and waited until morning to move into the hamlet of Raddon. At daybreak, they encountered no resistance; the village was empty. The Germans had retreated during the night.

Only later, by interviewing prisoners, was it determined what the enemy had planned during that epic series of battles. By overrunning the position held by Company L, the 3rd Battalion would have been split in two, and the enemy would have possessed the wedge they desperately wanted to annihilate the 30th Regiment and prove a threat to the flanking 36th Regiment to their left. But Love Company prevented a disaster.

As a result, the Presidential Distinguished Unit Citation would be awarded to Company L for its gallant stand. One of the men who'd fought with them in Italy and France, Sergeant Harold O. Messerschmidt, was posthumously awarded the Medal of Honor, having given his life on the battlefield.

But there was no time for Phil or his exhausted men to rest on their laurels. Unfortunately, there was a lot of extremely cruel combat left to fight.

---

iii   A bandolier is a pocketed belt for holding either individual bullets or belts of ammunition. It's usually slung sash-style over the shoulder, with the ammunition pockets across the midriff and chest.

28

AN EXPLOSIVE WAR

"I don't think any man can exactly explain combat. It's beyond words. Take a combination of fear, anger, hunger, thirst, exhaustion, disgust, loneliness, homesickness, and wrap that all up in one reaction, and you might approach the feelings a fellow has. It makes you feel mighty small, helpless, and alone."[i]

—**Private Paul Curtis of Oak Ridge, Tennessee**[150]

By nightfall on September 23, 1944, the 30th had reached the Moselle River, but they found the waterway swollen by heavy rains. The approach was so rutted and mired, only vehicles that weighed less than a quarter of a ton could get close to the riverbanks. Squads were sent out to search for possible crossing points.[151]

Around midnight, a platoon from the 7th Infantry, just on the 30th's left, realized a stroke of luck when they discovered an intact bridge amid the surrounding devastation. No one made a move to cross the Moselle, however. Their immediate concern was that the Krauts had fixed explosives to the bridge and were poised to blow it up as soon as they saw the American soldiers crossing en masse.

---

i   Three days after writing this letter on May 28, 1944, during the Battle of Anzio, Private Paul Curtis was killed in action.

Phil happened to be in the vicinity. When he heard that an undamaged bridge had been discovered, he grabbed one of his guys and took off. Upon their arrival, they volunteered to inspect the bridge for dynamite charges, even though that put them at significant risk. After all, an explosion could happen at any time. Even in the darkness, it didn't take Phil and the private very long to find seventeen dynamite cases affixed to the bridge with wires leading to the other side.

"What do you say we cut ourselves a few wires, private?" Phil brandished a pair of wire clippers in his right hand. "Stay on the lookout. Cover me."

"Roger that," the private replied.

Just then, they heard a noise and noticed a shadowy form sneaking up toward the TNT charges. Phil shouted out the code phrase of the day—"Brooklyn"—but the person didn't have the correct answer—"Dodgers."

When the man heard the challenge, he yelled across the bridge in German. That was all it took for Phil to throw his M-1 to his shoulder and fire a single shot, dropping the man like a limp doll. Fortunately, the Germans on the other side must not have heard him call out due to the river's roar. Phil quickly finished the job of defusing the TNT while the private remained on the lookout.

The twenty or so American soldiers watching were astounded by how Phil coolly handled things—from disarming the dynamite to killing a soldier in a split-second encounter. They were grateful that he had saved their lives. If they had tried to cross the booby-trapped bridge, they would have been blown to smithereens.

When they could safely cross, they were amazed to see that the German who yelled out had been shot right between the eyes. Of the privates muttered, "I want to shake that man's hand. Hell of a shot! Saved his life and ours. He ought to get a medal."

For Phil, it was just another night's work.

❧

The next day, Phil received a stack of letters from home. He quickly flipped through them until he came to a lightly scented one with Marilyn's handwriting. In his mind's eye, he could see her smile, feel her hand, smell her perfume, and taste her sweet lips. Sure, there had been some tension in some of their recent letters, but he still couldn't wait to be with his girl again.[152] Then he ripped the letter open and immediately wished he hadn't:

Dear Phil,

> *There's no other way to say this but to tell you that*
> *I've fallen for another guy. He's a sweet boy. We met when*
> *he was here in Gulfport for a week to visit. He's returned*
> *several times. He visited my mother in Des Moines, and she*
> *likes him. And now he's asked me to marry him. I've agreed.*
>
> *We haven't set a date yet, but I want you to know*
> *that you were my first love, and I'll always remember our*
> *wonderful times together. I pray that the tradition of the*
> *Friendship Oak will not be broken and that we can remain*
> *friends. And I know that there's just the right gal for you,*
> *Phil. She'll be one lucky lady.*[153]
>
> *Marilyn*

Phil felt his shoulders slump. He was stunned and caught completely off guard. Even though numerous men in his unit had received the dreaded "Dear John" letters notifying them that there wouldn't be a girl waiting for them back home, Phil was sure Marilyn would be there for him. He had *never* loved anyone like her. At that moment, life sucked.

In his next letter to his mother, Phil vented his pent-up feelings:

> *I still can't believe the news about Marilyn. But I'm not*
> *the only guy in this war who's been stiffed.*[154]

He never imagined he would be one of them.

The letter from Marilyn had arrived just as Phil's regiment was given a brief respite from the war. On September 27, Phil wrote this to his parents:

> *Most of my men are sitting around, shooting the bull*
> *with each other. Mostly a lot of dirty jokes. They feel fairly*
> *good now. They have had a hot meal, and for the first time*
> *in six days, they are dry and warm. The last two weeks*
> *have been hell. I know now what the soldiers of the last war*
> *mean when they cuss the rains of France.*[155]

That evening, the officers were given a copy of a letter from General Truscott, which Phil read to his men:

> *In thirty-eight days, you have traversed 500 miles*
> *and have defeated a desperate enemy at every stand.*

*You have forced a crossing of two major rivers. You
have overcome every obstacle that a resourceful enemy
could devise. You have...managed to move yourselves,
your weapons, and your supplies over distances almost
logistically unbelievable.*

*You have, by your successes, not only contributed
immeasurably to the advance of the northern Allied Forces
by preventing the movement of reserves against them but
have eliminated the German Nineteenth Army as an effective fighting force. Your operations have been a most vital
factor in clearing the enemy from almost all of France.*

*Your country has reason to be proud of your accom-
plishments and grateful for the services that you have
rendered. This campaign will stand as a monument to you
Americans of the VI Corps—a tribute to your training,
initiative, ingenuity, aggressiveness, boldness, determination, and fighting spirit and to the leadership of the officers
and non-commissioned officers of all ranks.*

With respect and pride, your Commander salutes you.[156]

☙

Phil folded up the letter and looked over his platoon. "And I salute you too,"
he softly said as he stood to attention and saluted his men, who immediately
rose to attention and snapped salutes in return.

For the next three weeks, the 30th Infantry continued to push
northward against increasingly stiff resistance, hill by hill and mountain
by mountain. From mid-September until the end of October, though,
it rained at least twelve hours a day, which kept the Allied tactical air
forces on the ground and allowed the German Army to make massive
and unhindered rail and road movements of troops and equipment.
Phil had heard the old military adage that the weather is neutral, but he
and his men found out that poor weather favors the defender in almost
every category. Thus, it became more difficult for Phil and his A&P
platoon to get ammunition to the frontline troops through the muddy,
dripping-wet conditions.

On October 2, General Truscott made a surprise visit to the 30th Infantry
command post north of Bruyères to visit General O'Daniel and Colonel
McGarr. The Army brass called Phil into a meeting to discuss the idea of using

mules again. Based upon Phil's innovative experiences with mules during the Battle of Anzio, General Truscott wanted Phil's opinion. The 1st lieutenant enthusiastically recommended bringing in mules to the Vosges Mountains, as well as experienced mule skinners and a veterinarian or two to treat any injuries or illnesses.

Phil assured his commanders that he and his men could oversee a program using the mules to haul rations and munitions to infantry units by night. Although providing forage for the animals could be a problem, Phil reported that the mules showed no signs of anxiety or skittishness when exposed to German artillery in Italy. The mules were also almost miraculously adept at sensing mines and booby traps, even in the dark, while carrying supplies in the most challenging terrain. Phil said he did not doubt that mules would have been useful during the earlier part of the Vosges campaign.

General Truscott stood. Before Phil could salute, the general extended his hand and said, "I appreciate your recommendation, Lieutenant. General O'Daniel tells me you're a fighting man. A good man."

Then, nodding at O'Daniel, he added, "We're all equestrians at heart here. You, Iron Mike, and me. But I'm glad for your example using mules back on Anzio. Brilliant. And I believe it will make a difference here."

Phil saluted and left. Following their meeting, General Truscott requisitioned 300 mules from Italy and a veterinary detachment. Since they would not arrive until November, he approved Phil acquiring a barren of mules from local farmers.

On the morning of October 17, Truscott was called to the army command post at Épinal, the capital of the Vosges départment, to confer with General Eisenhower and General Patch about the operation. While meeting, Truscott learned he was being promoted to lead the Fifteenth Army. Truscott wanted to retain his command of the VI Corps, but Ike said he'd decided that the Fifteenth Army needed him more, and that Major General E. H. (Ted) Brooks was already on his way to take over command.

To his credit, and coming as no surprise to his men, Truscott stayed on another week to visit his commanders and welcome General Brooks before leaving the field on October 25 for a short leave stateside. The long trip would be his first home visit in more than two years.

Following the meeting, Phil wrote to his mother:

> I want some nose drops and some handkerchiefs. The weather is getting cold, and now it rains almost every day. I have a bad cold and cough, but I had one last year on Anzio and got over it, so I guess I'll get over this one when you send me some nose drops. I hope everyone is swell and feeling good. We're all very, very tired. Pray for us.[157]

Phil and his men had reason to be exhausted. They had been continuously engaged since landing on the French Riviera two months before. The dog-tired and drained troops were finding it increasingly difficult to keep up their day and night advances, but one thought drove them on:

The sooner we get to Berlin, the sooner this godforsaken war is over and we can go home.

29

THE VICIOUS VOSGES

"The Infantryman sure takes a beating in this war both
physically and mentally. Nobody knows what combat is
like until he has fought in the Infantry."

**—Staff Sergeant Bruce E. Egger, Company G, 328ᵗʰ
Infantry, and co-author of G Company's War:
Two Personal Accounts of the Campaigns in Europe,
1944–1945**[158]

O n October 24, 1944, at 1000 hours, the push for the mountain village
of St. Diè began with the 30ᵗʰ Infantry acting as the lead element
entering the Mortagne Forest.[i] Phil's 3ʳᵈ Battalion took the lead from the
center position.[159]

A cold drizzle and considerable ground fog slowed their advance.
Nevertheless, under battalion commander Lieutenant Colonel Richard H.
Neddersen, the men found a hole in the enemy lines. They quickly exploited
its discovery, pushing forward and moving east along the ridge of the St. Diè
hill mass, followed by the 1ˢᵗ and 2ⁿᵈ Battalions. By dark, the 3ʳᵈ Battalion

---

i   All the roads from the Moselle River led steadily upward into the thick Vosges' forests, where the
Germans had every conceivable defensive advantage. The steep, wooded hills were rarely traversable by
vehicles, even by the lighter American tanks and half-tracks, while the narrow mountain roads were
nearly impassible and easily defended. Furthermore, heavy vegetation made it difficult to direct accurate
artillery and mortar fire, and impenetrable cloud prevented direct air support. The forests also tended
to compartmentalize the battlefield, making it easy for advancing units to become widely separated and
vulnerable to infiltration and enemy flanking attacks.

had knifed an 8,000-meter salient[ii] into the enemy lines. The battalion dug in at 1840 hours, prepared to meet possible enemy counterattack, but the enemy was utterly unaware of their presence.

After a cold, fitful night, the 3rd Battalion pushed forward on the morning of October 25th to the northeastern edge of the woods and seized the high ground looking east over St. Diè. Phil and his A&P Platoon remained at a spiderweb junction of primitive roads just behind the front lines with their mules.

Supplies had been trucked in on a paved mountain road from the regimental command post, established in Bout du Milieu, only three miles to the rear. From there, the mules made resupplying the three battalions a daunting but accomplishable goal. The hills were steep and muddy, but the mules made the job much more manageable since it would have been nearly impossible to transport ammo without them. In the Vosges Mountains, Phil decided the mules deserved the designation "warhorses" every bit as much as his men.

On October 26, Task Force Greer, headed by Captain Harold E. Greer, assistant to Regimental S-3 Ross Calvert, moved the regimental right flank into a gap between the 7th and 30th Infantries. When nightfall arrived, Captain Greer sent the Regimental Raider Platoon of twenty men, which had been attached to his task force, to a small, wooded hill that dominated a road leading from the west to St. Diè. This was done to deny the enemy use of the road. The command of this high ground ensured excellent observation to the south and east of the valley below.

The enemy realized the impending threat by the 30th Infantry's penetration and was determined to cut off the GIs' bulge through their defensive line. As a result, the ferocity of the fighting and the terrain's difficulty would lead numerous 3rd Infantry Division veterans of the Italian Campaign to report that the action was worse than any they had seen during the Battle of Anzio or the drive to Rome.

Every battalion was quickly engaged in either attacks or repulsing counterattacks up the numerous valleys leading to the St. Diè hill mass ridge. Phil, his men, and the mules were frenetically hauling supplies and ammunition up the muddy, mountainous slopes and returning as rapidly as possible to load up once again. The men worked around the clock, only taking short naps while the mules were loaded or unloaded.

Just after midnight, Greer's raiders were attacked by dozens of fanatical enemies, who charged again and again from the west, south, and east of their south-facing ridge, probing for a weak point. One enemy soldier made it past a raider OP[iii] before being cut down by a rifleman.

---

ii   A salient, also known as a bulge, is a battlefield feature that projects into enemy territory and is therefore surrounded by the enemy on multiple sides, making the troops occupying the salient vulnerable.
iii   An OP is an outpost that is a small detachment of troops stationed at a distance from the main force or formation.

where the next attack was coming from until a land mine exploded or the Germans began raking the path of attack, often a matter of yards from the camp perimeter.

Because they were surrounded and cut off from their supporting task force, Lieutenant Morris had Phil command one half of the Raiders while he commanded the other. Due to the lousy weather, they knew there was no way they could call in air, artillery, or armored support. At one point, after a BAR automatic rifleman was killed near Phil, he raced over and grabbed his still-smoking rifle.

Although the attackers were firing directly at Phil, he began spraying the screaming and charging enemy from point-blank range. The enemy seemed to multiply in the firefight—as if two enemies sprung up for every one he shot down.

When he and Private Vales ran out of ammunition, they reached for hand grenades from their belts, pulled the pins, and let them fly. As the grenades exploded, a flood of fiery rounds and tracers blazed among the trees around them, shredding the bark, mud, and rock. Phil and Vales dove to the ground, but as Phil did so, he felt a sudden, searing pain in his right thigh, like someone had hit him with a giant baseball bat swung by powerful arms. The force knocked him backward.

As he was falling in the air—and for some reason, he could never explain whether it was instinctive or intuitive—he pulled out his .45 pistol.[iv] Hitting the ground almost knocked his breath out of him, but at that moment, a German soldier leaped over the camp perimeter, spraying his machine pistol wildly. Phil steadied his .45 and unleashed three quick shots that exploded into the German's chest, flinging him back onto the concertina wire. At least for the moment, the attackers retreated, likely to regroup and come at them again.

"Happy," he quietly called to his partner. "I've been hit."

Fear engulfed Phil since he knew they were surrounded and were at least a couple of hundred yards away from the task force and the nearest medic. In the dark, he couldn't even see his hand in front of his face, but he could feel his warm blood soaking his long underwear and pants. Quickly pulling off his belt, he cinched it tightly around his right leg as a tourniquet, stemming the blood flow. Vales crawled over to him and used his fingers to explore the wound.

"Seems to be a clean 'through and through,' Lieutenant," he declared. "Don't think it hit bone. May have got an artery, but there's no more bleeding."

As he had been trained, and as he had done for dozens of his wounded men over the previous seven months, Phil had Happy pull out his first aid kit[v]

---

iv   The Colt .45 was a single-action, semi-automatic, magazine-fed, recoil-operated pistol that served the standard-issue sidearm for the US Armed Forces and was widely used in World War II.
v   Individual first aid packets were worn by each frontline solider. Each packet contained a tub injectable morphine, eight sulfadiazine tablets, an envelope of crystalline sulfanilamide, first aid dress

The men quickly determined that they were being counterattacked l fresh, well-armed, aggressive rifle squads from the crack 201st Mountai. Battalion, based upon the soldiers' clean uniforms, markings, and the aston-ishing amount of ammunition and grenades they carried. The American GIs were now facing 600 of Germany's best infantrymen—all of whom were well-equipped Austrian mountaineers. The enemy's initial attack was beaten off only after an intense hour-long firefight, but the men knew their respite was only temporary.

After the skirmish, the men radioed the battalion CP for more ammu-nition and supplies. Phil and Private Happy D. Vales were the only A&P staff still at the spiderweb junction. Vales had been with the battalion since their first landing in Fedala, French Morocco, nearly two years earlier. At thir-ty-three years of age, he was one of the oldest of the enlisted "old men" in the unit.

They loaded up the two remaining mules with ammunition, rations, AP mines, and rolls of wire. Climbing the mountain slopes was a struggle. The muddy paths were difficult enough during the day, but even more so in the pitch-dark night and driving rain. After a couple of hours of torturous slip-ping, stumbling, and scaling, they reached the Greer Task Force perimeter.

Upon their arrival, Captain Greer greeted Phil and Private Vales. Then the captain ordered some of his men to help them unload ammunition and place the ammo boxes on a medic's stretcher for Phil and his partner to carry down a steep ridge path to the raiders.

Arriving at the raider OP, Phil was greeted by his friend 1st Lieutenant Morris E. Porter, who directed his men where to unload the supplies. After several fatiguing trips hauling ammunition, Phil and Vales put on thick leather gloves to string concertina wire around the OP and quickly laid many land mines down the slope. They were planning to head back down the mountain to get more supplies when the 201st Mountain Battalion instigated a predawn surprise attack with almost one hundred elite combatants. The odds against the Americans were a staggering five-to-one—in both men and guns.

Phil and Vales quickly joined the ferocious battle. The superior enemy numbers drove a wedge between the raiders and the rest of Task Force Greer, thus isolating the raiders. Although the enemy was supported by at least five machine guns and countless machine pistols laying down intense fire, they were repeatedly beaten back. Phil was thankful he had decided to lay down the wire and mines, which effectively helped the raiders repel one unsuccessful drive after another, along with hand grenades and gunfire.

The Germans attacked again and again. Failing one spot, they would simply shift to another. Because of the dense darkness and endless sheets of heavy rain, accompanied by an eerily thick fog, the GIs never knew

from his belt, rip open a sulfa powder pack, sprinkle one-half of the powder on each wound, and then stuff a gauze pack into each hole. Happy then wrapped Phil's thigh with a roll of gauze and had Phil swallow two sulfa tablets.

Phil loosened his belt tourniquet. To his relief, the gauze stemmed the profuse bleeding. He knew leaving the tourniquet on for too long could damage the nerves and tissues of the right leg, so he was relieved he could slacken it. But he left the released belt in place in case any further hemorrhaging began.

When dawn broke, Happy made his way among the dead Germans to gather their guns, grenades, and ammo. When finished, he distributed the arms and the remaining ammunition from the small dump Phil had set up in the middle of their little OP. The goal was to be sure each man was as equipped as possible.

After a lull, the battle restarted and dramatically intensified. All morning the raiders, armed with BARs, small arms, and several German rifles and pistols, continued to hold off wave after wave of ever-more-frenzied attackers. At one point, Phil and Morris ordered their men to fix bayonets on their rifles. They were hoping they wouldn't have to use them, but bayonets, knives, pistols, and hand-to-hand combat would be their only defense if they were overrun.

The remainder of the task force was still unable to reach the raiders due to the 201st Mountain Battalion's aggressive attacks against them. The cloud cover still hung over the mountain ridge, which turned out to be a blessing since it prevented the Germans from using tree bursts, which would have likely ended the men's lives quickly and mercilessly.

By early afternoon, their ammunition nearly exhausted, Phil and Morris had the men disperse the remaining ammunition so that each man at least had a few rounds. Happy told Phil he had counted at least fifty enemy soldiers lying around the hill occupied by the raiders. Most were dead, but some were still moaning and crying.

Although several of the raiders had been wounded, only two were dead. Morris' radio, crackling as its battery began failing, informed the lieutenants that Company F was preparing to attack and relieve pressure.

"It can't come soon enough!" Morris said into the mouthpiece, just before a bullet exploded into his handheld radio, knocking it to the ground. Morris, Phil, and their courageous men began fighting off what they were sure would be the final attack. As man after man ran out of ammunition, the small squad prepared to be overrun. Phil found himself uttering a quick prayer.

Just then, the forest exploded with an astonishing eruption of suppressing fire and hand grenades. The men automatically positioned themselves for what was undoubtedly the end. Vales silently crossed himself and then drew and

and a field tourniquet.

held his knife in one hand and his bayonet in another.

"Thought you were Methodist, Vales," Phil commented, smiling at his partner.

"Just adding a little insurance to my prayers, Lieutenant," the private chuckled.

"If this is it for us, Happy," Phil added, "I'm honored to have fought alongside you."

"It's been that way since you joined us at Anzio, hasn't it, Lieutenant? Ain't a lot of us old men left."

Phil shook his head.

Vales growled. "If I had any ammo, I'd kill one German for you, one for me, and one each for our mothers, Lieutenant."

"I've got six bullets in my .45, Private," Phil said. "I'll see your four and raise you two."

The two men chuckled.

"How about we split my six bullets?"

Vales smiled and expertly rotated his knife and bayonet, one in each hand. "You're a better shot, Lieutenant, and I'm better with these. I'm kinda looking forward to the first line of Germans charging and leaping over our wire perimeter. It'll be the last thing they do before tasting my steel and meeting their maker."

"Or mine." Phil touched his wounded leg, but he wasn't feeling any pain.

He was as ready for death as he'd ever been, but he was not crossing the Styx—the boundary separating the living from the dead—without taking as many Krauts with him as possible.

30
POINT-BLANK RANGE

"The pride of the Infantryman comes not from knowing that he's doing a job that others can't, but that he's doing a job that others simply won't."

—Unknown[160]

Within seconds, a trio of German soldiers, each screaming at the top of his lungs, came from nowhere, leaping over the perimeter wire. As Phil raised and shot his pistol at point-blank range, hitting two of the men, each man's chest spewed eruptions of blood and tissue as they were blown backward. Phil shot the third German between the eyes. His face exploded, and he crumpled to the ground at Phil's feet.[161]

Two more shrieking Germans rushed up the hill. Phil aimed, but his .45's trigger only clicked as he pulled it again and again. Throwing the empty pistol down, he reached for his last weapon—his knife. Time slowed as he thought to himself, *This is it! Kill or be killed!*

Then Phil suddenly heard and felt a flurry of bullets whizzing just above his head. The fusillade was coming from behind. He couldn't believe his eyes as both Germans were cut down, landing in a heap at his feet. The tracer bullets, every fifth bullet fired by a BAR or Tommy gun, were red. They were American!

Unless the Germans had replaced their white or green tracers, help had arrived—and an answer to their prayers! Phil felt his lungs fill with air and escape in a slow exhalation of gratitude. Then the forest and slopes below them erupted from a torrent of mortar fire, creating tree bursts that rained down on the Germans, literally cutting them to shreds. Phil had never seen such a beautiful sight. He had *never* been so thankful for the support.

Within moments, men from F Company and the task force were swarming into the OP. The first men hit the perimeter, laying down suppressive fire. The second wave of GIs rushed in and descended on the raiders, indicating the escape route up the hill to the task force OP.

Lieutenant Morris came to Phil's side. "I'm having you hauled outta here, Phil!"

"The hell you are!" Phil replied. "Pretty sure I can walk if Vales will give me a hand."

With assistance, Phil stood and tried to put his weight on his wounded right leg. The pain was excruciating, and he felt sure he was going to faint. He tried keeping the leg stiff, but the pain was overwhelming.

"You're a tough nut, you sonofabitch," Morris commented. "But no limping up the mountain allowed. I've got to get you and the rest of these guys out of here fast."

The lieutenant directed Happy and another man to put Phil on the stretcher they'd used to bring ammunition to the Raider's OP. "Get him to safety and a medic!" Morris commanded. The men took off with him as fast as they could up the slippery slope.

A medic met him at the Task Force OP. Phil felt instant relief for two reasons. First, he received an injection of morphine, which reduced his severe pain immediately. Second, he knew that once he was in the hands of the medics, his chances of survival soared.

The next thing he knew, one end of his stretcher was strapped to one of his A&P mules, and the other end was carried by Private Vales, who let the mule go first, reining it from behind like he was plowing a field. Phil drifted in and out of consciousness but woke when they reached the level ground at the spiderweb intersection. Four stretcher-bearers from the forward aid station were waiting to evacuate him. They loaded him into one of the four litter holders mounted on the Jeep, and then they shot off to the battalion aid station, a couple of miles to the rear.

Although his mental status was foggy, Phil, like most injured men from the front, was stunned by how rapidly he was moved. Barely an hour had gone by from the time he'd been shot. Once inside the aid station, Phil knew his chance of survival was excellent.[i] He and his men were convinced the army had a regulation against dying inside an aid station.

---

i   In World War I, approximately four out of every 100 wounded men could expect to survive; in World War II, the rate improved to 50 out of 100. A soldier who received treatment within an hour of being seriously wounded had a 90 percent chance of recovery.

Phil found the light inside the field hospital to be blinding. He was used to total darkness. Besides, the heat from the stove was overbearing, and he thought he was going to faint or vomit. The staff pulled off his heavy field jacket and seated him in a chair. One of the men gave him a drink of water, which felt terrific going down his parched throat. A technical sergeant removed his blood-soaked combat boot and cut the trousers from his right ankle to just below the groin.

For the first time, Phil saw his wound. The bullet had made an ugly, bloody, three-inch gash on the outside of his right thigh, and had left a slightly larger hole on the back of the thigh. The battalion surgeon checked his strength and sensation below the wound.

"You're one lucky man," the surgeon, Captain Hilard Kravitz, said. "Doesn't look like it hit any vital structures. If it'd hit an artery, you'd have lost a lot more blood than you did. I think it missed the bone too, or else you wouldn't be able to stand. Most importantly, it missed your family jewels—your children will be thankful for that. We'll move you to a stretcher, Lieutenant, and give you some plasma and another dose of sulfa tablets."

Phil nodded, wondering what was going to happen next.

Captain Kravitz looked around to be sure no one was looking. "Here, take a dose of my private medicine. It ought to hold you 'till then." He pulled out a pint bottle of bourbon and let Phil take a long, slow swig.

Phil smacked and licked his lips, shaking his head. "That tasted better than any medicine I've ever had. Thanks, Doc."

The surgeon smiled, took back his flask, and tucked it into his coat pocket. He patted Phil on the back.

As a technical sergeant sprinkled more sulfa powder into each wound and redressed them, Phil heard footsteps behind him. The man attending him sprung up to attention and saluted.

"At ease!"

Phil turned to see his 3rd Battalion Commander, Lieutenant Colonel Neddersen, and tried to stand.

Neddersen put his hand on Phil's shoulder. "Don't even think about it, Lieutenant."

The colonel knelt. "Hell of a job out there, you and Vales getting as much ammo to those guys as you did. They would've been wiped out without your work. Well done. But that's what I've come to expect of you."

"And so have I," said a gravelly voice behind him. Phil turned to see Colonel McGarr. "They tell us it's just a flesh wound. So you get to the hospital, get taken care of, and get back here. We need you back, Larimore, but not until you're 100 percent. You understand me?"

"Yes, sir. Just hold my position at the platoon if you would."

Colonel McGarr's eyes softened. "You know we can't do that, Lieutenant. But we've had it in our minds for some time to get you out of our command staff and into commanding a company. You're young, but you've got more experience and wisdom than most. So, you just do your job—get well. And we'll absolutely guarantee you a job with us when you get back. You hear?"

"Yes, sir."

As the colonels stood, Phil saluted, and they immediately returned his salute. They turned and quickly left.

God, I love those men, Phil thought. Their confidence in him lifted his spirits and was like a balm to his wounds.

31

RECOVERY WITH MURPH

"My time in the Army was important in my life. I wouldn't want to repeat it, but having survived it, I can say I'm glad it occurred. The army taught me discipline and respect for authority. It taught me a great deal about living and a few things about dying."

—Private Sydney Fierman, F Company, 410th Infantry Regiment[162]

As Phil moved through the military medical triage system, he felt he was on an assembly line. And he was. The remarkable recovery rate for wounded GIs in World War II was based on medicalized, mass-production, assembly-line practices that had been honed to operate like a fine-tuned machine.[163]

Arriving at the field hospital in Épinal, he was quickly X-rayed to be sure there was no fracture, shrapnel, or bullet fragments. He was clear on all counts. Then, before he knew it, he was spirited off to the operating room.

His surgeons later told him they had explored and irrigated the wound, declaring it a clean, through-and-through wound that had torn up a bunch of muscle but missed any critical structures. They laid Vaseline-impregnated rags on the wounds so they wouldn't heal up before ten days—any sooner would have increased the chance of infection and the dreaded gangrene, which could lead to amputation, or even death.

Through the night, between penicillin and morphine injections, Phil's sleep was interrupted by recurrent, fitful nightmares. The next morning, he had no appetite and could only hold down juices. He penned this to his mother:

> I don't know how to write this letter. But it has to be done. I was shot in the leg on the morning of 27 Oct 1944 at 0300. But please don't worry, for it was a nice clean wound, and now I'm in a warm, comfortable hospital, out of the rain and cold, and am being well taken care of. So, I beg of you, again, don't worry about me. I'm much better off now.

> It was in the right leg halfway between the knee and hip. It went in one side and came out the other. So, there are just two holes. I'm not going to write much. I just wanted this to get to you before the War Department telegram, if possible.[164]

His letter did not reach her until November 11.[165] However, on the evening of October 27, less than twenty-four hours after he was wounded, Phil's parents received this telegram:

Western Union Telegram

> REGRET TO INFORM YOU YOUR SON FIRST LIEUTENANT PHILIP B LARIMORE WAS SLIGHTLY WOUNDED IN ACTION 27 OCTOBER IN FRANCE. YOU WILL BE ADVISED AS REPORTS OF CONDITION ARE RECEIVED.[166]

Phil's mother breathed out a long sigh of relief and a prayer of thanks that he was alive, and the wound was "slight," whatever that meant. Other mothers told her of similar telegrams, even though their sons had been severely wounded. She could only wait for more news. As part of processing her emotions, she began sewing a Blue Star Flag,[i] completing it in a few hours. The small, rectangular flag was made of white linen with a red border and a dark blue five-pointed star in the middle. She hung it that day from her front porch. She was proud of her only child and began praying daily that she would not have to cover the blue star with a gold one[ii] if she were to lose him. The telegram was a reminder that she needed to be prepared for that possibility.

---

i   Blue Star Mothers were those with a child in active military service. The blue star flag was their unofficial symbol. The Blue Star Mothers' original goals were to bring their children home, ensure they received the benefits they deserved, help service members' families and each other, and to be there if something happened.

ii   Gold Star Mothers were those with a child killed in active service.

Phil was transported by a hospital train ninety miles south to the Army's 46th General Hospital in Besançon. The trip took six hours. Once there, he required very little morphine, and his appetite quickly increased. He was able to shower, and the meals in the officer's ward were both hot and delicious. The doctors examined his wound daily and felt he was doing well, with no signs of infection. Then on November 1, they took him to the operating room to further debride and suture up both wounds.

Phil wrote to his parents:

> Just another note to let you know that I am still doing fine. They have operated on my leg and sewed it up, so all I've got to do now is lay in bed and let it get well. But they won't let me get out of bed, and that's bad! Bedpans, how I hate them! And they make me use them.
>
> I'm inside, warm...eat three meals a day and use the damn bedpan. Oh yes, I'm in a general hospital. They tell me I may be sent to a hospital further in the area. I don't know for sure, but I don't think I'll be shipped out of France. Well, Mom, I'll close now but will try to write very soon again.[167]

On November 7, 1944, election day in America, he wrote:

> Dearest Mom and Pop,
>
> Well, today is the big day. I guess almost everyone at home is going to vote today. I wish I could place some bets on who is going to win. I know who most of the men over here want and expect to win (again). But that's just us guys here.
>
> They took the bandage off my leg, so I get to see what they had done to me. The stitches were put in the 1st day of November, and today they took them out. I have two cuts on my leg, each about three inches long. There were seven stitches in one and nine in the other.... I'm getting well and will be back to duty before very long.[168]

Phil was now able to walk, but with a decided limp.

On a radio broadcast the following morning, the men and nurses learned that President Roosevelt was reelected President of the United States for an unprecedented fourth term.

On November 12, Phil was placed, along with several carloads of wounded troops, on another hospital train. It took almost a full two days for the train to travel 350 miles to Aix-en-Provence in the south of France. The city of 40,000 had been liberated by the 3rd Infantry Division on August 21, just two months earlier. Phil was admitted to the Army's 3rd General Hospital. His first impression of the facility wasn't just its excellent medical care, but also the delicious French cuisine served to the men.[169]

Phil mistakenly thought his stay would only be a few days, but the doctors caring for him knew he would be of no use to himself or his unit unless he were back literally to 100 percent. Given the amount of injured muscle that needed to heal, he would need plenty of time—likely several weeks, maybe a couple of months—to heal, rehabilitate, and retrain his large leg muscles. Given the pain and stiffness he felt anytime he tried to stand or walk, it didn't take him too long to accept his prognosis.

Phil was admitted to a bed next to the nurses' station in the officer's surgical ward. Next to him was an officer who looked as young as Phil.

"Whatcha here for?" the young infantry officer asked, with a slow Texan drawl.

Phil explained his wound and asked the young man the same question.

"On twenty-six October, I took a German sniper bullet in the right hip. But I got the sonofabitch right here," he said, pointing to his forehead, right between his eyes. "Because of the weather, I didn't get out of the evacuation hospital for three days. It was a damn deep wound, and I came down with gangrene. Guess I'll be here a while, but I sure want to get back to my guys."

"What's your unit?"

"B Company, 1st Battalion, 15th Infantry. Ike was the Battalion Commander back in 1940, long before I joined 'em. How about you?"

"I command an A&P Platoon for the 3rd Battalion, 30th Infantry. My first action was Anzio in February '44."

"Guess we've been fighting together in the 3rd for almost nine months. And you don't look any older than me. You started as an officer?"

"Yep," Phil said, "and I was born in January of '25."

"Sonofabitch! I'm June of '25. We're about the same age."

"How'd you get in the Army? How long ya been over here?" Phil asked.

The young man laughed. "On my eighteenth birthday, I tried to enlist with the Marines and Paratroopers. Got turned down by both. Said I was too small. That pissed me off. So, I joined the Army. I went through Basic, started out as a private. Landed at Casablanca in February '43. Trained under Truscott in Algeria, preparing for Sicily. I worked my way up the ranks and made 2nd lieutenant just last month—a battlefield commission. Been in Army hospitals three times, twice for malaria, and another time, just sick as hell. This is my first for a wound."

"You've got a lot more experience than me," Phil said, smiling. "By the way, I didn't get your name."

"Murph's what my friends call me," the soldier said, "Audie Murphy."[iii]

Just then, Charge Nurse Lieutenant Carolyn Price looked over the counter of the nurses' station. "Penicillin rounds, gentlemen!" she hollered.

The soldiers nicknamed her "Pricie."

While giving Phil his penicillin shot—via a six-inch-long needle deep into his buttocks—Pricie looked at Murph and said, "Gentlemen, let me formally introduce you two boys to each other. Second Lieutenant Murphy, 1st Lieutenant Larimore has a Silver Star, a Bronze Star, and a Purple Heart."

While giving Murph his shot, she said, "First Lieutenant Larimore, 2nd Lieutenant Murph here has outdone you. Besides the Silver Star, Bronze Star, and Purple Heart, he also holds the DSC and a second Silver Star. You boys will each get another Purple Heart to add to your impressive collections while you're here. Around here they throw them on the beds like candy."

For the rest of their recovery, Phil, Audie, and the other men in the officers' ward continued to receive superb medical care. Phil passed the hours shooting the bull, playing cards, reading books and magazines, or reading and writing mail. During the night shift, he would wake up only to see Murph—who had insomnia—limping to the nurse's office to talk to Pricie.[iv] After a few minutes, she would chase him back to bed.

The admiration that Phil, Audie, and other wounded soldiers had for their nurses was enormous—and the feeling was mutual.

The next morning, Phil was reading the military newspaper, *Stars and Stripes*. He came across an open letter to the frontline men from Lieutenant Frances Slanger, one of the first nurses to come ashore at Normandy. Assigned to the 45th Field Hospital to aid casualties in the wake of the Allied invasion of France, Frances shared these observations in the *Stars and Stripes*:

---

iii   Audie Murphy, called by some the "most decorated U.S. combat soldier in World War II," earned twenty-eight awards and medals, including the Medal of Honor. He fought in nine major campaigns and was wounded three times. After the war, he returned to the U.S. to a hero's welcome and was featured on the cover of *Life* magazine. Hollywood called, and he went on to star in more than forty films and publish his wartime memoir, *To Hell and Back*. On the downside, he struggled with post-traumatic stress syndrome (PTSD), battled depression, slept with a gun under his pillow, and lost a ton of money gambling. He died in the crash of a private plane in 1971 at the age of forty-six.

iv   Lieutenant Carolyn Price was Audie's first big romance. He proposed marriage to her three times. For some reason, perhaps the fact that she was four years older than him, she turned down his marriage proposals. She married C. Andrew Ryan on February 23, 1946. After returning to the States, Carolyn ran into Major Leon Ginsberg, the doctor who had cared for Murph and Phil. He told her, "Well Pricie, I see our boy made the cover of *Life* magazine. I healed him and you held his hand and neither one of us got our names in *Life*!"

We had several articles in different magazines and papers sent in by grateful GIs praising the work of the nurses around the combat zones. Praising us—for what? We wade ankle-deep in mud—you have to lie in it. We have a stove and coal. We even have a laundry line in the tent.

Sure, we rough it, but in comparison to the way you men are taking it, we can't complain, nor do we feel that bouquets are due to us. The men behind the guns, the men driving our tanks, flying our planes, sailing our ships, building bridges—it is to you we doff our helmets. To every GI wearing the American uniform, for you, we have the greatest admiration and respect.

We have learned about our American soldier and the stuff he is made of. The wounded don't cry. Their buddies come first. The patience and determination they show, the courage and fortitude they have is sometimes awesome to behold. It is a privilege to receive you, and a great distinction to see you open your eyes and with that swell American grin, say, "Hi-ya, babe."[v],[170]

On November 20, Phil's medical classification was changed from Class III to Class II, meaning he was reassigned to a convalescent camp several miles from Aix-en-Provence. Once there, he started working on getting back into shape.

One thing Phil sensed was there was a lot of war left to fight, and he didn't want to let himself or his combat buddies down. He needed to get back to the front to do what he was trained to do—kill the German enemy, free Europe, win a war, and get home safe and sound.

---

v   Hours after writing this letter, Germans shelled the field hospital and Frances Slanger was killed by an artillery barrage, becoming the only American nurse to die in the European Theater of Operations during World War II. She was buried in a military cemetery in France, flanked on either side by the fighting men she served.

32

BACK TO THE FRONT

"I have been in combat for only about two months, but I am so weary of it all. Sometimes I feel awful discouraged when I think of what the future holds and the long bitter months ahead. I can make it with the help of the Lord, but not otherwise. I am glad so many people are praying for me because I sure need them."

—Staff Sergeant Bruce E. Egger[171]

Through Thanksgiving and the first half of December, Phil commanded platoons of Class II enlisted men—all former Class III patients—in exercises and drills meant to increase their mental and physical conditioning, as well as his own. Once they were determined to be Class I, they would be sent to a replacement depot for assignment to frontline units.[172]

Staying at the convalescent camp near Aix-en-Provence gave Phil more access to information about what was happening on the front line. He learned that after he left the 30th Infantry, the Third Army crossed the Meurthe River, and by the end of November, they were the first troops to reach the Rhine.

After more than two years of pushing the Krauts out of French Morocco, Tunisia, Sicily, up the Italian boot, out of Rome, and through southern France, the 30th Infantry finally and triumphantly crossed into territory regarded by Germany as part of the Reich—Alsace, an area in eastern France on the German border. The German Army's hopes of holding in the Vosges Mountains were now completely smashed.

General Truscott had this to say about the U.S. Army's superiority in the Vosges:

> With all of the support made possible by mechanization both in the air and on the ground, it was the Infantryman who bore the brunt.... It was the Infantryman who scaled the heights and stormed the German positions. The whole campaign depended upon the physical and mental condition, the state of training, and the morale of the individual soldier, and, particularly, of the individual Infantryman.[173]

Acutely aware of these facts, Phil wrote his parents on December 12th and shared this:

> Well, now I am out and on my way back to the outfit. With good (or bad, however you wish to look at it) luck, I should be back within 7 or 8 days.[174]

He boarded a train in Aix-en-Provence heading north. Most of the men sent to the replacement depots were returned to their original units, but some were shipped to new companies. Although the journey north to Besançon took the most of two days and two nights, the train trip from there to Épinal was much slower, taking another day to travel the final ninety miles—a total of three days and nights with no heat. After arriving at the replacement depot, the days lumbered by as Phil waited for his orders.

❧

At first light on December 24, 1944, the sky was cloudless, the air crisp, and the temperature well below freezing. Not long after daybreak, Phil and a number of replacement soldiers loaded themselves into trucks to make the slow fifty-mile journey over the Vosges Mountains to the 30th Infantry CP in Kaysersberg, France. As they boarded the troop carriers, they looked up in amazement to watch a formation of American bombers, shadowed by P-47 fighters to protect them, roaring overhead. The men cheered and waved.

At least two feet of snow covered the ground, but this time around, the trucks were comfortably warm. The mountainous route through tall, majestic pines and firs draped with snow took the men past abandoned German equipment, overturned and burned vehicles, and overrun roadblocks—all attesting to the rapidity of the 30th Infantry's advance from the crest of the Vosges down toward the Alsatian plains.

Phil and the soldiers arrived on Christmas Eve. He reported immediately to regimental headquarters and was welcomed back with a rowdy cheer and applause from the regimental command staff. His warmest hug was from his close friend Lieutenant Ross Calvert, now the regimental S-2, or intelligence officer. His previous boss, 3rd Lieutenant Colonel Richard Neddersen, now the Interim Regimental Commander, greeted him warmly as well.

"Don't worry," Neddersen assured Phil with a smile. "Colonel McGarr has been given a temporary promotion to the Acting Assistant Division Commander under General O'Daniel since twelve December. We're expecting him back here any day now, Lieutenant. He's asked me to put you back with our old battalion. Lieutenant Colonel Chris Chaney's commanding it now, so I'm pulling the battalion back into reserve in the next couple of days. Why don't you hang out here at the CP? Get your land legs back."

"Sure, that would be great. Thank you, sir," Phil replied.

Neddersen nodded and turned away. After a step or two, he turned back. "Good to have you back, Lieutenant. You've been missed."

Phil enjoyed dinner with Ross and getting caught up. On the center of the table was a small fir tree decorated with makeshift ornaments made from war debris—bullet casings and tinfoil chaff dropped by bombers to fool radar. Pulling out a small map and laying it across the mess table, Ross said, "I've got some good news and some not-so-good news, Phil."

"What's the not-so-good news?"

Ross spread a map open. "Here's our situation. To our north, units of the Seventh Army are pushing east to the Rhine. To the south, the First French Army, with our 36th Infantry Division attached, has also reached the Rhine. In between, right here"—Ross placed his index finger on the map—"is what the commanders are calling, quote, 'an embarrassing German bulge' west of the Rhine and centered around the Alsatian city of Colmar. It appears the Germans are determined to stay here as long as possible, and the area is becoming more strongly fortified every day. Looks like a full-scale coordinated attack will be required to eliminate them."

"What's the area called?" Phil asked.

"At first, it was called the 'Bridgehead around Colmar,' because the enemy, in their desire to retain a bridgehead west of the Rhine, decided to defend Colmar, a city ten miles west of the Rhine in Alsace. But as resistance in the area has grown and persisted, it's been given a new name: 'The Colmar Pocket.'"

"What's the good news?"

Ross lit a cigarette. After his first puff, he added, "That *was* the good news. The not-so-good news is that you won't be going back to your boys in the A&P Platoon."

Phil was disappointed because he badly wanted to return to the guys he'd fought with the previous nine months. With another lieutenant already in command, however, it wouldn't have been the proper thing to do.

"So, what's going to happen?"

"I hear you're being assigned as the interim XO for Company K, effective 26 December. Phil, McGarr wants you as a company commander. There's not a job open now, but you'll get the next one. So use this position to get ready."

Company commander, Phil thought. He liked the sound of that. Usually, that was a position reserved for captains, so maybe there'd be a promotion coming also. He knew he was ready to lead, despite the inherent dangers of becoming a frontline company commander.[i]

All of them were acutely aware that since American troops had landed in Sicily, the turnover of lieutenants had exceeded 100 percent. Casualties were so common that an infantry could expect to lose its entire allotment of 132 2nd lieutenants in less than three months of combat. It wasn't unusual for frontline units like Phil's to report that more than 80 percent of 1st and 2nd lieutenants were KIA, or killed in action.

Late on Christmas Eve, Phil was in the cellar of the house used as the company CP. Just before midnight, he and Ross stepped outside to share a smoke with several of the men. They mingled in a courtyard, where the glow from their cigarettes could not be seen by the enemy.

The men were quiet, each alone in his thoughts. A wave of homesickness swept over Phil, who looked out over the snowy landscape and suddenly became aware of a strange phenomenon—silence.

He looked at his wristwatch. It was 2345 hours, and there wasn't the sound of gunfire in the air. Could both sides be momentarily standing down?

In the distance, Phil heard American soldiers singing "Silent Night," which moved him greatly. Heavy snowflakes gently fell, covering everything in sight. Then, to his astonishment, German voices joined the Americans in singing the same Christmas carol in German—"Stille Nacht." He bowed his head in prayer, asking the Lord that next Christmas, he would be safe at home and with his parents.

To his surprise, he even muttered a prayer for Marilyn and wondered how she was doing.

♋

Phil and most of the men attended a church service on Christmas morning conducted by their chaplain in a village church. Except for some shattered windows, the church had suffered little damage from the shelling. Phil noted the contrast between the dirty, unshaven men and the pristine, beautiful

---

i   Of the roughly 300,000 frontline combat soldiers in the European Theater of Operations (ETO) at the time, turnover had been the greatest in the junior officer ranks—almost three quarters. The source of desperately needed junior officers came from veterans who'd won battlefield promotions—one of the highest honors a soldier can receive—most of them going to men in their early twenties, or even nineteen-year-olds like Phil.

church, with the sun pouring through the stained glass windows that had survived bombardment.[175]

After the Christmas service, the men enjoyed a special meal—roast turkey, creamed potatoes, and other trimmings that the division quartermaster had obtained for the holiday. A special surprise was the arrival of several Christmas packages delivered by the Quartermaster staff, which had made a special effort to distribute as many letters and packages as possible to the men. He wrote to his mother the following day:

> *I can't tell you and Dad how much I enjoyed opening each and every package. It was almost like being home. I could close my eyes and see the two of you standing together, arm in arm, watching while I opened one of mine. That wasn't too many years ago, was it? But you can bet your boots that we will have one gay one next year. And I'm going to make a gallon of eggnog, then drink the whole thing myself."*[176]

After lunch, a single German fighter plane flew over the CP at treetop level, likely on a photo-reconnaissance mission, because he didn't strafe the men. A .50-caliber anti-aircraft gun opened up, striking the Messerschmitt. Black smoke erupted from the engine. The pilot used his momentum to gain altitude, then he rolled the burning wreck, and bailed out. The men broke out in cheers.

That should have been the end of it—just another Luftwaffe pilot sitting in a POW cage. But the pilot, swinging from his parachute harness as he drifted down, pulled out his pistol and began firing at the men. The Americans didn't hesitate. In an instant, dozens of infuriated GIs unleashed their weapons. One of them said, "By the time he hit the ground, there was hardly enough of him to bury. He shot first; we shot last."

Later on Christmas Day, the 3rd Battalion was ordered off the line and brought back to Kaysersberg and placed in regimental reserve. That night, Phil joined K Company as the Company Executive Officer. The company commander and the men welcomed him with open arms. Phil considered himself fortunate to be with his new company for several days before going back into combat. He wanted to get to know the men as much as possible before returning to action.

Phil knew they needed to be prepared to fight again should a counter-attack occur, but for now, it was time for hot food, warm showers, clean uniforms, and much-needed sleep.

The war could wait for another day.

33
COLD MISERY

"From the sunny beaches of the Riviera to the frozen forests of the Vosges, the campaign gave the average American soldier a tour of the European heartland that he would not soon forget. One said, 'I wouldn't trade the experience for a million dollars, but I wouldn't give a nickel to do it all over again.'"

—Jeffrey J. Clarke and Robert Ross Smith, authors of
Riviera to the Rhine[177]

New Year's Eve provided Phil and his men another unique memory. Just like Christmas Eve, before midnight, all shooting stopped. Then, precisely at 0000 hours, the American artillery began a fireworks show by sending illuminated rockets into the air.[178]

The rockets' shimmering light allowed Phil to watch the frontline GIs get out of their foxholes, dance, and shoot their weapons into the air. Before the Memphis native could scream at the men to get down, the Germans began firing off their own set of illuminated rockets and flares, as well as shooting their weapons into the air. The entire valley lit up. The joy was contagious, lasting about five minutes, before slowing and then stopping. Then both sides quietly disappeared into their respective foxholes and shelters.

Phil felt his eyes mist. Christmas and New Year's Eve in 1944 were beautiful experiences for him. For a few peaceful moments, frontline men on both sides had shared happiness, humanity, and hope.

When an icy dawn arrived on January 1, 1945, shooting resumed in earnest. But a new hope dawned for Phil—a belief that his prayers would be answered that this was the last winter of the war he would experience, and soon he'd go home.

❧

The first week of January brought welcome arrivals and a memorable party. The arrivals included Colonel Lionel C. McGarr, who returned to command the men of the 30th Regiment, and the welcome additions of the 254th Infantry Regiment, the 290th Engineer Combat Battalion, and a French Parachute Battalion that were all attached to the 3rd Division to help hold the wide divisional front. The 3rd Division was now better prepared to hold their twenty-one-mile front on the north end of the Colmar Pocket, from the Vosges on the west to the Rhine River on the east.[179]

The party occurred on Thursday, January 4, 1945, the celebratory occasion being Phil's twentieth birthday. After hitting the Anzio Beachhead on February 20, 1944, and fighting for nearly eleven grueling months, the passage of time seemed like an eternity to him. He was no longer a teenager fighting a war.

Phil shared this description of his birthday party with his mom:

> *Don't seem like I am any older than before. But I don't think I could feel much older. At least I no longer have to use a cane to walk with. During lunch, one of the mess sergeants came out with a large cake decorated with twenty candles of various sizes. The men took up the "Happy Birthday" song with robust voices. It was all I could do to keep back the tears of gratitude. The cake was crude but delicious. They called me the "Old Man," but the real Old Man gave me a carton of Lucky Strikes.*[i,180]

The *real* Old Man happened to be Colonel McGarr, who led a toast in Phil's honor. Two days later, in a brief ceremony at the division command post, Major General O'Daniel, with Colonel McGarr at his side, pinned the Bronze Star with Valor and the Oak Leaf Cluster—indicating it was his second Bronze Star award—on Phil's chest for his heroic actions at the Ognon River crossing in September.

---

i   The most popular brand of cigarettes among the men was Lucky Strike, followed by Camel. In the foxholes, the men smoked Pall Malls, Raleighs, or Chelseas. Phil wrote his mother, "Yes, we're getting our cigarettes all right. In combat, we are given one package per day, per man in the company. Some men don't smoke so it means the officers get all they want most of the time. When we are out of the line in the rear areas, we buy them at 5¢ per package and we can buy all we want. I wish I could send you some!"

After they saluted each other, McGarr smiled. "You're a hell of a fighting machine, Lieutenant! I'm glad you're on our side!"

∽

It was northern Europe's coldest winter in forty years, making eastern France an absolutely miserable place. Dusk began around 1600 hours, and by 1645 hours, it was completely dark. First light didn't come for another sixteen hours. Each day the wind blew like a gale, driving pellets of snow and ice into the men's faces.[181]

Temperatures were bitterly cold, with a high during the day barely reaching ten degrees Fahrenheit. Night temperatures plunged to minus ten degrees at times. Several feet of snow covered the ground.

The battle to reduce the Colmar Pocket was stalemated because of the frigid temperatures, leaving the regiment dangerously and thinly extended over their broad front. Their mission was to hold an MLR extending 2,000 meters along a line north, east, and south of the mountain village of Kaysersberg.

Daily, the company stayed active with deep patrolling. Phil's old A&P men worked with Companies K and L to help improve their defensive positions by clearing fields of fire, laying mines, and installing tactical and protective wire.

Phil taught his men a lifesaving winter TTP,[ii] an easy way to dig a winter foxhole in frozen soil. He instructed them to shoot eight rounds from their M1 into the same spot, then quickly dig out the loose dirt and ice with their trench knives, place a half stick of TNT in the hole, light the fuse, run like hell for thirty meters, hit the dirt until the explosion, get up and run back before the loosened earth and ice dust settled, and begin digging in the softer soil with their trench shovels. Within minutes, the men would have a habitable foxhole without expending too much effort, and even more importantly, not breaking a sweat that would then freeze.

Occupying a frontline foxhole proved to be fatal to some and miserable for all, however. Two men were assigned to each foxhole, each spending two hours on watch while the other slept during the night, which wasn't restful at all in the sub-zero temperatures. Soldiers tucked newspapers inside their uniforms to insulate their bodies and covered themselves with leaves and boughs for added warmth. Most wore two pairs of woolen long johns, two pairs of woolen socks, their relatively thin uniform, and their regular field jacket, which still left them cold.

---

ii   A TTP, or Tactics, Techniques, and Procedures, incorporated the men's evolving knowledge and experiences.

How cold was it?[iii] So cold that if a man didn't do his business in a hurry, he risked a frostbitten penis. It was so cold that the oil in the engines froze and weapons locked up. Men urinated on their rifles to get them working again.

At least half the patients in field hospitals were suffering severe cases of trench foot,[iv] where the men's feet turned purple and swelled to almost twice their normal size. The most severe cases became gangrenous, which often led to amputation.[v]

Phil's philosophy was that trench foot was preventable. He believed that if he and his men took care of their feet, they wouldn't succumb to the serious affliction. He demanded his men change two pairs of wool socks and the felt pads that lined their shoepacs daily.[vi] Every night, he'd have them take off their combat boots, rub their feet, dry them as much as possible, and put on dry socks. He instructed them to put the wet socks under their jackets and promised them that the socks would be dry the next night.

Phil had another technique he taught them—one he had learned at Anzio that involved shaving cream. Frontline men like him had discovered the many virtues of shaving cream, which could be used to treat sun and windburn, as a makeshift hair shampoo, and even as a balm for fleabites and cracked fingers. Best of all, massaging feet with shaving cream once a day, along with his other tips, helped prevent the dreaded malady of trench foot.

Not one of his men came down with it.

☙

For Phil and his company, the endless days and interminable glacial nights featured the normal firefights that came with vigorous patrolling, as well as some of the most bitter give-and-take small engagements the division ever had

---

iii   Historians have concluded that the GIs went through worse physical misery during the Battle of the Colmar Pocket than the brave souls at Valley Forge, or in the ice-filled trenches of World War I. Historian Stephen Ambrose marveled: "All but forgotten today, the battle that raged through January was for the GIs among the worst of the war. It was fought in conditions so terrible that they can only be marveled at, not really imagined. Only those who were there can know. More than once in interviewing veterans of the January fighting, when I ask them to describe the cold, men have involuntarily shivered."

iv   Trench foot is a type of foot damage from prolonged exposure to cold, damp, and unsanitary conditions. Unlike frostbite, it usually occurs at skin temperatures above freezing and can begin as rapidly as ten hours into exposure. Risk factors included overly tight boots and not moving. Initial symptoms include tingling or itching followed by numbness. The feet become red or bluish and then start to swell and smell of decay. The skin then breaks down and becomes infected.

v   Trench foot put more men out of action in the ETO than German artillery, mortars, or machine gun fire combined. During the winter of 1944–45, over 45,000 men had to be pulled off the front lines because of trench foot—the equivalent of three full Infantry divisions.

vi   One of the first cold-and-wet-weather footwear solutions for the World War II soldier was the shoepac (or shoe pac), which was developed in the early 1940s and widely distributed in 1944–45. Although it had many deficiencies, the shoepac was still the best available specialized boot for winter conditions.

encountered. The wear and tear on Phil and the frontline men was palpable. There were times when they were upright and walking, but they were practically sound asleep. Exhaustion took a dreadful toll as many reached their physical and mental limits. The unimaginable conditions were so terrible that Phil could only marvel at the resilience of his men.[182]

There were two men to a hole, taking turns watching out for the enemy or catching some z's. Looking out into the pitch darkness, the men would hear a variety of frightening, nerve-racking sounds. Alternating two hours on watch with two hours of sleep did not allow much rest. After a strenuous day of work and patrolling, the men had to resist falling asleep on guard duty because falling asleep on guard duty was one of the most serious offenses in the Army.

One night, while freezing in their foxhole, two of his men were startled by the noise of one of their booby traps exploding. For the rest of the night, they held their weapons at the ready, expecting an attack. In the morning, however, to their relief, they discovered it had been a false alarm. Two rabbits had triggered the trap, and their dead bodies lay sprawled on the ground, frozen fragments of flesh and fur—which resulted in a warm, wonderful stew for the squad later that day.

During January, the 30th instituted what they called "Local Rest Camps." Each platoon received a "drying tent" equipped with a stove and facilities for washing feet, shaving, and cooking. Every twenty-four hours, soldiers were rotated to the drying tent for at least two hours to get warm and clean up, which cut down considerably the chance of developing frostbite and trench foot. The drying tents raised morale, as did finding wandering chickens at small cottages and farmhouses that had been evacuated. The chickens weren't killed, however, because they lay eggs, which the men loved to scramble and eat.

Each morning patrols were sent out with two objectives: Keep the Germans at bay and recover as many eggs as possible. In one abandoned farmhouse, troops found hams and sausages hanging from a beam. There was nothing better than a warm plate of ham and eggs, a welcome change from the usual canned rations.

On another day, a much perturbed and highly irritated French woman ran screaming into a company CP, complaining to the commanding officer that six of her prize chickens had been stolen. The officer reimbursed her for her trouble and wrote a report about the missing chickens. "Two were KIA, two were MIA, and the other two were last seen were being 'coaxed' down the road at bayonet point, as POWs," he inscribed for the record.

Another night, the Germans set up a loudspeaker near the frontlines and treated the GIs to a round of jive music and a plea to come over to their side and surrender. The German voice informed the men that "the Communist, Jew-loving Roosevelt had involved them in a hopeless war." The GIs were hardly impressed and called for a heavy artillery barrage in the direction of the loudspeaker. The pinpoint-placed fire from a Yankee artillery unit silenced the music.

Morale was raised another notch with the far-overdue arrival of winter clothes—mountain boots, fur-lined caps, fur-lined jackets, heavy-lined pants—and mountain sleeping bags. The men were finally warm!

After the winter gear arrived and was distributed on January 16–17, Phil and his men boarded trucks and were moved into reserve, about twenty miles behind the lines in the area of Sainte-Croix-aux-Mines. The trucks made so much noise that the Germans started throwing in a few artillery rounds, making the GIs nervous since the trucks only moved about five miles an hour.

Two of Phil's men jumped off the truck at one intersection and ran into an abandoned farmhouse. A moment later, they raced back, carrying a ten-liter jug. With the assistance of the men inside, they boosted the pitcher onto the truck and scrambled on.

"Calvados!"[vii] exclaimed Staff Sergeant Charles Beardslee. Then he looked at Phil. "And don't ask, Lieutenant!"

Phil could only assume the men had found a stash while patrolling. Nevertheless, upon arriving at the camp, the men were rather tipsy and bellowing the division song, "Dogface Soldier."

Phil was called to the regimental CP to meet with Colonels McGarr and Neddersen. They wanted him to go back to his previous command since the A&P Platoon leader had been seriously wounded.

"I need you back there, Lieutenant," McGarr said. "More importantly, your men need you. We've had a lot of replacements, and I need you to get them ready for this upcoming campaign. It may be our toughest one yet."

Throughout the period of January 17–21, the 30th Regiment rested, rehabilitated, reequipped, and retrained for an all-out attack to eliminate the Colmar Pocket and prepare to invade Germany.

While there, the leaden skies released another foot of snow, but it didn't matter much as the GIs managed to get cleaned up, see a couple of movies, write letters home, and get their mail.

All armor and combat vehicles were painted white, while mattress covers, sheets, pillowcases, and everything available in the way of white cloth was set upon and redesigned into camouflage suits for the snow.

---

vii   Calvados is a powerful apple brandy, and ten liters could get a whole army drunk.

❧

On January 20, the 30ᵗʰ Regiment held its usual pre-battle awards ceremony, this time in a blinding snowstorm. Ceremonies usually marked the conclusion of one regimental campaign and almost always foretold the launching of another—and this ceremony followed that pattern. Phil received his second Purple Heart—called a Purple Heart with an Oak Leaf Cluster—for his leg wound in the Vosges. The medal was personally pinned on him by Colonel McGarr, assisted by Lieutenant Calvert. As was now his custom, after McGarr pinned Phil, he saluted and said, "Like General O'Daniel says, to a hell of a fighting man!"[183]

The ceremony was another proud moment for Phil, as very few twenty year olds had been awarded two Purple Hearts, two Bronze Stars, and a Silver Star. His mind, however, was set on the next battle looming ahead—the Colmar Pocket.

34

THE MAISON ROUGE BRIDGE

"…days of struggling, toiling, and praying, with very little food and sleep. It was…unremitting hell. In fact, the comparison is hardly fair to hell."

—An American soldier named Hugh, fighting in France[184]

The Colmar Pocket was in the heart of Alsace, where most of the citizens spoke French and German. The Allied soldiers found it increasingly difficult to tell whether they were still in France or already in Germany. Towns had German names, swastikas adorned buildings, and shopkeepers accepted German Reichsmarks.[i] Because of the German feel to the area, and the antagonism of the locals, for the first time in the war, the men began to feel more like conquerors than liberators.[185]

On top of this, German resistance was growing fiercer and more fanatical by the day. Phil and his men placed the blame directly on the back of the U.S. Secretary of the Treasury, Henry Morgenthau, Jr., a confidant of President Roosevelt.

The longtime treasury secretary had authored the "Morgenthau Plan," which would subdivide Germany into separate independent states once victory was attained, and intentionally wreck all its factories and industrial

---

i   The Reichsmark was the basic monetary unit of the Third Reich, replaced in 1948 by the Deutschmark.

capabilities. This would force a return to a pre-Industrial Revolution agrarian society. In effect, Morgenthau was proposing the wholesale destruction of the German economy and widespread deaths in a population that wouldn't be able to produce enough food to feed each other or themselves.

Even worse, President Roosevelt was reported to have approved the plan, which was leaked to the press, causing a public firestorm. German Propaganda Minister Joseph Goebbels seized the opportunity to fire up the German people and soldiers, saying that Morgenthau—a Jew—was set on turning Germany into a wasteland and starving many millions of Germans.

At 30th Regiment headquarters, Ross Calvert threw a cut-out newspaper article on the breakfast table.

"Got this in the mail from home," he said to Phil. The headline of the op-ed piece screamed, "Stop Helping Dr. Goebbels."

"Damn politicians," Ross grumbled. "You know, if the Krauts believe they're facing complete destruction when they lose this damn war, they're just going to fight like hell—even harder than they even are now."

Phil's friend took a sip of coffee and continued venting. "I've heard the War Department's pissed off. They're telling Morgenthau that the German reaction is like throwing thirty divisions at us."

Phil lit a cigarette and measured his words. "If you think the War Department's mad at Morgenthau, you ought to talk to my guys," he commented. "Hell, we're the ones facing these fanatical bastards. Ross, it's probably a good thing the Secretary doesn't come visit the men on the front."

He had this to say in a letter home:

> From the way things look now, it may be some time before we finish here. Not that we won't, because we will. People who make speeches like Morgenthau aren't doing anything but causing the Germans to fight more and harder. Why can't people at home learn to keep their damn mouths shut? Well, I guess I'd better close for now before I blow a fuse. Write soon.[186]

The fact that this letter wasn't censored spoke volumes.

&

There was still a lot of war to fight since the Allies were still in France. The elimination of the Colmar Pocket was assigned to the French First Army in September 1944, but once the French proved incapable of the mission, U.S. divisions were sent in.[187]

The kickoff for the Battle of the Colmar Pocket began on January 22, 1945, the one-year anniversary of the landing at Anzio. The massive armed conflict took place in daytime temperatures that never exceeded 14 degrees Fahrenheit, and it was carried out under thick clouds that limited artillery shelling and precluded any support from air strikes.

The landscape was uniformly flat, covered with thick, frozen snow, and offered virtually no protection to the infantrymen. Innumerable streams, brooks, and canals flowed across projected routes of advance. The considerable bridging equipment needed to span these waterways remained critically scarce and was carefully rationed.

The enemy had also assembled its elite 2nd Mountain Division, which had been transferred from Norway, and joined them to an estimated twenty-five German battalions, each with about 500 men. By committing this elite division to the action, Hitler was demonstrating the crucial importance of holding the bridgehead west of the Rhine.

The elimination of the Colmar Pocket under these difficult wartime conditions would result in the third most costly campaign, in terms of casualties, in the history of the Dogface Soldiers of the 30th Infantry Regiment.

ः

Past midnight, Phil's 3rd Battalion, commanded now by Major Robert B. Pridgen, trudged slowly through the deep snow, cutting southeast through a thick forest known as the *Forêt Communale de Colmar*, or Community Forest of Colmar. Each rifleman, in addition to his semiautomatic M1, carried four bandoleers of ammunition, three fragmentation grenades, one white phosphorous grenade, a day's worth of C-rations,[ii] one blanket, one shelter-half, toilet articles, packs of cigarettes, and other miscellaneous personal items, including letters and pictures from home.[188]

The clouds briefly parted at one point, revealing moonlight almost bright as day, which made the snow and ice sparkle. Phil was walking single file with his men, each one careful to step in the tracks of the point man. That way, he thought grimly, they'd only lose one man if one of the soldiers stepped on a mine.

Phil heard a loud pop and instinctively ducked. In half a second, he knew what had happened. The lead soldier had stepped on a mine. The sound was the cap going off—meaning, thank God, the main charge didn't explode. The detonation of the small cap stung the man's foot, but he wasn't hurt.

Skirting the minefield, the men continued through the forest, crossing three waist-deep streams and advancing steadily as their frozen pants stuck to their legs. Heavy snow began to fall, and the temperature dropped to fifteen

---

ii The C-ration was an individual combat food ration consisting of tins of meat stew, biscuits, coffee, tea, and a sweet. A shelter-half is a simple kind of partial tent designed to provide temporary shelter and concealment.

degrees below zero. At least the Colmar forest cut the wind, which made the advance more tolerable.

Sergeant Beardslee ran back to Phil and Ross. "Sirs, you're not going to believe what we found," he said.

They walked forward to find a surreal scene that magically appeared in a forest clearing with thick swirling fog—almost like a fantastic dream or mirage.

"Looky there, Daddy-O!" Ross exclaimed.

In disbelief, they saw three Jeeps parked by the side of the road with Red Cross girls passing out hot coffee and doughnuts. The American GIs could not believe their good fortune. The cute young women had so many pastries that the men put extras in their packs for later.

The soldiers moved on without encountering any enemy resistance. At daylight, they broke out of the woods near the Ill River. They were astonished to find that they were not more than fifty feet from their goal—the Maison Rouge Bridge.[iii]

At this point, the river was steeply banked and over sixty feet wide. Their orders were to secure the bridgehead so that two division battalions could pass through and attack southward toward Colmar. The solid masonry bridge, which had been studied in aerial photographs, could easily hold tanks and armor and was the only available crossing.

Since intelligence indicated the Maison Rouge Bridge was solid and didn't need any additional support, no bridging material was available to the Dogfaces. Therefore, upon their arrival, Phil and Ross were dumbfounded to see the stone bridge smashed to bits.

"The damn Krauts musta blown it up!" Major Pridgen said as he walked up beside them.

"No, sir," said Phil. "Looks like it's been bombed. Probably our Air Corps. And look over there!" He pointed to what appeared to be a newly constructed timber replacement bridge close to the demolished Maison Rouge Bridge.

Pridgen studied the new development. "Phil, Ross, disperse your men around the farm complex. I'll radio for the engineers to come inspect the bridge."

Once the bridgehead was secure, the men walked across the replacement bridge. The timbers looked large and stable, but Pridgen wasn't sure. "Will this bridge hold tanks and armor?" the major asked.

Army engineers arrived quickly and debated whether the replacement bridge was strong enough to allow tanks, artillery, and armor to cross the river. The consensus was that the bridge could not withstand the weight, so no heavy machines could cross until the bridge was reinforced.

---

iii   The Maison Rouge Bridge was named after a prominent red barn and farmhouse found on the other side—"maison" being the French word for "house" and "rouge" for "red."

❧

At 0755 hours, General O'Daniel radioed McGarr, impressing on him the need for speed and the necessity of immediately pushing several miles south. Against McGarr's better judgment, he ordered two of his three battalions to get moving. They quickly crossed the bridge and fanned out, heading south and east, encountering light resistance as they plunged across the flat-as-glass snow and ice-covered fields.[189]

Unbeknownst to the 30th, they were now moving into a massive ambush—a murderous buzzsaw made up of a division of enemy soldiers, a brigade of tanks, and scores of other armored vehicles, all hidden and waiting for the right time to be unleashed. Without their own tanks, artillery, and air support, the men of the 30th could hardly have been in a worse tactical position.

Phil and his A&P Platoon were attached to Lieutenant Darwyn E. Walker's I Company and Lieutenant Ross Calvert's K Company. Most of the men entered the village of Holtzwihr from the north and began clearing houses on each side of the streets, while others remained in support. At 1630 hours, Walker, Calvert, and Phil felt a surge of confidence and began setting up their CP on the second floor of a building that overlooked the main square while their men continued to clear the village. Calvert sent a patrol to the town's main street, which would be a perfect approach for attacking armor. He had them position a bazooka team inside a walled-in yard several houses down from the new CP.

The hope was that the bazooka team would be able to get in a good shot at any armor coming down the street, turning a lead tank or half-track into flames so that nothing else could come down the road. The men were arranging a defense plan when they spotted German Tiger tanks coming in their direction.

From their vantage point, Phil and Ross observed the lead tank pulling up beside to their bazooka team, which was perched behind a wall. The bazooka man fired two rounds at close range, but the shots bounced off the tank—like BBs off a steel barrel. The tanks began to retreat, but an enemy machine gun in a church bell tower opened fire, keeping Calvert's platoon and a section of heavy machine guns temporarily immobilized.

Phil and Ross watched as one of their heavy machine gunners set up in a slight curve of the street, which would allow him to cover the length of the road. He opened on the tank, and the tank's machine guns fired back. The GI was hit and started to crawl away. Then he changed his mind and crept back to his machine gun and resumed firing. This time the tank swung its main cannon and killed him in place. A second American machine gun nest came under fire from a German sniper in the church tower, killing the gunner and pinning down his platoon.

"Shit!" Calvert exclaimed. "Let's go, Phil."

They ran downstairs, found a soldier with a grenade launcher, and moved to a point in the street where the rifleman could get a good shot. The grenade hit the tank but did no damage. In response, the tank swung its main cannon and fired, just missing Phil and Ross. The tanks retreated and backed around the corner, putting them out of view. Phil, Calvert, and Walker knew this was only a taste of things to come.

Phil's primary concern was that there was no radio communication with Colonel McGarr back at the bridgehead. They had no idea when American tanks and other armor would arrive, or if they could call in artillery. Phil and Ross spent some time damning the designers of the SCR-300 radio, which had a reliable range of only three miles in the best of conditions. Since the men were at least three or four miles south of the Maison Rouge Bridge, Phil realized they were likely not in range due to the radio's "short sticks."[iv] He came up with an idea.

"Ross, I'll take one of our SCR-300s a mile or so north of town. I'll be your relay communication point to coordinate artillery and anything else you need."

Calvert and Walker agreed to Phil's plan, so Phil took off. As he and his men were leaving, they could hear the sounds of a massive German counterattack beginning on the south side of Holtzwihr.

About halfway between the village and the Maison Rouge Bridge, Phil and his platoon set up a heavy machine gun nest and their radio unit. They were quickly able to establish communication with the bridgehead, but they could not raise Walker, Calvert, or any of their men.

"Larimore," a staticky voice said, "this is Rattler."

Phil recognized the voice of Colonel McGarr, who was using his code name.

"I've got some real bad news, Lieutenant," the colonel said. "The engineers didn't have enough bridging material for the entire timber bridge, so the middle of the structure, which they thought was the strongest, was not reinforced. They thought for sure the bridge was safe, so they tested it with a Sherman. The damn tank broke through the bridge, and now it's sitting in the middle of the river. You'll be getting no armor or tank support for several hours, at least. I'm setting up artillery on the west bank of the Ill, but it's not available to you right now. As soon as it's ready, I'll let you know. In the meantime, I'll get artillery FOs on the line to coordinate with you."

"Got it, sir," Phil responded.

---

iv   The SCR-300 was equipped with one of two antennas: a thirty-three-inch "short stick" and a ten-foot "long stick." The shorter one had a more limited range.

"Oh, there's one more thing, Lieutenant." McGarr paused, as if he were measuring his words. "To make matters worse, the forces on each of your flanks have been held up by fierce enemy stands. You're on your own."

Phil physically shuddered and felt ill. "I'll let Walker and Calvert know when I can, sir," he coolly said. He knew that to advance further with no air or artillery support would be difficult. Actually, with no armor or tanks at their disposal, and no protection on either of their flanks, any forward movement would be suicide.

But McGarr's direct orders to the battalions were clear: Move forward as rapidly as possible, and at all costs. He also knew that the men of the 30th had never backed down from a fight and never retreated—not once.

Lieutenant Phil Larimore and his men had no intention of being the first to do so.

35

A DISASTROUS RECEPTION

"I hear a lot of crap about what a glorious thing it is to die for your country. It isn't glorious—it's stupid! You don't go into battle to die for your country. You go into battle to make the other bastard die for his country."

—General George S. Patton, Jr.,
speaking to troops in 1941[190]

P hil's thoughts were interrupted by hearing and feeling the tremors from massive detonations. He looked back at Holtzwihr. Several buildings exploded while others erupted in fire. GIs appeared at the back of the town, running for their lives toward him. He watched in horror as they were mowed down by German rifle and machine gun fire. His heart sank as he realized his own perilous position.[191]

There's no way Calvert would go down without a fight! He thought. Phil helplessly watched a brigade of German Panzers, which had not been stopped in the town, rumble out of the city. The tanks spread out in front of him and cut down the final remaining men, whether they were running for their lives or had their hands up in surrender.

As he said a quick prayer for Ross, he realized that if the bastards were killing men who were surrendering, then they were killing every GI in the town, confirming his suspicion that Ross was gone—of that he had no doubt.

His thoughts were interrupted, however, as vicious gunfire from one of the tanks erupted around their position. He could see not only the surge of onrushing tanks, but also armored vehicles and infantry pouring out of the town. Lacking armored support, having no available artillery, no chance of relief from the air, and no way to dig into the frozen earth, Phil and his men had no defense.

The Germans began blasting them with five tanks, with shells hitting all around them, tearing into the frozen soil, making huge black craters in the snow. Machine gun bullets cracked right over their heads. Phil had no choice but to order his men, made up of small groups from several units, to withdraw back to the Orchbach stream bridge, which was about 450 yards just east of the Maison Rouge Bridge. He thought he could at least try to have his men set up a defense line, using the bank and a few trees for cover. As he set the line, other terrified GIs sprinted back without weapons, packs, or any equipment—only a few even had rifles or helmets. He and a couple of other officers began to organize the panicked men.

Phil set up his men near the stream, while other officers positioned their infantrymen in defensive positions just to their east. Unfortunately, their frantic attempts to dig foxholes in the frozen earth made them easy targets for the oncoming Germans, the rings of brown dirt on the snow forming perfect bull's-eyes for the onrushing tanks.

Phil watched a nightmare unfold in front of him as some of the German tanks pivoted to steer over the shallow holes, mercilessly crushing the soldiers. Any troops making a run for it were raked and shredded to pieces by tank machine gun fire. One young lieutenant trying to surrender his platoon was mowed down, and all his men were slaughtered. Within moments, German infantry had taken any remaining men east of the Orchbach prisoner and were trotting them back to the woods.

"Rattler!" Phil yelled into the radio, reaching Colonel McGarr. "Our defensive positions on the east bank of the Orchbach are getting blasted. We have only a few weapons and little ammo left. Can you support our position? We need help *now*, or we're dead. Just shred the area in front of us with any artillery you have. You may kill some of us, but the damn Krauts will kill all of us."

"Rattler, here. Artillery is ready and available. Bridge repair ongoing, so no armor. First Battalion's pulling back also. Now that I know your positions, we'll blast the shit out of the squareheads and lay down smoke. When it's thick enough and you deem it safe, get the men back here."

As soon as Phil acknowledged the order, the artillery opened up. Seven American field artillery battalions and two French battalions swept the area from the Orchbach to the Riedwihr Woods, laying down the heaviest fire put out by division artillery since the Anzio Beachhead breakout. Between 1952 and 2050 hours, artillery fired 565 rounds on the enemy counterattack, while from 2050 to 2200 hours, it delivered another 244 rounds of harassing fire. Under this protection, Phil ordered his men to cross the neck-deep, icy Orchbach and retreat to the Ill River. The men plunged into the freezing current in a desperate attempt to make the other side. One of those soldiers was a machine gunner from Company L, Edward L. Drabczyk, who was lugging a heavy .30-caliber machine gun.

"I hit that damn stream with ice up to my chest," he remembered. "Then I slipped, and the thirty-pound gun fell in the water. I dove to pick it up, but I felt like I was going to faint. I got it on my shoulder but couldn't stand. I knew I was going to drown—I was a dead man—but I could *not* abandon the weapon. This was drilled into me at boot camp. Suddenly, I felt someone pull the gun off my shoulder and pull me and my gun out of the water. It was my commander, Phil Larimore. He said, 'Come on, Drab. Let's go!' So, we got to the opposite bank, and we made it."

The men, lashing out with a fury born of desperation, struggled their way back through the frozen snow to the Maison Rouge bridgehead. As they approached the Ill River, Phil was met by First Battalion Commander Lieutenant Colonel Mackenzie E. Porter. "Larimore," he commanded, "Get the wounded and soaked across the Ill. The engineers have set up a foot bridge. Then get back and meet me at the farm—you and those who can."

Phil, cold and soaking wet himself, thought about protesting, but after getting most of the men across the river, he and several of the men returned to meet the colonel at the stone farmhouse. Porter quickly organized Phil and the other junior officers in setting a line of defense to protect the bridge. As additional retreating stragglers appeared, they were directed across the river if they were either wounded or hypothermic. Those who were able stayed to fight. Although terribly chilled, the offensive spirit was still present. Most came from the remnants of at least six companies.

Phil was given the task of organizing a series of OPs in front of and beside the farm buildings. The A&P men who had come up with Porter and had lost their lieutenant operated under Phil's command and began setting up concertina wire and mines around the OPs, while Phil and the rest of the men stockpiled as much ammunition as they could from the rear.

Behind them, frustrated tank and tank destroyer crews on the west bank of the Ill River watched the debacle. Shortly after, as the sunlight began to fade, they spotted German assault guns moving up two by two, each section covering the advance of the other. Anti-tank and artillery fire kept the counterattacking force at bay for a while, but sometime after dark, the boundaries of the bridgehead appeared to be in German hands, though no one could tell for sure.

At 2000 hours, Regimental Executive Officer Lieutenant Colonel Richard H. Neddersen, the acting interim commander as Colonel McGarr had rushed to the front to meet and reorganize his men, ordered all available artillery to "pound the ground" a thousand yards east of the bridgehead. Every five minutes, he pulled it in 200 yards. This was to give the final escaping troops a chance to get back.

Under cover of darkness, as fresh uniforms and coats were brought up to the farm buildings, Phil would send the men, two at a time, to change, warm up, eat, and then return to the battlefield. Once dry and warm, with their weapons at their sides, one of the men told Phil: "Yes, sir, we can hold! No damn Kraut is going to kick the hell out of us and get by with it!"

Then, terrible news began to fall from the heavens—literally. Enemy artillery shot canisters filled with propaganda leaflets claiming that over one hundred members of Companies I and K of his 30th Infantry had been captured.

The leaflet read:

NOTHING BUT LIES!!!!
GERMAN MILITARY DEFENSE HAS BEEN LAMED!!!
THE GERMANS HAVE NO MORE TANKS!!!

Didn't they tell you so? Well, it was nothing but lies!!!
SOLDIERS OF THE 30TH INFANTRY!!!

What is the real truth? You know now your best formations
were flung hit-or-miss in the battle for Colmar.

REALLY SOMEBODY PLAYING DIRTY TRICKS ON YOU!!!!

You fought bravely but during the attack across the open plain,
the violent artillery fire caused you severe losses.
Lt. Darwin[i] Walker, Co I, 30th Infantry,
Lt. A.H. Stevens, Co K, 30th Infantry, and over
100 men are glad enough to have escaped
out of this senseless bloodshed.
They have not been shot nor have they been tortured
as your newspapers keep telling you.
After having a good dinner, they were transported to a POW camp,
which like the rest is supervised by the International Red Cross.
They are awaiting the end of the war in peace and comfort.
For them the war has already had a happy end and
peacetime has already arrived.

AND YOU????[192]

---

i   The German's misspelled Lt. Walker's first name, Darwyn.

Receiving those dispiriting leaflets may have been the lowest point in the regiment's history. After Phil read a leaflet, he wadded it up and threw it to the ground. With tears welling up, he bowed his head to pray for his dear friend Ross Calvert. If he had been captured, the Germans certainly would have mentioned him in the leaflet.

36
TAKING A LICKING

"The most difficult and responsible duty any young officer can be assigned in action is the command of a rifle company of an Infantry Battalion."

—Lieutenant General Benjamin Lear[193]

In the darkness after midnight, German armor freely roamed the fields around the Maison Rouge Bridge. General O'Daniel, 3rd Division Commander, informed Colonel McGarr of their plan to hold the bridgehead and a line along the Ill River. The engineers were working to get the bridge back in service after the tank fell through. Lieutenant Colonel Mackenzie E. Porter, Phil, and their men continued to hold the Maison Rouge farm complex.[194]

After getting off the radio, Colonel Porter said, "Neddersen's running the regiment."

"Was Colonel McGarr injured?" Phil asked. It was an almost unimaginable possibility to consider he might be out of action.

Porter chuckled. "They couldn't kill the SOB if they tried. Colonel McGarr left the CP and is working the front, up and down the Ill's west side. For hours, he's been assembling the men lost from their units, giving them talks of reassurance and making arrangements for their re-equipment and prompt return to the battle. Now they say he's touring the regiment's entire front, stopping at each foxhole, encouraging each man, and repositioning men as needed. The men returning to the CP say he's ignoring the fire from enemy tanks and machine guns that are blanketing our 2,000 to 3,000-meter sector—the one he's been walking the last five hours. There are rumors he's been hit by a bullet but is still going."

"McGarr's one tough bastard!" one of the men said.

"Damn right! And it's Colonel Bastard to you men!"

Phil turned toward the gravelly voice striding into the farmhouse. It was Colonel McGarr, smiling at his new nickname. The men sprung to attention and saluted.

"At ease. What you've heard are rumors. It's not a 3,000-meter front— it's 5,000 meters, just over three miles. It's tough trudging through the thick snow and ice, and almost impossible to see given the heavy snowfall. And about that bullet that hit me, it ricocheted off one of our vehicles. Just a damn flesh wound.

"But nothing I'm going through compares to what you Dogfaces have done and are doing. You're the tip of our spear right now. Know that stoves, hot coffee, blankets, beaucoup ammunition, guns, and mortar, along with fresh jackets, are all coming across the foot bridge to you. You're going to be backed up to the hilt, but know this: If we lose this bridge, we may not be able to push the damn Krauts out of France and back into Germany. I'm depending on you men. Don't let me down."

Before they could respond, the colonel spun around and left as rapidly as he had entered.

∽

At approximately 0430 hours on January 24, 1945, another furious German counterattack began. Porter and his executive officer, Captain William G. Stucky, manned the stone farmhouse as Phil commanded his men from a nearby stone barn. From their CP, the men of the 30th directed another furious American artillery barrage on the enemy infantry and tanks while having their men fire every available weapon to hold the bridgehead.

The Germans briefly backed off. Then at first light, the enemy began a new series of counterattacks with infantry, half-tracks, and a steady barrage of mortars and shells. By 0800 hours, German fire grew to a roar as the German Panther tanks and Jagdpanther TDs[i] began rolling out of the Riedwihr Forest, about a mile southeast of the farm complex, in a concentrated attack to push the GIs back into and beyond the river.

---

i　The Panther was a German medium tank designated as the Panzerkampfwagen V Panther. Some reports refer to it as the Mark V. The Jagdpanther (German for "hunting panther") was a German tank destroyer (TD) based on the chassis of the Panther tank.

At the height of the early morning push, several enemy tanks drove across the Orchbach stream to within one hundred yards of the farmhouse complex. Wave after wave of German armor and infantry were hurled against the GIs. Despite hopeless odds, the regiment held on tenaciously to the bridgehead.

Phil was intensely concerned that the German 2nd Mountain Division's superior forces and its supporting tanks would overrun the Maison Rouge, killing them or forcing them to surrender. The 30th had never been defeated, which spurred Phil to direct mortar and artillery fire that temporarily disorganized the German infantry, knocking out one enemy tank as four others began pulling back across the Orchbach.

Finally, after thirty-six hours of nonstop fighting, the men from the 30th holding the Maison Rouge bridgehead were relieved by men from the 15th. After orienting their replacements, Colonel Porter, along with Phil and their men, bolted across the Ill River on the new treadway bridge[ii] that engineers had just finished north of Maison Rouge. Behind the lines, they were quickly and joyously reunited at the regimental command post in an old stone farmhouse in the woods.

After Phil and two of his men wolfed down a hot C-ration feast, they fashioned a dessert out of the now-frozen doughnuts they'd received from the Red Cross girls. Necessity being the mother of invention, they worked their forks into their fried dough confections and heated the doughnuts slowly over a Coleman burner.[iii] Sergeant Charles Beardslee had a small jar of strawberry jam in his pack, so the three spread some sweet jam on their warm doughnuts. They felt like they were eating a dessert fit for kings.

While Phil savored each sweet bite, he listened to radio reports that said the new treadway bridge across the Ill River was allowing American armor to pour across. The result: a furious tank and artillery duel raged across the Colmar Plain throughout the day. He could see smoke staining the sky from the burnt-out carcasses of American Sherman and German Panther and Tiger tanks.

Every time the enemy tried to move in, the superior American artillery opened up and created more casualties to be recovered and evacuated by the German medics. In the process, more surviving members of the 30th Infantry were found, cold and exhausted, but alive. They made their way to the welcoming arms of their regiment, where they were met with blankets, hot coffee, cigarettes, and food delivered by regimental supply personnel. The shivering men were also supplied with fresh, warm clothes and more rifles and machine guns.

---

ii   A treadway bridge was a floating bridge, having two tracks as a roadway.

iii   The GI pocket stove at the time was a portable, pressurized-burner, liquid-fuel stove designed by the Coleman Company that was lightweight and no larger than a quart-sized thermos bottle. A Coleman stove could burn any kind of fuel and operate in weather from –60 degrees to 125 degrees Fahrenheit. Ernie Pyle ranked it "just behind the Jeep" in its usefulness.

Phil found the 30th Regiment survivors dazed. They were the fortunate ones, as the frontline rifle companies' strength had fallen from about 200 soldiers to just seventy. But they were also embarrassed and angry. They had no time to mourn the losses of their buddies, but they needed time to recover, recuperate, and regroup. They also wanted an opportunity to redeem the regiment's reputation.

Phil knew, as did most of the men, that the debacle was *not* their fault. The command decision from above—to attack with no support—had put them in an extremely perilous position. He assigned no blame, however, as he was acutely aware of the terrible costs that sometimes came with command decisions made in the heat of battle.

But the men and officers were also conscious that this was the first time the unit ever had to make a "strategic withdrawal." Phil and every man he talked to, whether an officer or enlisted man, never wanted that to happen again. A spirit of revenge, along with a desire to bowl the Krauts over for good, began to well up throughout the 30th Regiment. Phil wrote home:

> *It was a bloody battle, one of our worst, and I lost a lot of men and my best friend. For a day and a night, some of my men and me had to hold on by our fingernails...but we did. And now we move on.*[195]

On January 26, while the 30th Infantry Regiment was resting and recuperating, the 1st Battalion of the 15th Infantry was passing by, heading to the front. Phil asked one of the men if he knew a 2nd Lieutenant named Audie Murphy.[196]

"Coming up behind," the man said. "He's a 1st Lieutenant now and is commanding Baker Company."

When Phil saw his old hospital mate, he yelled out, "Murph!"

"Phil, how the hell are you?"

The two men embraced.

"You look no worse for the wear," Murph said. "Heard they kicked your asses yesterday. Glad you made it."

"A lot of guys didn't. We just softened 'em up for you guys."

"Win any more medals?"

"Not if I can help it!" Phil replied. The men shared a laugh. "Be careful, Murph. Break a leg."

The men hugged. Then Murph took off at a trot to catch up with his men.[iv]

On January 27, after the brief respite, a vengeful 30th Infantry was pronounced "ready to go" and sent back into action as if nothing had happened. Morale was high, and the men were determined to keep the Krauts reeling. More than ready to shove off on another attack, the regiment rejoined the division to begin the drive south toward Colmar.

They successfully reached their first objective, the Colmar Canal, on January 29, completing Phase I of reducing the Colmar Pocket in the north. Preparations had been made to blow across the Colmar Canal in force and to move far and fast. This time, there was no repetition of the grinding battle of attrition that had characterized their recent fighting.

The next phase of the battle for the warhorses of the 30th was ready to begin. Codenamed Operation Kraut Buster, the offensive was initiated at 2100 hours after twenty-four hours of over 16,000 artillery-fired rounds, while the 441st AA Battalion issued 22,300 rounds of .50-caliber shells into enemy positions across the canal and into nearby towns.

The terrific artillery barrage knocked the Germans punch-drunk. Before the Krauts could reorganize, at midnight, American assault troops from the 7th and 15th Regiments paddled over the water in rubber boats and established secure bridgeheads. Engineers shoved over footbridges. The two Infantry Regiments were on the south bank of the canal and had established a secure bridgehead.

The GIs had reclaimed the momentum.

&

In the following days, all three regiments drove south several miles, slashing across the countryside, battering down points of resistance and mopping up areas of thinly scattered resistance. They relentlessly drove forward as town after town was taken and liberated. The whole strategy now hinged on speed—to hit the enemy before he could get back on his feet. Phil had to tell his men, "Sleep is not among our options."[197]

On January 31, the 30th prepared to drive to the southeast toward the Rhine River for the final phase of cutting off Colmar from Germany's supply lines.

---

iv   Later that day, just north of Holtzwihr, Murphy's company was attacked by six tanks and waves of infantry. Murphy ordered his men to withdraw while he remained at their forward CP and directed artillery fire. He climbed on a burning TD and used its .50-caliber machine gun for an hour to hold his position. With Germans getting as close as ten yards, he killed over fifty while receiving a leg wound. He continued the fight until his ammunition was gone and then made his way back to his company. He refused medical attention and organized the company for an attack that forced the German Infantry and tanks to withdraw. For this action, he was awarded the Medal of Honor.

Jumping off at 0100 hours on February 1, the 1st and 3rd Battalions attacked under the advantage of "artificial moonlight"[v] through the heavily wooded Bois de Biesheim and Schaeferwald Forest. The men overcame heavy small arms fire, but both attack battalions took heavy casualties from tree bursts of 120-mm mortars firing from positions east of the Rhine River.

At 0200 hours on February 1, the L Company commander got hit during a fierce firefight as the company was subjected to heavy artillery, Flakwagen, mortar, machine gun, and rifle fire. Phil was sent up to take his place and assume command. He had been waiting the entire war to command a front-line company, but he had two major concerns as he went to meet his men.

He was aware that many GIs at the front believed that after any man was seriously wounded, he was never as good in combat again, which automatically meant his men were suspicious of him. Phil didn't think this would be true in his case, but he understood the sentiment. Furthermore, he was also cautious because Love Company was the most storied in the regiment and had been led by superior officers. Although he would be their youngest commander ever and knew he had big shoes to fill,[vi] he felt calmer and more prepared than ever before.

Upon Phil's arrival, he quickly saw that the company was frozen in place by the sub-freezing temperatures and withering enemy fire. Phil feared that acute combat fatigue had set in since many men were reliving their Maison Rouge horrors.

The new commander quickly reorganized the shaken company, moving from platoon to platoon. Working with his FO, Phil organized a blistering artillery barrage, followed by leading his men from tree to tree through the thick woods while under steady artillery, mortar, and heavy small arms fire. They cleared 3,000 yards of ground in record time, killing scores of the enemy with no American losses.

At one point, about forty German soldiers began a fanatical and what-appeared-to-be suicidal attack toward Company L, but small arms, artillery, and mortar fire stopped and dispersed them, allowing the company to capture even more German POWs. The expressions on the prisoners' faces ranged from anger and exhaustion to relief. In one stomach-turning episode, a German SS officer about to be taken prisoner grabbed a grenade, held it against his body, and shouted, "Heil Hitler!" before blowing himself apart.

---

v   Artificial moonlight referred to the placement of powerful searchlights 4,000 to 6,000 yards behind the front line, adjusted to reflect off the low clouds to give light equal to that of a half-moon which aided in detecting and defeating German patrols. Since the Germans faced the light source, it did not aid them as much as the GIs, who had their back to the light source. Furthermore, even in diffused light, a considerable shadow effect was produced on the far side of hedges, tanks, and houses. From the concealment of these shadows, Allied troops could more easily observe German troops and installations.

vi   In Italy, Company Love had been led by Captain Maurice L. "Footsie" Britt, who had been awarded the Medal of Honor, the Distinguished Service Cross, a Silver Star, Bronze Star, and a Purple Heart. Captain Britt wrote Phil's parents, "You can bet your life that he really has something on the ball to be placed in command of a company as young as he is."

Once the prisoners were dealt with, the men finally stopped for a brief rest. Using Phil's TNT technique, they were able to quickly dig safe foxholes to huddle up in and get some rest while enduring the penetrating cold.

A sentry woke Phil just before dawn. He found his company in a bone-chilling, thick-as-soup fog that billowed in a thick layer five to six feet or more above them. The soldiers' matches couldn't light stoves or cigarettes because the air was so damp. He couldn't see a thing in the fog, but it was crystal clear just above it.

Suddenly, they heard the clanking sound of a tank approaching. Sergeant Edward L. Drabczyk stuck his head up just above the fog blanket and quickly ducked down.

"There's a black X on the turret. It's a Kraut Panther."

The hair on the back of Phil's neck stood up. He stood to take a quick look and didn't know whether to fire or not, given the horrible visibility. Some of the men wanted to attack, but Phil shook his head. "Let's wait. There might be a group of Kraut infantry following behind the tank, looking for a fight. Spread the word to the men to stay down, be ready, and wait without a sound."

In a few moments, the tank ambled off. Phil was surprised by how the thick fog muffled the sound of it.

The men celebrated the German tank's departure after Phil called up a field kitchen to serve his new company a piping-hot breakfast. At 1600 hours, Phil's men were counterattacked by two enemy tanks and forty infantrymen, but his reinvigorated company quickly repulsed the attack. Once again, they killed Germans with no casualties of their own. When it was over, the men captured a battery of 150-mm artillery pieces intact.

As a result of his first battle as Company Commander, Phil was nominated by his men for his second Bronze Star "for meritorious achievement in actual combat." As a result of his aggressive leadership and bravery, his company was the first to reach the battalion objective and seize the bulk of the battalion's prisoners.

On February 4, Phil wrote his parents:

> I owe both of you quite a few letters, and this is no attempt to answer them all—but rather as a note just to let you know I'm still well. We are on the line now, so a good long answer will have to wait until we get relieved. I'm back in L Company, but this time I'm the company commander. Don't know how long it will last though. Maybe it will be for good. I don't know.[198]

Phil was put to the test the following day when Company L was caught in an intense artillery concentration while clearing the town of Biesheim.

Besides contending with fire from well-fortified bunkers, the GIs had to beat off constant counterattacks by enemy infantry. Some German soldiers were wearing stolen American uniforms, which made for a chaotic battlefield. Despite suffering heavy losses, the company took 500 German prisoners.

By 1115 hours on February 6, Phil heard over the radio that the final fortified city on the Colmar Plain, Neuf-Brisach, was clear of the enemy and the flanking of the city of Colmar was complete. The enemy was now unable to supply or reinforce its troops in Colmar or any other location in the Colmar Pocket—a German island amid an Allied sea.

After light enemy resistance, the city surrendered on February 8. When the fury of the battle subsided, some observers quickly labeled the 3rd Infantry Divisions' actions as "the best bit of maneuvering on the Western Front."[199]

છ

Phil was proud of having earned his second Bronze Star, this one also with valor, but he was still sick about the loss of his dear friend, Ross Calvert. Even though still officially listed as MIA, Phil would trade every medal he'd earned to have his friend back.

37

THE BIG DANCE

"War was an introduction to an adult life marked by outrunning death every day."

—Unknown[200]

During February and early March 1945, the regiment enjoyed some hard-earned R&R time. Even then, they continued training with an eye toward the coming invasion of Germany. Each soldier knew that every mile deeper into Germany had to be purchased with someone's blood.[201]

On February 11, 1945, Phil wrote this to his mother:

> *Again, this is just a note. But one of these days I'm going to sit down and write you a long letter. Being a CO puts one heck of a strain on a person, so I don't know if I want the job or not.*

> *I got a big stack of mail yesterday. All written in Sept. & Oct. had been sent to the hospital and just now caught up with me. Maybe I will be able to write tomorrow night. Hope so. With all my love.*

> *Phil*[202]

Besides rest and rehabilitation were the inevitable training and the addition of a steady stream of replacements to their dwindling ranks. Training periods highlighted street fighting, attacking fortified positions, training with tanks and infantry fighting together, and physical hardening. Other sessions emphasized basic weaponry, map reading, use of the compass, and squad- and platoon-level tactics to work new soldiers into their seasoned units.

Phil and the other company commanders also had to fight numerous rumors unsettling their men. Because the Germans were known for booby trapping, some of the "old men" advised the rookie infantrymen to never lay on a bed or flush a toilet upon entering a captured house. Why? Because explosives could go off.

They told them that the enemy would even wire their dead, knowing that GIs couldn't resist pocketing a Luger[i] or a few Reichsmarks. Souvenir collecting was also discouraged by the rumor that if a GI were caught with German plunder, he would either be poorly treated as a POW or summarily executed since the Germans would think he was responsible for the death of one of their comrades.

The battlefield hearsay created great unease through the ranks, especially as combat intensified and the number of casualties climbed in early 1945. Phil noticed that attendance at the Sunday worship services grew dramatically, and Catholic priests heard more confessions than ever. One of Phil's men, Sergeant Norman Mohar, told him, "I finally got to confession—I had to since we're entering Germany. My time might be running out."

"How does that make you feel?" Phil wondered.

"Like I'm clean and absolved. I've never felt better."

The Protestant chaplains were similarly busy, receiving new converts and baptizing them as fast as possible.

ೞ

At the end of the first week in March, a regimental ceremony was held in a beautiful meadow overlooking the charming city of Nancy, France, which showed no signs of the war, unscathed by even a few shells. The trees were budding, and the French villagers had started to spade their gardens. The men were gloriously happy to watch the coming of spring. To them, the thawing and muddy fields drying in the warming winds would soon be ready to support armor. A record number of almost 250 awards were presented by Major General John W. "Iron Mike" O'Daniel, as well-deserved accolades began to pour in for what the 30th Regiment had accomplished.[203]

"Iron Mike" had this to say to the officers and men at the start of the ceremony:

---

i   The Luger is well known from its use by Germany during World War II. For GIs, it was the most prized war souvenir and is still highly sought today.

> *In crossing the Fecht and Ill Rivers, the Colmar and Rhine-Rhône canals, and in your attacks toward Colmar and Neuf-Brisach, culminating in the routing of the Germans and the capture of the area, you have participated in the most outstanding operation in the career of your division. You drove on relentlessly day and night through the worst of weather. Your action not only enabled you to advance, but also made possible the advance of all other forces in the bridgehead and hastened the collapse and elimination of the German-held Colmar Pocket. As your commander, I congratulate you on your outstanding performance and am proud of the honor of being in command of such a superb group of fighting men.*[204]

During the last sixteen days of the Colmar battle, the 3rd Infantry Division liberated twenty-two towns. General Charles de Gaulle's[ii] Provisional French Government recognized what the American soldiers had accomplished by awarding the entire 3rd Division the French Order of the Croix de Guerre with palm.[iii] President Roosevelt awarded the Distinguished Unit Citation to the 3rd Division,[iv] saying, in part, "In one of the hardest fought and bloodiest campaigns of the war, the 3rd Infantry Division annihilated three enemy divisions, partially destroyed three others, and captured over 4,000 prisoners."[205]

The German Nineteenth Army recorded over 22,000 casualties and ceased to exist as an effective fighting force, as approximately 75 percent of its personnel were either killed or captured. The Wehrmacht's last gamble was at an end.

ᗧ·ᗤ

For his valor, Phil received his second Bronze Star with a "V" device[v] from General O'Daniel, with Colonel McGarr standing beside him, beaming

---

ii   Charles de Gaulle (1890–1970) was a French army officer who led the Free French Forces against Nazi Germany in World War II and then chaired the Provisional Government of the French Republic from 1944–1946. In 1958, he came out of retirement and was elected President of France.

iii   The Croix de Guerre was a French military decoration to honor people or organizations who fought with the French against the Axis forces during World War II. The "palm" was issued to military units whose members performed heroic deeds in combat and was the highest-level Croix de Guerre that could be awarded. This was the unit's second Croix de Guerre, the first coming from fighting in the Vosges.

iv   This was one of the few times in World War II that an entire division received the Presidential Unit Citation, which was normally awarded only to smaller units for especially outstanding actions.

v   A "second Purple Heart" is also called a "Purple Heart with a single Oak Leaf Cluster" while a "second Bronze Star" is called a "Bronze Star with a single Oak Leaf Cluster." A "V" device is awarded on certain decorations to distinguish an award for heroism or valor in combat instead of for meritorious service or achievement.

from ear to ear. General O'Daniel paid homage to Phil, saying, "To a helluva fighting man." Then he smiled and leaned forward. "And I'll soon find out if you can dance," he whispered.[206]

Phil had no idea what the general meant until he received a coveted and rare invitation to the Regimental Officers Dance in Nancy on March 9. Division Commander Major General O'Daniel and his staff, along with Regimental Commander Colonel Lionel McGarr and his battalion staff, would all be there.[207]

During dinner, Phil sat around a table with several junior officers at the back of the room. After the dessert dishes were cleared, many of them danced with nurses from the American hospital to a live band. While Phil was sipping a drink, a senior officer walked over to him.

"You're wanted at the head table," he said in a commanding tone.

Phil followed the officer to the table where General O'Daniel and Colonel McGarr were in deep conversation, each with a drink in one hand and a lit cigar in the other. Upon seeing him approach, McGarr stood. "Lieutenant Larimore," he said, nodding at the general, "you've met General O'Daniel."

The general put down his cigar, stood, and shook Phil's hand. "Have a seat, son."

Phil pulled up a chair.

"Get the man a drink and one of my cigars," the general commanded one of his staff colonels. Then he looked at Phil. "How many medals have I pinned on you so far, young man?"

Phil felt color come to his face and his head drop a bit.

"Nothing to be embarrassed about," the general said. "No brag, just fact. I'm told it's a Silver, two Bronzes, and two Purples. Is that correct?"

Phil nodded. "Yes, sir."

"Like I said early today, a helluva fighting man."

"Just turned twenty years old, and last week I promoted him to company commander, General," McGarr interjected. "Youngest graduate out of Benning's OCS. Youngest officer in the Army at the time. Bright future, I'd say."

The general nodded, taking a deep puff off his cigar. "But more importantly, Lieutenant, McGarr tells me you're an equestrian."

Once again, Phil nodded and kept quiet.

"Damn proud of your work," the general continued. "Herding up all those horses around Montélimar. Fabulous. Your mule work on Anzio and in the Vosges. Brilliant stuff. Not only saved who knows how many lives of my men, but cost Germans their lives. I like that."

The general turned reflective. "When I was a newly commissioned officer, I learned to ride at the Reserve Officers Training Camp at Fort Myer. The horses there are magnificent, and the stables are top tier. Loved every minute on the back of a horse. After I shipped out for overseas duty in 1918, I served on the Western Front as part of the American Expeditionary Force, commanded by General John Pershing. I got to ride a couple of times with him once I became a company commander. He had his personal horse, Kidron, over there, and rode him during our victory parade in Paris."

The general took another puff and watched the smoke rings he blew rise to the ceiling. "Tell me about your interest in the noble beast, son."

Phil shared briefly about riding as a boy, meeting the Lipizzaners, fox hunting at Fort Benning, learning about draft horses in Nebraska, his experience in French Morocco with the *moukhalas* and *lab al baroud*, and dressage in Naples.

O'Daniel shook his head and looked at Phil directly. "When this damn war ends," he said, "you and I need to get together at a redoubt or hunt club and ride."

"I would like that, sir," Phil quickly assented.

Sensing his time with the senior officers was coming to an end, Phil leaned his head toward the dance floor. "If you don't mind, sirs, there's a pretty little nurse waiting for a dance."

O'Daniel threw his head back again, laughing. "I told you I'd be finding out if you can dance. You're dismissed, Lieutenant. Enjoy your night! That's a direct order."

ﮩ

On March 13, 1945, the 30th Infantry began moving by truck to an assembly area sixty miles away near Schmittviller, France, still in the Alsace region and about fourteen miles from the German border. The regiment traveled under cover of darkness and in complete secrecy. The numbers on vehicle bumpers were covered over, and shoulder patches were blotted out with adhesive tape strips, as were the blue-and-white patches of the 3rd ID that decorated helmets. Other combat units of the 3rd began moving to assembly areas also just inside the Franco-German border. Almost all were anxious about what lay ahead.[208]

The frontline men debated in great detail the attitude they thought the Germans would take about fighting on their own soil—in defending their dear *Vaterland*, or Fatherland. While some believed resistance would quickly collapse because they sensed Allied victory was inevitable, most men were confident the enemy would make a last-ditch stand. Desperate German soldiers, no doubt spurred on by propaganda regarding the "Morgenthau Plan" to leave Germany a wasteland, would make the fight increasingly difficult as the GIs drove deeper into their homeland. Given the fanatical response he'd already seen on the front lines, Phil and most of his men were certain the latter would be the case.

The men were poised, awaiting the signal for attack. D-Day was to be March 15, 1945; H-hour was 0100. In a special, last-minute briefing, General O'Daniel told his regimental commanders: "Within one hour after the jump-off, you will be in Germany." At long last, the 30th Infantry was about to smash through the portals of the enemy's Fatherland. The end was in sight.

And Phil and his men were ready for the final dance.

PART IV:
THE GERMAN CAMPAIGN

"When men take up arms to set other men free, there is something sacred and holy in the warfare."

—**Woodrow Wilson, 28th President of the United States (1913–1921)**[209]

38
DRAGON'S TEETH

"Previous combat experience has taught us that casualties are lumped primarily in the rifle platoons. For here are concentrated the handful of troops that must advance under enemy fire. It is upon them that the burden of war falls with the greatest risk and with less likelihood of survival than in any other of the combat arms."

—Sergeant Charles O. Beardslee of the 3rd Infantry Division[210]

On March 14, 1945, the Dogface soldiers gathered behind the border to Germany like an angry rattlesnake, poised and prepared to strike a venomous and final blow at their enemy. That evening, the 3rd Battalion trucked about ten miles to an assembly area just outside the village of Epping, France, where they awaited the signal to ruthlessly attack the Germans' vaunted Siegfried Line[i]—located about a mile inside the German border. The mission: Destroy the defensive line and put a dagger in Hitler's thousand-year Reich.[211]

The defensive line itself was between 500 to 600 yards deep, though additional well-camouflaged pillboxes in secondary positions dotted knolls and rises for several kilometers. Most of the dug-in, concrete fortifications were

---

i   The Siegfried Line was a German defensive line Hitler had built in 1938 so that the perpetual German fear of fighting on two fronts, East and West, could be obviated. The German military fortified nearly 400 miles of its western boundary that stretched from the Netherlands to Switzerland. The Siegfried Line featured more than 18,000 bunkers, 14,000 reinforced concrete pillboxes and bunkers, tunnels, and tank traps.

covered with earth and vegetation. The entrance tunnels giving access to the pillboxes were as much as 150 meters to the rear.

The anti-tank obstacles were three- to four-foot-tall pyramidal fortifications of reinforced concrete called "dragon's teeth." Laid between the individual teeth were countless land mines and endless strings of razor-sharp barbed wire to inhibit infantry, along with diagonally placed steel beams to thwart Allied tanks.

Similar to Anzio and in the Vosges, the enemy had ample time to prepare. During the stalemate of the previous two months at the Colmar Pocket, the Germans feverishly improved their defenses. But the greatest danger during the first days of the attack would come from the tens of thousands of deadly mines[ii] scattered in front of the German's main line of resistance (MLR). The entire front, especially the usual avenues of approach, was heavily mined up to over on mile from the German border back to the Siegfried Line.

Promptly at 0100 hours on March 15, 1945, the 1st and 3rd Battalions of the 30th Infantry pushed off. Ten battalions of artillery simultaneously opened fire, plus an additional six battalions of XV Corps artillery providing reinforcing fire. The initial barrage lasted twenty minutes.

When the American battalions advanced, they ran into the worse minefields yet, which inflicted heavy casualties. One platoon, slogging through a muddy farm corral, had nineteen men killed or wounded trying to find a way through. A call went out to men from the A&P Platoon—known as "sappers"—to clear paths through the dangerous minefields and the gummy, sticky ground created by recent rains.

Under the illumination of German flares, Phil could see the guys from his previous platoon, still with many of the "old men" that had served with him, probing every inch of ground with trench knives, gently working the blades at an angle in the dirt, hoping to hit only the sides of the mines. The sappers came upon many devilish mines handmade from cottage cheese-type crocks and sealed with wax. The only metal was the detonator, which was too small to be picked up by their mine detectors. Finding and clearing each minefield was painstakingly difficult and extraordinarily dangerous work that had to be one of the war's nastiest jobs, knowing that each probe could be a man's last.

The men worked day and night on what had to be one of the war's nastiest jobs, knowing that each probe could be a man's last. As they inched their way forward, Phil and his men covered them with suppressing fire, calling in murderous artillery when needed.

ii The Germans lay two types of mines designed to mutilate GIs rather than killing them: the S-mine or "Bouncing Betties" and the *Schützenmine 42*, which consisted of a simple wooden container the size of a box of kitchen matches containing seven ounces of TNT. A slot in the lid pressed down on a detonator, and the explosion could tear off a foot. With little metal, it was almost impossible to detect with metal detectors.

The minefields, though dense, did not extend for more than a mile in depth. The anti-personnel mines significantly slowed the advance, but as soon as the sappers outlined several clear paths through a minefield, marking them with a band of fluorescent tape on each side, Phil and Company L quickly moved out.

Tanks and howitzers were employed to great advantage by the 30th in detonating the remaining mines to widen the paths even more, which helped evacuate the wounded. As for the troublesome anti-tank ditches, armored bulldozers filled in the trenches with dirt so that tanks and self-propelled guns could follow.

From the outset, the two attack battalions, the 1st on the left and the 3rd on the right, drew a barrage of automatic fire from the pillboxes and a virtual storm of machine gun and small arms fire from narrow gaps in the minefields. On top of that, hefty, casualty-inflicting fire from self-propelled artillery either raked or rained down on them.

All enemy fire was sighted to cover the avenues of approach with a web of death coming in all directions from the front. Division artillery, as always, played an essential part in the initial attack—from 0100 hours until daylight, March 15, the battalions fired a hundred concentrations in support of the attacking infantry units, in addition to their massive opening barrage.

As a warming sun cleared the eastern horizon, the infantry received tremendous support from the air. When a 1,600-yard breach had been effected, the work began to eliminate the pillboxes systematically. The weakest part of a pillbox were the front openings, called "loopholes," from where the Germans fired their weapons. GIs unleashed tons of chemical smoke in front of the openings to blind the enemy and employed flamethrowers[iii] or pole charges[iv] to attack the loopholes, which took a lot of guts since they were up close and personal with frenzied German soldiers firing away.

For Phil and his company, though, howitzers were their most powerful tool in shattering the concrete boxes. Major James Lamar Boutwell commanded a 155-mm howitzer[v] group, providing direct support for Phil's battalion. Each gun in his battery of four howitzers required six men to load the ninety-five-pound projectiles, which were fitted with armor- or concrete-piercing fuses.

---

iii   The M1 and M1A1 were portable flamethrowers used by the U.S. during World War II. The M1 weighed 72 pounds, had a range of 50 feet, and a fuel tank capacity of five gallons of gasoline or diesel. The improved M1A1 weighed 65 pounds with the same fuel tank capacity, and had a range of just under 150 feet.

iv   A pole charge is a quantity of fused explosives fastened to the end of a pole and used in military attacks against pillboxes, dugouts, and cave positions.

v   A howitzer is a tube-fired artillery piece, larger than a mortar and smaller than a cannon. The M114 155-mm howitzer (designated the 155-mm Howitzer M1 or just 155) was a towed medium artillery gun, and along with mortars, one of the two types of artillery guns which normally were in close support of frontline infantry.

Major Boutwell had one of his gunners lower the howitzer's muzzle and open the gun's breech block. The major peered through the barrel at the target. Satisfied with the aim, he had the loaders stuff in a round. A tap of the helmet, and the shell was on its way. In a second or two, the pillbox exploded in a sheet of flame, and a perfect smoke ring popped out of an air vent at the top.

Boutwell punched the air with his fist. "Scratch one pillbox!" he exclaimed.

"It's still standing," Phil retorted.

"True, but there's no one left alive."

The major had Phil get behind one of the howitzers for its next firing. "You can watch the shell all the way to the target."

The soldier zeroed in on another pillbox. Another tap of the helmet. When the gun fired, Phil saw a black dot arc flash across the horizon. Same result: another pillbox put out of commission.

"See that!" Boutwell yelled. "We obliterated a pillbox from a half-mile away!"

More earth-covered concrete blockhouses met a similar fate, allowing Phil's 3rd Battalion to stealthily enter Dollenbach Woods, where they made slow, steady progress against heavy small arms and direct fire from self-propelled artillery. As they slowly advanced, the enemy opened up with heavy concentrations of artillery fire. The resistance was fast and furious. Brisk firefights raged throughout the morning.

Piper Cubs were employed extensively by Major General O'Daniel and Colonel McGarr to radio information to ground troops. Thus, pockets of the enemy were weeded out expeditiously with surprisingly little loss to the regiment. As a result, the troops picked up speed, and the 30th became the first regiment to completely penetrate the Siegfried Line. The deed was done in three days from start to finish.

෴

The grinding, slashing, grueling fight continued for several days, made more difficult when the retreating Germans demolished every bridge in the path of the advance. Nevertheless, the 30th Regiment moved so fast that the Germans had no time to counterattack.[212]

One time, the men seized an enemy military switchboard still in full operation, which proved to be a windfall for intelligence officers. They were able to overhear an SS captain issuing orders for withdrawal and pass that information along to the Army Air Corps, which sent planes to harass a convoy of enemy vehicles, three abreast and extending for several miles. The fighter bombers inflicted horrific destruction on the retreating Germans. So intense was the attack that scarcely a man or a man-made thing remained when they were finished.

On March 20, 1945, the 30th Infantry attacked and quickly cleared Zweibrücken, which had been nearly flattened by an Allied bombing raid a few days earlier. Chaotic conditions prevailed. Rubble and ruins were everywhere. Parts of the town still burned, while craters pitted the streets. Thousands of released Allied prisoners and forced labor workers roamed aimlessly. Dead horses were strewn on the roads leading out of town. Phil tried not to breathe in the terrible stench. One of his men said, "It's a deathly smell."

General O'Daniel and Colonel McGarr entered the city at 0830 hours to set up a Regimental CP. An hour later, a Jeep from the 45th Division drove up and asked where they would find their CP. General O'Daniel replied, "My 30th Infantry CP is the only CP you will find in this town!"

The rapid collapse of the German defenses was augmented by the massive air support, which played a leading part in blasting a path for the ground forces. Phil and his men found it difficult to describe the devastation that the fighter bombers wrought. In some towns, it was even difficult to find buildings suitable for CPs.

"Lieutenant," one of his men muttered, "*this* is scorched earth."

As the drive's momentum increased, American units overran large quantities of German guns, ammunition, explosives, and other equipment. It was looking like Supreme Allied Commander Dwight D. Eisenhower's prediction that the war would be won west of the Rhine River was fast becoming fact. Phil and his men heard estimates suggesting that the German 1st and 3rd Armies had lost 75 percent of their combat effectiveness. More than 100,000 prisoners were taken.

Phil was thrilled when he heard that orders had come down that the 30th Infantry was to be entirely motorized for a nearly sixty-mile dash to the Rhine.

Once Germany's major river was crossed, Phil knew Germany would fall, and the sooner that happened, the sooner he could return home—hopefully in one piece.

39

CROSSING THE RHINE

"Those who have not been in the forward areas can never hope to fully comprehend the awful reality of Infantry combat. However, we can arrive at a deeper understanding of the grimly determined, glorious men who are serving throughout the world as our spokesman for freedom—our combat Infantrymen."

—Lieutenant General Benjamin Lear, Commander of the U.S. Second Army[213]

The 30th Infantry Regiment, with Phil's 3rd Battalion in the lead, covered sixty miles in three days to assemble directly west of Mannheim and the Rhine River. The German autobahn, built originally for military traffic, served its purpose well. On the night of March 24–25, 1945, under a scudding moon periodically obscured by clouds, the assault elements moved up to the Rhine and assembled two to three miles from the river for Operation Rhineland.[214]

The Rhine was about 1,000 feet wide and up to seventeen feet deep at the crossing areas, flowing swiftly between revetted banks. The country on both sides was flat and sparsely wooded, so men and equipment had to be concentrated under cover of darkness. H-Hour was set for 0230 hours, March 26. Division artillery opened fire at 0152 hours with a terrific barrage: 10,000 shells crashed on the east bank, hitting the Germans' defensive positions over a thirty-eight-minute period, while assault troops from the 3rd Infantry tensely crouched on the western bank. The artillery bursts painted the dark sky a lurid red.

At 0225 hours, a sudden, eerie silence descended on the Rhine as the Allied artillery barrage ceased. Five minutes later, the hush was broken by the throbbing of skiff engines as the first wave of "storm boats"[i] headed across the river. Once in the water, each crossing took less than thirty seconds.

American machine guns fired tracers to guide the first wave as it penetrated the fog and smoke. Colored landing lights showed the way for those who followed. The massive bombardment and chemical smoke blinded and stunned the German defenders, lifting just as the first wave hit the shore. Communication wires that had been destroyed by the opening barrage kept German forward observers from calling in fire missions.

The east bank, defended by the enemy in double foxholes equipped with machine guns, was attacked immediately, resulting in tense, close-quarter firefights which forced the Germans to retreat.

After his successfully crossing, Phil observed a larger boat carrying some of the battalion aid station personnel capsize ten to twenty yards from the riverbank. Without a thought, he and several of his men stripped off their coats, boots, and equipment and dove into the ice-cold water. Phil grabbed the first man, who was panicking and fighting to keep his head above the water. Just as Phil did with his good friend Billy in the Mississippi River, he dove below the surface, turned the man to face away from him, wrapped him up in a cross-chest lock, and dragged him to shore through the churning water.

Phil was pleased to learn that he had saved the life of Captain Hilard Kravitz, the battalion surgeon who'd tended to his leg wound in a field hospital and offered him a swig of his "private medicine." Kravitz was lucky to escape drowning; nine of the seventeen men drowned.

Despite the enemy resistance and artillery fire, the last of the 3rd Battalion assault boats crossed the swift-flowing Rhine by 0305 hours.

When machine gun and small arms fire ceased to harass the crossing sites, engineers began building a pair of floating bridges while still under artillery and mortar fire. They brought in two heavy pontoon rafts and two infantry support rafts to help them complete a 948-foot treadway bridge and a 1,040-foot heavy pontoon bridge in just over nine hours.

During the first twenty-four hours of floating bridge operation, 1,000 support vehicles were transported across the mighty Rhine. Evacuation of casualties back across the river was carried out by DUKWs[ii] and ferries, as all bridges were one-way only.

i   These high-speed assault boats, equipped with a 55 HP outboard motor, were deployed by the Combat Engineer Battalion and designed to hit the shoreline at high speed. A two-man crew could ferry six soldiers at a time.
ii   The DUKW (colloquially known as a "Duck") was a six-wheel-drive amphibious truck used in World War II for the transportation of goods and troops over land and water. The name DUKW comes from General Motors nomenclature: D: designed in 1942; U: utility; K: all-wheel drive; and W: dual-tandem rear axles. Surviving DUKWs have found popularity as tourist craft in marine environments.

✌

Under cloudy skies at Lampertheim, five miles inland from the river, the regrouped enemy offered the most resistance of the day. Phil's 3rd Battalion met 500 German infantry supported by 88s, Flakwagens, and armor, all determinedly holding out. Phil's company knocked out a complete battery of 88-mm guns, and his bazooka men destroyed two tanks that attempted to counterattack their positions. The hard fight ended when the town finally fell at 1300 hours.[215]

After taking Lampertheim, the 3rd Battalion took out four more 76-mm anti-tank guns, clearing the woods east of the city and securing high ground. Approximately 300 enemy prisoners were taken. With the 1st and 3rd Battalions spearheading forward movement, the 30th boarded trucks and raced nearly forty miles to seize bridges across the Main River at Wörth-am-Main, a town of several thousand only forty miles southeast of Frankfurt. In just two weeks after crossing the Franco-German border, the regiment's rapid advance to the Main River covered 130 miles.

While passing through village after village, Phil was surprised to see anything white—bedsheets, nightgowns, and even panties—hanging out of the windows, just like in France. It looked like wash day back in Italy.

Equally shocking was that Nazi swastikas were nowhere to be found. The glum German citizens who lined the streets and sidewalks stared menacingly at the incoming troops. Some glared in open hostility. Others appeared to be in a daze, as if they were finally waking up to the fact that they'd been told a string of lies on the radio by Hitler and propaganda minister Joseph Goebbels about how well the Germans were doing and how victory was inevitable. They gave the GIs no trouble at all, however.

Phil leaned over to his Jeep driver. "Not quite as friendly as the French, eh?"

The 30th rolled eastward, steamrolling through the German countryside. Towns where German soldiers resisted were leveled by artillery and tanks; those that surrendered were left unmolested.

In one village, a German civilian met the GIs with a white surrender flag and escorted them to a large wooden building, where they found a room full of German Luftwaffe personnel eating supper. The airmen said they were hoping to surrender to the Allies because in a day or two, they were going to be transferred to an infantry division—a certain death sentence. With no fuel left for their planes, their war was over anyway.

Phil and his men spent their nights in German houses, giving the indignant owners five minutes to clear out. The GIs had no sympathy for them at all.[iii] After eight months of constant combat while battling

---

iii   In France, American GIs did not forcefully "requisition" French houses for overnight stays and camped outside in tents because France was an ally. The situation was different for Germany, viewed as a belligerent adversary.

merciless Germans through France, the men reveled in the creature comforts of electricity, hot water, flush toilets, soft white toilet paper, and clean, comfortable beds.

The next plan was to cross the Main River, a barrier nearly as wide as the Rhine, which called for another spearhead by the 30th Infantry. A reconnaissance team patrolling the Main River's banks in the vicinity of Wörth, southeast of Frankfurt, drew considerable fire from the enemy.

As Phil's 3rd Battalion drove south to their assigned river crossing, they destroyed a tank, two twin-barreled 37-mm anti-aircraft guns, a pair of 20-mm Flakwagens, and killed a surprisingly large number of German snipers. Lieutenant Colonel Christopher W. Chaney tasked Phil and his company with procuring a German barge to carry the entire battalion across the river. The crossing began at 0300 hours on the morning of March 30.

For Phil, it was déjà vu all over again, remembering the time when he and his men had used a barge to cross the Ognon River in France.

This time, there was no enemy fire.

◈

On March 31, the weather turned cloudy and cold, but the men of the 30th were given a time of rest over the Easter weekend as they went into division reserve. Phil and several of his men attended Easter Sunday services in a village church, where GIs and locals filled the pews.[216]

Every now and then, one of the rifles would slip on the hardwood and crash to the floor, causing congregants to jump or shudder. The men also placed their steel helmets under the pews in front of them, but when the local people knelt during the service, they often kicked the helmets, making a racket.

All the commotion made for a noisy service, but for Phil, it was his most memorable Easter service ever. In a letter home, he wrote:

> *The men and I were dirty and unshaven, standing in a war-damaged but once beautiful church. Sun was pouring in, illuminating and warming us. It was as if we were being cleansed. The sense of comfort, well-being, and safety was amazing.*[217]

∾

On a rainy, cold Monday, April 2, the day after Easter, the 30th Regiment was preparing to move by motorized vehicles about twenty miles to a new assembly area, but Phil was not with his men.[218]

Those who knew where he was going could be counted on the fingers of one hand. On fear of court-martial, they could tell no one about his upcoming mission.

A top secret mission.

40

A SECRET MISSION

"Courage is rightly esteemed the first of human
qualities, because, as has been said, it is the quality
which guarantees all others."

—British Prime Minister Winston Churchill[219]

On Monday, April 2, 1945, just before dinner, Phil was outside his company CP smoking a cigarette with his executive officer, Lieutenant Abraham Fitterman. Suddenly, a Jeep raced up and skidded to a halt. In the passenger seat was a man Phil didn't recognize, wearing a major's insignia on his impeccably clean and pressed uniform.[220]

Phil and Abe looked suspiciously at each other as they popped to attention and saluted. The officer hopped out of the Jeep, stood, saluted back, and barked, "At ease. I'm Major Hugh A. Scott, Division G-2.[i] I'm looking for Lieutenant Larimore."

"That would be me, sir," Phil replied.

Major Scott shook Phil's hand and gestured to step away from the Jeep for a private conversation. After hearing what the major had to say, Phil hopped in the back seat of the Jeep with Major Scott and raced away, ending up at the Battalion CP, which had taken up residence in a nicely appointed German villa.

---

i   A G-2 is an intelligence officer or section of a major command above brigade level.

Phil followed the rapidly walking major into the manor and up the stairs to the command room, where Colonel McGarr was on the telephone. After finishing his conversation, he dismissed all men except for Major Scott and his two valets.

"I'm going to have dinner brought up for us, if that's okay," McGarr said. It was not a request, and the two young officers nodded. As the valets set the table, McGarr handed Phil a cigar and poured tumblers of scotch all around. As they lit up, he asked, "Any idea why you're here, Lieutenant?"

Phil glanced dubiously at the major, who sat stone-faced, and then back at the colonel. "No, sir."

McGarr took a sip of his scotch and leaned back. "Damnedest thing. Cobra tells me he has it on good authority that there are rumors of a bunch of highbrow horses just across the border in Czechoslovakia that need to be saved. But we need confirmation, which means we need an equestrian to find out if it's true."

"Cobra?" Phil asked.

"O'Daniel's code name."

"And the general wants me to go there?"

"Cobra has sent his G-2 to explain this to us." He nodded at Major Scott, but three men entered before he could start, each carrying a tray of food. The officers sat at the table and were served dinner.

As they enjoyed their hot meal, Major Scott began his story. "There's an Army intelligence unit working near the German-Czech border, about ninety miles east of Nuremberg, interrogating German POWs. They learned about a large stud farm, formerly owned by the Czech royal family but confiscated by the Nazis, near a tiny Bohemian village called Hostau, about ten miles east of the German border as the crow flies. Intelligence says Hitler and his underlings have gathered what may be the finest collection of mounts in the world. Apparently, it's some experiment to purify the breeds the same way he wants to purify the races."

Phil's interest peaked. "Which breeds?"

The major pulled a small notebook out of his chest pocket. "Says here they have Arabians, Andalusians, Friesians, Anglo-Kabardas—don't exactly know what those are."

"Those are all considered royal breeds, horses preferred by and bred for kings and queens," Phil explained. "They've all been used as warhorses throughout history across Europe. Amazing creatures."

The major looked back at his notes. "He also spoke about the farm having Thoroughbreds stolen from the capitals of Europe, including several famous racehorses that won Europe's top sweepstakes."

"Must be quite a farm," Phil said.

"It's even better than you think, Lieutenant. They've also gathered Lipizzaners."

"The dancing white horses of Austria!" Phil exclaimed. "I saw them perform when I was a kid, and I've seen pictures of them at the Spanish Riding School in Vienna. The best classical dressage mounts in the world. Ever see that famous painting of Napoleon crossing the Alps? That one shows him leading his troops from the back of a prancing Lipizzaner stallion."[ii]

The major nodded, looked down at his notebook, and continued. "Intelligence reports that as far back as 1939, Hitler put out orders for his men to capture every single Lipizzaner they could find. Adolf Hitler coveted the Lipizzaner for its white coat and its perceived racial purity. The super race he planned needed splendid stallions beneath them. They've netted about 250 of the horses, which may represent most of the suitable breeding stock in the world."

Phil softly whistled. "What do you need me to do?"

The major smiled again. "I like a man who gets to the point. Intelligence tells us that over the last month or so, more and more horses—some Lipizzaners, some not—have been pouring into the Hostau stable from the eastern part of Czechoslovakia, which is being overrun by the Red Army. Things appear to be getting desperate. One report says, and I quote, 'In the path of the Russian armies, nothing is safe. Men and boys are killed, women and girls are raped and murdered. Animals that can be eaten are sent back to the starving Soviet Union, where famine continues,' end quote."

Phil sat straight up. "You don't think the Russians would harm the Lipizzaners, do you?"

The major flipped a few pages of his notebook and found what he was looking for. "We have this report from just a week ago, twenty-four March. Quote, 'A German convoy was intercepted by Soviet tanks an hour from the Austrian border. Inside the trucks were more than twenty Lipizzaners. The Russian soldiers found the sometimes-temperamental steeds too difficult to control, so they slaughtered eighteen of the most high-spirited ones, then harnessed the others to ammunition carts,' end quote." The G-2 closed his notebook and put it back into his pocket.

"General O'Daniel tells me, Lieutenant Larimore, that you know of his love of horses. He's been riding horses his whole life. Loved the cavalry, loves the hunt, and loves the steeplechase. He's not an Olympian like Patton, but he wants to do something. He's suggesting one of our Piper Cubs carry a soldier, an expert equestrian, behind enemy lines to either confirm or refute this information. If confirmed, the general will propose to senior command that these

---

ii   Phil was referring to a masterpiece painting by French painter Jacques-Louis David called "Napoleon Crossing the Alps," commemorating the crossing that French emperor Napoleon Bonaparte conducted through the Great St. Bernard Pass in May 1800. In reality, he rode a mule over the crest of the Alps, which would hardly be impressive for an emperor looking to enhance his image and legacy.

steeds be saved. Unfortunately, his superiors will not *officially* sanction such a mission. Fortunately for us, they are not forbidding it either. But should the mission fail, the Army's official comment would be that any participants were just plain lost in western Czechoslovakia—or worse, that they were AWOL or attempting to defect."

The gravity of the situation fully rested on Phil's shoulders. He leaned back and sighed deeply.

"Let me be clear, Lieutenant," the major continued, "if you volunteer for this mission, the plane that'll transport you will have all the markings painted out, and you will not be in uniform. You can carry a sidearm and keep your dog tags with you, but you can bring no other identification. No papers. No wallet. Being an unauthorized mission, if you are captured, any future career in the Army would likely be kaput. You'd also be at risk, should the political backlash from the Russians become too heated. The Army might be forced to declare you AWOL or a turncoat. Worse yet, should you not survive, there may be no benefits for your family, including no life insurance benefit."

The possibilities are going from bad to worse, Phil thought.

"Even if you're successful, officially, this mission never happened. There will be no record of it whatsoever."

Colonel McGarr leaned forward. In a soft, almost fatherly voice, he said, "Lieutenant, this is a completely volunteer effort. If you say no, that's fine with me. I need you here, and I need you in our final few days of attack so that we can end this godforsaken war. We need to finish what we started long ago."

The colonel leaned back and took a puff on his cigar. "But if you decide to go, you'll have my full, albeit unofficial, support. As the major says, there will be no written record either way."

"How long do I have to decide?" Phil asked.

"I need to know now," the G-2 answered. "We have the plane prepared and a volunteer pilot ready to go. The scheduled takeoff is 0400 hours tomorrow. The horse farm is about 160 to 170 air miles from here. Weather is predicted to be cloudy and cold with limited visibility, but the moon is just past full. The pilot says the partial cloud cover and the moonlight diffused through the cloud cover will be perfect. He says he can bounce in and out of the clouds so that you'll be protected from AA fire and won't have to worry about the Luftwaffe. But you'll be flying through mountains, which increases the turbulence and the risk."

He paused a moment to take a sip of his scotch. "For obvious reasons, I don't want you or the pilot to know any of the ground arrangements. We've promised this to the Czech resistance with whom we've made arrangements for your care on the ground."

Phil knew the G-2 didn't want him to have any information that could be tortured out of him or the pilot. A concerning thought crossed his mind as he remembered his days flying the Piper Cub at the Gulf Coast Military Academy. "You said it's about 160 miles from here?"

"Yes."

"That's the maximum range of the Cub, isn't it?"

The major was silent for a moment. "Actually, one-eighty or one-ninety. Should be enough."

Phil chuckled. "Sure hope so, because we'll be on fumes when we're trying to find the landing strip."

The major nodded. "Not much room for error on several fronts. But I'll tell you this much: Once there, you'll be escorted through a forest to the farm. While you're scouting, fuel will be delivered to refill the plane."

The colonel took a deep breath and let it out. "Lieutenant, once you're on the ground, don't dillydally around. Do your scouting, and then get the hell outta there. We want you back by sunset."

Phil didn't have to think twice. "I'll go!" he announced with a grin. "A chance to save the Lipizzaners. How could I say no?"

McGarr slammed the table. "I knew you'd do it!" he exclaimed. "More scotch all the way around!" he commanded his valet. The men clinked their glasses.

In Phil's mind's eye, he could see his friend, Ross Calvert, smiling from ear to ear and slapping him on the back. He still wanted to believe that his friend was alive and doing well in a POW camp somewhere in Germany.

Phil could almost hear his buddy laughing at him and saying, *Hell— being a POW ain't that bad, Phil. You'll enjoy your time off in a camp. And if I can survive, so can you!*

☙

Takeoff for Operation Lipizzaner, as Phil was calling it, was precisely at 0400 hours on Tuesday, April 3. General O'Daniel and Colonel McGarr were both there to see him off and wish him luck.

"Find those horses," was Iron Mike's last command. Phil and the pilot were not to exchange names or any personal or military information about each other. "Mission talk only," growled O'Daniel.

The flight was surprisingly uneventful, and the pilot, obviously an expert, darted in and out of the moonlit clouds. Phil calmed his anxiety by staring at the semi-dark mountainous landscape passing underneath them at their leisurely cruising speed of eighty miles an hour—and by saying a silent prayer or two. Fortunately, they encountered no flak, for which Phil was grateful. He even caught forty winks, but he was awakened when the pilot called out, "Hey, buddy! Wake up!"

Phil sat up and rubbed his eyes. The first rays of the sun were lighting up the landscape.

"We should be close," the pilot said. "Help me keep an eye out. I'm going to fly a bit south of the coordinates and then turn back and forth, working our way north, until we see something."

"How's our fuel?"

"Don't ask. We need to find the strip pretty soon. Remember, look for something straight. Nature doesn't make straight lines; men do. Look for fire, smoke, or a pattern in the landscape."

Phil was now wide awake, straining his eyes, front to back, side to side. They made a couple of passes back and forth, spotting a small town that the pilot assured him was Hostau.

"Should be a bit northwest of here," the pilot said.

A shrill buzz filled the cabin, causing Phil's heart to skip a beat. He noticed a red light blinking on the control panel. "What's that?" he asked.

"That's our almost-out-of-fuel signal," the pilot replied in a strained voice.

Phil felt his chest and throat tighten. His observation was even sharper as he scanned the landscape. Phil thought he saw something unusual. He rubbed his eyes and focused his gaze.

"There!" Phil yelled. "Five o'clock. A fire."

Off their right wing was a field with a small campfire burning on the border of the woods.

"I see it! There's the strip!" Phil called out. There were also a series of lanterns along the forest edge.

"Dumbasses," the pilot snarled. "Should have put the lanterns more in the open. Had we come from the other direction, we'd have never seen 'em."

He banked the plane to the right as the engine began to sputter. The incessant high-pitched buzzing continued as the plane quickly dove. When the engine sputtered to a sudden stop, the propeller stilled. They were now gliding.

With his extensive glider experience, Phil quickly calculated their ground speed, elevation, rate of descent, and distance to the landing field.

"We'll make it!" he shouted.

"How the hell do you know that?" the pilot barked.

"One year of glider training."

The treetops were getting closer and closer.

"Better say your prayers would be my advice. We hit those trees, and it'll be bad."

Phil felt calm. "Nah. You've got it."

But his apprehension and heart rate increased when the Cub's wheels clipped the last tree's top branches at the forest's edge. The pilot pulled up the nose just before a bumpy landing in a farm field.

"Damn! That was close!" the pilot muttered. "But we're safely down."

Several men in dark overcoats rushed toward them, carrying rifles. Phil's hand instinctively reached for his holstered Colt 45.

"Hope those guys are friendly," Phil said.

He would soon find out.

41

OPERATION LIPIZZANER

"To find a horse like this, in the middle of this filthy abomination of a war, is for me like finding a butterfly on a dung heap. We don't belong in the same universe as a creature like this."

—Sir Michael Morpurgo, British author and playwright[221]

Phil and the pilot quickly exited the plane as several men with baying dogs ran up to greet them. The lead man stuck out his hand, and the canine handlers pulled their dogs back with the leashes.[222]

"We're ÚVOD," he said in a thickly accented voice. Phil recognized the acronym of the Czech resistance network as he shook the man's hand.

"We brought camouflage netting," the man said. "Let's push the plane over by the forest edge."

Several men covered the Cub while others extinguished the lanterns, no longer necessary in the dawn's first light. The lead man then directed Phil and the pilot to a campfire that the partisans had made next to the woods.

"We're safe here," the man said. "Anyone passing will think we are a hunting party."

"What's the plan?" Phil asked as cups of dark, piping hot coffee were poured.

At that moment, several hunting dogs began barking, stretching their leashes in the direction of the forest. Two men instantaneously shouldered their rifles, while another pair cautiously walked behind nearby trees. Another partisan rolled behind a log and aimed his rifle in sniper fashion.

At that moment, a single horseman exited the forest's edge about fifty yards away and pulled his mount to a halt. Even at that distance, Phil was astounded by what he saw. The man, dressed in traditional hunting garb, sat upright on one of the most beautiful horses he had ever seen. The stallion's grayish-white coat glowed in the dim light. Phil estimated it a bit more than fifteen hands and a stocky 1,200 pounds.

The horse nickered, then lowered and shook his massive head. His long white mane flowed from the arched carriage of his sturdy neck and broad, deep chest. His tail was long, well set, and carried high as it swished from side to side, slapping its well-muscled, strong legs with broad joints and well-defined tendons.

"Marvelous. Stunning. Glorious," Phil whispered to himself. "A Lipizzaner!"

The rider expertly dismounted and led his white horse toward the men. As he approached, Phil noticed another horse in tow—a bay-colored stallion that was a good sixteen hands. His first thought was this: *That animal has a mighty ugly head.*

But the animal was otherwise well-built with an unusual small, white star-shaped marking on the lower middle of his chest. As Phil looked at it more closely, he noticed the long neck, high withers, deep chest, short back, lean body, good depth of hindquarters, and long legs. *Definitely a Thoroughbred*, he thought.

The rider shook hands with the men and then turned to Phil. "My name is Captain Lessing," he said in a German accent. "I'm one of the staff veterinarians at the Hostau stud farm."

Phil recognized the name from his pre-mission briefing. Lessing had grown up in Mecklenburg, Germany—horse farm territory east of Berlin. He'd joined the Hitler Youth in his teens and had attended veterinary school in Hamburg, graduating in 1939.

"Good to meet you, I'm—"

The captain cut Phil off. "I expect no trouble, sir, but it's best I don't know your first or your last name. I do need to know your rank."

"Lieutenant, Sir. First Lieutenant."

The captain nodded. "Best we leave these hunters and go about our ride, don't you think? Are you comfortable on a mount?"

"I am, sir. Have ridden most of my life. I am in awe of your Lipizzaner. He makes even this magnificent Thoroughbred look positively common."

The captain smiled, turned, and quickly remounted his horse, indicating that Phil should do the same.

As Phil settled into his saddle, under the watchful eye of his host, the captain explained, "Your mount is sometimes a bit lazy and has to be prodded with a spur or soft whistle to run or jump. I call him Tuckern."

Captain Lessing reigned his mighty stallion around and took off at a canter. Phil whistled and reined Tuckern around to follow. Once Phil and Tuckern caught up with them, they trotted together and then slowed to a walk as they entered the dense forest.

"My men and I walk or ride the horses once or twice a day," the captain said. "That way, if we are seen from a distance, no worries. If someone comes close…well, do you speak any language other than English?"

"I speak pretty good French," Phil replied. He'd been speaking *beaucoup de français* ever since the Allies landed in southern France.

"Then I'll introduce you as a visiting veterinarian from France—a Nazi sympathizer who escaped. What city shall I say you are from?"

"Aix-en-Provence would work. I spent several weeks in a hospital there."

The captain nodded. "I'm told you're here to confirm our stock. We'll ride to the forest edge above the farm. You'll get a good look from there."

"You sound German, not Czech."

The man smiled. "I'm a German Army officer. I was an adjunct to Hitler's Chief Equerry of Germany and Master of the Horse, Gustav Rau. He's world-renowned as an expert in breeding horses."

"I didn't know Hitler was into horses."

"It should be no surprise," Captain Lessing explained, "for two reasons. First of all, as you probably already know, the German Army is heavily dependent upon horses. About 80 percent of their entire transport is equestrian. With the way the war is going, we're churning through them at a rate of about 6,000 killed or lost to disease per month."

Phil mulled that number. "I've seen countless dead and dying horses across France, but I had no idea they lost that many."

The captain nodded. "The second reason is that Adolf Hitler's ultimate dream is to create the perfect German—blond, blue-eyed, strong, lean— through selective breeding. He wants to do the same with horses, so he got his hands on what he considered the most perfectly bred horses in Europe. The perfect horses for the perfect humans—'the quintessential German warhorse,' he called it."

"Kinda funny, isn't it?" Phil wondered aloud.

"What?"

"I mean Hitler's a short, pudgy, dark-haired man."

"Who never sat on a horse," Lessing added, chuckling. "Anyway, Gustav

Rau is considered the equestrian equivalent of Hitler, and he set up fourteen stud farms to produce purebreds. He brought prize Arabians from Poland as well as other breeds. But as time went on, he and Hitler became much more interested in the Lipizzaner. They sent me to procure for the Reich all of the Lipizzaner stock from Yugoslavia and Italy. We set up two centers for the Lipizzaners: the one here in Hostau, and another in a small Austrian town, Sankt Martin im Innkreis, about 200 kilometers[i] south of here.

"Herr Rau also had the entire bloodstock of the stud farm owned by the Spanish Riding School in Vienna—stallions, mares, and foals—loaded into specially designed train cars and brought here to Hostau. He gathered any others he found in small pockets scattered around Europe. He corralled virtually every one of the world's Lipizzaners in these two stud farms, at first far from the war zone."

Phil changed the subject. "Are you a Nazi?"

The German captain took a deep breath and slowly released it. Looking into the forest ahead, he softly explained. "As I said, Herr Rau sent me to procure for the Reich all of the Lipizzaner stock from Yugoslavia and Italy. As I toured the Reich, I traveled at the highest level of comfort. One day I was on a train, enjoying a meal in a well-appointed dining car with high-ranking Gestapo and Army officers. I was by far the youngest officer. During a pause at a rail station, as we were all drinking champagne from crystal flutes, a medical train pulled up next to us. I could see cars stuffed with wounded soldiers from the Eastern Front, stacked three-deep on tiered bunks. The men looked pitiful and exhausted, wrapped in tattered bandages sodden with blood; they looked only half-alive."

Lessing paused and shifted in his saddle. "One of the Gestapo ordered his valet to close the curtains. He said, and I remember it like it was yesterday, 'Those men have no understanding of the National Socialist lifestyle.' While his fellow Germans were being transported in cattle cars, our horses moved about in plush, padded train cars, specially equipped for their protection, always accompanied by grooms who cared for their every need. I've never gotten that out of my mind. I think, for the first time, I'd seen up close and in person the ruthless contempt the party leaders had for their men who were suffering and dying."

He nudged his horse to begin walking. "Traveling around let me also see the depredations and atrocities being committed by the Reich, especially in Poland. It was awful, Lieutenant. But a trip to Auschwitz...."

Phil remembered reading about the liberation of the Polish concentration camp in late January by the Russians. The reports were awful: Nearly a million Jews had been systematically killed in gas chambers, and their bodies burned in a crematorium. Those who survived were nothing more than skin and bones.

i   Two hundred kilometers is close to 125 miles.

The captain paused, and his eyes moistened. "There, I learned the Reich was gassing the Jews. From my train window, I saw black ashes spewing into the air, blackening the gray sky like a spreading blot of ink. I couldn't help but recoil, but I could not avert my eyes. It was then that I first thought, *If the Germans win this war, there is no God Almighty.* The smoky residue settled into my uniform. I could not wash it out. I got a new uniform, but the smell still clings to the inside of my nostrils."

"Auschwitz has been in all the newspapers since January. But our intelligence knows that there are more—at least a half dozen large concentration camps. Who knows how many smaller ones there are," Phil said.

The captain continued. "After working for Herr Rau for under a year, I gave up believing in the Nazi cause. In my mind, my vow of loyalty was no longer to the Führer, but only to the horses. Fortunately, it was then that I was assigned to Hostau."

He looked at Phil directly. "To answer your question, sir, no, I'm not a Nazi—at least not anymore. Certainly not in my heart or soul, even though I'm required to wear the uniform."

Phil pulled out a pen and small notepad to take notes. "Why do you want us to know about this farm?"

Captain Lessing shook a finger at him. "No notes! It's too dangerous for you or me."

Phil apologized and put his notepad away, while willing himself to remember each word, each sentence, and each thought from the captain.

There would be a lot to remember.

42
RIDE OF A LIFETIME

"When I bestride him, I soar, I am a hawk; he trots
the air; the earth sings when he touches it."

—William Shakespeare, English playwright[223]

Phil and Captain Lessing continued to ride toward the edge of the forest overlooking the horse farm.[224]

"When I was assigned to Hostau, it was a heavenly assignment at first," Captain Lessing explained. "It's spacious, peaceful, and well-run—the Reich's most sheltered and stunning stud farm. Even in the middle of the war, right here, all has been deceptively tranquil. The scenes of rural, pastoral life to which I awaken each morning seem to have no relation to what is happening anywhere else in this godforsaken war."

"You're a lucky man," Phil commented.

"You would be correct, and I am grateful. I can concentrate on my day-to-day routine, which is steeped in centuries-old tradition. Our grooms meticulously care for our horses—their feeding, grooming, walking, washing, pasturing, even performing the geldings.[i] I lead a team of veterinarians who care for their every medical or dietary need. We inspect the horses daily, are on call to go to the stables to look after sick horses, and we assist in the births of the Lipizzaner foals. Did you know they're jet black when they're born?" he asked.

---

i   A gelding is a male horse that has been castrated.

234

"I didn't!" Phil exclaimed.

"Most people don't. But I wasn't here long before I saw, to my horror, I might add, what Dr. Rau was doing. Yes, that's what we were forced to call him, although he is no such thing—neither a physician nor a veterinarian. He only has an honorary degree, but people call him 'Doctor' in deference to his authority. Anyway, I saw what Herr Rau called 'modern changes in breeding.' But they were awful."

"Like what?"

"Mares that were far too young were to be covered by stallions,[ii] instead of waiting until they were more mature. Close relations were mated to each other. Yugoslavian stallions were paired with Austrian mares rather than keeping each strain separate. He was experimenting, but the horror was that he was experimenting with the Lipizzaner breed. With virtually every pureblood Lipizzaner under his control, he was embarking on linebreeding—father to daughter, brother with sister—to reshape the Lipizzaner to accentuate specific certain characteristics he liked. He was unleashed to put his theories to test, with Austria's most extraordinary natural treasure as his guinea pigs. The fate of history's most prized horse is now entirely in the hands of an insane Nazi.

"Herr Rau's program at Hostau is identical to the Nazi's most infamous breeding project: the *Lebensborn*. Have you heard of it?"

Phil shook his head.

"At special birth clinics, SS officers had sex with specifically selected women who exhibited quintessential Aryan traits. The babies produced by these liaisons were baptized in a special SS rite, cradled beneath a symbolic SS dagger. At the same time, incantations pledged that these Aryan babies would have lifelong allegiance to Nazi beliefs."

"That's sick!" Phil said.

"In a similar way, Herr Rau has a special rite for each foal at Hostau. They are each branded with the letter *H*, which is pierced through with a dagger. This is the mark of Herr Rau's pure new race of Lipizzaner. But now, thank God, it's coming to an end."

The men approached the edge of the forest. Phil looked out over hundreds of acres of beautiful pastures, with grazing mares and frolicking foals as far as he could see. In the distance were row after row of well-maintained stables and barns, surrounded by riding arenas.

"This place is huge!"

Lessing nodded. "As I said, one of the most remarkable stud farms in the world. This facility was owned by a family of nobles that bred cavalry horses

---

ii   "Covered" means "bred" or "mated to." "Live cover" is when the mare is covered by the stallion in a breeding shed. "Pasture bred" is when the mare is turned out in a pasture with the stallion for several days to breed. Live cover is often preferred as it provides a more controlled environment, allowing the breeder to ensure that the mare was covered, and places the handlers in a position to remove the horses from one another should one attempt to kick or bite the other.

for centuries and served as imperial equerries[iii] for the Habsburg Crown.[iv] The entire establishment covers just over 600 hectares[v] and can accommodate more than a thousand stallions, mares, and foals."

"How many are here now?"

"Over 1,200, including about 250 Lipizzaners, 100 Arabians, 200 Thoroughbreds like Tuckern, and 600 purebred Russian, Polish, and Yugoslavian horses. Any horse felt not to be pure is eliminated."

The German captain looked down at Tuckern. "I'm afraid that's the sentence for the champion you're riding today."

"Why?" Phil muttered incredulously. "He's spectacular."

The captain nodded. "But it has been determined he is only seven-eighths pure Thoroughbred. So, he's doomed."

Phil could only shake his head.

"Which brings me to why you're here today. We're directly in the path of the Russian armies. The only hope for us and the Lipizzaners is you Americans. That's why I'm risking my life, Lieutenant. I need you to let your superiors know we're here and convince them to save the horses."

The captain looked across the fields, his face betraying the emotion of the moment. "Oh, I don't think I mentioned the POWs working for us, did I?"

Phil's heart skipped a beat. "No. What POWs?"

"We have British, French, Polish, Russian, and American prisoners working as forced labor on the farm. Mostly they're Americans and British."

Phil couldn't believe his good fortune. He pulled out his notepad and wrote down Ross Calvert's name. "If this man is one of the POWs, can you get a message to him?"

When he finished writing, Phil pressed the note into Captain Lessing's hand.

"I'll try," he said as he pocketed it.

"I've seen all I need to, Captain. Best for me to get out of here. I'll make sure headquarters knows everything you've told me, everything I've seen. I can't imagine them not wanting to help."

"Hopefully soon, Lieutenant. I'm not sure how long until the Russians arrive. But we best get you back to your plane. My guess is that you've never ridden on a Lipizzaner before?"

"Actually, on my twelfth birthday, I spent a day with the Lipizzaners from the Spanish Riding School when they were visiting my hometown. One of the riders actually let me sit on one."

"Yes, but did you ride?"

iii   An equerry is an officer of honor who historically was a senior attendant with responsibilities for the horses of a person of rank.

iv   The Habsburg Crown was an umbrella term coined by historians to denote the numerous lands and kingdoms of the Habsburg dynasty, especially for those of the Austrian line beginning in 1273.

v   Six hundred hectares is around 1,500 acres.

Phil shook his head.

"Then today, you're in luck."

They switched mounts and rode back into the forest. Phil could not believe his good fortune. Nor could he believe the sensations he felt. The stallion's rippling muscles sent waves of movement through his legs and chills up his spine. His gait was so smooth that Phil felt like he was riding on a magic carpet.

Phil's mind was completely immersed in the moment—the bob of his hips above the saddle, the billow of the stallion's thick, flowing mane, the resplendence of the forest and the shadows he cast. The American soldier was struck by an overwhelming impression of symbiosis—of two separate organisms in intimate closeness in a relationship that benefited both. Not becoming one but acting as one. His respect for the Lipizzaner welled up, and he somehow sensed the sentiment was mutual.

As they came to a halt, Lessing almost whispered, "Few men in the world know what you're feeling now, Lieutenant."

Phil couldn't help it. He was so overjoyed that as his eyes filled with tears, he bent over to softly stroke the Lipizzaner's neck. He noted that Lessing's smile was warm, and he looked emotional as well. No words were exchanged, but Phil knew instantly they were kindred spirits.

After a few more minutes of riding, Lessing had them exchange horses.

"Why don't we take these stallions on a run and a jump?" the German captain suggested. "There's a cross-country steeplechase course we could follow back to the plane. Are you up to it? It's an advanced course!"

It was Phil's turn to smile. "I am! But is Tuckern?"

"He may only be seven-eighths Thoroughbred, Lieutenant, but he's one of the fastest and best jumpers we have. That's why I brought him. My guess is he's more than ready to try *you* out, sir."

Lessing spurred his Lipizzaner. Phil only needed to lean forward and to the side, and Tuckern, sensing his rider's wishes, bolted in chase. The men raced over creeks and log obstacles, around copses, and through clearings. With each seemingly more difficult jump, Phil leaned forward in the saddle, and Tuckern would take off like a rocket. Phil had not felt such happiness since he'd rescued horses in southern France. The war—no, the whole world with all of its anxieties and trauma—melted away.

After several heart-pounding but exhilarating minutes, they approached the clearing. Captain Lessing indicated they should slow, and they then carefully approached the forest's edge. All looked peaceful across the field. The men were still seated around the fire, which had a curl of gray smoke wafting up to the sky.

"Race you again!" Lessing yelled, and the men were off. The horses pounded side by side across the field with Tuckern pulling away at the end.

Phil and Tuckern slid to a muddy halt at the camp first. Both men laughed. Phil thought, *Two warhorses mounted on two splendid warhorses.*

He quickly dismounted, handed the reins to Lessing, and held out his hand. The two men shook, smiling, with silent words of respect passing through the eyes of each equestrian and bonded by their love and dedication to these amazing animals. The war may have made them one-time enemies, but these magnificent animals gave them a common ground—and friendship.

"I'll take your message back," Phil said. "Pray for a safe journey for us."

"I will. I'll let you know if your friend is here as a POW." He reined his horse around and, with Tuckern in tow, trotted off.

Quickly, Phil tensed his lips and whistled. Tuckern's ears shot forward, and his front legs extended as he skidded to a halt and tried to turn back toward Phil.

Lessing laughed as he pulled on the Thoroughbred's reins and turned around. "I think he's taken a liking to you, Lieutenant."

Phil smiled and waved as the German captain and the horses trotted away.

"Get what you needed, Lieutenant?" the pilot asked.

"More than I imagined." Phil looked at the pilot. "Fuel?"

He looked up at the low-lying clouds. "Filled to the brim. Weather's still in our favor. Plus, the resistance guys got word your regiment has moved by truck over twenty miles to a town called Rieneck. Turns out we only have to fly 150 miles home. We should have a safe flight."

The pilot was right on target. After an uneventful flight, Phil and the pilot landed safely, not far from Rieneck.

Phil couldn't wait to tell the big brass about what he'd seen and learned.

43

HELMET TRICK

"War was the most selfless work I ever did. The
experience was dreadful, sobering, and maturing, but
when you survived it, it was elevating."

—Unknown[225]

Upon arrival from Czechoslovakia, Phil spent the rest of the afternoon
debriefing with division intelligence. That evening, he was honored to
share dinner at the Division CP with General O'Daniel, Colonel McGarr, and
Major Scott. His report engrossed his superiors.[226]

"Something will come of this," General O'Daniel predicted.

Then it was back to the war. The next morning, Phil returned to his
company with cheers and a rousing rendition of "For He's a Jolly Good
Fellow."[i] Of course, he could not discuss his mission with anyone. He could
only say he had been on an assignment for Cobra.

After being in division reserve for five days, the 30th Infantry returned to
action on April 5, 1945, leaving its assembly area west of Rieneck early that
morning in cold, rainy conditions. The men encountered steep terrain and
quickly outpaced their armor, thwarting the speed of their advance. The men's
progress was radioed back to battalion as "slow, but sure."[227]

---

i   "For He's a Jolly Good Fellow" was a popular song sung to congratulate a person on a significant
event, such as a promotion or a birthday. The tune is of French origin and dates to the 18th century.

At 1305 hours, they met their first resistance entering the town of Wolfsmünster. Phil's Love Company pressed forward, followed by several tanks. When one of his rifle platoons encountered stiff resistance, the officer leading the platoon was shot through the head and instantly killed by a sniper. He was an OCS grad, a recent replacement, and must have been leading from the front. The phrase *Follow me can be fuckin' fatal* from Benning flashed through Phil's thoughts once again.

"We're pinned down and can't move up!" the radio blared. Phil and his Executive Officer, Abe Fitterman, ran up and found the men crouched behind a building. The officer's body was lying in the middle of the street; what was left of his head rested in a pool of blood.

"Helluva sniper," the sergeant warned them. "He can shoot a fly off the top of your helmet. We think he's shooting from the town square—maybe an office building or the church. About 250, 300 yards up the road. There must be Krauts in every building up and down the street, firing on anything that moves. Want to call in artillery?"

Phil took off his helmet, leaned over his sergeant, who was kneeling, and slowly pushed his helmet around the corner. He was not surprised when the helmet was cracked out of his hand by a sniper bullet.

"Damn! He *is* good!" Then again, Phil knew that most German snipers were accurate up to 400 yards.

"German sniper rifles have a five-round internal box magazine, right?" Abe asked.

"Haven't seen one with more," Phil answered. "Yet."

"If he didn't reload, and I doubt he did, he's got four shots left."

Abe came around Phil and crouched down behind him and the kneeling sergeant. "I've got an idea, Lieutenant."

"I'm all ears."

"You guys each have a fifteen-round magazine in your Garands?"

Phil and the sergeant nodded.

"Sergeant, you take the low position. Phil, you take high. On my signal, aim your rifles around the building and begin rapid fire toward the church, but don't expose any body parts and only release six or seven shots."

"What do you have in mind?" Phil asked.

"After he shoots back, I'm going to sprint across the street and see if I can get a bead on the guy. I ought to have a better angle from over there. So, cover me by blasting out the rest of your magazine."

Phil nodded and moved into position alongside his sergeant, their rifles poised.

"On the count of three," Abe instructed. "One-two-three!"

Phil and the sergeant began firing blindly. Within seconds, three or four sniper bullets blasted the corner of the brick building, spraying fragments over the men, who pulled their guns back. A second later, Abe hotfooted it to the other side of the street without drawing a shot.

The three-second rule, Phil thought, happy that Abe had just enough time to sprint the thirty feet or so across the road. Fortunately, the sniper had emptied his magazine and did not have time to snap in another and shoot.

Safe behind a building on the other side of the road, Abe yelled to Phil, "One more time, Lieutenant!"

Then he pulled a hand mirror out of his belt pack. "On my signal, do the helmet trick again."

"Damn, Abe! We're gonna run out of helmets before the bastard runs out of ammo."

Abe smiled as he lay on the ground, positioning the mirror around the edge of the building so he could examine the street. Several blocks away, on the other side of the town square, sat an ancient stone church with a rectangular stone steeple and a stone balcony around it.

That's probably it, he thought. *That's where the sonofabitch is perched. Either on the balcony or in one of the windows. I'm guessing a window. Safe from grenades or mortar.*

"Okay!" he yelled. "Now!"

The sniper took the bait and easily nailed the sergeant's helmet, allowing Fitterman to see the muzzle flash emitting from a small window near the top of the steeple.

"He's in the top of the church steeple. About three blocks up the street."

"I'll call in two bazooka squads and a tank to come up pronto," Phil said.

Within a matter of minutes, all arrived. Phil signaled the tank to go around the corner and take out the steeple.

Machine gun, rifle, and small arms fire erupted from buildings on either side of the street, ricocheting off the tank's front and turret. Phil knew the sniper would not fire on the tank and give away his position.

The Sherman moved up to—but not over—the officer's body. The tank barrel slowly raised. Phil smiled as he realized the sniper now knew he'd been found out. *Probably crapping in his pants and jumping down the steps as fast as possible*, Phil thought. *But we're gonna nail his ass!*

With one single blast from its 76-mm cannon, the steeple disintegrated. Fragments of lumber and limestone rained onto the town center. One of the intact church bells tumbled to the cobblestone street below, releasing several resounding gongs as it careened off the side of the church and bounced along the road, making more noise. As if in slow motion, Phil watched the sniper tumble through the air until the lifeless body thudded onto the cobblestones.

Phil had the tank provide cover while he ordered one bazooka team and half his men to cross the street quickly. The bazooka men blasted an entry into the closest building on their side of the road. Using the technique they had perfected in France, the bazooka handlers moved inside and began blasting holes from one building to another, one at a time. By the time they reached the town square, where all resistance had ended, the men had killed five, wounded eleven, and captured 125 German soldiers.

As they walked into the town square, Abe checked out the dead sniper.

"Lieutenant!" he yelled. "Come see this." He was rolling the dead body over when Phil walked up.

"Well, I'll be!" Phil exclaimed as he and the men gathered around. At their feet was a young and attractive woman dressed in civilian clothes. The GIs had seen increasing numbers of civilian snipers, but this was the first German female fighter any of the men had seen.

"Why the hell didn't she shoot and scoot?" Abe asked.

"Suicide mission?" proposed one of the men.

"Maybe an SS mistress?" wondered another. "No matter. Her sorry ass is dead and headed straight to hell."

"Let's move out!" Phil barked.[ii]

Throughout the night, the regiment advanced east and northeast, taking all assigned objectives en route, inflicting severe damage to enemy equipment and taking many more POWs.

ଏଓ

The following day, April 6, 1945, a cobalt sky couldn't decide whether to issue sprinkles or deliver a dousing rain shower.[228]

Company L joined Company I in clearing several villages before moving out toward the east. Their goal for the day: the village of Oberthulba. That morning, they passed upturned and bombed-out enemy vehicles with dead drivers and crew scattered about, the result of sweeping strikes from P-47 Thunderbolts that strafed and bombed the German column to oblivion. Phil watched impassively as two gray-haired civilian men struggled to lift and toss the stiffening corpses onto a horse-drawn wagon.

The lieutenant studied his map, which showed pastureland bordered by thick forests on each side. Between their position and Oberthulba was a main north-south highway—Motorway 7—which could be an excellent defense point. Because of their rapid movement, Phil was concerned that their artillery was lagging and wouldn't be available to support them in case of an attack. He cocked his head toward the clearing heavens, where the developments were more welcoming.

---

ii   Later, Phil nominated Abe Fitterman for a Silver Star "for gallantry in action," which he was awarded.

Looks like we'll be able to call in some air support if it's needed, he thought.

He assigned his 1st Platoon to penetrate the forest to the north and his 3rd Platoon to the south. His 2nd Platoon, trailed by tanks and TDs, would stay with him and follow a single-lane road slicing through green pasture-land. From his vantage point, he observed flanking riflemen working their way slowly through thick underbrush and woods. The platoons stayed in touch with him by radio but encountered no resistance.

Phil was apprehensive that they might be walking into a trap—and wished his command had given him time to send scouting patrols up front. As he surveyed forested land up ahead with his field glasses, a battalion Jeep drove up with Colonel James E. Chaney in the passenger seat. After Phil briefed the colonel, Chaney said that he didn't share his concern about being attacked.

"Lieutenant, resistance has been light," he said. "Intelligence doesn't see that changing as long as we keep moving, so get your men out of the woods and onto the road. Let's get across the motorway and into Oberthulba as quickly as possible. I'd like you to clear the town before dark. If you move your men to the road, they'll make a hell of a lot better time."

Phil was unsure what all the rush was about, but his job was to follow orders. "Yes, sir," he said, immediately radioing his men with instructions to make their way back to the road and double-time it.

As the men moved out of the woods, however, an enormous eruption of small arms and machine gun fire burst out from the woods directly ahead. The GIs instinctively hit the ground and returned fire. A tsunami of bullets whistled overhead and was so concentrated that Phil couldn't initially differentiate between friendly and enemy fire. He motioned to Fitterman and the rest of his CP staff to follow him as he moved them up and into a gully.

The road ahead curved slightly to the left as it left the pastureland and entered a strip of forest. Phil could not see Motorway 7, but he knew that the highway was nearby. Then the enemy fire suddenly stopped. Only an occasional rifle shot could be heard. He called the platoon leaders to determine what was happening.

"Hit a thick line of Krauts," answered one of his lieutenants. "Damnedest thing. Looks like a company made up of young boys and old men."

"I don't care what their ages are. We gotta take them out," Phil said.

Yelling to one of the radiomen, he issued an order: "Call battalion. Get the A&P platoon up here pronto with as much M1 and BAR ammo as they can carry." Next, he radioed his up-front men and found out that both platoons had taken a few casualties but were intact and ready for orders.

"Ammo's coming up," Phil said. "We need to advance immediately, before those bastards have time to reach the protection of Oberthulba. What about moving forward with marching fire?" he asked.

Phil had trained his men to use their M1s, BARs, and even machine guns while using marching fire. Infantrymen kept the butt of their rifles halfway between their belts and their right armpits, shooting one round every two to three steps. For machine gun units, one man carried and fired the heavy gun while another walked alongside him with the ammo belt.

"Hell, yes, we can do that," his lieutenant answered.

"When mortar fire and tanks start firing over your heads, that's your go signal."

"Roger."

On Phil's command, the mortars began their fire, followed by powerful fusillades from the tank and TD machine guns. As their tracers lit up the air, the riflemen separated into one long skirmish line. After a minute or two of fierce covering fire, Phil gave the attack order. The men rose in unison and walked forward with an unremitting march of fire.

"Damn!" Phil exclaimed as he watched the action through his field binoculars, "What a beautiful thing."

"You got that right," Fitterman commented.

Together, they saw virtually no return fire as the infantrymen moved quickly up to and into the forest that had been shredded by the covering fire.

Radio reports streamed back to Phil. No casualties on the American side, but many enemy soldiers were killed or giving up. The rest were racing to Oberthulba, where they could regroup and reorganize.

"Let's go!" Phil yelled as he jumped into a company Jeep, followed by Fitterman. In no time, they arrived at an intersection marked by the highway overpass. A massive log roadblock stopped their progress, but one of his Sherman tanks with a heavy steel blade easily pushed the barricade out of the way.

Up ahead was Oberthulba, a quaint farming village of a couple of thousand people, smack dab in the middle of Germany. Phil radioed Battalion S-3 and learned that artillery was ready to support him. A small amount of air support was also available if needed. That was the good news. The bad news was that Oberthulba was likely heavily fortified and defended.

Phil and Abe drew up a quick battle plan for a three-platoon frontal attack.

The time was four o'clock in the afternoon. Phil relayed the news to his lieutenants in the field that if the next couple of hours went well, then they would billet inside a lovely home in Oberthulba that night.

Phil knew the idea of a hot bath and a soft bed would keep his men motivated and morale high for one more day.

And war was a day-by-day proposition, wasn't it?

44

PERFECT TIMING

"I'm convinced that the Infantry is the group in the Army which gives more and gets less than anybody else."

—Bill Mauldin, American cartoonist famous for his sardonic drawings about the lives of World War II combat soldiers[229]

On the approach into Oberthulba, Phil had three Sherman tanks and TDs at his disposal, one for each platoon. Using the tanks as cover, the three platoon leaders set up heavy machine gun nests in shallow ditches.[230]

As the platoons began to move forward, significant fire came from enemy machine guns in the forests on both sides of the village. Phil's tanks and heavy machine gunners quickly silenced them. Several white flags were raised above one enemy machine gun nest, but the flags disappeared when a mortar shell disintegrated the nest and presumably the men in it.

Phil had his flanking platoons use their BARs and light machine guns to lay down suppressing fire along the forest edge. Then he looked at his watch. In two minutes, a ten-minute-long artillery barrage would commence. The shelling aimed at the town center would give him and his men a distinct advantage. He called the timing to his platoon leaders and heard the roar of tanks as they prepared to move forward with the infantrymen advancing behind them.

"Do not move forward until 1708 hours, two minutes before the artillery ends," Phil barked into the radio handset. The goal was for the men and tanks to hit the edge of town just as the barrage ended.

Precisely on time, at 1700 hours, the preparatory barrage began. Like all frontline men, Phil loved the sound of artillery—as long as it was his own. Wave after wave of artillery shells whistled overhead, as if taking flight from the forest directly behind them, sailing over the treetops and the advancing men, and pouring into the town in one roaring explosion after another. A cacophony of smaller eruptions from M1 mortars[i] joined in the fiery mayhem. Then an unusual and unexpected surprise descended upon the Germans.

A half dozen roaring and shiny P-47s emerged from the skies, the setting sun's rays reflected on their silver bodies and wings. They swooped down over the village and unleashed their 50-caliber machine guns while raining down more bombs. In a few short minutes, the combination of artillery and air fire-power had turned Oberthulba into a fiery inferno.

The P-47s roared back up into the sky, each steeply banking, and then returned for a second strafing run with their machine guns and cannons unloading out a hailstone of red-hot lead and explosive shells before disappearing to the west. Meanwhile, artillery continued to whistle overhead and explode in the town.

Two minutes before the artillery was scheduled to stop, Phil radioed out commands to prepare to seize the village. He could see his trained veterans, with scattered but now battle-tested replacements, crouched and ready to spring. Phil wondered how anyone could have survived the thrashing the town had taken, but he knew that the stone buildings contained cellars where the enemy could patiently wait out the barrage.

The tanks began to rev their engines. Phil counted down the seconds: ten, nine, eight….

"Attack!" he yelled into the radio. "All platoons attack!"

He prayed he had the timing right as artillery shells continued to fall. The tanks edged forward with some of the men following behind them. Other soldiers spread out, using marching fire in their approach formation. The tanks moved slowly enough for the men to keep up. The tank machine guns and cannons spewed fire. Time almost seemed to stand still. Rounds from the light and heavy machine guns, punctuated by tracers, once again formed an umbrella of molten lead and steel over the advancing men's heads.

When the men were within fifty yards of the town's outer edge, the artillery fire stopped. Beyond thick billows of swirling smoke, orange flames reached into the air from an untold number of burning buildings.

Phil's chest swelled with pride, and his spirit overflowed with gratitude. The coordination and formations of men, air power, artillery, and armor were

---

i   The M1 mortar was an American 81-millimeter caliber mortar.

textbook perfect. He hadn't seen an attack this precise and well-coordinated carried out for the entire war—even since training back at the Alliance Air Base. He wished his superiors were here to see his men perform.

He heaved a sigh of relief as the men and armor quickly infiltrated the edge of town and vanished into the smoke and maelstrom. Phil was just about to command his CP men to move forward when a pair of German machine gun nests opened up from each side of the town. The nest to the north was perched in the upper part of a large barn, while the machine gun nest to the south sat behind a large haystack.

Without having to radio a command, the 1st Platoon Sherman turned, and with one expertly placed shell from its 76-mm cannon, disintegrated the barn into a ball of fire and smoke. On the other side of the village, almost at the same moment, two of his 3rd Platoon's heavy machine guns rained scorching hot lead shells into the haystack, which instantly erupted ablaze. He saw at least two Germans, their bodies engulfed in flames, trying to escape. They didn't get but a few steps before machine guns cut them into flaming pieces of flesh.

Phil and his CP men, including his Executive Officer Abe Fitterman, began to double-time toward the village center. To his utter surprise, the main road was littered with dead and dying Germans of every imaginable age—from young teens to older men.

So, this is what the end looks like.

Phil had heard from Colonel McGarr that the German High Command had ordered fanatical "last man" stands at every town to give the Nazis more time to prepare defenses in larger cities. The Krauts were sending their least effective soldiers—the very old and very young known as the *Volkssturm*ii—to the front lines, no doubt saving their best troops for the very end.

As he entered the main road into the burning village at 1730, after just twenty minutes of overwhelming, stiff—but fleeting—opposition, Phil spotted a parade of around one hundred dazed and shocked German soldiers being marched to the rear, their hands clasped behind their heads. Many were wounded and bleeding. All seemed stunned and confused. As Phil and Abe moved down the street, his men were shoving other German prisoners out of buildings on either side of the road. The Kraut soldiers looked terrified as the GIs shouted commands and pushed them forward with the tips of their rifle barrels.

The German POWs were generally easy to handle. Still, Phil knew that it was the officers he had to watch out for, especially those who were part of the SS, the military branch of the Nazi Party's organization. There were stories

ii   The *Volkssturm* was a national militia established by Nazi Germany during the last months of World War II. The militia was not set up by the German Army but by the Nazi Party on the orders of Adolf Hitler. It was staffed by conscripting males between the ages of sixteen and sixty years who were not already serving in some military unit, and it comprised one of the final desperate components of the war.

that SS officers were shooting fellow German soldiers who waved white flags, advanced toward the Allied lines with their hands up, or surrendered. Maybe that's why these prisoners looked so nervous.

Phil recalled how just a week earlier, in the center of one small German town, one of his men had brought out an older man, a German civilian, in a crumpled suit, carrying a small white handkerchief that he waved over his head. "He's the mayor," the private explained. "Here to surrender."

The town mayor kept looking nervously over his shoulder, which aroused Phil's instincts. He put his hand on his holstered Colt .45, unlatched the holster flap, lifted the gun slightly, and clicked off the safety. At that moment, an SS officer stepped out of the shadows with his 9-mm Luger drawn.

The German SS soldier shot the old man in the head, to everyone's shock. Then he immediately swerved to fire at Phil when Phil dropped to one knee, drew his pistol, and rapidly fired twice, using a combat two-handed grip. The SS man's forehead and chest exploded as he was blown backward, dead before he hit the pavement. Phil's men were not surprised; they had seen his expert marksmanship many times.

In Oberthulba, four SS officers were shoved out of a building and onto the street by several GIs. Suddenly, an SS officer lunged at one of his men's rifles. The GI hit the German in the shoulder with the steel butt plate of his Garand, knocking him to the ground.

Like an angry bull, the frenzied SS officer leaped off the ground and attacked. The GI hit him in the head with the butt plate, sending him reeling to the cobblestoned street a second time. The SS officer, dazed and bloody, slowly pulled himself to his knees and then charged again.

This time the German soldier was struck so hard in the head that he never got up.

"Damn," Abe Fitterman muttered to Phil. "SS officers are unpredictable SOBs."

Phil nodded. "No doubt, they're the elite of the German Army system. Unfortunately, they're worshiping the wrong god. Hitler's leading them all to hell."

"Happy to send this one there early, Lieutenant," the GI with the rifle said.

෴

That evening, after everything was buttoned up in Oberthulba, Phil was hoping for orders to find a CP and billet for the night, but it was not to be. The men were ordered to keep moving. Three miles further east, the company arrived just outside the town of Albertshausen at midnight, where they were met by light enemy resistance. By 0225 on the morning of April 7, 1945,

Company L had taken and cleared the town. The men's morale was excellent. It had been, by all counts, a perfect day.[231]

Phil made sure his Love Company men billeted in the best houses in town. Residents were awakened with a loud knock and were told they had *fünf minuten*—five minutes—to leave. Following one family's hasty departure, Phil and his men entered the home, where one of the men started a fire in the living room fireplace. Smoke began to fill the room. Turned out the chimney wasn't drawing. After opening the damper and clearing the air, one of his men investigated and found the chimney flue stuffed with smoked hams and sausages that the family had tried to hide. The banquet was shared with several houses. With full tummies, the GIs luxuriated with a hot shower and slept in duvet-covered beds with thick, soft mattresses.

For some reason, though, Phil couldn't sleep, even though he was pleased most of his men were inside a warm home with a full stomach and a comfortable bed. He spent time visiting each of the sentries and men in the outposts.

He loved leading Company L, loved his guys, and admired the tenacity they were showing in the last stages of a long war. He sensed the Germans couldn't hold out much longer, not after what he'd seen that afternoon. There were rumors that the Russian Army would arrive at the city gates of Berlin any day now.

Phil didn't care who got there first.

Now that victory was in sight, he just wanted this war to be over and go home.

45

NO SPA DAY

"Officers and men under my command…established records that were not equaled by others in this war and have not been excelled in any other to my knowledge. In large measure, these magnificent accomplishments… passed without full recognition."

—Lieutenant General Lucian K. Truscott, Jr.[232]

After daybreak and a warm, filling breakfast on a chilly spring morning with unlimited visibility, Phil and his men in Company L jumped off from Albertshausen in the direction of the town of Bad Kissingen, which boasted a world-famed spa noted for its fine mineral springs and numerous resort hotels.[i] Twenty-eight hostelries had been converted into German military hospitals, whose red-crossed roofs had saved the city from Allied bombing.[233]

In the early afternoon of April 7, 1945, at 1315 hours, Phil received an unusual radio call from one of his platoon leaders, Lieutenant Emil T. Byke, who was leading a reconnaissance patrol.

---

i   Bad Kissingen had first been developed as a spa in the 1500s and grew to be a fashionable resort in the 19th century, when it was rebuilt during the reign of King Ludwig I of Bavaria. Crowned heads of state, including Empress Elisabeth of Austria, Tsar Alexander II of Russia, Imperial Chancellor Otto von Bismarck, and King Ludwig II of Bavaria (also called "Mad King Ludwig" and best known for his construction of Neuschwanstein, the castle Walt Disney used to model his own Sleeping Beauty Castle at Disneyland) were among the guests.

"Love 6," Byke began, "one of my squad leaders reported a vehicle just outside Bad Kissingen, displaying a white flag. I went to verify the report and found three German military personnel in the vehicle. I approached the Germans with coverage all around and was greeted by two German officers who, in broken English, asked if I would go into the town of Bad Kissingen with them and meet their commander. They want to surrender."

"Were the officers SS?" Phil asked. The memories of what had happened in Oberthulba the day before were fresh in his mind.

"Nope."

"Permission granted. Just be sure to take a well-armed Jeep or two with you."

"Yes, sir."

As the HQ Company moved forward, Byke radioed back an hour later. "Love 6, the damnedest thing just happened."

"What?"

"When we arrived in Bad Kissingen, we were met by a German soldier who couldn't have been more than fourteen years old. He was carrying a white flag and spoke excellent English. We followed him to the town square, which was filled with German soldiers who had stacked their arms in piles before us. Two bodies were hanging from the city hall balcony. They were two local officials who wanted to surrender. SS troopers had hung them as traitors."

"Are the SS guys still around?" Phil asked.

"Flew the coop," Byke replied. "The German officers presented me to their commander. Through the kid, this commander told me that he wished to surrender and wants me to convey the message up the ladder. I agreed to do that, but before we departed, he took us to a nearby hospital. We found a bunch of our wounded GIs there. They were all crying with joy at seeing us. Some of the boys hugged me and wanted to know if they were going home. I told them that we were at the gates of the city and that I would return as fast as possible."

"Good work," Phil said.

"Thanks, but that's not all. You should have seen the dirty looks we got from the wounded and sick German soldiers. I especially remember one proud Kraut. He was sitting in front of a large window with his hands folded, medals all over his chest, giving everybody the evil eye. I could have shot the SOB!"

"I bet you could have. Well done," Phil said. "I'll pass your report on."

Phil radioed battalion and was put in touch with Lieutenant Colonel James E. Chaney, the battalion commander. After relaying the news, Chaney told Phil to meet him outside of town at Byke's Jeep.

When Phil and Abe arrived, they found Lieutenant Byke had placed his men at advantageous points on the hills surrounding Bad Kissingen. At the same time, Company M, commanded by 1st Lieutenant Harold J. Saine, brought up mortars and placed them in firing position "just in case." He then sent two squads inside the city for reconnaissance.

While they waited for a report, Byke gave Phil an update on the resort town's military hospitals. "All the wounded GIs appear to have been well cared for. They said the bedding, bandages, and entire area was as clean and orderly as any hospital you might imagine. They're impressed with everything; except they say the nurses look like battle axes. Big and mean-looking. Nothing like our gals."

Just then, Colonel Chaney's Jeep screeched to a halt. Phil and Byke updated him on the latest developments. It was looking like they could safely meet the German commander in the town center to discuss terms of the surrender. With two squads of riflemen providing protection, they slowly drove their Jeeps into the resort town, encountering no hostile fire. As they drove through the quiet streets, the colonel whistled.

"Look at this. The buildings are completely unscratched," Chaney said. "I guess our guys in their hospitals saved their asses. Otherwise, this place would have been destroyed."

Their delegation was met at the center of town in front of City Hall, where a German general and his command officers were waiting for their arrival. All were unarmed.

After handshakes, they sat down in an office. The first question Colonel Chaney asked was this: "Do you understand what unconditional surrender is?"

The reply from the German side was affirmative.

"As you know," Chaney continued, "Bad Kissingen is an important rail and highway center. Because its spacious buildings can easily accommodate thousands of troops, Bad Kissingen is a highly desirable military prize. I must emphasize that the 3rd Division will not accept Bad Kissingen as an 'open city,' however. It will be used as a military base for United States troops. Is that acceptable?"

As if you have a choice, buster, Phil thought.

The general nodded his approval, and that was that.

Phil walked back with Chaney to a Jeep with a radioman. The colonel called Regimental Commander, Colonel McGarr, at 1650 hours.

"I accepted the surrender of the Germans in Bad Kissingen," Chaney told McGarr. "There are around 2,800 patients in two dozen or so hospitals in the town, and the German general said he and his staff would be responsible for the German wounded. I've arranged to get our Red Cross folks up here with cigarettes and chocolate for our American POWs."

After the report, Phil, Abe, and several of their men walked around the town, rifles slung over their shoulders. They came across a factory that manufactured dress suits. They went inside the factory, where they took turns putting on high hats and bow ties with their dirty uniforms, laughing at the incongruous look. There were also bolts and bolts of silk fabric—white, shiny, and smooth to the touch. The men didn't have the foggiest idea why the Germans were still making such finery in time of war. The men cut off pieces of the satiny fabric to make handsome scarves, which they draped around their necks and under their collars, giving a regal appearance.

For a fleeting moment, the war was forgotten.

Meanwhile, the 3rd Battalion rounded up German prisoners in Bad Kissingen, capturing 2,825 that day, a record for the division. That night, the Regimental CP set up in a beautiful hotel just on the outskirts of town. When Colonel McGarr arrived, he made the men wipe their feet before they walked into the marble-floored lobby.

Phil and his men stayed in a ritzy hotel in the center of town that night. After placing guards and outposts, the men were served a hot meal, received clean clothes, and were handed their mail. Most of the men were nearly giddy with the opportunity to write letters and enjoy some good food. For the second night in a row, they slept on mattresses.

The Love Company officers enjoyed a nightcap and cigars together, dog-tired but proud of the battles and victories of the three previous days. In many ways, everything had gone perfectly.

Abe blew a ring of smoke and looked at Phil. "I can feel it in my bones," he said. "This damn war is almost over."

"Hope you're right, Abe," Phil said softly. "Hope you're right."

❧

As Phil and his men slept, Colonel McGarr received orders just after midnight that jump-off was scheduled for 0730 hours the next morning, April 8. An Intelligence officer, however, warned McGarr that his troops better be prepared to enter the long-predicted buzzsaw as they continued their easterly advance. American forces could expect to meet considerable artillery and anti-tank fire and even more fanatical infantry.[234]

Phil and his command officers were awakened at 0300 to receive their orders and prepare for a difficult day. During the early morning briefing, the men were told that the Germans could be expected to try, once again, to slow the 3rd Division's relentless attack, most likely to give the Nazi "bigwigs" a chance to withdraw to the Redoubt area in the Austrian Alps.

What lay ahead for Phil was a day he would never forget.

46

NOWHERE TO GO

"After weeks or months in the line only a wound can offer him the comfort of safety, shelter, and a bed. Those who are left to fight, fight on, evading death but knowing that with each day of evasion they have exhausted one more chance for survival. Sooner or later, unless victory comes, the chase must end on the litter or in the grave."

—General Omar N. Bradley[235]

O n the morning of April 8, 1945, Phil and L Company jumped off Bad Kissingen at 0730 with K Company on their right flank. Passing through pastureland bordered by forests, they reached several successive objectives with minimal resistance, overcoming a small firefight at 0950 hours and another at 1005 hours, followed by defeating Germans at three log roadblocks and bypassing another two.[236]

Several of the skirmishes involved hand-to-hand fighting to the death—in this case, resulting in all German deaths. Phil had to take out a German officer at point-blank range when he tried to pull out his Luger in the process of surrendering. The pistol never left the German's holster before he crashed to the ground, killed instantly by Phil's quick-draw response.

By 1330 hours, both lead companies began encountering significant machine gun and small arms fire from forested areas bordering their zone of advance. Phil hated hearing the guttural blasts from the German Schmeisser machine guns[i] that GIs called "burp guns." After fifteen months of nonstop fighting, he detested the fact that Schmeissers fired at twice the rate of the best American-made counterparts, giving the Krauts a battlefield advantage.

Phil called in heavy artillery time and time again, which stalled progress—a development that neither his officers nor NCOs liked. At 1800 hours, they found themselves moving slowly through a wooded section outside the tiny village of Rottershausen.

As the light began to fade, Phil's company made a flanking move through the dense thicket of trees. They slowed their advance and moved carefully.

Phil found the silence of the woods unnerving. He and his men could feel apprehension in every fiber of their beings. None of them wanted to be the last to die in this war.

The tension was sky-high among his men—higher than any time in the last three days. These were desperate times for the enemy. Intelligence told them that trigger-happy Krauts were infesting the countryside, especially in forested areas, setting up traps and ambushes. Phil was greatly concerned about the dangerous situation developing. His men crept low, darting from tree to tree, most with fingers on their M1 triggers, others hand signaling man to man.

Death could be lurking anywhere in the forest surrounding them. Snipers could be nestled in towering firs or behind their massive bases. Machine gun nests might be hidden behind a camouflage of evergreen boughs prepared to annihilate Phil's frontline troops in a hailstorm of gunfire. On top of that, one well-hidden artillery piece could fire its rounds into the tree canopy, raining splintered wood and white-hot shrapnel that would cut through flesh like hot knives through butter. Death lurked in every direction.

Three of Phil's fast-moving platoons advanced to the south and east as he, Fitterman, and his radioman followed. Phil had his compass in one hand and a field map in the other, continually scanning it with trained eyes and an intuition gained from over a year's experience fighting Germans. He almost always knew what the Krauts were thinking and doing.

Rule of War #15 passed through his mind: *Direction: The compass is the infantry officer's most reliable guide.*[ii] More attacks failed from the loss of direction than from any other cause.[237]

Suddenly, Phil saw something he had missed—a small clearing ahead, surrounded by a forest edge that was slightly elevated over a small meadow. He had Fitterman radio the point men to skirt the field and remain in the forest.

---

i   The Schmeisser, or MP 40 (Maschinenpistole 40), was a submachine gun heavily used by German Infantrymen.
ii   In World War II, the Army used inexpensive lesantic compasses because the "marching compasses" of World War I were too large, too elaborate, and too costly. Phil memorized the "Rules of War" at military board school when they were published in 1939.

The woods ahead suddenly crackled with small arms fire and the deep rasping sounds from the German burp guns.

Damn, he thought. *Too late!*

Suddenly, his radioman's backpack SCR-300 sizzled with distress. "Love 1, this is point squad alpha." It was one of his point squad leaders. His strained voice said, "We've been ambushed in a glade." The sergeant added, "There are nine of us and probably 150 Krauts around us. The rest of the platoon behind us is pinned down. We have four wounded. We're low on ammo. We're in a clearing. Help needed now, sir!"

"Shit," Phil whispered to himself, remembering it was one of his least-experienced squads. He could hear German-type potato masher grenades exploding, answered by American grenades and machine gun fire, adding to the pandemonium. Projecting a calmness he didn't feel, Phil ordered the 1st Platoon on the left flank and the 3rd Platoon on the right to begin an immediate pincer move to save the trapped squad. He also called for a tank. "I need a medium can now!" he bellowed into the radio handset.

He always wondered why he had to call tanks "cans" over the radio. Any German monitor would know what he was referring to. As the battle sounds intensified, he spread his field map on the ground and studied it with Lieutenant Fitterman and their FO, who had just come to the front.

"Our trapped squad must be here," Phil said, pointing to the northwest edge of the only nearby clearing. Turning to his FO, he said, "I need fire massed on the other side of the clearing."

He ran his finger along what appeared to be a forest lane on the map. "Abe, you take over the CP staff. When the first tank gets here, I'll take it to the clearing to get to my guys."

"I'll go," Abe offered. "We need you back here."

Phil remembered Rule of War #14—*Supervision: Leaders must supervise the execution of their orders*. The more untrained the troops, the more detailed the supervision must be.[238]

"This one's on me, Abe."

Phil radioed the trapped patrol. "Fire coming in. Ammo is on its way. First and 3rd platoons are pinching toward you now."

Surprised to hear the rumble of three Sherman tanks behind him instead of the one he'd called for, he radioed his frontline men. "We've got three cans here. We're coming up now!"

The reply was filled with panic. "We're pinned down with marching fire, Love 1! We need help fast!"

As the lead Sherman pulled up, Phil yelled, "Abe, I'm hopping a ride on the lead can! Get artillery firing now!"

Before Abe could object, Phil jumped up on the back of the tank with his radioman in tow. Climbing in behind the turret, he had his radioman hand him an intercom handset that was kept in an empty ammunition container on the back of the tank and stretch the long cord up to him. That would allow him to communicate with the tank commander inside as he signaled to his radioman to hunker down behind him. As the tank lurched forward, Phil prepared the turret-mounted .50-caliber machine gun, unlocking the safety and cocking it. There was not a lot of ammo, but he hoped it would be enough.

His head snapped up at whistling sounds whizzing overhead, just seconds before American artillery projectiles exploded on enemy positions. *That'll sure as hell help me save my guys*, Phil thought. *Maybe help save me too*.

The German MG-42 medium machine guns[iii]—nicknamed "Hitler's buzzsaw" by American GIs—continued erupting at 1,000 to 1,200 rounds per minute to his front. His own men's machine guns gave studied answers at less than half the rate—the American guns sounding like Model Ts compared to the murderous reverberation of the enemy's heavy automatic firearm.

Approaching the clearing, Phil crouched behind the turret as green tracer bullets from enemy machine guns peppered the air from the front, while friendly red tracers came from behind on either side of the tank.

"Our guys are fifty yards ahead! Friendly platoons are coming up from behind on our left and right!" Phil called to the tank commander. Into the radio, he yelled, "Second Platoon, send up your remaining squads, pronto! Each one behind a can as we can move up!"

His men sprinted from the forest to the shelter of the tanks, fanning out across the western edge of the clearing, one on his left flank and the other to his right, bullets churning up dirt around them.

"Shermans, move into the clearing!" Phil commanded into the tank handset. He quickly identified three machine gun nests on the other side of the clearing. The tanks lurched forward as fire poured in, the bullets from multiple snipers missing him by only inches. Phil ordered the gunners inside the tanks to use their 76-mm cannons and .30-caliber machine guns to lay down suppressing fire, while he manned the hundred-pound, turret-mounted .50-caliber machine gun, firing and taking fire all the way. He sprayed bursts across the forest line, silencing several snipers and destroying at least three machine gun nests, momentarily quelling the enemy attack.

"I see our guys!" Phil shouted into the SCR-300 handset. "Between the center and left cans! Twenty yards ahead. Let's get 'em outta here!"

His men emerged from behind the protection of the tanks. As he had trained them, his forward troops laid down a torrent of marching fire as they

---

iii   The MG 42, short for Maschinengewehr 42 or "machine gun 42," was highly reliable and easy to operate. It was most notable for its high cyclic rate, averaging about 1,200 rounds per minute compared to around 450 to 600 rounds for American machine guns like the M1919 Browning or Bren.

advanced toward the trapped soldiers, while others ran up and grabbed the wounded. Enemy fire erupted again, and Phil emptied his remaining ammunition, killing several Kraut soldiers and drawing more hostile fire his squads used the diversion to withdraw.

Out of machine gun ammunition, Phil jumped off the back of the tank to direct his men, miraculously eluding another hail of bullets, dozens missing him by inches. Suddenly the back of his head took a staggering blow as a sniper's bullet blew his helmet from his head, knocking him to the ground. Phil, seeing stars, was momentarily stunned.

As if on autopilot, his eyes quickly scanned the trees as he swung his M1 in the direction of the enemy. Spotting a solitary German sniper in a tree, he took aim and triggered several rounds. The sniper's head exploded, and his body crashed to the earth.

"Got the sonofabitch!" Phil screamed.

The radioman jumped off the tank and pulled Phil closer to the Sherman's hull so they could take cover. The radioman then knelt down and carefully ran his hands through Phil's hair, soaked with blood.

"Just nicked your scalp, Lieutenant, but it's bleeding like hell." He reached into his overcoat, tore the wrapper off a gauze bandage, and pressed it against the wound. He tied the gauze cloth in a knot as another flurry of bullets ricocheted off the tank.

"You okay, sir?" the radioman asked.

Phil refocused his eyes as he became more alert. "Yeah," he said. "Just a scratch."

"It's more than that, sir, but we gotta get out of this hellhole!" the radioman exclaimed.

As Phil and the radioman moved back between the tanks and his retreating men laid down suppressing fire, enemy fire from the far side of the clearing intensified, coming from three directions. His men started running as fast as they could for the protection of the trees. Phil was beside the last tank backing out of the clearing, rapidly firing his M1 Garand as bullets shredded the earth around him.

"Take cover!" Phil yelled. He and the radioman grabbed their M1s. The radioman made it behind the rear of tank's hull as Phil followed. Bullets whooshed through the air, just inches away.

"Sniper! Eleven o'clock!" the radioman yelled.

Phil quickly turned and spotted movement in another tree a hundred yards away.

Another bastard is aiming at us!

In a practiced motion, he raised his M1 and squeezed off two swift rounds. The sniper tumbled out of the tree, hitting the ground like a limp rag doll.

His action drew more fire in their direction, intensifying by the second and coming from a wider radius. Phil quickly realized that their position was being overrun. They were too exposed. They needed to get to the safety of the trees.

"We're surrounded! Get the hell outta here! That's an order!" Phil cried out to his radioman. "I'll suppress 'em!"

He and his radioman began firing as they and the tank moved backward and the radioman started sprinting for the wooded forest behind them, a distance of fifty yards. As Phil turned to get a better angle on yet another sniper, a sudden, burning pain seared just below his right knee, as if someone had hit him with a giant club.

He instantly knew he'd been shot in the leg.

Phil crashed to the ground, groaning in pain. His entire right leg felt numb as blood gushed from a massive wound. Fear surged through him as warm liquid filled his boot.

Then his training kicked in. Phil ripped off his belt and tightened it around his upper leg. Relief flooded him as the spurting flow of blood slowed, but the searing pain brought on nausea.

Looking up, he saw his radioman had also been hit and had fallen to his knees a few yards away. He was holding his hand over an oozing shoulder wound.

"You okay?" Phil yelled.

"Yes, sir. I think it's a through-and-through. Almost no bleeding."

Suddenly, out of the clearing, angels appeared. A number of his men from Headquarters and Headquarters Company (HHC) rushed to their defense and laid down a steel curtain of suppressing fire, giving his executive officer, Abe Fitterman, enough time to come to Phil's aid.

Fitterman squatted next to Phil and pulled up his pants leg. What he saw caused the XO's face to pale a bit.

Phil's first look nearly caused him to faint as well. Just below the right knee, a gnarly wound the size of a golf ball was still leaking blood. The torturous pain was something he'd never experienced before—way beyond all his previous wounds, including the major injury he'd suffered in the same leg in France.

Abe reached over to the radio on the back of the radioman and grabbed the handset.

"S-3, this is Love-5. Larimore's been hit."

"How badly?" It was the gravelly voice of Colonel McGarr.

Abe smiled at Phil. "He's tough. He'll live, but he has a hole through his leg about the size of a silver dollar."

"Get him out. Now!" came the order from the colonel.

"Yes, sir. Love-5 out."

Abe handed the handset to the radioman. "Phil, the men are safe. Let's get the hell out of here and regroup in the woods."

Phil, his face twisted in pain, looked at Fitterman. "Abe, you get my radioman outta here."

"After I help you, Phil."

"I think it missed the bone, Fitt."

Phil wasn't sure if that was true. What he saw was a much bigger wound than he expected. "I can walk! I'll use my Garand as a crutch. I'll be right behind you."

Fitterman looked at him, skepticism written on his face.

"Abe," Phil said sternly, "get him out and call down a TOT[iv] on this clearing and the woods behind. We've gotta stop this now. You hear me?"

"I don't like leaving you. You can't walk. You'll be a sitting duck."

"Go! The TOT will protect me."

Abe grabbed the radioman, and they ran behind the retreating Sherman as enemy fire from the far edge of the forest intensified and poured in from three directions.

Suddenly, as mortar fire began to shred the clearing, scores of Germans poured out of the woods. Phil tried to stand, but an unimaginably excruciating pain shot up his leg. He collapsed as bullets shredded the dirt around him. Seeking cover to save his life, he managed to quickly roll away from the tank treads and into a shallow ditch.

Although his artillery and armor fusillade had broken the attack momentarily, Phil could tell they had only temporarily slowed the enemy advance. He could only pray Fitterman would call in the more concentrated TOT he had ordered to end this onslaught and end it now.

As the Krauts inched closer and closer, an ear-deafening concussion was followed by dirt and mud raining across Phil's body. A mortar had landed only a few yards from him; thank goodness the shallow bank of the ditch provided some protection.

As the TOT intensified, he began to quietly pray—that he'd survive the wound, that he'd see his parents again. In the craziness and danger of the moment, a tune flashed through his mind:

I'll be home for Christmas. You can plan on me.

The melody was shattered by the growing fusillade from his guys, mixed with the fanatical shrieking of onrushing Krauts and their hail of small arms

---

iv   Time on Target (TOT) is the military coordination of artillery and mortar fire by many weapons so that all the munitions arrive at the target at roughly the same time. The military standard for coordinating a time-on-target strike is plus or minus three seconds from the prescribed time of impact.

fire, causing him to rub the dirt from his eyes. Tracers and bullets screamed past, inches above his head. Despite the unbearable agony, Phil slowly rolled over and peeked out of the ditch. He felt the color drain from his face as he saw crazed Germans running toward him, screaming wildly like banshees, firing as fast as they could. Less than twenty to thirty yards from him, and they were closing fast.

Phil pressed his head into the ground, suppressing the urge to vomit. As waves of pain, nausea, and mind-numbing fear shot through him, he turned limp and played dead. The ruse worked; within seconds, the enemy soldiers leaped over the ditch and kept running.

Not daring to move, Phil thought, *They didn't see me moving. Maybe I'll make it.*

Then, the same melody played in his mind:

Please have snow and mistletoe and presents on the tree.

A tsunami wave of friendly artillery exploded around him. The earth shook mercilessly from blast after blast.

Thank God for the 155s. They'll save my men. Maybe me too.

Phil felt clumps of moist loam shower down on him. He knew the earthen covering would not save him from a direct hit, but maybe it would hide him from the enemy surrounding him.

The violent blasts of the raging battle around him strangely began to wane. Phil's eyes clouded, and his peripheral vision dimmed. The overwhelming pain began to melt away.

He understood what was happening: he was bleeding out, and he didn't have the strength to tighten the belt around his leg that was serving as a tourniquet. Soon the world around him was silent, and his body completely numb.

So, this is what it feels like to die. Not as bad as I imagined.

Tired beyond measure, he closed his eyes. He felt strangely at peace. His breathing slowed. He began to recite the Lord's Prayer.

Although he would miss his mother and father terribly, he looked forward to meeting his Father in heaven. On the eighth day of April 1945, he knew that his long, grueling war was over.

I'll be home for Christmas, if only in my dreams.

47
THE SOUND OF A GUNSHOT

"This war proceeds along its terrible path by the slaughter of Infantry.... It is the fighting part that is the true measure of your military, and the only true measure."

—British Prime Minister Winston Churchill[239]

On Sunday, April 8, 1945, at 11:30 a.m., Philip Sr. and Ethyl Larimore were attending a worship service at St. Luke's United Methodist Church in Memphis. As the pastor prayed, Philip felt his wife startle.

At first, he wondered if she had dozed off. He looked at her and noticed she had broken out in a sweat and was trembling. After their eyes met, he recognized the fear in her face. Then Ethyl stood and walked rapidly out to the vestibule, pulling a handkerchief from her purse.

Philip followed her to the foyer, where he found her seated on a bench, crying uncontrollably. He sat down and embraced his crying wife, not knowing what else to do.

After a moment, her sobs turned to moaning and then quiet weeping. She was able to mutter the words, "While the pastor was praying, I heard a gunshot."

"I didn't hear anything," Philip said, tightening his arm around her.

"Not here. In Germany. Junior's been shot. I know it."

It was precisely 6:30 p.m. in Germany—the moment Phil had taken a German bullet to the leg.

Philip Sr. believed his wife. He just did not know if his son was dead or alive.

☙❧

At 1850 hours, Colonel McGarr's Jeep skidded to a halt. He and two other men jumped out and ran up to the Love Company CP.[240]

"Update!" McGarr demanded.

"The TOT worked," Lieutenant Fitterman reported. "The enemy line was destroyed. Our guys are mopping up."

"Casualties?" he asked.

"Several wounded. Phil is MIA, but it hasn't been safe to look for him, sir."

"Follow me!" McGarr commanded. The colonel spun on his heels with Fitterman and two of McGarr's men, a medic and a radioman, trailing. "I'm going to find him!"

Headlights off, the Jeep moved slowly in the increasing darkness, the sounds of small arms fire, grenades, and machine guns erupting in spurts from the forest and pastures in front of them. As they came to the edge of the woods, there was just enough light to see that the clearing appeared empty. Smoke, the smell of gunpowder, and the stink of burned flesh clung to the ground. The men moved forward, carefully checking the German bodies to be sure there were no wounded or fakers that could shoot them in the back after they passed.

"Where'd you last see him?" McGarr whispered.

"Just up here, sir," Fitterman answered. His heart sank as he passed several craters, still smoking from a recent shelling, each containing parts of men who'd been blown apart.

As the men moved slowly forward, Colonel McGarr moved up beside Fitterman. *How many colonels would do that?* Abe thought. But he and McGarr's men were used to this. Abe knew Phil had a great admiration for McGarr. The two had fought together since Anzio—413 days of one bloody battle after another. Phil was one of McGarr's longest-lived company commanders. It was no surprise the colonel would be out here looking for him. Abe prayed—hope against hope—that they'd find his body, or at least body parts and his dog tags.

"There!" The colonel ran forward in a crouch. In a shallow ditch lay the half-buried body of a GI, his American boots sticking out of a covering of mud, dirt, and bits of grass.

McGarr threw down his rifle and began to gently dig with his hands. "It's Larimore!" he exclaimed. "God Almighty! He's alive! Medic!"

As the medic ran up, McGarr told his radioman, "Get a stretcher! Get my Jeep! Now!"

McGarr and Fitterman quickly uncovered Phil. McGarr sat on the ground and gently lifted Phil's head and placed it in his lap. "Larimore, can you hear me?" he said softly.

Phil slowly nodded. "Colonel, that you?"

"Damn right, it's me!"

He stroked Phil's hair back from his blanched face. "I'm ordering you to live, damn it. Don't die on my watch, son!"

A slight smile creased Phil's face. "Yes, sir," he whispered, lapsing back into unconsciousness.

⁂

Phil was roused into semi-consciousness when the medic gave him a shot, removed the tourniquet, field-dressed his wound, and inserted an IV. McGarr and Abe lifted and carried him to the Jeep while the medic held the bottle of plasma. Together they carefully placed the stretcher across the back seat.

"It's a miracle you're alive, sir," the medic observed. "Not to mention the men you saved."

Phil, awake from the movement, smiled. "Rule of War No. 26 is called 'Miracles.'"

"Which is?" the medic asked.

"Resolute action by a few determined men is often decisive."[241]

"Damned right on that one, Larimore," McGarr said.

Phil grimaced when the colonel's Jeep hit a bump, causing an electric shock of pain to shoot up his leg. He was nearly unconscious when they arrived at the battalion aid station, where the medic started another IV.

His first visitor was waiting for him: General "Iron Mike" O'Daniel, who leaned over and whispered, "Helluva fighting man."

Not anymore, Phil thought.

He saw that Colonel McGarr was still at his side, holding his hand. "We'll get you fixed up," the colonel promised.

"Yes, sir," he weakly replied.

Phil was carried into the surgical tent, where Captain Charles S. Williams, a Regimental surgeon, introduced himself. In the haze, Phil recognized the other doctor, also in surgical scrubs: Captain Hilard Kravitz, the battalion surgeon whose life he had saved while crossing the surging Rhine River two weeks earlier.

Dr. Kravitz, grim and businesslike, took Phil's hand. "The colonel called me up to help Captain Williams. He knows I owe you one, Larimore."

The doctors explained some sort of procedure they needed to do with his right leg. Phil was pretty sure they'd give the wound a good cleaning, just like they had done with the injury to his right thigh six months previously.

Then a gas mask was placed over his face, and the bright lights inside the operating room turned to black.

☙

Phil woke up inside a jostling truck. A medic gave him two shots; he assumed they were morphine and penicillin. He hoped that both shots were *not* morphine. He'd heard whispered rumors of terribly wounded soldiers given "terminal doses" of morphine when the medic was sure the man would not survive his devastating wounds. He could imagine they'd comfortably go to sleep—no more distress, no more agony, no more suffering. Was this happening to him? He whispered the Lord's Prayer as he drifted off.

He awakened while being carried into a building on his stretcher—two men carrying him while another held up nearly-empty bottles of IV fluids, plasma, and blood.

I musta lost a lot of blood, he reasoned.

Then his thoughts turned darker.

My God! They're not taking me to the morgue, are they?

He must have received a fatal dose of morphine.

Before he could scream out, he lapsed again into oblivion.

48
HOMEWARD BOUND

"One cannot go to war and come back normal."

**—Richard Proulx, World War II Infantryman,
U.S. Army**[242]

When Phil woke up, he had no idea where he was. He felt no pain and wondered for a moment if this was heaven. His blurred vision cleared as he rubbed his eyes. He felt like his tongue was swollen, and his mouth was as dry as a ball of cotton. He slowly pushed himself up on his elbows and quickly realized he was in a hospital ward.[243]

Suddenly, Phil felt excruciating burning and itching on the bottom of his right foot. He sat up to scratch his right foot, and then his eyes widened in shock.

There was no right foot. There was no right lower leg. A beige elastic bandage was wrapped around a stump. He slowly scooted down and picked up the clipboard hanging from the end of the bed. The description of what happened in the operating room was stark: "Amputation, guillotine type, leg, right, below knee, performed 9 April 1945, sequela to perforating bullet wound of right leg." Further down the page, his chart read, "Circulation was so poor in the leg that an amputation was performed at a distance of five inches below the knee joint."[244]

Burning tears streaked down his face as he stared down at what remained of his leg. The word *remnant* came to mind, followed by *vestige, leftover*, and *scrap*. *Is that what I am now?* he wondered.

Questions poured through his mind. *What will I tell Mom and Dad? Will I ever walk? Will I ever ride a horse again? What am I going to do?* Overcome with terror and nausea, Phil began to wretch.

"Here's a pan," said a warm, comforting voice. It was as if an angel had appeared in front of him. "Hold this, Captain," she said softly.

"I'm a lieutenant," Phil answered, before throwing up into the pan.

"Not anymore," she answered. "You've been promoted, sir."

When he finished puking, she laid him down and had him turn to the side so she could give him a shot in the left buttock. "This'll calm your tummy, Captain."

Later that day, Phil awoke and was able to sit up with her help. She fluffed the pillows behind his back.

"Hungry?" she asked.

He nodded. "That would be nice."

She brought him a bowl of chicken broth and a ginger ale. Both tasted heavenly.

"Where am I?"

"10th Field Hospital in Alsbach-Hähnlein. We're about halfway between Heidelberg and Frankfurt and just over a hundred miles behind the front. At least we were yesterday. The boys on the front are moving so fast, it's hard to keep up with them. Heard this morning that your unit, the 30th, spearheaded another river crossing—the Main River, a second time. But today, we need to get you bathed, cleaned up, and your dressings changed."

Her smile was radiant. He lay down and fell back into a deep sleep.

ﾋﾟ

Phil was used to the routine based upon his previous hospitalization. Doctor visits and wound changes twice a day, meals three times a day, penicillin shots every four hours, morphine and smoke breaks as needed.

A couple of days later, on April 13, 1945, Phil chose to write his father, knowing that the news would be painful to bear for his mother:

> *Dad:*
>
> *By now, I hope you've gotten the letter from Capt. Williams, our Regimental surgeon, about just what happened to me.... I was wounded by what I think was a*

dumdum sniper bullet. Try as they did, they couldn't save my right foot. So, they had to cut it off about halfway between the knee and the ankle.... The main thing I'm interested in is getting my new one and getting back with the 3rd Div. I don't intend on letting them discharge me just on account of this. My promotion will be through here in a few weeks, so I'm told, and I'm all ready to get back to work.

Now, Dad, the job comes for you. I won't be getting any mail from you from now until I get home. (Which I am now on my way.) But you've got to tell Mom, so when I write her all about it in a few days, she will know about it. Most likely, I'll be sent to the General Hospital there in Memphis when they get me in the States. Now, Dad, I don't want any of these damn people crying over me or any of that crap. I'm all well, and as soon as I learn to use my new foot, I'll be ok again, so you tell them, huh? Must lay down again but will write you again. But am going to wait a few days before I write Mom.[245]

That same day, terrible news spread through the ward like wildfire: President Roosevelt was dead, having died the day before at his Warm Springs, Georgia, retreat. All of the men were shocked and felt a tremendous loss since FDR had been the only leader of the United States they'd ever known. They'd grown up listening to his "fireside chats" on the radio and were motivated by his speeches of encouragement as they went off to war.

General Eisenhower ordered all unit commanders to hold a short memorial service for Roosevelt on Sunday, April 15. Phil was unable to attend because he was being transferred 250 miles by train to the 195th General Hospital near Reims, France, in preparation for being shipped home.

On April 23, Phil received the news his promotion had gone through—he was now a captain after having served only a bit over two years—sixteen months as a 2nd lieutenant and eleven months as a 1st lieutenant. He was only twenty years old.

The news was delivered to him via his favorite nurse, Lieutenant Mary Lona Hicks, a Tennessee girl trained at Methodist Hospital in Memphis. They had long discussions about their hometown. He wrote to his dad the next day:

Dearest Dad,

    Hope I haven't kept you waiting too long for a letter, but I haven't felt like writing lately.... Still don't know when I'm leaving, but all I'm waiting on is a plane. It will take about 36 hours to get to Mitchel Field[i].... I'm still getting along very well, Dad. It has amazed me how little this losing of my foot has affected me. The docs tell me that it is getting along very well, much better than expected and that I have a very good stump and that it will take a new leg well. I'm all ready to get that new leg and try it out. When I learn to use it, Dad, look out, cause I'm going to find out just how many sports I can do, and you are appointed the likely one to help me find out. Hope you can read this as I am lying down. Love to everyone and hope to see you soon.

Your son,
Phil[246]

☎

Until his flight to the U.S., all Phil could do was keep tabs on the war from his hospital bed in France. It was becoming clear that the Third Reich would fall any minute. On April 30, Nazi leader Adolf Hitler committed suicide by shooting himself in his *Führerbunker* in Berlin. His longtime lover and wife of about forty hours, Eva Braun, died beside him after taking a fatal dose of cyanide.[247]

Meanwhile, the 30th Infantry was entering Munich, having covered an estimated 700 miles from March into the end of April and capturing more than 25,000 German prisoners. Phil learned that only thirty-two officers and 498 enlisted men of his original regiment of over 3,000 men who landed at Fedala, French Morocco, on November 8, 1942, were still active members of the 30th Infantry Regiment.

On May 5, the 30th Regiment took Salzburg, Austria. On May 8, the Nazi surrender was ratified in Berlin and proclaimed as "Victory in Europe Day" or V-E Day. Phil was glad that the war was finally over for the courageous men he'd served with, but his joy was tempered by the stupendous losses within his regiment, which sustained 8,308 total casualties: 1,876 killed in action, 5,788 wounded in action, and 644 missing in action.

---

i   Mitchel Field was an Army Air Force base located on the Hempstead Plains of Long Island, New York. The flight plan usually involved refueling stops in the Azores and Newfoundland.

Few entire divisions in the Pacific or European Theaters of Operation, much less a single regiment, suffered as high a casualty rate as the 30th Infantry did. They were the only U.S. Army regiment to participate in *five* separate divisional amphibious landings,[ii] not including another two battalion-level D-Days on Sicily, which made seven in all for Phil's 3rd Battalion. The 30th Infantry became one of the most highly decorated regiments in the U.S. Army.

Colonel McGarr wrote this to his surviving men:

> We, whom God has spared, offer this, our record of achievement, half humbly, half proudly. Humbly, because we know the terrible price in life and limb our regiment paid for victory. Proudly, because we, as an Infantry Regiment in thirty-one months of almost continuous combat, never failed to take an assigned objective.[248]

After 912 days of combat, the fighting men of the 30th continued to make their proud boast: "On countless battlefields, we have never yet failed to take our assigned objective! We never will!"

On May 9, Phil was scheduled to depart on a specially equipped C-54 military hospital plane from Reims, France, to Mitchel Field. While waiting in a wheelchair to board the aircraft, several military vehicles rapidly drove up. One of the front sedans had flags attached, each displaying five stars in a pentagonal pattern with points touching.

Phil knew instantly the flags meant that General Eisenhower—"Ike" to the men—was in the car. The general quickly exited the sedan and began to work his way down the line of wounded men. His entourage followed as he greeted each man, ordering them to stay seated and "at ease."

When he came to Phil, one of Ike's men, reading from a clipboard, gave the general a quick summary of the soldier's background. He shook Phil's hand and bent over. "How are you feeling, Captain?"

"Better, sir. I'm getting great care. And I'm heading home today."

Eisenhower smiled. "I served as a Marne Man in your 3rd Division slightly more than a year in '40 and '41. I hold General Truscott in high esteem. He served as one of my deputy commanders in my forward tactical headquarters. But what you men have done over here is spectacular. Some never saw the Germans; most saw too many. Not a single instance when your division failed; I can't recall a single instance when the division gave up a foot of ground."

"We had great commanders," Phil said.

"Yes, that's true. But more importantly, *they* had marvelous men. It's you men that I look back to in our moment of triumph. But I can't look back on you men without looking forward to the future for which you

---

ii   Fedala, French Morocco; Sicily; Salerno, Italy; Anzio, Italy; and southern France.

fought. It's now our task to build the future on the solid foundation laid by those who have left us forever—and those forever wounded. Thank you for your service and sacrifice."

"Thank you, sir," was all Phil could think to say.

The general started to stand, but then he knelt on one knee in front of Phil. "I'm told that the most pleasant things that old soldiers can talk about among themselves are the memory of successful battles. I think the future reunions of the 3rd Division will be the most enjoyable affairs. I hope to see you at one." Then the general stood and moved quickly to the next man.

The journey by air was a long one. After arrival in New York, where he spent the night, a U.S. Army military hospital transport plane flew him to the Naval Reserve Air Station near Atlanta.

While Phil was en route, his parents received a letter from Captain Williams at the 30th Infantry's Medical Detachment in Salzburg:

> *I hope by now both of you have been able to see him.... Knowing Philip as I do, I believe he can make the adjustment without too much difficulty. The Infantry is where...one proves himself very quickly as to be a man or not. Age means nothing. Your son proved himself a man from the beginning.*[249]

Adjacent to the landing strips at Naval Air Station in Atlanta was Lawson General Hospital, a cantonment-type[iii] army hospital with rows of one-story buildings built from Georgia pine. It was here that Phil would spend the next twelve months receiving additional surgeries and undergoing intensive rehabilitation.

In many ways, Phil didn't realize that some of the most significant battles of his life lay ahead of him.

---

iii   Cantonment refers to a group of temporary buildings or a camp where soldiers live.

PART V: AFTERMATH

"American soldiers…share a bond of pride, of courage, of sacrifice forged on the battlefields of Europe….They fought to free us from the darkest of tyrannies and restore a sense of hope to the world."

—National World War II Museum in New Orleans[250]

49
BITTER OR BETTER?

"Only the dead have seen the end of war."

—George Santayana, influential American thinker in the early 20th century[251]

L awson General Hospital in Atlanta was known across the United States for its care of soldiers with amputations, including fitting them with the newest prosthetic devices and rehabilitating them. More than 90 percent of soldiers like Phil were cared for at seven amputee centers.[i] They received wound care and revision surgery to close the residual limb, a series of temporary prostheses, and their initial rehabilitation.[252]

These centers ensured that consistent, high-quality care was provided for patients with amputations. Rather than having individual practitioners treating amputees in various ways, amputation care protocols were established based on the best available evidence to provide the best care possible. The patients stayed at the centers until they were completely rehabilitated and in their permanent prostheses.

Phil was personally attended to by Lieutenant Colonel Edward C. Holscher, MD, who was in charge of the orthopedic and amputation service. Unfortunately, even with all of his expertise, Dr. Holscher could not save Phil's knee because of the severe damage to his leg. Ten days after Phil's arrival, on May 21, 1945, Dr. Holscher had to perform an above-knee amputation. Phil's medical record read, "Leg amputated, second time."[253]

---

i   Of the soldiers in the U.S. Army wounded in action during World War II, Phil was among the roughly 15,000 (or 2.5 percent) who required major amputations.

Dr. Holscher promised Phil that he would receive all necessary physical therapy and rehabilitation, and in the months following his horrific wound in Germany, that was true. As could be expected for any amputee victim, Phil wrestled emotionally and spiritually with his future. After all, he was twenty years old with his whole life in front of him. But for the rest of his days, nothing would change the fact that he had lost most of his right leg. That was the harsh reality.

A series of heartfelt conversations with a chaplain was life-altering for Phil. One afternoon, he was feeling incredibly depressed about his status as an amputee. His self-image was shattered; his future was uncertain. His parents seemed to be pulling away from him, almost as if his stump repelled them. Though his mom and dad were nice and loving, Phil sensed a change in their attitude toward him when they visited.

After Phil confessed these awkward feelings to his chaplain, he heard this soul-stirring advice: "Phil, your wound will either make you a bitter person or a better person. It will either harden your heart or soften it. It will either result in a more-angry Phil or a more-aware Phil—one who is more pessimistic or more positive. You will either be a soldier and a person changed for the worse, or one who chooses to make the world better. In my opinion, the worst disability in life isn't being disabled; it's being disabled with a bad attitude. If you spend time focusing only on your inabilities, you will become blinded to your abilities. The Germans smashed your leg, but don't let them shatter your heart, your talents, your gifts, or your will. The choice is really up to you."

Phil's prayers began to change. He asked for God's guidance *through* the storms instead of some sort of miraculous rescue *from* the storms. He asked for a sense of peace to reign in his heart.

During his rehabilitation, Phil's spirits soared the day he received word of two commendations. The first was a telegram from the public relations office of the 3rd Division stating: "Capt. Philip B. Larimore, of Memphis, Tenn., has been awarded a second Bronze Star with valor for meritorious achievement in actual combat while fighting with the 3rd Infantry Division in France." The men of Company L had nominated him for this medal after his first night serving as their Company Commander.

A second telegram delivered to his bed said this:

> *You have been awarded a second Silver Star for gallantry in action. Please accept my sincere congratulations on your heroic actions. You have upheld the high standard of the 30th Infantry without thought of your personal safety. It is the work of men like you that makes the United States Army the powerful fighting machine that it is. You will receive your medal at an appropriate ceremony in the near future.*

> *Lionel C. McGarr, Colonel, 30th Infantry,*
> *Commanding*[254]

Colonel McGarr, who had always liked Phil and treated him like a son, had nominated him the Silver Star for his final fight in Germany.

❧

As Phil's spirits were refreshed and renewed, a thought formed in his mind. He wanted to make the military a career and pursue a return to active duty. That summer, he began a drive to stay in the Army by contacting various commands about working for them. Surely, with his vast experience on the field of battle, there was something he could do.[255]

At the same time, he knew this would be an uphill battle. U.S. Army policy stipulated that any officer suffering an amputation would, at the end of their rehabilitation, receive a medical discharge and be forced to leave the military. Enlisted men were treated differently. Those with amputations could remain in the army if they convinced their superiors that they could still do the job.

He wrote this to his mother:

> Wish you would look in the '42 G.C.M.A. catalog and see if the PMS&T[ii] was Lt. Col. Howard Clark II and also look in the lower right-hand drawer of my desk and inside a little wooden box is a bunch of letters. One of them is a letter written by Col. Clark. I wish you would send that to me. I think Col. Clark commands a post not far from here, and if it is him, I want to go down to see him about a job.[256]

His mother also began a letter-writing campaign to support him. A letter from Memphis attorney Abe D. Waldauer to U.S. Congressman Cliff Davis wrote:

> Captain Larimore...is an honest-to-goodness front-line soldier. He commanded a company at twenty years of age and received his commission as a 2nd Lieutenant before he was eighteen, having to wait until his eighteenth birthday to be sworn in. He has lost his right leg, which was amputated following wounds. He desires to remain in the service and does not wish to be discharged by reason of this disability.
>
> Please look into the matter and ascertain whether or not it is the policy of the Army to keep in service those who

---

ii   PMS&T means Professor of Military Science & Tactics.

> *are wounded in action. In the last war, they would have*
> *discharged a man with an amputation. But it occurs to me*
> *as possible and likely that in this war...the Government*
> *might find ways and means of retaining Captain Lari-*
> *more's service.*[257]

One evening, a nurse interrupted a discussion he was having with other amputees in the officer's mess.[iii] "Captain Larimore, there's a call for you."

He wheeled over to the nurses' station and picked up the phone. His face paled, and his jaw dropped. Then he fumbled the phone, which fell to the floor.

The nurse picked up the receiver and placed it in his trembling hands. "Are you okay, sir?"

Phil nodded and quickly put the phone to his ear. "What did you say? Who is this again?"

He heard a voice repeat: "Phil, this is Ross."

He almost dropped the phone a second time. His closest buddy, Ross Calvert, was alive!

"Is that really you, Ross?"

"It's me, Daddy-O!"

Tears tumbled down Phil's cheeks. His best friend was alive and recovering from malnutrition and severe pneumonia at an army hospital in Nashville. Ross said he had been liberated by American troops while in a POW hospital in Germany.

They were now only about 250 miles from each other. Being the "healthier" of the two, Phil promised to visit as soon as possible.

❧

As his recovery progressed, Phil became an expert at ambulating with crutches and a wheelchair. By mid-June, he'd recovered to a point where he was awarded a thirty-day leave. The first thing Phil did with his newfound freedom was to take a train to Nashville, where he enjoyed a wonderful visit with Ross at Thayer General Hospital.[258]

Ross explained what had happened when the Germans overran the village of Holtzwihr in the Colmar Pocket. "Several of us sheltered in a barn near a house. We later crawled into the hayloft and covered ourselves with hay. That was a miserable night. The Germans put a CP in the house and billeted their men in the barn. One of my men snored, so I spent half the night choking him. Somehow, we got through the night without being discovered," Ross remembered, laughing.

---

iii   A mess (also called a mess deck aboard a ship) is an area where military personnel socialize and eat.

"The next day, the old Alsatian who lived in the place crawled up to the loft to throw hay down for his stock. He uncovered a GI boot, let out a yell, and fell back. Pretty soon, a voice, in excellent English, said that we could either come down or he would burn down the barn, but if he set the barn on fire, they would shoot any man trying to escape the flames. Of course, we came down, cold, tired, and sleepy. I wasn't too worried because I knew the Germans had a POW enclosure in Colmar and that Colmar would soon be encircled. Again, too much knowledge is a dangerous thing. They marched us straight to a ferry to cross the Rhine. A squadron of French fighter planes tried to blow up the ferry, but they never got a direct hit. We were taken to POW camps in Stuttgart and then Hammelburg, near Bad Kissingen, and that ended the war for me."

"Did you ever try to escape?" Phil asked.

"Hell, yes! Actually did, but developed severe double pneumonia, and I was weakened to the point where I had no run or fight left. I'm told that I was easily recaptured walking down the middle of a paved road, but I don't remember that. I finally ended up in a POW hospital in Nürnburg. I overheard an American medical man say he didn't think it likely I would last much longer. But to hell with that, I thought."

The men laughed together.

"I was there when the 3rd Division took the place. I couldn't make contact with anyone from the division and was evacuated to Nancy, Paris, New York, and finally here to Thayer."

It was there that Phil and Ross began to strategize how they might work together in the Army.

From Nashville, Phil took a train to Memphis for his first visit home since the fall of 1943, when he dropped by to see his parents before boarding a Liberty ship bound for French Morocco. His reunion with his parents was a media sensation. Reporter Dick Lane with the *Memphis Commercial Appeal* wrote this:

> *Fighting outfits breed fighting commanders. And the 3rd Division's famed Company L, 30th Infantry, is no exception. It's the old outfit of Capt. Maurice L. Britt[iv] of Lonoke, Ark.—the nation's most decorated man—and also that of Philip B. Larimore, beribboned 20-year-old Memphis hero who'd like nothing better than to be back with it. Captain Larimore, who served under Britt before taking command of Company L himself, is now home from Lawson General Hospital in Atlanta visiting his parents...while recuperating from battle wounds.*

iv   Britt was wounded, losing an arm on Anzio on January 22–23, 1944, and was evacuated before Phil arrived on Anzio in February 1944. Therefore, Phil never served with Britt, but he later became the Company Commander of Love Company, which was Britt's company.

"Sure, I'd like to stay in the Army. I like it—its bull and all," Captain Larimore mused yesterday. And you knew he meant it, too. You knew it by his surprise at being asked his service point total.[v] He modestly admitted that he had never bothered to add them, but a casual count showed more than 100 points, which increased over the weekend by the addition of a second Silver Star for gallantry in action. Along with his first Silver Star for laying mines within 100 yards of German positions during daylight on Anzio, Captain Larimore wears the Bronze Star with Oak Leaf Cluster,[vi] the Purple Heart with two Oak Leaf Clusters, a Presidential Unit Citation with Oak Leaf Cluster, the Combat Infantryman's Badge, and the European Theater ribbon with four campaign stars and one arrowhead.

What is the future now that his combat days are over?

"If the Army doesn't let me stay in—and I certainly hope they will—I'd like to get around to taking that engineering course at the Massachusetts Institute of Technology that I've always wanted. Maybe the Army can use another engineer—even with a wooden leg," he added reflectively.[259]

After Phil returned to Lawson in mid-July, he continued his campaign to stay in the Army. He received a glimmer of hope about his potential future in the Army when Congressman Davis notified him the War Department had responded to his inquiry, saying:

Captain Larimore's wish to remain in military service in spite of his disabilities is appreciated. If Captain Larimore will write directly to the Adjutant General, Attention: Captain Dross, when his hospitalization is completed, it is possible that there may be a vacancy in the Army Service Forces in which he could be assigned.[260]

Buoyed by the response, Phil was more upbeat and chattier in his next letter home:

---

v   The "service point total" or "adjusted service rating score" was used by the U.S. Army at the end of World War II. The score was determined as follows: months in service, one point each; months in service overseas, one point each. In addition, combat awards (Medal of Honor, Distinguished Service Cross, Silver Star Medal, Bronze Star Medal, Purple Heart, etc.) or campaign participation stars were worth five points each.

vi   The Oak Leaf Cluster represents one additional award. In this case, it represents a second Bronze Star.

*I'm feeling as well as can be expected. Anyway, I feel
no pain. I have been to town only a couple of times. But
other than that, I haven't done much but work on my rehabilitation, eat, and sleep. Lazy huh?*

*Got a lovely card from Grandmom yesterday. Tell her
I sure do miss her good cooking and for her not to let you eat
all the chickens cause I'll be home again one of these days.*[261]

As Phil continued to make steady progress, he went out more and more.
He started attending a Methodist church close by and accepted invitations to
dine with various families after the service. Phil also began to take an interest
in some of the young ladies from nearby Dunwoody who visited the hospital
to lift the men's spirits. Maybe he'd even start dating again. There was always
that hope.

☙

On August 6, 1945, stunning news swept through Lawson. Phil and every
wounded patient gathered around radios to listen to the startling news that the
U.S. military had dropped the first atomic bomb in history, leveling the city of
Hiroshima. The reports noted that Japanese residents had been warned—via
dropped leaflets—to flee in the days leading up to the bombing.[262]

The reaction from the servicemen? A roar of approval from most, while
others broke down and cried with relief and joy. All were in favor of doing
anything that would end the war. They were well aware that an invasion of
Japan promised to be the bloodiest seaborne attack of all time, with estimates that a prolonged offensive would cost two to four million American
casualties, including 400,000 to 800,000 fatalities, and five to ten million
Japanese deaths.

Also, Japanese forces were causing the deaths of between 100,000 and
250,000 noncombatants *each* month. On top of this, thousands of Allied and
Asian prisoners of war were dying daily throughout the still-occupied Japanese
Empire and would do so as long as Japan could pursue the war. Dropping the
atomic bomb would end all that.

Three days later, Phil and the men on his floor gathered around the radio
again to listen to the news of a second atomic bomb destroying the city of
Nagasaki. On August 15, 1945, Japan announced its surrender to the United
States, ending the most devastating war in human history.

Phil and the estimated 672,000 U.S. troops wounded during the war
could only wonder what would happen next. Would their sacrifices be
forgotten? Would life ever return to some semblance of normalcy?

The only thing certain, Phil knew, was that he faced an uncertain future.

50

BACK IN THE SADDLE AGAIN

"My horse's feet are as swift as rolling thunder;
he carries me away from all my fears.
And when the world threatens to fall asunder,
his mane is there to wipe away my tears."

—Bonnie Lewis, author of *Riding a Dead Horse*[263]

When Phil received his new prosthetic wooden leg on September 7, 1945, he could not believe what the artificial limb did for his soul and spirit. Although most of his lower right leg was man-made, the prosthesis allowed him to feel like a man again, not like a cripple. No longer did he have to use crutches or a wheelchair. No longer was the right leg of his pants pinned up. No longer did people outside the hospital stare at him and quickly look away. No longer did he feel like an outcast—an amputee. His attitude and self-image improved dramatically.[264]

More importantly, his traumatic memories seemed to be dissolving. He wasn't having the terrible nightmares that had plagued him since his leg took a dumdum bullet in Germany. Certain aromas no longer triggered harrowing visions and recollections. The horrible smells of war tattooed into his nostrils were finally dispersing. He could inhale the aromatic scents of roses and wisteria in the hospital gardens and find them bringing both joy and hope. He could even differentiate the various fragrances worn by the girls.

And then he saw *her* for the first time at the Methodist church near Lawson in Dunwoody—a tall, willowy, remarkably attractive brunette standing in the foyer. She even approached him to introduce herself.

"My name's Mary Katherine," she said, in an almost sultry voice.

That was all the encouragement Phil needed. He waited a couple of days and then called her. With a tender, "Yes, absolutely, yes!" she accepted his offer to a dinner date at the fine dining room of one of Atlanta's fanciest hotels, the Winecoff.[i]

That night, he looked spiffy in his dress uniform, and she was resplendent in a shimmering black evening dress with a lovely drape front and a gathered band running from shoulder to shoulder across the neckline, leaving a small peephole opening. The romantic restaurant had live music and a small dance floor. Between courses, she asked, "Phil, are you a dancer?"

"I used to be. I loved to dance. But now…." He looked down.

As the band began to play "A Nightingale Sang in Berkeley Square," Mary Katherine stood and took his hand. "It's a slow one. What say we get you back in the saddle, soldier?"

Phil took a deep breath, let it out, and stood up. This was the most nervous he'd felt since the war. She led him to the dance floor and took him into her arms. Matching the leisurely cadence of the number, they slowly began to dance.

Mary Katherine sang along with the soloist but changed the lyrics, singing, "This special time, the night we dined, there is magic around in the air. There's a twosome dining at the Winecoff, and a soldier dancing on a dare."

She giggled, and he melted against her as her perfume drifted over him. They hummed the rest of the song together. Suddenly, the band struck up Glenn Miller's up-tempo hit, "In the Mood." He took her hand to go back to their table, but she pulled him back.

"It's too fast," Phil complained, feeling his face blush. "I feel like a scarecrow."

Her smile radiated, and she gave him a gentle tug. "Let's give it a go. I won't let go of you! Come on!" She laughed as the singer began and exclaimed, "Don't keep me waiting, soldier! *I'm* in the mood!"

They started slowly, and Phil was astounded at how well his artificial leg worked, even though it had to be evident to everyone that he was wearing a prosthetic limb.

"I can dance!" he cried.

"My heart is skipping!" she answered as several couples joined them. Others watching from their tables applauded and cheered them on.

---

i   The Winecoff Hotel (now the Ellis Hotel) opened in 1913, and at fifteen stories, was one of the tallest buildings in Atlanta. The hotel was touted in advertisements and on its stationery as "absolutely fireproof," but on December 7, 1946, the Winecoff suffered the deadliest hotel fire in United States history at the time, killing 119 hotel occupants, including the hotel's original owners.

When the dance number was over, they returned to their table. Phil was radiant—and a bit bushed. As he settled back into his chair, an older couple stopped by their table.

"Please forgive us for interrupting," the dapper gentleman said, "but I want to thank you for your service and your sacrifice, sir. Your bill is taken care of." Before Phil could object—or even thank him—the couple turned and left.

Their glorious evening together hit a crescendo when Mary Katherine shared that not only did she love horses, but her family had a second home on a horse farm just north of the city. Her parents, she said, had joined a group of horse and hunting enthusiasts to help the Fulton County Commissioners construct a stable and polo field in one of the city parks. When Mary Katherine invited him to come riding with her, how could he say no?

That night, as she pulled up at Lawson to drop him off, she gave him a gentle kiss on his cheek. Pulling away, she whispered, "Is this a dream, or is it real?"

That's exactly what Phil was thinking.

❧

That week, Phil worked overtime with one of the physical therapists on successfully mounting a horse while wearing his wooden leg. The therapist found an old western saddle and attached it to a gymnastics pommel horse, with the pommels removed, of course.

Phil quickly became an expert at locking the prosthetic knee, lifting his good left leg into the saddle's left stirrup while facing his horse's rump, then using his left hand to hold the saddle horn while lifting himself and then throwing his right thigh and prosthesis over the saddle. When he was in place atop the horse, he placed the prosthetic foot into its stirrup. His confidence increased dramatically as the week went on.

When the Saturday morning ride arrived, he was nervous. But Mary Katherine was understanding and accommodating. Within a fenced riding arena, Phil successfully mounted one of her father's Thoroughbreds on his first try. He couldn't believe how good it felt to be in the saddle again. As he settled in, taking in the rich leather aroma, he felt his lip tremble and tears form.

What happened next stunned him: Mary Katherine removed his right wooden foot from the stirrup, replaced it with her own, and standing up in the stirrup, she leaned next to him, gently wiped his tears, and gave him a soft kiss on the cheek.

"Let's go for a ride," she said, hopping down to the ground. She replaced his artificial foot in the stirrup, mounted her horse, and they started with trotting and advanced to a canter. At one point, his horse inexplicably and suddenly bucked, and before he knew it, he was face down in musky riding arena loam.

Phil was embarrassed, but before he could pull himself up, Mary Katherine quickly dismounted and was at his side, helping him sit up while comforting him. She was incredibly tender. Their third kiss was on the riding arena floor—and this one was not on his cheek! It was soft and sweet, and he did *not* want to stop.

"All right, soldier," she coaxed, laughing. "Back in the saddle. But be more careful. I think your artificial knee may have pinched him. Let's switch your saddle to one with a fender."

Phil felt his forehead furrow. That was a horse term he hadn't heard before.

Mary Katherine laughed. "It's a piece of leather that goes between the stirrup and the seat. Here, I'll show you."

They walked back to the barn, changed saddles, and were off again. This time, their ride together was delightful and without incident. Before long, they departed the arena and were galloping through forested paths, jumping small obstacles, and wading through streams. Phil could see she was as pleased with his progress as he was. After dismounting in the late afternoon, they walked the horses back to the barn, holding hands. They put up the tack, brushed and fed the horses, stabled them, and then sat on a bench to continue talking.

Phil decided this was the happiest he'd been since he arrived home.

∾

That evening over dinner with her family, Phil discovered they were members of the only foxhunting club in northern Georgia—the Atlanta Hunt Club.

"It's the oldest hunt club in Georgia," her father explained over after-dinner scotch and cigars.

Mary Katherine stifled a chuckle. "Phil, it was established only two years ago, in 1943."

Her father blew a puff of aromatic cigar smoke into the air. "We're hoping to be officially recognized by the Master of Foxhounds Association someday, but that's likely to take some time. Actually, our first official hunt of the season is next weekend. Interested?"

Phil could not believe his good fortune. "Why," he stammered, "I'd love to join you!"

Her father set his tumbler of whisky down and turned to his daughter. "What do you think, darling? Do we start Phil in the Second or Third Field?"

Her father was referring to the terms used by hunt clubs when rating riders. The First Field was for confident, experienced foxhunters with proficient horses. The Second Field closely followed but did not jump coops,[ii] although they did jump over fallen logs and smaller ditches. The Third Field

---

ii   A coop is a brace of boards placed over a wire fence, providing a "safe" place for mounted riders to jump when crossing a boundary.

was for novice riders and horses that would be challenged by the speed of the First and Second Fields.

Usually, Phil would have considered the question an insult. He was more than experienced and had never ridden in a hunt except in the First Field. But given his new leg and the fact that he and his horse were only newly introduced to each other—and he had already been thrown once—he blurted out, "How 'bout I start in the Third Field?"

"Daddy," Mary Katherine interjected. "Phil's ridden First Field many times before."

"No," Phil broke in. "With my new leg and a new horse, I think it's best I start slow."

"Okay," she conceded. "How about this, Daddy? We'll start in the Third Field, and if it goes well, as I know it will, can we ride up to the Second Field?"

Her father smiled. "Agreed."

Phil had a question. "What are your dogs?" he asked.

"Mostly Penn-Marydel hounds,"[iii] he answered. "But we also have some crossbred foxhounds."

"I know the breed," Phil said, sipping his scotch. "A true American hound. I'm told they are a derivative of hounds that came to America from England and France in the early 1600s."

"Phil!" Mary Katherine exclaimed. "How do you know *that*?"

"Not my first hunt. And what *do* you hunt?"

"Mostly red and gray foxes, although we see more coyotes and bobcats," her father explained. "Oh, and all participants in the hunt must obtain and carry an annual Georgia hunting license."

"Phil, don't worry. I can drive you to get the license," she assured him.

"I can't wait," Phil said, almost giddily. Then he remembered. "But what will I wear? I had pinks when I hunted at Fort Benning, but I borrowed them."

"Well, of course, you couldn't wear colors as a newcomer *here*," Mary's father explained. "Our rules for those without colors is that they wear a plain black hunt coat with black buttons. No facing on the collar, of course. Your breeches should be a heavy material and can be buff, canary, gray, or rust. You'll need plain black calf boots without tops, a canary vest with plain brass, and a black velvet riding helmet with a harness."

"Daddy! Don't scare Phil away!" Mary Katherine put her arm through his. "Don't worry about it, honey. I'll get everything you need."

Honey, she'd said. He almost swooned.

---

iii   The Penn-Marydel (PMD) hound is a variety of American Foxhound developed in Pennsylvania and the Eastern Shore of Maryland/Delaware, hence the name. Although only formally recognized by the Masters of Foxhounds Association as a separate breed in 2008, PMDs were developed in the early 1900s. The dogs are driven and enduring hunters when in pursuit of game, yet they are said to be generally playful and amicable at home.

That night, when Mary Katherine dropped him at the hospital, she pulled him close. Their kiss was passionate. As she withdrew slightly, her smile radiant and welcoming, she said, "Don't be late for curfew. I want to see you again."

Before hopping out of the car, he kissed her on the forehead. "Thanks for a great day, Mary Katherine. A *great* day."

"Off to bed, soldier!" she commanded, laughing.

"Mary Katherine, I'm so thankful. You've made me feel whole, and I now know that I'm recovering not only physically but emotionally and spiritually as well. You're a big part of that."

"Me or that beautiful Thoroughbred?"

Phil chuckled. "Maybe both?"

She laughed and kissed him again.

As he watched her drive away, he looked up at the stars. They seemed to shimmer and sparkle more vividly than he could remember. It had been *so* long since he had felt like a whole man.

Could it be that romantic love had dawned once again?

51

IN THE HUNT

"A man on a horse is spiritually, as well as physically, bigger than a man on foot."

—John Steinbeck, author of *The Grapes of Wrath*[265]

During the week, Phil counted the minutes until the hunt. He didn't want to be thrown again. The therapists and some of his buddies rigged up a 55-gallon barrel strung up by four ropes hung over two thick mattresses. They took an old English saddle and strapped it on the barrel. One man would mount "the beast," as they called it, and four others would pull on the ropes. The harder they pulled, the more violently the beast bucked. The men laughed uproariously as one after another was conquered by the barrel.[266]

When it was Phil's turn, his buddies took it easy on him at first, but by the end of the week, they couldn't buck Phil off. He was ready to hunt with both the beauty and the beast.

On the morning of the hunt, Mary Katherine picked him up early. He was decked out in a borrowed "uniform" she had brought to the hospital the day before. Once they arrived at the country estate where the hunt would begin, they found her father at his horse trailer. He already had the horses out and brushed. Together they tacked the horses, and when the first bugle call came, they mounted and rode out to the pack. Mary Katherine introduced Phil to everyone she could, which he deeply appreciated. And he was incredibly honored when she introduced him to the Master[i] just before he addressed the riders and explained the rules of the hunt.

"We have more guests than usual," the Master began, "so allow me a moment to review our rules. These foxhunting guidelines are commonsense rules of safety, courtesy, and the traditions of the sport we enjoy together.

"First of all, leave gates open that you find open. If the gate is closed, the first one there opens it. The last one through is to close and latch it securely. Stay to the headlands[ii] when navigating around planted fields. Following the pack will keep you out of trouble.

"Be sure to slow down and ride slowly around livestock so as not to excite them or make them run. Be extra careful around loose horses. They tend to jump fences behind you."

The Master stopped to see if there were any questions. Hearing none, he continued. "If your horse refuses to jump a coop, please go around to the end of the line to attempt the coop again. A hunting day is *not* a training opportunity for green horses. When the hounds are running, pass slower horses only in a safe and open area. Remember, foxhunting is not a competitive sport. The winners are those who come home safely; the losers are those who spoil the sport for others. If you see a situation that you think is dangerous or improper, report it quietly and confidentially to me."

All the riders in their colorful attire nodded.

"Above all, keep your horse's heels away from any passing rider or the hounds to avoid accidents," the Master continued. "Safety for our riders, our hounds, and our horses is our priority. Understand?"

Again, everyone nodded. Phil was duly impressed. He loved the emphasis on rules, order, and safety. Before they knew it, the bugle sounded, and the hounds were off, baying like crazy. The First and Second Fields led the way, and he and Mary Katherine rode with a rather large Third Field. The pace increased, and soon they were trotting. Phil couldn't believe how comfortable and relaxed he felt.

By midmorning, Mary Katherine had moved them up, with their Field Master's permission, into the Second Field. After a delightful picnic lunch, they were admitted to the First Field and performed admirably. The hunt was not successful in cornering a fox, but the participants did tree a bobcat, which the dogs quickly abandoned. In the late afternoon, the huntsman bugled "End of the Day," and they rode back to where they started.

Back at the trailer, they put up the tack and began brushing down the horses. Phil and her father brushed with one hand and held a glass of scotch on the rocks in another. Phil had never felt so welcome or so at home. Once

---

i   The foxhunt is led by a "Master of Foxhounds," sometimes called a "Master of Hounds" or "Master" for short.
ii   The headland was a strip of land left unplowed at the end or side of a field.

the horses were trailered, Phil and Mary Katherine offered to follow her father home to help stable the horses, but he refused the offer.

"You kids go and have a nice night on the town." He looked at his daughter and peeled off several big bills from his money clip. "Make it on me, honey. We owe this soldier our gratitude for all he's done for our country." Turning toward Phil, he set his jaw, stuck out his hand, and took Phil's hand into his. "Thank you, soldier!"

That night was an evening of dining and dancing, this time at the famous Empire Dining Room at the Biltmore Hotel.[iii] A small orchestra played swing music tunes as couples drifted off and on the dance floor around them. After a delicious dinner, Phil and Mary Katherine joined them on the parquet floor. His confidence was surging, although he was careful not to make any fast moves with his feet.

"I don't think I'm ready for the Lindy Hop[iv] just yet," he said between songs.

Mary Katherine caught her breath. "Don't worry about it. You're doing great."

His favorite time on the dance floor was when the orchestra played leisurely tunes that allowed them to slow dance. As he held Mary Katherine close, Phil felt pampered, spoiled, and appreciated. He sensed she had chosen this venue to get him even more used to dancing with a new prosthesis and a new partner. The more they talked and danced, the more he came to know her and like her.

Mary Katherine had him back at the hospital by the midnight curfew, walked him to the door, and sent him off with a kiss. "I'll pick you up for church tomorrow," she promised.

"I may need to go to confession first," Phil said, laughing.

"For what?"

"Having impure thoughts."

Mary Katherine laughed as she turned on her heels. Looking back over her shoulder, she said, "Take a cold shower, soldier. See you tomorrow."

She smiled and blew him a kiss. After returning the gesture, he felt like he floated into the officer's ward. The men still up that evening teased him with catcalls. He didn't care one iota.

Phil Larimore was falling in love.

---

iii   Built in 1924, the Biltmore Hotel was the focal point of Atlanta's business and social life for almost sixty years. The Empire Room was a dancing-and-dining venue known for its with exceptional food. The Biltmore closed its doors in 1982.

iv   The Lindy Hop, named after Charles Lindbergh's "hop" across the Atlantic Ocean in May 1927, was an American dance that began in the African-American community of Harlem in New York City. The Lindy Hop became a popular dance during the swing era that lasted into the 1940s.

❦

That fall, he and Mary Katherine attended horse shows, hunted several times with her father, and continued to cut the rug on dance floors. The more she took him dancing and dining, the more proficient he became with his prosthesis. Riding and dancing became more comfortable. Even the foxtrot and swing dance moves became effortless because Mary Katherine was such an excellent dance partner and companion. Without even trying, she taught him to lead her. She brought out the gentleman in him. He was a better man due to Mary Katherine.

The riding barrel at the hospital was a very popular success with the PTs and the men. So much so that Phil was enlisted to help establish an equine-assisted physical therapy program. Mary Katherine and her father provided the horses at the nearby city park stable. The horses proved themselves as being naturally intuitive and able to sense and mirror their rider's mood. They became excellent therapeutic animals and helped the men's balance, strength, and confidence. It was a resounding success that he enjoyed doing with her.

Their long talks became comfortable to the point where, for the first time, he was able to start talking about the war. The gruesome battles. The hand-to-hand combat. The horrific sight of his buddies with their heads blown off or bodies cut in two. The tremendous losses. His final battle.

She listened carefully, helping Phil clarify his thoughts and sort through his emotions. She asked probing questions, gently at first, and more penetrating as time went on. He felt comfortable sharing with her. She didn't judge; she listened and learned. She brought him out of a deep, dark foxhole of horrific memories and quickly became his true and trusted friend.

Phil celebrated a southern Thanksgiving at her parents' home: a roast turkey, green bean casserole, scalloped potatoes, and hot buttered biscuits. He wanted to reciprocate by taking Mary Katherine to Memphis at Christmastime to meet his parents, both to introduce them to her and also to assuage his mother's increasing complaints about him not coming home as often as he had in the past.

Mary Katherine declined the invitation, however. "Not yet, honey."

It was the first red flag he noted. Soon there were others. She was getting harder to reach by phone and was less available for dates. Her parents seemed more distant and less welcoming.

"What's going on?" he asked Mary Katherine as they shared dinner in early December.

She looked away and lowered her head.

"What is it?"

She began to cry. "Oh, honey, I don't want to ruin our evening."

And then she proceeded to do just that. "Mommy doesn't approve of us," she tearfully confessed.

Phil was dumbfounded. He had never been more surprised at any news in his life. Not even Marilyn's *Dear John* letter had stupefied him as much as this. He felt utterly blindsided.

"Why?" he muttered. "Because I'm an amputee?"

Mary Katherine vigorously shook her head and continued to cry.

"Did I do or say something wrong?"

Again, she shook her head.

"Then what?"

She sniffled. "You're *not* from Atlanta!" she exclaimed. "She and Daddy want me to marry someone from our social circles. You know, Mommy thinks Memphis is *not* the South. And...."

"Is she saying my family's not good enough?" Phil felt his face reddening. "That *I'm* not good enough?" Meaning that he didn't come from a wealthy family, wasn't of the same class.

Mary Katherine nodded, hung her head, and began crying again.

Now he knew. His love affair with Mary Katherine was over.

❧

As Phil fell asleep that night, the chaplain's words rumbled through his mind: *You can choose to be bitter or better.*

He knew he was a better man—a man beginning to heal—because of Mary Katherine. Sure, she would leave a giant hole in his heart, but he determined that he would fill that space with thankfulness, not bitterness.

He had to let her go. He was confident that God had someone else out there for him. All he had to do was to be patient.

52
A CHRISTMAS REUNION

"My idea of Christmas, whether old-fashioned or modern, is very simple: loving others. Come to think of it, why do we have to wait for Christmas to do that?"

—Bob Hope, famous comedian and Hollywood actor[267]

Phil asked for and received a long pass for the Christmas season. He felt that leaving Atlanta and being home in Memphis among family and friends would help mend his broken heart. He remembered the chaplain's advice after talking about how Mary Katherine broke up with him: "Don't let it shatter your heart. The choice is really up to you."

Phil repeatedly wondered if he could have done anything differently with her, but he could think of nothing. And then he began to think about all the positives that had happened between them. He had learned to ride again and love again. He had started to process his emotions about the war, the horrors he had seen and experienced. That's when Phil realized that the time they were together had been good. *Very* good. And he began to feel thankful, truly thankful for what Mary Katherine and her family had done for him.

His moods improved even more once he spent a few days with Ross, who was out of the hospital in Nashville, and then was back home in Memphis. He stayed with his parents and spent time with old friends and buddies—especially Bill O'Bannon and Luke McLaurine. Christmas was always his favorite season of the year, and he was ready to enjoy an old-fashioned family Christmas. After two severely cold and bitter winters on the European front, being home for Christmas was an answered prayer.

Phil's mother told him she had arranged what she hoped would be an extra special Christmas surprise for him—dinner at the Peabody Hotel on Friday, December 21, with a special friend from the past. She refused to tell him who it was—no hints whatsoever, adding to the mystery by saying, "Oh, and be sure to wear your full-dress uniform."

This request left him wondering if he would be seeing one of his buddies from the war. He hoped the special guest was Ross Calvert. But why the dress uniform? Did that mean Colonel McGarr and even General O'Daniel would be coming for a visit? His mother told him he should have a seat at the lobby bar, and his friend would meet him there for a drink at about half-past five.

Phil decided to drive to town early.[i] He entered the enormous two-story lobby of Memphis' best hotel—where Presidents Andrew Johnson and William McKinley had once stayed. He smiled as he recognized the magnificent black travertine marble fountain populated by the world-famous "Peabody Ducks," always five mallards—one drake and four hens.

Since it was five o'clock, the Duckmaster was rounding up the mallards for their return trip to their "Duck Palace." The excited kids around the fountain brought back fond memories of his ninth birthday party. After the ducks departed on the traditional red carpet, Phil made his way to the hotel bar, where he ordered a scotch on the rocks.

As he sorted through his thoughts at the moment, it struck him he had much in his past to be thankful for. A feeling of gratitude swept over him. Lost in a cacophony of warm memories, he twirled the ice cubes with one finger. His concentration broke when a strikingly long-legged woman scooted onto the barstool immediately to his right. His eyes moved up her beautiful evening gown, cut low in the front, which magnificently displayed the young lady's beauty. He noticed the absence of jewelry on her ring finger.

She was looking slightly to the right as if searching for someone. Phil wondered for an instant if she might be looking for her date. When she turned to face him, he felt the blood drain from his face. His jaw slightly opened as he gasped.

Sitting next to him was Marilyn Fountain.

She looked into his eyes, initially displaying no emotion at all. She took in a deep breath and then slowly let it out. Phil began to say something, but she lifted her finger to his lips.

"Shush," she said, removing her hand and looking down for a moment. When she looked up, her eyes were brimming with tears.

---

i   By this time, Phil was feeling comfortable driving an automatic car, using his left leg for accelerating and braking.

"I came in from Des Moines," she began, "because I want to see you face-to-face. I need to apologize to you. I need to ask your forgiveness. I don't *expect* to be forgiven based on the way I treated you. But let me tell you what happened." She reached into her small handbag and pulled out a handkerchief.

His mind was reeling. Sitting before him was his first real love. A young lady he had admired and adored. They had so much in common, and he had thought they were fated to be together. Then came her *Dear John* letter while he was in the Vosges Mountains in eastern France. He had never expected one. Not from Marilyn, not from *his* girl.

She dabbed her tears and gently sniffled. "Phil, you had been gone from me for so long, and you were *so* far away. I heard from you so seldom. Part of that was because your letters were terribly slow to arrive. Many other times, I knew you were too busy fighting the damn war to write. Your mother told me it was the same for her. But Phil, I *needed* to hear from you. I needed to know you still cared for me and loved me. Your letters didn't tell me that. At times, when I read them, the real you seemed so distant. You talked about your buddies and the sights you were seeing. I know you wanted to protect me from the awful brutality you were suffering, but I needed to hear my Phil's heart. I needed his words to caress me, not inform me. I needed to hear from my love, not a war correspondent."

She paused, and he felt like she had taken a red-hot dagger and shoved it into his heart. He could hardly breathe.

"I'm *not* saying what you did was wrong. I'm just saying I needed something else. And then, when I was least expecting it, and when I hadn't heard from you for several weeks, I met this sweet guy. I guess I was vulnerable. He said he understood I was yours and was willing for us just to be friends, but the more time he and I spent together…." Her voice trailed off.

"Well, he was there. He was with me. He visited my mother, and she liked him. *A lot.* Then he offered me himself and a ring."

"That was a long time ago," was all he could whisper. "Over a year ago."

"Yes, it was. During that time, I learned a lot about that boy I was engaged to. I learned he wasn't what he made himself out to be. He became more and more controlling. From time to time, he'd get outraged over something I said or did, and he'd slap or punch me. I tried to rationalize it—he was drinking a lot. I blamed myself. But I came to realize it wasn't *me* that was the problem. It was *him.* When I gave him back his ring, he went crazy—threatened to kill me. Said he'd make me regret it forever. Fortunately, Daddy was still serving with General Patton. I'm guessing Old Blood and Guts[ii] made some calls, and the next thing I knew, the police chief came by the dorm one night. He told

---

ii   General George S. Patton insisted the officers who served under him knew what they could expect in battle. He would tell them, "You're going to be up to your neck in blood and guts," which made quite an impression, leading to the nickname "Old Blood and Guts."

me that my former fiancé had been visited by a couple of MPs and a couple of G-men."[iii]

She smiled. *That* smile. A smile he had loved. "The chief told me the meeting scared the silly out of that boy." She softly laughed. "That's what he said. 'Scared the silly outta him.' Anyway, he hightailed it out of town and hasn't been seen since."

There was a pause in the conversation as Phil digested this revelation. "Can I get you a drink?"

"Sure," she smiled.

Phil snapped his fingers, prompting the bartender to come their way. As we wiped off the bar with a damp towel, he glanced at Marilyn.

"I'll have what he's having," she said. "Scotch on the rocks, with a twist."

"Another one for me, please," Phil said, tapping his empty glass. "No twist."

He turned his attention back to Marilyn. "And then what happened?"

"Well, I threw myself into my job as a stewardess with American Airlines. I had moved to DC to live with some of the other stewardesses. I enjoy the work because it allows me to travel and see the world for a while before starting law school."

The bartender delivered their drinks, and they clinked them in a toast. When Marilyn set her tumbler down, Phil noticed that she also stirred the ice cubes with her right index finger. Some things never changed.

"Mind if I have a cigarette?" she asked.

"By all means, but here. Let me—"

Phil reached into his coat and pulled out a pack of Lucky Strikes. He lit one for her and another for himself.

Marilyn blew a long stream of smoke up toward the ornate ceiling. "I thought traveling all over the country as a stewardess might allow me to forget you."

She took another sip and directly met his gaze. "Not a chance," she said. Then she smiled. "You've always had my heart."

Hearing those kind words allowed Phil's emotions to settle. Initially, he didn't know whether to blow up, be angry, get up and walk away, or say some of the nasty thoughts he had contemplated about her. When she'd broken off their relationship, he'd felt greatly discouraged, especially during lulls between battles in France and Germany. But he had a job to do over there, and he had done it—despite the costs. Now all that was in the past. He took a sip of scotch and a deep drag on his cigarette.

"Why did you decide to see me tonight?" he asked. That was all he could think to say.

---

iii   The MPs were military police. G-man was short for "government man" and became a slang term for agents of the US government, especially agents for the Federal Bureau of Investigation (FBI).

"I called your mother a few weeks back to see how you were doing. I told her everything that had happened to me, and she told me such stories about you. Your wound. Your promotions. Your courage and bravery and medals. I didn't doubt a word. She told me you were home, and you were recuperating. That you were finally seeing other girls. I'm happy for you, Phil. Glad you survived the war and you're doing well. I really am."

She took a sip of her drink and continued. "I told your mother I couldn't get you out of my mind, and I wanted to see you. To face you and tell you what happened."

She looked up from her drink and turned toward him. "I wanted to apologize to you face-to-face. Not in a letter. Not over the phone. I told her I was hoping you'd at least hear me out, even if you couldn't forgive me. She told me when you'd be home and told me she'd arrange for us to get together."

Marilyn shrugged. "So that's it. I was hoping you'd hear my apology. I was praying you might be able to forgive me, but if you can't—and I would completely understand if you couldn't—then at the very least, we might share a last meal and conversation. That perhaps we could be friends from here on out. You'll remember that that's the Friendship Oak tradition."

He chuckled, remembering the massive oak in Gulfport under which they'd met.

"So, that's my confession, and that's why I'm here."

He sensed a cacophony of emotions in himself, but most of all, he felt a great deal of warmth and sympathy for Marilyn. She was as beautiful and sensitive and wonderful and unique as he had remembered. He wondered if he hadn't always secretly hoped that she would come back one day. But never in a thousand years did he think that might happen. Before he knew it, his hand reached out and took hers. He felt his eyes misting and his lips trembling. He looked down and felt her squeeze his hand.

"Thanks for being here tonight," he said. "It's great to see you again." Phil lifted his head, and their eyes met. "And yes, I'm willing to forgive you. I am." He tried to blink back tears.

She took both of his hands in hers. "Your mother made us dinner reservations at the Skyway."

"The fine dining room?"

She nodded. "For dinner and dancing. My treat." She chuckled and blushed. "Well, actually, my daddy's treat."

Phil reached for his wallet, but the bartender leaned over. "Your drinks are on the Peabody, sir. Thanks for your service." The uniformed barkeep smiled warmly.

"I appreciate your support," Phil said.

"And congratulations on the reunion, you two."

❦

The evening was indeed remarkable. Phil and Marilyn shared a delicious dinner in the Skyway Room and a wonderful time dancing to a live big band in the adjoining Plantation Room.[iv] They enjoyed dancing the rumba, the foxtrot, the jive, and even the swing. He loved holding her in his arms during the slow dances, relishing the feel of her curves, and smelling her scent.

When he dropped Marilyn at a friend's house, they kissed for the first time in almost two years on the front porch. As he walked back to the car, he shook his head at the turn of events.

Marilyn was back in his life.

---

iv   The original Peabody Hotel existed from 1869 to 1932. The "new" Peabody opened in 1934 in time for Phil's birthday party and served as the business and social center of the Mid-South throughout the 1930s and 1940s, hosting one of only three national live radio broadcasts. The Plantation Roof and adjoining Skyway Room were popular spots for big band music—that was broadcast nationwide on CBS radio—and dancing to the sounds of Tommy Dorsey, Harry James, and the Andrews Sisters.

53

A HOPEFUL FUTURE

"The war now is away back in the past, and you can tell what books cannot. When you talk, you come down to the practical realities just as they happened....There is many a boy here today who looks on war as all glory, but boys, it is all hell. You can be the warning voice to generations yet to come. I look upon war with horror."

—**Union Civil War General William Tecumseh Sherman**[i,268]

The day before Christmas, Phil and Marilyn flew on a military transport to Des Moines and spent Christmas with Marilyn's parents. Her father and Phil had many war stories to exchange.[269]

During a private time in his study, drinking scotch and enjoying a fine Cuban cigar, Ray Fountain—a colonel who served under General George Patton in the Third Army—told Phil about how Patton ordered soldiers from the 2nd Cavalry Regiment to save the Lipizzaners and free over 150 Allied prisoners at the end of the war.

i   General Sherman said this in a speech in Columbus, Ohio, to 10,000 veterans fifteen years after the Civil War ended. This is the phrase from which the adage, "War is Hell," originated. During the Civil War, Sherman felt the need to punish the South for starting the war and wanted the Southern people to feel the cold hand of war so they would never contemplate it again. The Ulysses Grant-William Tecumseh Sherman philosophy of fighting a war carried on to World War II, ensuring the Germans and Japanese felt the cold hand of war as well.

"General Patton, a well-known horse enthusiast, was aware of your secret mission," Colonel Fountain said. "As far as I'm concerned, you deserve a medal for that, Phil. Too bad there isn't some type of reward for your bravery."

The next morning, just past dawn, Phil awoke to the most beautiful and magnificent sounds—church bells were simultaneously ringing across the whole city. He sat up and grabbed the crutches leaning by his bed and hurried over to the window, opened it, and stuck his head out into the clear, crisp air.

He smiled to himself and was startled as he felt Marilyn at his side. He pulled her close as they listened together. All he could think was, *This is the best Christmas I've ever had!*

"It's wonderful," she whispered.

"The sound of freedom!" was all he could say as the pealing of bells echoed far and wide, floating through the Christmas air from every direction.

With the benefit of flying military transport, Phil and Marilyn met as often as they could. On January 4, 1946, they celebrated his twenty-first birthday during a weeklong visit with his Aunt Leota and Uncle Walter at their Park Avenue brownstone in Manhattan. They returned to New York City for a long weekend in February and took in a Broadway show.

Later that month, Phil began to experience increasing pain in his stump, and his prosthesis became more and more uncomfortable. The prosthetists worked hard to alter the artificial leg, to no avail. Most of the time, he needed to use crutches, which lowered his spirits. The doctors finally diagnosed his stump pain as coming from a growth on one of the nerves. He shared this news with his mother via a letter:

> Well, Mom, they have made their minds up to do a bit
> more cutting on me. It shouldn't keep me in bed much over
> a week if even that long.... Of course, I will write all about
> it as soon as I am able. This will set me back a month or so
> in my walking, but I still think I'll be out by September. Do
> hope so anyway.[270]

Phil also attended his first reunion with some Army buddies at Fort Bragg in North Carolina, where he met up with a bunch of friends from the 326th Glider troop. He had trained with them but never fought with them. Their time together was meaningful.

After returning from North Carolina, he had his final surgery, with the surgeon writing:

> Because of painful neuroma of the sciatic nerve, an
> excision of same was performed 27 February 1946; recovery
> was uneventful.[271]

Phil's post-operative course went far better than expected; his recovery was far ahead of schedule. By April, he was walking comfortably in a prosthesis made of new composite materials much lighter than his last wooden leg.

Things got interesting when doctors began talking of an early discharge, which meant Phil needed an Army assignment. He knew he would need some time to prepare his appeal and defense. Men in the Army's Judge Advocate General's (JAG) Corps advised him to complete this process before receiving notice of pending discharge.

Then another exciting development occurred: Phil discovered that his friend, Ross Calvert, had been assigned to work with their former commander, Colonel McGarr, who was serving as Post Commanding Officer at Fort Myer, Virginia, right across the river from Washington, D.C. Also, McGarr's boss was Brigadier General Robert N. Young, who had served both as an assistant and acting division commander of the 3rd Infantry Division from 1944–1945, and was given command of the Military District of Washington in July 1945. Of course, Marilyn was based in Washington as a stewardess for American Airlines. If there were an opening at Fort Myer, he'd be walking into a veritable beehive of friendly faces.

It took only a couple of phone conversations with Ross until Phil got the uplifting news that his old boss, Colonel McGarr, wanted to give him a job as his executive officer and assist him with his fight to stay in the service. Living in Washington, D.C., where the decision-makers lived and worked, would benefit him.

During the call, Ross told Phil about the uniqueness of the unit under his command. "I'm in charge of the 2511 Special Ceremonial Detachment assigned to Fort Myer, and we provide all of the ceremonial duties for the Military District of Washington," he explained.

"Doing what?" Phil asked.

"Well, first of all, we have the mission of performing memorial affairs, which includes standard and full-honor funerals at the Arlington National Cemetery. We also execute all of the dignified transfers of fallen soldiers from overseas returning to the D.C. area. If there's to be a military ceremony at the White House, the Pentagon, or any national memorial in the D.C. area, we get the call."

"Guess I'll need to update my dress uniforms if I come to work for you, eh?"

"That's right," Ross answered, chuckling. "Including your dress tuxedos. We also have the mission of performing ceremonial tasks such as a full-honor guard for the arrivals of visiting dignitaries, wreath ceremonies at the Tomb of the Unknowns, and full-honor reviews in support of senior army leaders and retiring soldiers. The Military District here provides details for hundreds of ceremonies each year."

"Sounds like a lot of work."

"It is, Phil. But it's also a lot of fun. We're in high cotton here as we get to rub elbows with some bigwigs. Whenever the head of a sovereign state visits D.C., we provide salutes, music, and honor guards. Some of my guys even get to serve as ushers at the White House and escorts for the President and Vice President. I've done events with both, and best of all, they get to know you by name before you know it. In fact, we had a swell event recently."

"Do tell."

"It happened just after General Eisenhower moved into Quarters One here at Fort Myer—that was the end of January, I believe. Then on March 9, he and his wife, Mamie, had Winston Churchill over for dinner."

"That's amazing."

"Yup. And I was on the honor guard that evening. Then I and some of the men helped with dinner service. Incredible to see the two famous men enjoying cigars and a drink on the front porch and laughing about old times. Later that evening, I got to shake Churchill's hand. I told him we had seen him on his boat just before landing in France and how we had appreciated the gesture. He told me he remembered the day—that it was Napoleon's birthday, and he was traveling under the assumed name of 'Colonel Kent.' He said he opposed the invasion of southern France, but that Eisenhower and Roosevelt were not, as he said, 'so moved.' But once the decision was made, he prayed for its success and did everything in his power to help—including coming to see us off and support us GIs. Swell stuff, eh?"

"I'd say!"

"But my main job may be the best assignment on the post. I'm Commander of the Tomb Guards at Arlington Cemetery. I'm in charge of the best-known group of men here. In their role of protecting the Tomb, we call them 'sentinels.' There has been a military guard at the Tomb of the Unknowns every hour, rain or shine, snow, or ice, or sleet, tornado or hurricane, since 1926. Before that, a civilian security guard protected the tombs."

"You said, 'the Tomb of the Unknowns.' I thought it was the Tomb of the Unknown Soldier."

"Lots of folks call it that. But there's more than one unknown there. We also provide the 'Continental Color Guard,' which presents the nation's colors at special events across the Capitol region, like the Presidential Salute Battery, which renders honors to senior dignitaries at arrival. My personal favorite is the U.S. Army Caisson Platoon, which provides horses and riders to pull the caisson at military and state funerals."

"Hate to show my ignorance, Ross, but what's a caisson?"

"I didn't know what it was either, Daddy-O, but it's the wagon that carries the flag-draped coffin to the burial sites at Arlington. Caissons were common in the Revolutionary War and Civil War and used to carry ammunition. The caissons we're using were built in 1918 and used for 75-mm cannons. But they also carried ammunition, spare parts, and tools for the cannons. For our purposes, those items have been removed and exchanged for the flat platform on which the casket sits. Horses pull the caissons."

Phil's eyes lit up. "Oh, yeah. I've seen pictures of these processions in *Life* magazine. Tell me about these horses."

"We have four teams of matched blacks or grays," Ross continued. "Three pair from each team pull the caisson. The lead pair is in front, the swing pair follows, and the wheel pair, made up of the largest and strongest horses, are closest to the caisson. They serve as the brakes, if needed. All six horses are saddled, but only the horses on each pair's left side have mounted riders. This tradition carries over from horse-drawn artillery days when one horse carried the soldier, and the other horse carried extra supplies.

"Finally, there are two other horses per team. The commander rides one and the other, what they call the 'caparisoned horse,' has no rider, and is walked behind the caisson by one of our men. That horse has an empty saddle with a pair of boots reversed in the stirrups. They say the caparisoned horse symbolizes the officer's last journey. The backward boots in the stirrups imply that the warrior has one last look at his family, who typically walk behind the caisson. But to have a caparisoned horse at your funeral, you have to achieve the rank of colonel or above or be a famous politician. They say that Abraham Lincoln was the first U.S. president to have a caparisoned horse at his funeral."

"Guess that horse can take the day off when one of us kicks the can," Phil quipped, but inside his gut, his emotions were swirling since the position of XO was usually reserved for a major. If Colonel McGarr offered him the job, he'd have a lot to learn and he didn't want to fail his benefactor.

Simultaneously, excitement filled his heart because he would be around horses and living close to Marilyn.

ᑲᔑ

In a phone conversation on April 7, 1946, Phil's old boss said he was happy to offer him a job at Fort Myer as his executive officer, pending approval from above.[272]

"Thank you, sir. I'm delighted to accept," Phil replied.

McGarr then put Ross on the phone to instruct Phil on his next steps.

After they hung up, Phil immediately wrote Colonel McGarr using the exact language Ross suggested:

Subject: Return to Six Months Temporary Duty

1. As regards to my conversation with you on 7 April 1946, I would like to return to duty under your command for six months Temporary Duty.

2. The main reason for this duty is (1) I wish to give my prosthesis a good test before being retired from the Service. (2) I would like to return to duty for a while, even though it may be a short time.

3. I do not wish for this position if you think there is a chance that I might be reduced in grade before the end of my Temporary Duty.[273]

Good news arrived in early May when higher-ups approved Phil's request for six months temporary duty with the proviso that in November 1946, he would return to an appropriate medical facility, likely Walter Reed General Hospital[ii] in Washington, for reconsideration of his physical capacity for military duty.

The news gladdened Phil, who suddenly felt more optimistic than ever about his prospects. That morning at Lawson, he visited the small hospital chapel for a moment of prayer and reflection. As he knelt in one of the pews, he realized that a new chapter was being written in his life. He was becoming a new man, a better man, a whole man.

The rest of the day, Phil packed and made the rounds, saying goodbye to his friends, as well as the staff and doctors. The following morning, he hopped in his car and began driving northbound for Fort Myer, Virginia, a 600-mile journey that represented a new future.

Would he win his appeal not to be honorably discharged from the Army because he was an officer with an amputated limb? No officer had ever made—much less won—that appeal, but he sensed a new wind blowing across the land of the free and the home of the brave.

---

ii   The name of Walter Reed General Hospital was changed to Walter Reed National Army Medical Center in 1951. Named after yellow fever researcher Walter Reed, the medical facility was the U.S. Army's flagship medical center from 1909 to 2011. Walter Reed General Hospital closed in 2011 and was combined with the National Naval Medical Center to form the tri-service Walter Reed National Military Medical Center in Bethesda, Maryland.

54

BURYING HEROES

"These are the caisson horses, who quietly play an
important role in the U.S. military by honoring its
service members."

**—1st Lieutenant Austin Hatch, public affairs officer for
the 3rd Infantry Regiment caisson platoon[274]**

Phil immediately felt at home as he drove past the guard gate at Fort Myer.
The storied post abutted Arlington National Cemetery. He took a turn on
Lee Avenue, a well-kept, leafy residential area that could have been found in
almost any town in America.[275]

Most of the buildings at the north end of Fort Myer had been built
between 1895 and 1908. He passed Quarters One, home to the Army Chief
of Staff since 1908 and some of the nation's most famous generals, including
Douglas MacArthur and George C. Marshall. Its current resident was General
Dwight D. Eisenhower. Phil smiled when he saw Mamie Eisenhower on the
front porch, reading a book in a rocker. She waved to him. He sheepishly
waved back.

As he continued along the tree-lined avenue past Victorian-style homes
with inviting verandas and front yards filled with playful children, he found
the scene comforting since it reminded him of the grander residential streets
in his hometown of Memphis.

Phil drove by the extensive Fort Myer parade grounds, where aviator Orville Wright, during a military test flight in September 1908, set a world record for the longest time aloft in the air—a flight lasting one hour and two minutes. Traveling at a leisurely speed of thirty-eight miles per hour, Wright circled the parade grounds seventy-one times above hundreds of awestruck spectators.[i]

Coming upon the headquarters building, a striking Georgian red-brick structure, Phil noted the sharply dressed Army men entering and leaving the HQ, all spit and polish. Then his heart raced a bit faster when he came upon rows of magnificent stables and a riding hall. He recalled how Fort Myer's equestrian training facility was the primary training ground for Olympic equestrian entrants.

Phil had a little time before he needed to check in at HQ, so he parked and walked inside the front entrance to the stables. A specialist in full dress uniform immediately acknowledged him.

"Can I help you, sir?" he said.

"I'm Captain Larimore," he began.

The man snapped to attention and saluted.

"At ease. I'm Colonel McGarr's new XO and wanted to look around."

The soldier relaxed. "Well, Captain, welcome to the Caisson Stables. I have a few moments before we gear up for the next funeral. I'm happy to give you a quick tour."

As they began walking, Phil asked, "How many men and horses does the platoon utilize?"

"Sir, it's about fifty men, give or take, and about sixty horses—forty horses stabled here and twenty at Fort Belvoir. We're divided into four squads or what we call 'riding teams.' Each squad has its own set of horses matched by coat color. We have the grays on two teams—but of course, the gray horses turn white with age. Then we have the black coats on the other two teams. At any given time, only two squads are riding."

"Only black or gray horses?"

"Yes, sir. That's it. If a horse is born a bay,[ii] it has to find another profession."

"Eight horses per funeral?"

"Usually, seven. Eight only if we have the caparisoned horse, or what we call 'the Cap.' The lead horse is not harnessed and is ridden by the section chief alone, alongside the front left carriage horse to guide him."

---

i   Over five days, with and without a guest passenger, Orville set successive endurance records. The eleventh test flight on September 17, 1908, ended in tragedy when the aircraft crashed. Wright was severely cut and bruised, with a fractured left leg and four broken ribs. Unfortunately, his passenger, Lieutenant Thomas Selfridge, a West Point graduate, was seriously injured and died a few hours later after unsuccessful neurosurgery, becoming the first person to die in an airplane crash.

ii   A bay is a reddish-brown or brown hair coat color. Bay is one of the most common coat colors in many horse breeds.

"How many funerals are you doing?"

"On average, six to eight full-honor funerals a day, split between two teams. All day, every day, sometimes up to thirty a day. We're like the post office: we're at our appointed rounds in rain, sleet, snow, or ice."

"Who can be buried at Arlington?"

"Eligibility for in-ground burial at Arlington National Cemetery is the most stringent of all U.S. national cemeteries. The honor is reserved for officers, warrant officers, sergeant majors, or E-9s, the highest enlisted rank, and anyone killed in the line of duty. Priority is given to those killed in action."

"You said there were four riding teams. But only two work each day?"

"Well, the two teams not active on a given day have a lot to do. Besides all the stable work, there's constant training. It never stops. The training for both the horses and the guys is fairly intense because no words can be spoken during the ceremony. The men direct their horses with undetected foot or knee movements—what we call a 'two-leg lead.' These horses are trained to withstand all the different stimuli they are exposed to—trumpets, twenty-one-gun salutes, even cannons and low-flying airplanes. We look for the ones that don't spook easily. And then we train, train, and train. We prefer riders with little or no riding experience because we use a riding style not taught anywhere else, what we call an 'erect posture of solemn military attention.'"

"Do you tend to use any particular breeds?"

"Not really. The horses are chosen for their easygoing temperaments. But they must also be well-disciplined, often standing still for long periods."

"I can see why you need highly trained horses. I've been around horses my whole life," Phil observed. "They can be as different as night and day."

"Yes, sir. We find that horses are a lot like people. Some are social; some are antisocial. Some like to be washed and groomed; some don't. Some are nice and gentle; others can be mean as snakes."

The men walked up to the washroom and watched as two beautiful gray horses were splashed down with suds and their hooves cleaned. Phil noticed their traditional military look: clipped manes and forelocks and squared tails.

"How long do the horses serve here?" he asked.

"About ten years on average, then we usually adopt them out to the public. The Caisson Horse Adoption Program ensures that each horse is rewarded with a great home following a well-earned retirement."

Phil took in the musty stable smells, which he loved. "Sounds like you guys have long days," he commented.

"We do, sir. We usually begin our day at zero-four-hundred hours when we report to the stables. There's a ton to do before zero-eight-hundred when the first two caissons have to be ready to go. When the caisson squads are in the cemetery, the guys left behind clean the barn stalls and feed pails and shine the tack and the brass. We work steadily until about fifteen hundred hours."

"Quite an operation," Phil observed.

The soldier paused a moment. "Yes, sir, it is. But it's more than just an assignment or job. It's a pleasure and honor to serve our country's heroes and their families. We consider it part of our sacred trust that each funeral is executed with the utmost dignity and respect. We have the privilege of carrying a comrade for their last ride to Arlington National Cemetery. My sense is not only that the families appreciate it, but we create a lifelong memory and bring some peace and closure to them."

Phil glanced at his watch. "I have an appointment with Colonel McGarr in a few minutes. Served with him from Anzio until the end of the war in Germany."

The man's eyes widened. He stood straight and saluted. "Thank you for your service and sacrifice, sir."

Phil returned the salute. "Thank you, and I'm looking forward to working with you."

಄

As Phil approached the HQ, the front doors burst open. Ross Calvert rushed out, jumped down the steps, and embraced Phil. Both laughed and slapped each other's backs as they walked into the building, grinning from ear to ear.

"Gosh, Phil, you look great. And you're walking with a lot less limp."

"I am. These new prosthetics really help. They're made of composite materials. Much lighter than the first wooden leg I got. The ankle and knee joints are pretty realistic. Pretty soon, I'll be beating you in a hundred-yard race."

His old friend grinned. "I'm sure you will, Daddy-O, but let's get inside. The old man's waiting."

Once they were upstairs, Colonel McGarr's aide escorted them into his office. The colonel sat behind a formidable wooden desk signing papers, a cigar propped in his mouth. Upon seeing them enter and receiving their salute, McGarr exclaimed, "Well, I'll be damned! Captain Larimore in the flesh."

He circled the desk and briskly shook Phil's hand. They sat down on a group of overstuffed chairs, the windows overlooking the caisson stables. The colonel offered the men a box of Cuban Coronas.

"Cigars are in order, Phil," Ross offered. "Colonel McGarr's been put in for general. And, if I may say, sir, it's well overdue."

"Every commander needs a suck-up, brownnosing officer below him, right, Captain?" the Colonel observed, laughing.

Ross' face reddened. "No, sir! I mean it when I say it's overdue. How many colonels in the U.S Army commanded a regiment as long as you did? Twenty months, including a month as the acting assistant division commander of the 3rd Infantry Division. How many colonels in the war have a DSC, two Distinguished Service Medals, three Silver Stars, three Legions of Merit, five Bronze Stars, and seven Purple Hearts? And they didn't give those out because you led from the rear, sir."

Phil picked up the assault. "He's right, Colonel. You fought right beside us, on the front lines, in Anzio, Besançon, the Vosges, the disaster at Colmar, and the Siegfried Line. None of the men in the other regiments saw their commanders up front as much as we did. And when you weren't with your men, you were in a Piper Cub getting shot at. You didn't just order us, sir, you led us. When we were slow off the line, it was your boot in our ass. That's how close you stayed to us, sir. And when I was wounded, you got to me almost as quickly as the medics."

McGarr threw his head back and roared. "You two sons-of-bitches make me proud. God, I loved leading you and the men just like you."

The colonel took a puff off of his cigar and leaned forward toward Phil. "Tell you what, Captain. To switch subjects, I want you to know why I don't think you're an executive officer type of guy."

Hearing this surprised Phil, and it must have shown because the colonel chuckled again. "Not that you can't and won't do a great job, but being an XO is mostly a paper-pusher type of job. Coordinate my schedule, be sure my orders are carried out, travel with me here and there, occasionally attend some big ceremony.

"Captain, I see you more as a boots-on-the-ground type of guy, or in-the-stirrup, if you know what I mean. You're a natural leader. I saw it in Europe, and that's what you need to be doing here. But there are three reasons I wanted you here as my XO. First of all, it's the only opening I had. Second, I want to facilitate your efforts to overturn that damned ridiculous War Department policy whereby officers with an amputation are automatically discharged once rehabilitated.

"Now, don't get me wrong. After some men are wounded, they aren't the same. They've lost their luster. But most have the experience and leadership skills that this Army needs. I'm not alone in believing this war we just fought will not end all wars. In the future, we're going to need more good officers—war-hardened men, experienced men, good men—to lead. Amputee or not, Larimore, we need you. And having you here in Washington will expedite your appeal process by putting you close to the decision-makers in this town."

"I deeply appreciate that, sir," Phil replied. "Phone calls don't seem to be working very well, and as you know, getting letters answered by the War Department or a senator seems to take a long time."

Phil set his cigar on the edge of an ashtray. "But I'm curious. What's the third reason, Colonel?"

McGarr looked at Ross, who smiled. "I'll show you tomorrow." The colonel took the last drag off his cigar, crushed the butt in an ashtray, and stood. Phil and Ross followed his lead.

"Men, I'm up to my ass in paperwork," the colonel declared. "Calvert, give Larimore a quick tour of Arlington and get him settled in his housing. Then, I'll see you in the morning, and we'll get started.

"One more thing, guys. Your bridge-playing expertise at Fort Benning has been noticed. Ike wants you two to come over to Quarters One to play bridge sometime. He'll contact you."

ജ

Phil and Ross drove to the officers' quarters, where Ross helped him unload his bags. Then it was off for a quick tour of the post and Arlington Cemetery, ending up at the Tomb of the Unknowns. They were met and shown the underground facilities below the tombs by two members of Ross' guard platoon: Sergeant George H. Waple, III, and Private Pasquale "Pat" Varalla, both in full dress uniform. When Phil commented on their snappy appearance, Waple said, "We are probably the sharpest unit in the U.S. Army at this time, sir."[276]

Varalla added, "Complete spit and polish at all times, sir."

Ross looked at his watch. "It's about time for the next ceremony."

Once upstairs, Phil saw that quite a crowd had gathered around the tomb. Beyond the cemetery, Memorial Bridge and the District of Columbia perched at their feet. Below them lay a large marble sarcophagus with a single soldier marching back and forth on a long mat. His rifle rested on his shoulder as he slowly paced back and forth. Tourists wandered around the tomb, snapping photographs.

"Once a recruit is chosen," Sergeant Waple explained, "they undergo an intense two-week training period, in which they must pass tests on weapons, ceremonial steps, cadence, military bearing, uniform preparation, and orders. Although we as military members are known for our neat uniforms, the Tomb Guards have the highest standards of them all. If a trainee fails any test, they are assigned back to their company. In fact, let's test our private. So, Varalla, what's the mission of the Tomb guards?"

Private Varalla pulled himself to attention, puffed out his chest, and barked, "Sergeant Waple, the mission of the Tomb platoon is this: We are responsible for maintaining the highest standards and traditions of the United States Army and this Nation while keeping a constant vigil at this National Shrine, and our special duty is to prevent any desecration or disrespect directed toward the Tomb."

"Perfect!" crowed Waple, obviously proud of his charge. "Our goal as trainers is not to make our trainees as good as we are, but to make them better."

Waple pointed to the guard. "Note the cadence, Captain. We practice our steps with a metronome, set to ninety beats per minute, the tempo of a slow march. After the cemetery closes, groups of trainees will walk the steps over and over. Perfection is the standard. If they stop even a half-inch off their mark, boy, do they hear about it."

"How come the soldier walking the mat doesn't wear rank insignia?"

"It's on purpose," Ross said. "We don't want the sentinel to appear to outrank the Unknown, whatever his rank may have been."

As they turned to face the tomb, a bell tolled. The relief commander announced the Changing of the Guard. They heard him unlock the bolt of his rifle—the signal to begin the ceremony. Then the relief commander walked to the front of the tomb, saluted, and turned to face the several dozen spectators.

"Ladies and gentlemen," he barked, "may I have your attention, please! The ceremony that you are about to witness is the Changing of the Guard. In keeping with the dignity of this ceremony, it is requested that everyone remain silent and standing! Thank you."

The relief commander walked to the relieving sentinel, conducted an elaborate white-glove, two-minute inspection of the weapon, checking each part of the rifle, then returned it and carefully studied the soldier's uniform from top to bottom.

The relief commander and the relieving sentinel then marched to meet the retiring sentinel at the center of the matted path in front of the tomb in perfectly matched timing. After presenting their arms, all three saluted the Unknown Soldiers who had posthumously been awarded the Medal of Honor.

The relief commander spoke to the retiring sentinel: "Pass on your orders."

The retiring sentinel responded, "Post and orders, remain as directed."

The relieving sentinel responded, "Orders acknowledged," and stepped into position on the mat. The relief commander, along with the retiring and relieving sentinels, marched together in perfect harmony at the cadence of ninety steps per minute. Once at the end of the mat, the relieving sentinel turned while the retired sentinel walked a few steps further. After unlocking his bolt, he was ordered to fall out while the relieving sentinel began walking on the mat as the new Tomb Guard.

When the rite was over, Phil shook his head and commented, "What a remarkable ceremony. What a sacred place."

"To me," Ross added, "it's the ultimate symbol of the ultimate sacrifice. We've both served with more men than we can count who did not return to their loved ones, who were never laid to rest with the honors they deserve. We've both known many men, too many men, who could have been here. So, in a way, to me, the Unknown Soldiers represent them all."

Phil could only nod his head in assent. He turned away to keep Ross from seeing his tears—tears of relief that he had survived a horrible war when so many of his fellow officers and men had not. Their faces still flashed before his eyes, and he could name each one.

55

A FOUNTAIN OF HOPE

"The country is now peaceful, and long may it remain
so. To you soldiers, they owe the debt of gratitude."

**—Union Civil War General William Tecumseh
Sherman**[277]

After Phil reported to work and settled into his new desk the following morning, one of Colonel McGarr's aides came rushing in.[278]

"Captain, the boss is waiting for you in his car out front. You need to get out there pronto. The old man does *not* like to be kept waiting."

Phil hopped down the stairs as fast as he could. Even with his new prosthesis, he had to take each step one at a time, stepping down with his good leg, bringing the artificial leg down to the same level, and repeating the same steps again and again. As good as his updated leg was, the prosthetists at Walter Reed General Hospital said newer legs with much improved joints would soon be available. In the future, a new prosthesis would allow him to walk up and down steps more naturally and even run to some degree. He couldn't wait.

Phil spotted Ross, sitting shotgun. The driver stood next to the idling car, holding open the rear door, where Colonel McGarr sat cross-legged on a leather bench seat. Phil slid in and said hello to the colonel and Ross.

Soon they were cruising down Highway 1 through the lush Virginia countryside. Their windows were wide open, and the warm air of a spring morning in 1946 blew through the car.

"What's our mission?" Phil asked.

"We're going to Fort Belvoir, about twenty miles to the south, for some business and to show you around the stables," McGarr answered. "We'll inspect the advance horsemanship training course that some of the caisson platoon men and horses are attending. This training is somewhat of a break for the caisson soldiers and their horses. These men receive this advanced training every few months to sharpen their skills.

"The Fort Belvoir stables are where new horses are medically evaluated, trained, and housed before their transfer to Fort Myer," the colonel added. "Once up with us, they're rookies on the caisson platoon. After two weeks working at Arlington, the horses are taken back to Fort Belvoir's stables for a week, where they have acres of pastureland to run, roam, and graze. After their rest week, they come back to Fort Myer and train for another week before going back to Arlington cemetery for two weeks. Then the cycle repeats itself. I want you to see and be familiar with the process. Plus, I love the drive down and back. It's relaxing for me to be away from all the bullshit paperwork and administration."

Phil was excited about the opportunity to understand the other side of the caisson operation. During the drive, the men smoked and shared stories.

"Calvert, you've been promising to tell me more about your POW time once Larimore arrived. No better time than now," Colonel McGarr said. "You were a POW from Maison Rouge to almost the end of the war, right?"

"Yes, sir. Three and a half months as a 'Kriegie.'[i] After the Krauts captured us, the officers were segregated in Stuttgart and put into jail cells, two or three to a cell. Then someone came up to our cell and said, 'Calvert? Come on. An SS officer wants to talk to you.' I figured, 'Hell, this is not a good thing.'

"I went down to this small room and was told to sit. The interrogator had a ledger, and he read from it: 'Your name is Calvert, and you are an intelligence officer with your regiment.' He had a roster of everyone, which one of our guys must have had tortured out of him. He asked, 'Third Division?' I didn't say anything. So, he reached over and ripped the camouflage netting off my helmet so he could see the insignia. I said, 'Okay, Third Division.' He asked a few other questions, but nothing seemed to need an answer, so he sent me back. That was it."

"Intelligence reported that our POWs were treated awful. Did that happen to you?" the colonel asked.

"It wasn't a day at the beach, but we were luckier than most. It must have been true," Ross said sarcastically, "because a Red Cross representative explained in great detail how our captors were doing all they could to keep

---

i   "Kriegie" was a term former POWs in Germany called themselves. It comes from the German word *Kriegsgefangene*, which means "prisoner of war."

us comfortable. He said we shouldn't be complaining because it made the Germans nervous."

"Those lying bastards!" McGarr exclaimed. "They didn't want the damn Germans to be nervous? Maybe they should have worried a bit more about my guys and not licking German asses!"

Ross smiled. "Well, 900 calories a day sure made *us* nervous. And we saw the German staff had quite a bit more. So food was of considerable interest to us. Each day, we were given a loaf of bread for seven men. They guaranteed that it wasn't more than 25 percent sawdust, but it did not always meet that standard. It looked like regular German bread, but it didn't taste like much of anything. We divided it very carefully. That was our ration for the day. Some guys would wolf down their piece immediately, while others would just nibble on it. Nobody ever knew which was the better approach.

"We never knew whether our breakfast beverage was coffee or shaving water. It came out about the same. Lunch was supposed to be the heavy meal of the day, although it was pretty light. It was mostly a dehydrated vegetable—I can't think of the name. Just dried-up leaves, which, of course, added to our dietary problems. No surprise that I lost about forty pounds."

Ross took a deep puff from his cigarette. "We were treated like hell, sir. I'm not sure I'll ever be the same."

❧

The colonel's driver took them directly to a lush green pasture next to the stables. A small brook ran down the middle of a verdant meadow dotted with dandelions and daisies. Several dozen horses were grazing, but one horse in particular caught Phil's eye: a gorgeous bay-colored Thoroughbred with high withers, a deep chest, a short back, and a lean muscular body. He admired the remarkable horse's deep hindquarters and long legs.[279]

But what caught Phil's attention was the horse's unique head. Not attractive or sleek, just clunky looking. An unusual sight, especially given the horse's beautiful and muscular line. Then the horse looked up at him as he chewed a bit of fresh grass. Phil's eyes widened when he noticed an unusual and small white star-shaped marking on the lower middle of the Thoroughbred's chest. His mind immediately returned to his covert mission to Czechoslovakia just days before a bullet shattered his right leg. For a moment, he couldn't believe his eyes.

Could it be him? But how?

He looked at Ross and the colonel, who were both carefully watching him. Then McGarr broke into an ear-to-ear smile and nodded. "It's him."

"Tuckern?"

McGarr slapped a hand on Phil's shoulder. "I believe you've met before."

Phil looked back at the stallion in utter disbelief. At first, he felt his jaw drop ever so slightly as his eyes widened. Then his lips tightened. Without even thinking, he whistled. The horse's ears perked up and pointed forward to capture the sound.

Phil whistled again, and in an instant, the Thoroughbred charged toward them. Phil stepped up on a middle rail, then threw his new leg over the top railing, hopping the fence and landing in the pasture. For a moment, he thought the steed might run him over.

But then the sixteen-hander pulled himself up just a few feet away from Phil. He snorted and shook his ugly head. Phil squatted down, almost instinctively, and looked at the horse's chest. He'd noticed the same unique marking in Czechoslovakia. The horse walked up to him and allowed him to stroke his nose. Phil felt his eyes misting and glanced back at Ross and Colonel McGarr. He was speechless.

"After your mission," McGarr began, "word got back to me about you and that Thoroughbred—that there seemed to be a bond. Don't know why, but that fact stuck with me. It's a funny thing about the life of a commander. Thousands of things happen every day, especially in the pitch of battle. Most are forgotten. But some stick. This did."

Phil slowly stood and walked to Tuckern's side, gently stroking his neck.

"When you were wounded, exactly one month before the end of that godforsaken war, I took the news more personally than I usually did. I guess we all, after so many, many months of fighting and carnage, grew a bit calloused to losing men."

McGarr looked across the field, toward the forest. "When you were wounded, I thought of what I had heard about this horse. Once I knew the generals had approved the mission to rescue the Lipizzaner horses, I requested that Tuckern be brought out with the rest."

"How did they get out?" Phil asked incredulously.

"It's a story that can be told over drinks at the Officer's Club some evening, but to make a very long story very short, after I reported your findings up the chain of command, I'm not sure it was believed. Then General Patton's 2nd Cavalry Group, which had advanced west of Czechoslovakia in late April of '45, was contacted by the ranking German at the horse farm, a Colonel Holters.

"Most of the 2nd Cav's officers were horsemen, including the unit's commander, Colonel Charles M. Reed. Reed and Holters negotiated the groundwork for a surrender. Then Reed sent a message to General Patton at Third Army headquarters requesting permission to save the horses. After giving a wink and a nod, I was told that Patton's immediate response was, and I quote, 'Get them. Make it fast!'"

"That makes sense," Phil interjected. "Patton was known to be a lifelong horseman."

"It took until four days after Germany's surrender to work out the details and approvals. But on twelve May, 300 of the most prized horses, including all the Lipizzaners and Tuckern, were either trucked, ridden, or herded safely over the border to Bad Kötzting, Germany, thirty-five miles away. Miraculously, only two horses didn't survive the two-day march.

"Saving those horses, particularly the Lipizzaners, was a gutsy-as-hell move. I've heard there was no legal or historical precedent. All over Europe, we had soldiers and art historians whose mission was to protect cultural artifacts and recover stolen art. But the horses did not have the same official protection."

"What happened to the horses after they safely reached Germany?" Phil asked.

"The military decided to ship some of the horses, which had been declared 'spoils of war,' back to the States. Last fall, 151 of the world's most beautiful stallions, mares, and foals were loaded onto a liberty ship, the *Stephen F. Austin*. When they arrived in Newport News, most were transferred by train to the Army's Pomona Remount Depot in California. But Patton's Lipizzaners and one ugly-headed and mostly blue-blooded Thoroughbred were sent here."

McGarr turned to Phil. "General O'Daniel intervened on your behalf, along with one of Patton's staff officers, a Colonel Fountain, and a German officer, a Captain Rudolph Lessing. All helped us get Tuckern on that shipment."

Once again, Phil couldn't believe his ears. Now he knew what Colonel Fountain had been referring to when he'd visited Marilyn's family in Des Moines at Christmastime. And, of course, he never forgot meeting Captain Lessing from the Hostau stable. *Oh, my goodness*, he thought.

"Remember that the boss said he had three reasons he wanted you here as XO, Phil?" Ross said. "Tuckern is the third."

"And," Phil whispered, stroking Tuckern's neck, "the best of all."

"I'll have Tuckern put on the next transport trailer back to Fort Myer," the colonel said, smiling. "The Army officially owns him, but I'm having him assigned to us. You'll be able to train and ride him as long as you're at the post."

Phil could not believe his good fortune. He and Marilyn were an item again, and now this.

Life, he decided, was really looking up.

56

ONE-LEG LEAD

"We have raised our hands and said, 'Take me, America.
I am willing to kill for you. I am willing to sacrifice my
limbs for you. I will come back to America scarred and
disfigured for you.'"

—National Infantry Museum[280]

On Thursday, May 30, 1946, Memorial Day,[i] Phil had his first ceremonial assignment. Since Colonel McGarr was away for the week, Phil, Ross, and a small team were assigned to meet President Harry Truman at the White House for a Medal of Honor presentation. Afterward, the President invited Phil and Ross to ride with him to Arlington National Cemetery for a wreath-laying ceremony at the Tombs. Phil had never seen a United States president before, so this day, especially riding in the presidential limousine, was a highlight for him.[281]

Phil later wrote this to his mother:

> *As you know, we were quite busy on the 30th and the
> day before. We were with the President, so we had to look
> our best. I enjoyed the pomp and circumstance.*[282]

---

i   From 1868 to 1970, Memorial Day was celebrated on May 30. The Uniform Monday Holiday Act moved its date to the last Monday of May to increase the number of three-day weekends for federal employees.

During this time, with more exposure to caskets, funerals, and salutes from guns and artillery pieces, difficult memories began to explode unexpectedly in Phil's mind. He also started to experience an increase in extremely disturbing nightmares. When his mother complained about his infrequent letters, he wrote:

> *Honest, I promise to try to do better from now on, but when I get in one of these darn moods where I don't feel like writing, there just seems to be no way to get me out.*[283]

As Phil became more of a recluse, he lost his appetite for food and friendship. He contemplated seeing a psychiatrist, but with Ross' encouragement, he met with one of the post chaplains. He found the visits surprisingly encouraging, similar to what he experienced during his chaplain visits at Lawson. Ross also came by daily and recommended they begin attending the weekly Protestant service and get out together more often for social events around the post. Meeting new people lifted Phil's spirits, and he found his mood improving.

He focused on pleasures that brought him the greatest joy, such as having lunch with Ross on most days and riding Tuckern, usually when his workday was over. He loved feeding and grooming him afterward.

Phil decided that he didn't like the name Tuckern—too German-sounding to his ears. He played with a few names in his mind. First, he thought of "Chugalug," but then decided that he liked "Chugwater" the best. Something about that name reminded him of the mighty Mississippi River, so Chugwater he became. As his love grew for this Thoroughbred, Phil started calling him "Chug" as a term of endearment.

He and Ross would occasionally catch a movie in the evenings, but increasingly the duo played bridge against other competitive players on base. They found their years of working together made for an excellent bridge partnership. Word got around of their prowess at bidding and winning tricks.

General Eisenhower, an avid bridge player, invited the two of them to play at Quarters One from time to time. The joke around Fort Myer was that Eisenhower was planning to snatch them because one of the unwritten qualifications for serving on Eisenhower's staff was an officer's ability to play a decent game of bridge.

Phil remembered when Ike told them he had "augmented" his meager cadet stipend playing poker at West Point, but the card game did not sharpen his mind like bridge, a game of "strategy, percentages, and bluff," the general said. Ike considered anything less than total concentration to be a sacrilege to the game of bridge, but he could become quite animated during the playing of hands.

His wife, Mamie, would serve refreshments for the men as they sipped beverages and chain-smoked during their spirited games, which were always serious competitions. One time, Mamie bragged to Phil that a world-class bridge expert said her husband was a "fine player." When Ike was stationed in the Philippines in the mid-1930s, he would play with the country's president, Manuel Quezon, who called him a "bridge wizard."[284]

"Do you play bridge with the general?" Phil asked.

"Rarely," she replied. "He yells at me when I make mistakes," she added, winking.

ↄ৯

Phil was surprised that he didn't get to see Marilyn as often as he thought he would, even though they lived close to each other. Air travel was taking off after the war, and Marilyn was busiest from Thursdays to Sundays.[285]

When she was in town on weekends between flight assignments, they attended horse shows, participated in foxhunts, or enjoyed rides with Chug and a horse that Marilyn's father had purchased for her and was stabling at Fort Myer.

In August, Phil changed bosses. Colonel McGarr gave up his position as Post Executive Officer to attend the National War College, which had just opened a month earlier in downtown Washington. Phil was happy for him, sure that Colonel McGarr would become General McGarr one day.

He was equally happy that the new Commanding Officer of Fort Myer, Colonel John J. Albright, was even more supportive of his upcoming appeals to stay in the Army.

"Major, I'm going to have you spend more time with some of the legal skirmishes I have to deal with," said the colonel. "Working with the JAG folks will give you bug-on-the-wall insights about the inner workings of the Army's board hearings—especially what leads to successful outcomes and what results in failed hearings."

Phil's optimism rose after hearing that. It was as if divine providence was giving him a legal education without him even knowing it.

As well as things were going at work, his relationship with Marilyn hit a rough patch. Maybe it was the reality that Phil had lost a leg and what that would mean if they got married and lived the rest of their lives together. Perhaps it was because Marilyn always wanted to become a lawyer and go to law school herself. Maybe it was because she always wanted to marry a doctor.

If she married Phil—whose future was very much in doubt—those dreams might not ever happen. As she and Phil talked things through, Marilyn declared that she wanted to move back to Des Moines and attend Drake School of Law, where she had been accepted.

Phil didn't want to lose her, so he applied to the College of Engineering at Iowa State University in Des Moines. An admission acceptance would be a nice backup in the unlikely event he lost his appeal. But at the same time, he began to wonder if their relationship would go the distance.

While they agreed they weren't breaking up and would continue seeing each other, Phil wondered if they were delaying the inevitable.

↪

At least Phil still had Chug to take his mind off his foundering love life. By the fall, the Thoroughbred had completed basic caisson training and learned to respond to Phil's one-leg lead. Some of the more learned horsemen he knew said it was the first they had ever heard of a horse capable of following a one-leg lead. From time to time, Phil rode in a high-ranking officer's funeral, which was a privilege. During the memorial services, he would think of the guys he had fought with and lost.[286]

Meanwhile, life on the post revolved around ceremonial assignments, including wreath presentations at the Tomb, medal ceremonies at the Amphitheater, and riding with Ross to National Airport to meet some two-star or three-star general. Their most fascinating airport event was leading an Honor Guard to present arms to General Eisenhower and British Field Marshal Bernard Montgomery before returning to England.

Phil was also delighted to have increased opportunities to join Ross and his men at White House soirées. After the guests had departed, they would be invited downstairs to the White House kitchen to enjoy any leftover food or wine, of which there was usually plenty. From time to time, President Truman would join them and seemed to enjoy hanging with the servicemen away from the hustle and bustle of his responsibilities.[ii]

The President would cajole them into a game of poker, which he said was his favorite leisure activity and pastime. The game was accompanied by rounds of Kentucky bourbon. Truman liked to deal, left-handed, eight-card hands. Although he played for money with friends most Friday nights, he never did so with Phil, Russ, or their men. "Our country already owes you boys too much," he would tell Phil.

September 10, 1946, was a highlight for Phil. He had been told to report to Colonel Albright's office in full-dress uniform. When Phil arrived, he was surprised to find Colonel McGarr and Ross waiting for him. Colonel Albright announced that they were all accompanying him to a medal ceremony. To his shock, the ceremony was for him. A Pentagon press release explained this:

ii   Truman served as an artillery captain in World War I during the Meuse-Argonne offensive from September 26, 1918, until the Armistice on November 11, 1918. At the time, this was the largest American offensive in history with over a million men taking part.

> *The youngest man commissioned an Infantry Officer in this war, Captain Philip B. Larimore, Fort Myer, Virginia, was awarded the Médaille de France[iii], it was announced today by the Military District of Washington. This singularly high honor awarded to few Americans was presented to Captain Larimore at the Ceremonial Detachment, Fort Myer, Virginia, where he is Executive Officer. The medal was awarded for gallantry in action.[287]*

After noting his wartime injuries and loss of his right leg, the press release added:

> *"He has mastered the use of his new leg so well that he rides horseback as well as any horseman in Washington," according to Captain Hubert Andrews, the Cavalry chief at Fort Myer. Larimore is still very much on active duty and teaches swimming as a sideline at the Fort Myer pool and plays football with the men of his detachment.*

> *Captain Larimore wears the Silver Star with an Oak Leaf Cluster, the Bronze Star with an Oak Leaf Cluster, and the Purple Heart with six clusters.[iv] It is expected that the Distinguished Service Cross will be awarded to him shortly. Captain Larimore hopes to remain in the Army and eventually obtain a regular commission. A board of Medical Officers will meet on November 2, at Walter Reed Hospital, to determine whether he should be retired or accepted for continued service.[288]*

Although Phil was the recipient of four, not seven Purple Hearts, the bit about the DSC was news to him, and the last sentence was a tremendous encouragement.

It turned out, though, that Phil's hearing before a board of medical officers—officially known as the Army Retiring Board—would be postponed until the spring of 1947, which would give him more time to prepare his appeal of amputee officers being automatically discharged.

On November 11, 1946, Phil had an opportunity to accompany President Truman and Secretary of the Navy James Forrestal to the Tomb of the Unknowns, where a standing-room-only crowd waited for the solemn event

iii   By the Médaille de France, the reporter probably meant the Croix de Guerre with Palm.
iv   Each "Oak Leaf Cluster" indicates an additional award. In this case, Phil had been awarded two Silver Stars, two Bronze Stars (both with Valor), and only three Purple Hearts (the Purple Heart with two Oak Leaf Clusters).

in observance of Armistice Day.[v] After the President placed a wreath at the Tomb of the Unknowns, there was a traditional minute of silence, which stirred Phil's heart as he pondered all those he served with who didn't come home from the war. A single bugler played the moving and powerful "Taps" as President Truman held his black hat over his heart.

Phil noticed tears streaking down the President's cheeks. Afterward, President Truman pulled Phil aside and asked him if he knew the bugler who blew "Taps."

"Yes, sir," Phil replied.

"Then tell him he did one hell of a job."

"I will, sir," Phil said, snapping a salute.

As he watched the President being led back to his limousine, Phil was grateful that the Commander in Chief understood the sacrifices that men like him made on the battlefield.

Now, if only the Army Retiring Board could see things the same way.

---

v Armistice Day was initially celebrated in the U.S. in 1919 to commemorate the armistice signed between the Allies of the Great War and Germany. In 1954, the name was changed to Veterans Day to celebrate all veterans, not just those who died in World War I. While the legal holiday remains on November 11, if that date happens to be on a Saturday or Sunday, then organizations that formally observe the holiday will normally be closed on the adjacent Friday or Monday, respectively.

57
GAME OF THE CENTURY

"The most precious commodity with which the Army
deals is the individual soldier, who is the heart and soul
of our combat forces."

**—General J. Lawton Collins,ⁱ commander of VII Corps
during the Allied invasion of Normandy[289]**

During the fall of 1946, Phil and Marilyn saw each other several times, even though she had moved to Des Moines to begin her first year of law school. A highlight was attending the National Capital Horse Show in Washington and the National Horse Show in New York City. While in New York, they stayed with Phil's Aunt Leota and Uncle Walter in their Park Avenue brownstone and attended the Army-Notre Dame football game at Yankee Stadium as guests of General Eisenhower. Colonel McGarr and Ross Calvert joined them.[290]

Sportswriters breathlessly called the matchup of the top two teams in the country—No. 1 Army versus No. 2 Notre Dame—the "Game of the Century." The rivalry between Notre Dame and Army was the most popular and prestigious in college football. Army was unbeaten and untied

---

i   General Collins' nickname was "Lightning Joe." He was also a division commander at Guadalcanal. At the time of his appointment, he was the youngest division commander in the U.S. Army at the age of forty-six.

in twenty-five games and had been National Champions the previous two years, while the Fighting Irish had vengeance on their mind: Army had scorched Notre Dame 59-0 and 48-0 in the last two seasons when many of the Fighting Irish players were serving in the armed forces. Army was thirsting for an unprecedented third national championship.

The game was a sellout at Yankee Stadium, where scalpers were getting $200 per ticket.[ii] Despite the matchup of two high-scoring and much-hyped offenses before a frenzied sold-out crowd of 75,000, the game turned into a terrific battle of defenses, ending in a scoreless tie, 0-0.[iii]

After the game, Phil wrote to his parents:

> *Gosh, what a show! That was a wonderful game. You never knew from one minute to the next who was going to do what. Grand all the way through.*[291]

What he didn't tell them was that despite Walter and Leota financing their fine dining, dancing, and Broadway shows, Phil and Marilyn found themselves sniping at each other more and more. Once or twice this fanned into verbal fisticuffs. They always made up, but old wounds were festering and scars were beginning to form.

ᏸ

With the start of the new year in 1947, Phil was in and out of Walter Reed General Hospital undergoing extensive examinations regarding his official request to stay on active duty in the Army. The medical scrutiny involved overnight stays, giving Phil plenty of time to ponder whether the Army would allow him to continue to serve in the military or honorably discharge him.[292]

When he returned to Fort Myer, Phil's responsibilities included overseeing the soldiers' assignments to various soirées at the White House, which often requested up to ten soldiers to act as junior aides during the winter reception season. Phil or Ross would often accompany the men at these state functions, where the uniformed soldiers lined up four abreast preceding the receiving line of the President, the First Lady, and the guests of honor. After all the guests arrived, they were allowed to mingle before the state dinner.

By now, President Truman recognized Phil and some of his men by sight. One evening, after all the guests had left, the President sat down at the piano in the East Room and led the soldiers in a rousing rendition of "As the Caissons Go Rolling Along."[iv]

---

ii   This would be the equivalent of one month's salary for the average American at the time.

iii   Both teams finished the season unbeaten, and neither played in postseason bowls back then. Notre Dame was voted No. 1 in the final Associated Press poll, and Army finished second.

iv   "The Army Goes Rolling Along" is the official song of the U.S. Army and is typically called "The Army Song." The original version was titled "As the Caissons Go Rolling Along."

The President asked his head butler, Alonzo Fields, "an accomplished mixologist," to prepare several rounds of Old Fashioned drinks made according to the President's tastes—bourbon over rocks with water and nothing else. Phil decided not to point out that a true Old Fashioned would have included a sugar cube, a couple of dashes of Angostura bitters, and a slice of orange or a maraschino cherry.

For Phil, this was an evening to remember, which he shared with his father in a letter home:

> *He reminds me a lot of you, Pop. Full of wisdom and easy to talk to. Me and the men love being with him.*[293]

ↄ৲

Phil received some encouraging news on January 27, 1947, from the medical board at Walter Reed.[294]

The report summary said:

> *The officer was boarded on 2 May 1946 and given six months temporary limited duty, which he served without difficulty.... No active therapy was given to this officer. He had been going about his duties without any difficulty and had no complaints. This officer has an assignment awaiting him if he is given medical and surgical clearances.*[295]

Phil was now cleared to stay on active duty and continue his mission to overturn what he felt was an unfair policy that all officers who were amputees must be discharged.

On March 3, he received orders from the Army Retiring Board to undergo another evaluation at Walter Reed Hospital. Phil took this news as an ominous indication that the Army wanted to discharge him and give him a disability rating.

On March 9, while at the hospital, he wrote home:

> *I'm still in the hospital, sitting around doing nothing but waiting for this damn Medical Dept. to make up their minds. Do think I'm going to see Sen. McKellar[v] and see if he can help me in any way. I've been all over the War Department. Have had some people say they would help me, some say there is no chance, others say they would look into it and let me know. Anyhow, I'm not about to stop*

---

v   Senator Kenneth McKellar was the senior senator from Phil's home state of Tennessee.

trying until I'm sure in my mind that there is no hope. Then I'll let them kick me out. We will just have to wait a while and see.[296]

While Phil wasn't going to give up the military without a fight, he wasn't in a mood to fight for Marilyn, who apparently was moving on and seeing other guys. Phil wrote this to his mother in early March:

I've called Marilyn up several times, and the few times I got to talk to her, she was dated up too much for me to get a minute or so in. In spite of what I know Dad will say, I have tried 'cause I do want to see her. But guess we have every hope put away now. Maybe one of the two of us will see the light later on. Do hope so.[297]

Through all the emotional ups and downs, his greatest solace seemed to come from Chug. He shared this with his parents:

Don't have much to do now but ride all day Sat & Sunday and every Wed & Friday nite. Do have a lot of fun. As soon as it gets a bit warmer, we plan on trying to get a polo team started. We can have a bunch of fun. Also, if the government will let me, I'm going to try to get my horse in good enough jumping condition and enter him in some of the smaller nationally recognized horse shows to give both him and me some experience. If he turns out to be as good a jumper and hunter as I think he will be, then I plan on buying him. I can get him from the government for around $150, as long as I am in the service. He's only ten years old and 7/8 Thoroughbred, so he is a good mount.

Just walked down to the bar and got me a couple of beers, so guess I will settle down with the beer, my pipe, a good book, and get some rest. Have been riding my horse since 0930 this morn, an hour out for lunch, until 1630, so I'm kinda tired.[298]

On March 21, Phil had a complete physical exam by Major C. Highsmith, Jr., and 1st Lieutenant W. T. Swartz, both MDs and orthopedists at Walter Reed. They noted that he was in excellent physical shape besides the missing leg, a shade over six feet tall, and weighing a lean 139 pounds. What Phil found to be extremely discouraging, however, were the doctors' conclusions:

- *Permanently disabling, line of duty: yes.*
- *Corrective measures or other action recommended: retirement.*
- *Is individual permanently incapacitated for general service: yes.*
- *Is individual permanently incapacitated for limited service: yes.*[299]

Phil understood that they were just following written procedure and protocol, and both physicians told him they'd be willing to testify in his favor at the final hearing. He doubled down on his visits to congressmen, senators, and upper-level officers at the War Department.

Back home, Phil's mother asked Walter Armstrong, the attorney she worked for, to contact their congressman, Clifford Davis, on Phil's behalf. Armstrong and Davis knew each other well. The attorney received this reply:

> *My dear friend,*
>
> *Young Larimore was in last week. We had quite a nice visit, and I was most impressed with him. In his quiet way, he has something. It would have done your heart good to have heard him express so modestly the respect and esteem that he holds for you.*
>
> *We are having to work against time in his case. He is appearing before a Medical Review Board. The whole question to be determined is whether or not amputees will be permitted in the regular establishment.*
>
> *With all good wishes, I am,*
> *Cliff* [300]

Walter Armstrong also reached out to another political friend, Kenneth McKellar, the Tennessee senator who had contacted the War Department on Phil's behalf. Armstrong received this letter from Major General Edward F. Witsell, the Adjutant General:

> *Since my acknowledgment of 4 April 1947, to your letter of 27 March 1947, including correspondence from Mr. Walter P. Armstrong, in the interest of Captain Philip B. Larimore, I have checked further into the case. Captain Larimore was recommended to appear before the Army*

> *Retiring Board at Walter Reed General Hospital. In view*
> *of this, the reassignment of this officer cannot be considered*
> *until such time as the finding and recommendation of the*
> *board are received by the War Department. Your interest on*
> *behalf of Captain Larimore is appreciated.*[301]

After discussing his case with those close to him—his parents, Mr. Armstrong, Colonels Albright and McGarr, several JAG officers with whom he had worked, and close friend Ross Calvert, Phil decided to represent himself at the hearing. They all thought his presence would engender more sympathy and come across as potentially less adversarial. Army Retiring Board members, he was told, tended to be crusty enough without any added provocation.

Then came the anxiously awaited orders:

> *You are hereby notified to appear for a hearing before*
> *the Army Retiring Board on 15 April, at 1:00 p.m., in the*
> *Board Room, 2nd Floor, Walter Reed General Hospital,*
> *Washington, D.C. The Board will make findings with*
> *respect to whether you are permanently, physically, or*
> *mentally incapacitated for active service.*[302]

The last sentence gave Phil a sense of great hope. But he still felt a plethora of contradictory emotions; he was rattled and rosy, anxious and anticipative, petrified and positive, concerned yet confident.

Only time would tell which adjectives he'd use to describe a decision that would change the course of his life. For Phil, this was his "Game of the Century," one that would determine if he got back in the game or if he and his Army brothers with amputated limps would be sent permanently to the showers.

58

THE APPEAL

"In a war such as this one where the gain to be had was so great and the destruction of the evil force so necessary, great sacrifice was inevitable."

—Lieutenant General John "Iron Mike" O'Daniel[303]

Immediately after a burial service at Arlington on April 15, 1947, that had been delayed, Phil met Ross at the Fort Myer stables. Phil was running fifteen minutes late and knew the colonels on the Army Retiring Board would not take kindly to his tardiness, even if they had gotten the message.[304,305]

"I've called Walter Reed," Phil's buddy said. "They know the situation and will wait for you. The boss' car and driver are outside. Go!"

Although it was only about ten miles from Fort Myer to Walter Reed General Hospital, Phil knew the trip could easily take up to an hour. Fortunately, the traffic was light, and the driver had a lead foot. They arrived at Walter Reed just as the hearing was supposed to start at 1400 hours.

The walk down a long corridor to the front of the hospital and the elevator ride to the second floor seemed to take forever for Phil, who was looking smart in his crisp full-dress uniform with decorations and service medals.

When the elevator doors finally opened, Phil walked as quickly as his prosthesis would allow. Turning a corner, he spotted Lieutenant Colonel Alexander J. Rouch, the Recorder for the Army Retiring Board, waiting outside the door to the hearing room.

"Sorry, sir."

"No problem for me, Captain," Colonel Rouch said. "I received the message from Colonel Albright and relayed it to the board. I think they understand. After all, they *all* hope to be buried in Arlington one day."

Phil smiled and relaxed for the first time in nearly an hour.

"We have a moment," the lieutenant colonel said. "The board isn't back from their lunch break yet. Undoubtedly, they've had a smoke and perhaps a drink or two. It may relax them and play in your favor."

"Who's on the board today?" Phil asked. He had been notified of the officers assigned to his hearing, but wanted to double-check that there would be no surprises.

"Colonel Lindsay McDonald Silvester is Infantry, Colonels Pearl Thomas and James Kilian are Cavalry, while Colonel Louis Field and Lieutenant Colonel Leon Gardner are Medical Corps. One might think that having three from Infantry and Cavalry, at the very least, might also be favorable, but I'm not sure."

"Why's that?"

"Silvester was reverted from major general to the permanent rank of colonel when he was relieved of his command of the 7th Armored Division after the Germans badly mauled that division in November of '44. Several members of his division command were also released in the shake-up. He took it pretty hard and has been as crusty as month-old bread ever since."[i]

"And the other two?"

"Kilian may even be nastier, Captain. He was court-martialed at the end of the war for events that occurred at an infamous U.S. Army replacement depot near Lichfield, England. *The Stars and Stripes* called it, quote, 'a concentration camp for American soldiers accused of desertion,' a serious military crime. Kilian, known as the 'Beast of Lichfield,' was the facility's commandant and claimed he was unaware of the brutality going on under his nose. Many believe the trial was a whitewash, however. Instead of a bust in rank or the end of his career, he got off with the proverbial slap on the wrist—just a $500 fine and letter of reprimand. I wouldn't expect any sympathy from those two."

Phil knitted his brow. "The only bright spot is that I know Colonel Thomas. He's a crack equestrian. We've ridden together several times. We've even competed jointly."

"That's good," Rouch observed. "But watch out for Colonels Field and Gardner. They're Medical Corps and not very patient by nature."

"Thanks for the heads-up, sir."

Rouch nodded. "I understand you do not desire counsel, correct?"

---

i   In 1946, Silvester asked for an inquiry, which vindicated General Omar Bradley's decision to relieve him on the grounds of commander's discretion. Silvester retired in 1949 and maintained his rank of Major General on the retired list. In addition to the Distinguished Service Cross, his awards included the Silver Star, Purple Heart, and French Croix de Guerre.

"That's correct, sir. I wish to present my case myself. It's really a very simple request."

"But your request is unprecedented, isn't it?"

Phil nodded. "It is."

"And you've been denied through previous levels of request and appeal, correct?"

"Correct again, sir. This is my last and final chance. But I'm hopeful."

"Well, for what it's worth, I'm hoping they find in your favor. There are a lot of good officers who are amputees and anxious to continue to serve their country."

"No question about that, sir. I'm here to represent all of them. I hope I'll be the first of many."

Rouch smiled. "Me too, Captain."

A soldier opened the door. "They're ready for you, sirs."

"So then, let's get in there. And remember, there is no need to salute upon entry."

The soldier held the door open as they entered. Phil and Rouch walked briskly to a small table in front of the hearing board. Rouch indicated where he was to sit. Phil nodded at the two physicians seated in the chairs available for audience members. No one else was there except for a stenographer.

Colonel Rouch remained standing as he opened the hearing notebook at his seat. "Gentlemen, the officer before the board stated he did not desire counsel."

Colonel Silvester gaveled the Army Retiring Board for Officers to order and noted that he was serving as the board president. "Proceed," he said.

Rouch, after swearing Phil in, began the proceedings. "Captain, state your name, rank, serial number, and organization."

"Captain Philip B. Larimore, 0511609, Infantry, Army of the United States."

"State the nature of the disability or ailment for which you're now appearing before the board."

"I have an amputation of the right leg."

"How long have you had this?"

"The leg was amputated in April of 1945, sir."

"Do you believe that your disability or ailment was incurred in combat with an enemy of the United States?"

"Yes, sir."

"Do you wish to be relieved from active duty?"

"No, sir. Of course, presently it is War Department policy for officers who are amputees to be honorably discharged. I'm hoping that a decision in my favor will change that policy."

"Have you examined the records in your case?"

"I have, sir."

"Do you wish to make a statement to the board prior to the calling of the medical witnesses?"

"If I may, sir."

Phil slowly stood up and looked briefly at each of the officers seated at the table. "As I have mentioned, I am very desirous, sirs, of remaining on active duty until the War Department makes a decision about changing their policy. I don't know whether or not they will accept amputee officers in the regular Army in the future. I have been told that there are plans that they will do so. I have a position offered to me, and if War Department policy allows me to go on general service with a waiver for my leg, I feel that I am perfectly capable of holding down almost any job the Army can offer me."

"Bullshit!" interrupted Colonel Kilian. "You're a cripple! Mind you, a highly decorated cripple, but still a cripple."

Kilian looked at Colonel Silvester. "Pardon my French, Mac, but amputee officers simply don't have a place in *our* Army."

Phil felt the blood rush to his face but took in a deep breath and slowly let it out. "Sir, I've held nine months temporary duty at Fort Myer with superior ratings all the way through and have been second in line for the ceremonial attachment."

"That's all pretty dressing, Captain. But the Army is already preparing for its next war. We don't need one-legged handicaps!"

"Colonel Kilian!" interrupted Colonel Silvester. "This is a hearing. That means we're to *hear* the evidence. We can keep our considered opinions to ourselves until we adjourn to discuss the case. Is that understood?"

Kilian muttered something under his breath, crossed his arms, and nodded. "Understood, sir. But can we at least ask questions?"

"By all means," Silvester replied. "Please proceed."

Kilian glared at Phil. "So, who the hell would take a handicapped officer?"

"I have a job promised me at Fort Benning as an instructor."

"By whom?"

"Major General John O'Daniel, the commandant of the Infantry School and the Commanding General there."

"I know who he is, but why?" interrupted the colonel. "He knows as well as we do that amputees can't serve."

"I served in his 3rd Division from Anzio to Germany and was requested because of my fifteen-month combat experience with a line company, and because the Army is desirous of having experienced combat officers train new officers. I realize that the policy of the War Department is that enlisted men with amputations can go back to duty, but officers cannot. I feel in my mind and have been told that the Army is planning on changing that policy to match what the War Department is doing for enlisted men. If they do so, I wish to be the first one of the officers to accept a Regular Army commission under the new regulation."

It was Colonel Silvester's turn to express his displeasure.

"As president of this board, I must tell you that the board's mission here is to determine whether or not you are fit for general service. As to the policy of the War Department, the board has no authority to act upon it. Your request, however, will be included in the hearing and will probably be reviewed by the appropriate section of the War Department. However, I think that is something you should take up with the War Department separately, and *not* through this board."

The pushback attitude of these colonels didn't surprise Phil, given what Colonel Rouch had said beforehand. He had been hoping for a more sympathetic response, but he had prepared for this line of questioning. "I have looked into it, sir, quite a bit. It seems to be a period of time is all that they are waiting for."

Silvester nodded. "Colonel Rouch, if you could briefly review all of the submitted records that are contained in each of the board members' notebooks."

After Rouch answered several questions, Colonel Silvester asked if anything else was coming before the board. From Phil's chair, it looked like the colonel had made up his mind and was ready to end the hearing.

Rouch cleared his throat. "We have two medical witnesses waiting to be called, sir."

Silvester scowled. "Then proceed!"

This was the part of the hearing Phil had been waiting for. It was now a make-or-break time. The following testimony would either lead to valiant victory or crushing failure—not just for him, but for all the amputees he represented.

This appeal was bigger than him—and vitally important for so many of his brothers who came back from the war missing an arm or leg.

59

THE GREAT DEBATE

"The Infantry suffers the biggest number of casualties too,
and to my notion, they get the least praise.... Pray for me,
so I'll have courage and strength for whatever is ahead."

—Staff Sergeant Bruce E. Egger[306]

Two medical officers walked to the front and were duly sworn in. Lieutenant Colonel Alexander Rouch, the Recorder for the Army Retiring Board, nodded to the first medical officer. "State your name, rank, qualifications, and present assignment," he said.[307],[308]

"Captain Cornelius P. Frey, MC; Ward Officer, Ward Thirty-Three, Amputation Section, WRGH—"

Colonel Rouch interrupted. "For the record, that's Walter Reed General Hospital. Please continue."

"I'm a graduate of Johns Hopkins Medical School with eighteen months of surgical training prior to entry into the Army."

Rouch looked at the other witness. "Major, state your name, rank, qualifications, and present assignment."

"Major Charles Highsmith, Jr., MC; graduate, George Washington University School of Medicine, 1942. Present assignment: Assistant Chief, Surgical Services, Walter Reed General Hospital."

"Major Highsmith, did you personally examine Captain Larimore?"

"Yes, sir."

"And Exhibit K is your report to the board?"

"Yes, sir. It's our joint report." Highsmith tilted his head toward Captain Frey.

Colonel Rouch nodded to the board and sat down.

Colonel Silvester began the questioning. "This officer has obtained maximum benefits of hospitalization, has he?"

"Yes, sir."

"Is he wearing a prosthesis?"

"Yes, sir."

"Is the cause of the incapacity an incident of service?"

"Yes, sir. And as a matter of record, it was incurred in combat with an enemy of the United States, in the line of duty."

"Is further treatment, hospitalization, convalescence in this hospital, a specialized general hospital, or any other medical facility indicated?"

"No, sir."

Silvester turned to the other doctor. "Captain Frey, are you in full agreement with the testimony of Major Highsmith?"

"I am, sir."

"Do you have any additional testimony to offer?"

"None."

Silvester looked at his wristwatch and then at Phil. "Captain Larimore, do you have any questions to ask?"

Phil took a slow deep breath. He knew even asking a question at this point would be viewed as impertinent, but he also knew his next question could be the one that would settle the case for him. And he believed he knew what the physician would say—at least what he hoped and prayed would be said.

"I do have one, sir."

Silvester glared at Phil for a moment, who remained impassive.

Phil then turned to the doctors. "Major, do you believe that I am incapacitated for *all* types of military service? Do you believe that I am *completely* incapacitated, sir?"

"Well," the major muttered as if gathering his thoughts. "Uh, no. No, I don't."

"What!" interrupted Colonel Silvester, his face reddening as he hastily stood up, knocking his chair against the wall behind him. "Are you saying his considerable incapacity is not sufficient to render him *unfit* for general service?"

"I am."

"Why?" bellowed the now-red-faced colonel.

"Because, sir, of the fact he has been on limited service since last May. During that time, he had no trouble with his stump or prosthesis. He performed with excellence—above and beyond the call of duty."

"So," Colonel Silvester said, clearly flustered. "I'll ask once again. Based upon current Army policy, do you believe this soldier is incapacitated for general military service?"

"I do, sir, based upon *current* policy. But let me be perfectly clear. His incapacity would *not* prevent him from doing *some* types of military duty."

The physician's statement hung in the air. After a moment had passed, Rouch asked, "Does any member of the board desire to further question these witnesses?"

All five members shook their heads. Rouch thanked and excused the physicians. He then turned to Phil.

"Captain Larimore, do you wish to testify on your behalf, call witnesses, offer depositions or other evidence, or present any more oral or written arguments on any point involved in this hearing?"

"Yes, sir. I have reports to submit indicating my physical capabilities. Even though I am an amputee, sir, these reports demonstrate that I can outperform men even younger than me in many ways, including providing instruction to officer candidates. In addition, as this is a matter of precedence, I would personally be glad to answer any questions members of the board may have."

Several members scoffed, but Colonel Thomas began the questioning.

"Captain," the colonel began, his voice soft and reassuring. "What types of instruction could you successfully carry out?"

Phil was grateful to elaborate. "Sir, I have been fully trained in specialized warfare, paratroops, gliders, ski troops, and demolitions, but I'm also fully qualified to instruct in any type of company combat work, particularly front-line combat. The Army is looking for that, sir. And I believe I can provide that as well or even better than most any officer."

"Do you think your handicap—your amputation—would serve to reduce the morale of the gentlemen in training?"

Phil was quiet for a moment because he knew this was the main reason for the absurd policy that kept qualified amputees from continuing service to their country.

"I don't think so, sir. My service here in Washington has shown others what we amputees are capable of. At the Infantry School at Fort Benning, I would serve as a strong example to the men."

"How so?" asked Thomas.

"I would show them that should they also become impaired, then *their* Army will not discard them, that *their* Army cares for them, and that *their* Army can and will allow them to serve with honor and distinction."

"Do you think that your present disability would handicap you in any way in instructing?"

"In instructing, no, sir. Not even in most physical competitions, where I can still top most of the young officers. And not even in equitation, sir, as you well know."

Colonel Thomas managed a wry smile. "You and Chug make a formidable team," he allowed.

Colonel Kilian straightened up and scowled at Phil. "Wait a minute. Are you saying that you have no problem riding a horse? Before you answer, sir, know that I'm Cavalry."

"I ride a great deal on my own, sir. You heard Colonel Thomas refer to my horse, Chug. We both participate in caisson ceremonies at Arlington Cemetery. We're in horse shows nearly every weekend. We do Red Cross demonstrations. I also work with wounded men to get them on mounts also."

"You can actually mount?" Kilian asked, almost incredulously.

"Not only mount, but I can dismount and jump over any course with my horse, sir, in competition and in the wild."

"He and Chug also fox hunt," Colonel Thomas interjected. "I wish I were half as good as him, Jim."

The silent members of the board smiled and, for the first time, visibly relaxed.

Phil blew out a sigh of relief. There were a few more questions, but nothing he couldn't handle. When he finished, Phil was pleased with how he had held up to the grilling and couldn't be happier with his testimony.

He figured the two medical men—Colonel Field and Lieutenant Colonel Gardner—were on his side and would vote with Colonel Thomas. In that case, the board's recommendation to the War Department would make it far more likely he'd become the first amputee officer to not automatically receive an honorable discharge for a disability that shouldn't keep him from further service.

Colonel Silvester let the drama of the moment slowly subside before asking, "Does any member wish to recall any witness for additional testimony?"

There was only the shaking of heads.

"Then the board will be closed for deliberation and to maturely consider the case. Let the record show our hearing adjournment at 1501 hours."

When the colonel struck the gavel on the table, Phil felt confident that he had made a strong argument for staying in the Army.

Now it was up to the Army Retiring Board to see if they agreed.

60

DECISION TIME

"The cost has been great—almost at times, it seemed, too great. It is now our task to build the future on the solid foundation laid by those who have left us. We shall go forward in our traditional way, never forgetting those who march with us in memory."

—Lieutenant Donald G. Taggart, editor of *History of the Third Infantry Division in World War II*[309]

Lieutenant Colonel Rouch walked Phil and the pair of physicians out to the hall. After thanking the doctors, he turned to Phil. "You did a fine job, Captain."[310]

"Thank you, sir. I appreciate your help."

"You didn't need it. You did as well as any military attorney would have, and better than most. You knew when to speak and when to be quiet. Well done."

Phil nodded as Rouch continued. "As you know, we typically mail the hearing results in a week or two. But if you want to wait, I'm willing to make an exception to our standard operating procedure and find out the result right away for you."

This was beyond what Phil could have hoped for. He knew Rouch wouldn't extend this offer if he wasn't certain of a positive outcome. "That would be swell, sir."

"Why don't you sit tight here for a while? It shouldn't be too long."

"Do I have time to go to the lounge for a smoke?" Phil asked.

"You go do that. Figure about thirty minutes."

༄

At 1545 hours, Phil walked back from the lounge and had hardly settled into a chair outside the hearing room when the door opened, and Rouch came out.

As Phil started to stand, Rouch motioned for him to stay seated. The colonel took the chair next to Phil. His lips were tense, his face expressionless as he handed Phil an unsealed envelope.

Phil felt his throat dry up and his pulse quicken as he hurriedly opened it, removed the folded letter, and scanned past the administrative headers to get the heart of the decision:

> Captain Larimore is advised in writing that this Board carefully reviewed extensive written and oral evidence and has found that Captain Philip B. Larimore, 0511609, Infantry, Army of the United States, is permanently incapacitated for active service.[311]

The letter slipped from his shaking hands and fluttered to the floor. He had failed. He had failed himself. He had failed his brothers, who were officers and amputees.

Phil felt Rouch's hand on his shoulder. "I'm sorry, Captain. I truly am. And if it helps, it wasn't a unanimous decision. It fell three-to-two. You came damn close. Damn close."

As Rouch stood to leave, Phil's head fell into his hands. He could not hold back the burning tears.

༄

Phil slowly accepted the fact his military days were coming to an end. He and Marilyn began seeing each other again and flew by military transport to Atlanta to visit his former doctors and colleagues at Lawson General Hospital one last time.[312]

With their futures in front of them, Phil and Marilyn began talking about getting married. They traveled to Des Moines, where Phil asked her father for his daughter's hand in marriage. Colonel Ray Fountain was pleased to give his blessing. At a romantic dinner in Des Moines, Phil proposed, Marilyn accepted, and they became formally engaged.

During their stay in Des Moines, Marilyn's father was also delighted to inform Phil that Colonel McGarr's nomination for him to receive the Distinguished Service Cross, the nation's second-highest military honor, had been approved. Phil was told that he would receive his medal in a special ceremony the day before Memorial Day.

Upon his return to Washington in early May 1947, Phil wrote to his parents:

> *I know as little about what's going to happen to me as I ever have. I'm having a good time, and Chug and I are still getting along well. I'm trying to teach him all kinds of new things but not having much luck. He learns darn slow but mighty well. Which I think is best.*[313]

For some unexplained reason, he didn't mention his engagement.

In his free time, he and Ross spent their final days together. Phil visited other friends to say farewell and participated in several equestrian events, including the traditional spring steeplechase races in Maryland, such as the Maryland Hunt Club Race, the My Lady's Point-to-Point, and the Grand National, which was by far the nation's oldest and the longest race—at four miles—with twenty-two fences.

The Grand National was a huge social affair because the race hadn't been run during the war years. He and Chug joined the field, and during the grueling sprint at the end, warm memories of their dash with the Nazi horseman on his Lipizzaner stallion in Czechoslovakia flooded Phil's mind. They finished near the front of the pack, to Phil's immense satisfaction—a tremendous victory given their limited experience racing together. Despite her love of all things equestrian, Marilyn did not accompany him to any of the events.

In May, Ross and Phil had dinner with the Eisenhowers at Quarters One and a final bridge game together. General Eisenhower told him how much he regretted that amputees could not stay in the Army. He also mentioned, rather casually, that aides to President Truman had communicated the President's interest in his situation to him.

"Really?" Phil said.

"Yes," Ike replied, "and I was asked to relay an interesting proposition to you."

For the next five minutes, Phil listened intently.

"A major donor to the Truman campaign lives on a large estate just outside Charlottesville, Virginia, home of the University of Virginia," the general began. "The man is a significant benefactor to the university and an avid horseman. When he heard of you and your wartime injury, as well as your equestrian skills, he wanted to do something for you. He indicated he was willing to assist you in obtaining admission to the University of Virginia and to allow you to live at his estate, all expenses paid, in exchange for you managing his stable, including the stable hands and horses, and helping run his fox hunts. He'll also provide a small stipend, an automobile, and any stable and veterinary expenses should you have a mount."

The offer dumbfounded Phil. "I accept!" he said on the spot.

On May 12, 1947, Phil received orders to be released from Walter Reed General Hospital and revert to inactive status during sixty days of terminal leave.

The next day he also learned of his promotion to major at the tender age of twenty-two, meaning he had advanced from 2nd lieutenant to major in only fifty-one months and twenty-four days. His remarkable record in nearly sixteen months of nonstop, frontline combat facilitated this extraordinary feat.

On May 14, 1947, he wrote his mother:

> *Just a note to kinda let you get caught up on what your long-lost son has been doing. To start with, I am out of the Army and plan on being home around the 15th of June. Will just sit around with you and fish, I guess.*
>
> *Then I'm off to school at the University of Virginia. I'm sorry I couldn't get you on Mother's Day. I did try to call, but they never seemed to be able to reach Memphis. Did you get the flowers? I sent them through the Officer's Club, and some of the other officers have told me that they have had every kind of trouble from the flowers being late to not getting home at all.*
>
> *P.S. Oh yes, I am a major.*[314]

಄

Thursday, May 29, 1947, dawned cool and clear at fifty-five degrees, with gentle winds wafting through the fully budded trees at Fort Myer. It was the day before the country would celebrate its second Memorial Day after the end of the war, but also a day that would stick in Phil's memory for a lifetime.[315]

He paced around the packed boxes in the apartment he had occupied for nearly a year, wearing his full-dress uniform. Standing in front of a full-length mirror, he gazed at several rows of medals on his left chest, each of which evoked vivid memories, including the awful aromas and horrific sounds of each battle. He shuddered under the weight of his recollections. He looked with pride at the newly awarded golden oak leaf on his cap and uniform—the insignia for the rank of major.

Phil felt her hands on his shoulders, gently smoothing any wrinkles. He turned into Marilyn's arms. "Thanks for being here," was all he could say as tears filled his eyes.

She smiled. "Wouldn't have missed it for the world."

She kissed his cheek. Ross Calvert walked in then, also in full-dress uniform. "More time for romance later. You've got a big ceremony today, Daddy-O."

Ross drove them the short distance to the Fort Myer parade grounds, where they were met by Colonel John J. Albright, the Commanding Officer of Fort Myer and the Acting Commander of the Military District of Washington.

In front of a ceremoniously decorated stage at the edge of the large parade ground, all of the Military District of Washington troops stood—including the Tomb Honor Guard and the Caisson Platoon with Chug and several other horses.

After a welcome by Colonel Albright and the post chaplain's prayer, the colonel read Phil's Distinguished Service Cross commendation. This was followed by a retreat parade, a review of two battalions of troops, and the pinning ceremony itself—after which the troops saluted him and were dismissed.

Then Colonel Albright hosted a formal luncheon in Phil's honor. Afterward, the military issued a glowing press release that was distributed around the country:

> *Major Philip B. Larimore of Memphis, the youngest man commissioned an Infantry officer in World War II and believed to be the most-decorated Memphis hero of the war, received the second-highest Army decoration today.*

> *The War Department announced Major Larimore was decorated with the Distinguished Service Cross following a review of troops assembled in his honor at Fort Myer, Virginia. Major Larimore was commissioned a 2nd lieutenant at seventeen upon graduation from Gulf Coast Military Academy in 1942. He had to wait until he was eighteen in January 1943 for his first duty assignment. Major Larimore is retiring from the Army effective today because of disability.*

> *The ceremony marked the end of the twenty-two-year-old officer's military career. He has become so proficient in the use of his artificial leg that he played baseball with the Fort Myer soldiers and is an excellent horseman.*[316]

The *Washington Evening Star* carried a photo with this caption:

> *Major Philip B. Larimore gets a smile from his fiancée, Miss Marilyn M. Fountain of Des Moines, at the Fort Myer review yesterday.*[317]

In the picture, the young couple was radiantly smiling at each other, standing together arm in arm, but the reality was that their engagement was on the rocks. Within weeks of saying yes to Phil, Marilyn returned the ring, and the wedding was off. Since Phil was still on final leave, he returned to his hometown of Memphis while Marilyn flew to Des Moines, where she prepared for her second year of law school at Drake.

They would never write or speak to each other again.[i]

❧

Phil traveled between Memphis and Washington several times that summer. When in D.C., he would stay with Ross and ride Chug whenever he desired.[318]

President Truman invited Phil to join him for a Fourth of July celebration at Monticello, the historic home of Thomas Jefferson located a couple of miles from Charlottesville, Virginia. On July 3, they were driven four hours from Washington for a weekend visit.

Upon arriving at the home of President Truman's good friends, Stanley and Sarah Woodward, Truman invited Phil to join him and his entourage for drinks and dinner. The President stood for pictures on the back terrace for the press corps, which he called the "One More Club" since the photographers would frequently say, "Just one more, Mr. President."

Phil was also introduced to the Truman supporter who offered him the caretaking job at his horse farm. Plans were firmed up to Phil to live on the estate, take care of the stables, and enroll at the University of Virginia in the fall. He told his benefactor that he wanted to study international law.

Drinks were served on the terrace, and Phil was served his first mint julep. The President commented that it was a "real mint julep—Kentucky-style—frost and everything," followed by a grand dinner. Phil then spent his first night at the nearby horse farm.

---

i   Thus, the tradition of the Friendship Oak was broken.

Before a national broadcast on July 4 by the major radio networks, Phil enjoyed a luncheon with the President, his benefactor, and other dignitaries inside Monticello. Dressed in full uniform, Phil sat among the VIPs that included Virginia Governor William M. Tuck and Frank Houston, president of the Thomas Jefferson Memorial Foundation.

President Truman told the VIPs, "I'm going to have a grand weekend soon as I get past the damned speech." The President, who spoke at 1:30 p.m. from the east portico of Monticello, finished his address with these words:

> The life of Thomas Jefferson demonstrates, to a remark-
> able degree, the strength and power of truth. He believed,
> with deep conviction, that in this young nation, the survival
> of freedom depended upon the survival of truth. So it is with
> the world.
>
> This is the foundation for peace—a peace that is not
> merely the absence of war, but a deep, lasting peace built
> upon mutual respect and tolerance. Our goal must be not
> peace in our time but peace for all time.[319]

Back in Washington, Phil, still on the rebound, enjoyed an active social life. A gossip column in the *Washington Post* in July 1947 read:

> Major Phil Larimore is spending the weekend hunting
> in Warrenton with his pal Chugwater. The twenty-two-
> year-old major, still twitted by friends about becoming
> an Eagle Scout after receiving his commission as a 2nd
> lieutenant in the United States Army, plans to study
> international law at the University of Virginia. Inciden-
> tally, his favorite companion lately has been pretty Sallie
> Chamberlin, home with her parents Major General and
> Mrs. Stephen J. Chamberlin. She recently graduated from
> Hollins College.[320]

☙

On a lazy summer trip to Memphis, Phil fished with his mother, hunted with his dad, and visited old friends, including childhood buddies Billy O'Bannon and Luke McLaurine. He also attended equestrian events and dated "Miss Arkansas," Pam Camp of Little Rock, Arkansas, and Alma Jean "Boots" Henderson from Atlanta. His medal-laden uniform attracted young women like flies to honey.[321]

Upon his return to Washington, he wrote this about "Boots" to his mother:

> *I like this gal very much, and I want you and Dad to meet her. You might drop her a note if you wish to let her know that more than one Larimore would love to have her 'cause I know well that our house is open to all my friends.*
>
> *PS: I tried to get Chug to put his footprint on here, but he was chewing on hay and would have no part of me or this letter.*[322]

Chug not only carried him away from his worries and disappointments but also away from his horrific war memories and recurring nightmares. With each afternoon ride and brush session, Phil realized that when he left Washington for Charlottesville and the start of school at the University of Virginia after Labor Day, leaving Chug would be extremely difficult.

A reporter for the *Daily Mirror* newspaper in New York City, Sam Kahn, penned a column about Phil and his special horse:

> *In the old pre-war days, it was an Army tradition that a cadet or student officer, before commissioning, was forbidden to possess (1) a wife, (2) a mustache, and (3) a horse.*
>
> *Major Philip B. Larimore, one of the youngest combat officers of field rank in all of the rugged foot-slogging service, has neither a wife nor a mustache, but he does have a horse. And something of a horse it is. His name is Chug.*
>
> *One reason that Larimore is so fond of Chug is because when he is riding him, no one would suspect that most of the young veteran's right leg is made of wood to take the place of the one he left in Germany.*
>
> *Larimore and Chug established an understanding soon after the officer arrived at Fort Myer, Va., upon his release from an Army hospital. He took up riding as part of his rehabilitation course. Larimore taught Chug that when he wanted him to trot, he would touch him low on the side with his boot heel. When he wanted him to change from a trot to a canter, he would touch him a little higher on his side. And whenever the young officer wanted Chug to jump*

over a hurdle, he taught him to respond when his rider bent
forward low in the saddle.[323]

Everyone at Fort Myer knew about Phil and Chug. His military colleagues also knew that when the iconic caisson horses had served their time, they would either be auctioned off or become available for adoption by private parties. Prospective owners needed to pass strict muster before they could bring one of the retired equine veterans home.

Phil had no doubt he'd qualify, and Ross promised he'd let him know the second there was any indication Chug would be available.

61
THE AUCTION

"Everyone who fought was a hero."

**—Sergeant Murray Soskil, author of *From the Bronx to
Berchtesgaden*** [324]

Phil took one last drag off his cigarette and extinguished the stub into the sand of an outside ashtray. Pulling out his handkerchief, he wiped the beads of sweat from his forehead and exhaled the smoke.[325]

Best to get in there before it's over. He had arrived early that morning, at first light, for the War Assets Administration's auction of surplus army horses. The date was July 10, 1947.

Phil had learned from Ross that Chug was being put up for sale as one of sixty-one surplus horses at the Fort Myer Riding Hall. He knew a crowd of several hundred well-healed equestrians was likely to attend the Army auction. The minimum bid was fifty dollars, so he arrived with five ten-dollar bills in his pocket. Unfortunately, Phil learned Chug would not be auctioned until after the dinner break, which meant his buddy would likely go for much more money than he brought with him.

He watched the auction throughout the day, noting that most horses sold between the minimum bid of fifty and one hundred dollars. The "best" horses, of course, were being saved for last. Following the afternoon session, he shared dinner with Ross Calvert at the Officer's Club. Simultaneously, the bigwig bidders enjoyed a multicourse banquet in the Riding Hall's concourse underneath the stands.

After dinner, Phil stepped inside the auditorium's cool air and deeply inhaled the familiar fragrance of rich loam mixed with leather tack. Anxiety filled his heart as he worked his way through the wall-to-wall crowd inside the riding hall and found a single seat at the ring's edge.

As he scanned the hall, his heart sank. Around him, nearly every seat was taken, and the aisles overflowed with a standing-room-only crowd.

There must be more than 500 people here. They can't all be bidding, can they?

Auctioneer Byron Brumback sat at his table and spoke into a microphone. "Folks, if I could have your attention."

The crowd hushed.

"As you know, we're nearing the end of our auction for the sixty-one surplus horses of the War Assets Administration," the auctioneer boomed. "We've sold fifty-seven horses so far, and now we are down to our last lot—the four most amazing horses of the whole kit and caboodle: lots number six, five, two, and one. Each of these horses is in sound condition and has been certified by a veterinarian.

"At the end of this evening, I'll be offering lots number one and two. One will be Mrs. Eleanor Roosevelt's mount, Here's How, kept in the White House stables until President Roosevelt died.[i] He's a quite showy and strikingly good-looking animal. The second steed is well known to you all, and was General Patton's favorite horse."

The auctioneer's rich baritone echoed across the crowd from a bank of ceiling-mounted speakers far above the dirt floor. "The first horse this evening, lot six, is Reno Fantas."

At the far end of Fort Myer Riding Hall, dark curtains were pulled apart, and two spotlights clanked on to illuminate a beautiful chestnut quarter horse, led by a black groom toward the auctioneer's table in front of the grandstands. When Reno Fantas pulled to a stop, the magnificent horse stiffened in place—almost as if standing at attention.

"This gorgeous seventeen year old, as most of you know, was the favorite mount of former Army Chief of Staff and present Secretary of State, General George Marshall. She is a polo type and was used by the All-American polo team."

The stable hand quickly walked the horse to the center of the ring.

"Not only are you buying a marvelous horse," the auctioneer intoned, "but a piece of U.S. history. Reno Fantas would make a superb purchase for

---

i   In her "My Day" newspaper column the next day, July 11, 1947, Eleanor Roosevelt wrote, "A horse called Here's How, which was for a short time in the stables at Fort Myer allotted for the use of the President, is now being sold by the Army. I am not actually sure that we ever owned Here's How. I think we merely tried him out among other horses for a time. The horse that I rode for years was called Dot."

a child, or a small lady not used to riding. Who'll start the bidding? Who'll begin? As you know, the minimum bid is fifty dollars. Can we start at a hundred dollars?"

As the auctioneer began his rapid-fire banter, Phil became more concerned.

A hundred dollars! That's twice what I have!

Having seen the bidding for each horse increase throughout the afternoon and knowing Chug was still being held in the back, he realized that he didn't stand a chance.

He chastised himself. *Why'd you even think you'd be able to buy him?*

"One hundred dollars! Can I get two hundred? Anyone give two hundred? No one? Going once! Going twice!"

"Three hundred," cried a young woman in a bright floral dress and a floppy, wide-brimmed white hat. She looked to be in her mid-thirties.

"Three hundred twenty-five," thundered a man in a three-piece suit, leaning against the railing as the horse passed by.

"Three hundred thirty!" shouted the young woman in the floral dress.

The two stared at each other for an icy moment.

"Do I hear three hundred fifty?" the overhead speaker announced, the question reverberating around the arena. "Three hundred thirty going once. Three hundred thirty going twice. Don't let this piece of history get away from you."

The entire arena stared at the man, who smiled, shook his head, and tipped his hat to the young lady. Phil's eyes widened as he recognized the man from the morning auction sales.

I can't believe it! They brought in a ringer to run up the price. And he knows Chug. He knows what he's worth. I'm sunk!

The sharp bang of the gavel slamming onto the solid oak desk startled Phil. "Sold to paddle 279 for 330 dollars," the auctioneer announced with a grin.

The audience politely clapped and turned their attention to their programs as bank after bank of the overhead lights shut off. In seconds, the arena became pitch black, other than the lamps on the auctioneer's stand. Then a spotlight turned on, fully illuminating the men.

The auctioneer rapped sharply for attention. "Ladies and gentlemen, entering the arena is horse number five, Chugwater, a splendid ten-year-old bay gelding."

At the auctioneer's announcement, a second spotlight immediately bathed the black curtains, which were thrown back, revealing Phil's best friend. He fingered his wallet anxiously.

There was a gasp as another stableman led the immaculately groomed horse into the arena. Chug's coat was shiny and gleaming, his ears were at attention, and his eyes bright and alert as they darted around the darkened riding arena.

Don't be scared, Chug. You're gonna do fine.

Phil slowly rose and walked to the railing. *I'm here, Buddy.* He felt his lips pucker, and he let out an almost inaudible whistle. He smiled as he saw Chug look in his direction.

He knows I'm here. He knows it

The murmuring from the crowd grew.

They know you're special. Stand proud.

"Ladies and gentlemen, this horse, this amazing horse named Chugwater, is now available. You've likely seen him in pictures in newspapers and magazines leading the caisson at funerals for our war heroes at Arlington Cemetery. Chugwater has been specially trained by an Army man, a combat veteran, a hero, and an amputee, who spent all his spare time teaching the horse to respond to left leg cues. Far as we know, no other cavalry mount in history ever learned to master that trick."

Abruptly, the murmuring voices of the crowd hushed as a third spotlight clanked on and aimed at Phil, blinding him. He instinctively swung his left arm in front of his eyes as the overhead speakers continued, "At twenty-two years old, he's one of the youngest majors in the U.S. Army. His name is Philip B. Larimore, Jr., and, as you can see, he's here with us today."

Phil raised his arm to acknowledge the polite applause echoing around the cavernous arena.

"Ladies and gentlemen, Major Larimore would never tell you this, even if you asked, but the Army tells me he was the youngest man commissioned as an infantry officer in World War II. He was still seventeen when he graduated from Officer Candidate School at Fort Benning and was given the rank of 2nd lieutenant.

"He fought day and night for over fifteen months in the grueling European Theater of Operations. He survived two amphibious landings and is the proud holder of the Army's second-highest decoration, the Distinguished Service Cross. In addition, he was wounded six times in battles from Anzio, through southern France, and finally in Germany, where a Nazi sniper's bullet crushed the bone in his right leg.

"Nevertheless, after strapping a tourniquet around his leg, he still wiped out three machine gun nests and saved a trapped and surrounded platoon of his men. The next day his right leg was amputated only four weeks before the end of the war."

Although the story wasn't entirely accurate, Phil wondered, *How'd he know I'd be here? How'd he know any of this?*

"For that action, this hero received the Distinguished Service Cross last May twenty-ninth, when all of the troops in Washington paraded here at Fort Myer in his honor. For heroism in other engagements, he also received two Bronze and two Silver Stars, four Purple Hearts, along with the Médaille de France."

Every person in the crowd leaned forward, anxious not to miss a word or scene of this unexpected, one-act drama.

"Furthermore," the auctioneer continued, "he's still a crack horseman— despite a 100 percent Army disability rating that he never wanted or asked for. He plays football and baseball, coaches swimming, and can still outdistance his two-legged buddies in the pool at one hundred yards."

Chug shook his head and whinnied toward his former master. Pawing the ground, the horse took a step back. His full attention turned to the man he loved, pleading with his eyes for his former master to rescue him again.

"I wish I could, Chug. More than you can imagine," Phil whispered, tears welling up in his eyes. "Saying goodbye to you is gonna be harder than I ever imagined."

The auctioneer's voice mellowed. "Ladies and gentlemen, I have a favor to ask. Please listen carefully, as I've never made this request before and may never make it again."

The audience in the arena strained every eye toward the auctioneer as the silence deepened.

"I want to ask you *not* to bid on horse number five."

Then across the expanse of the arena, he smiled at Phil. "I'm opening the bidding at the fifty-dollar minimum…fifty dollars…who'll bid fifty dollars?"

Phil's trembling hand reached back and struggled to pull out his wallet for what seemed like an eternity. Then he fumbled the billfold, which fell to the floor. He quickly reached down, picked up his wallet, opened it, and pulled out the five ten-dollar bills.

"Fifty dollars, right here!" he yelled as he waved the bills above his head.

The bid had hardly been shouted when the auctioneer banged his gavel and boomed, "Sold! Sold to the soldier for fifty dollars!"

The crowd erupted in thunderous applause. Almost simultaneously, Phil whistled, and Chug jerked free from the stable hand and sprinted across the dirt arena. Phil quickly hopped down the three steps into the riding ring and walked briskly up to his buddy. After hugging Chug and getting nuzzled in return, he smiled in appreciation as he waved gratefully to the crowd and led his horse away to a deafening ovation.

Afterward, as Phil brushed his old friend in the paddock, several members of the press asked for interviews. One newspaperman reported, "No doubt Major Larimore is proud of the decorations he won during his fifteen months in Europe, but we'll bet that he's a lot prouder of Chugwater."

Another wrote, "It's the relationship between a young soldier with only one leg and his four-legged friend who seems to understand."

Phil said little more to the reporters, other than telling one, "He isn't much to look at. He's ten years old, and even I have to admit he's got a mighty ugly head. A dogface head, I'd say. But boy, can Chugwater jump! Just the other day, he thudded down the turf for a takeoff like one of those new jet planes and cleared the bar at the height of five feet, six inches, with me bent low in the saddle."

A final correspondent asked, "I understand Chugwater was going to be euthanized by the Germans at one time. Is it true you saved his life?"

Phil shook his head.

"Actually, he saved mine."

EPILOGUE
BY WALT LARIMORE

"They had a character like a rock, these members of the generation born between 1910–1928. They were the children of the Depression, fighters in the greatest war in history, builders of and participants in the postwar boom.

"They accepted a hand-up in the G.I. Bill, but they never took a handout. They made their own way. A few of them became rich, a few became powerful, and almost all of them built their houses and did their jobs and raised their families and lived good lives, taking full advantage of the freedom they had helped preserve."

—Stephen E. Ambrose, author of *Band of Brothers*[326]

My father never talked about the war when I was growing up—not even after I was married, and my children were young adults.[327] But I knew Dad was in the U.S. Army because of the certificates, pictures, and medals hanging in his small office at home.

I was certainly aware that his leg had been amputated during World War II, but he never talked about *how* he lost his limb. The war was in the past for him, like it was for so many veterans. I think he wanted a clean break because a year or two after V-E Day, he asked his friends and acquaintances—in the military and in civilian life—to call him Larry, not Phil.[i] Mom and all his friends addressed him by his nickname. To me and my wife, Barb, my three brothers, and the grandchildren, he was Pop.

---

i   I believe the nickname came from Colonel McGarr and Ross Calvert during their days together at Fort Myer. Both liked to call him "Larry," obviously a play off our last name.

I'm the oldest of four sons—Billy, Phil, and Rick are my younger brothers—and we knew very little of Dad's war exploits until the 1990s, when he began sharing some stories with friends and us. Then, on his 50th wedding anniversary in 1999—don't worry, I'll tell you more about my mom in a moment—he really opened up.

I'll never forget the moment at The Cabin, a Southern and Cajun restaurant near Burnside, Louisiana, about twenty-five miles south of our hometown of Baton Rouge. Along with extended family, my brothers and I were sitting in an oversized patio when I casually mentioned to Dad that I had been asked to preach a sermon at our church on the topic of "Freedom Isn't Free." I wondered if he might tell us a little more about his adventures during the war years.

After asking him this leading question, it was as if the moment was right for him. Perhaps Dad was feeling nostalgic after a half-century of marriage and keeping his stories hidden, but for whatever reason, he decided that the moment was right to share parts of the story that you just read.

Of course, he didn't have enough time to tell us everything that magical night, but when I heard—for the first time—the story of the battle that precipitated the loss of his right leg, I was mesmerized. I couldn't imagine what that had to be like, getting shot in the leg and playing dead while German soldiers jumped over him in the forest, shooting at the retreating Americans.

I was also captivated by Dad's story of purchasing Chug at the auction, which, by the way, was recorded in the Congressional Record of the Senate[328] and an Associated Press story printed in newspapers across the country. Here are just a few of the many headlines I found:

- A Horse and His Trainer Reunited (*New York Times*)
- Bidders Mum, Let Amputee Have Horse (*Baltimore Sun*)
- 500 Attend Sale: Disabled Vet Gets Show Horse for $50 (*Washington Times-Herald*)
- Purple Heart Pays Off at 300 to 1 (*Boston Herald*)
- The Auctioneer Asked for No Other Bid (*Pittsburgh Post-Gazette*)
- Amputee Hero Gets Horse at Auction (*Seattle Post-Intelligencer*)

And finally, these two from his hometown newspapers:

- A Soldier Will Be Home Soon with His Understanding Horse (*Memphis Commercial-Appeal*)
- And the Auctioneer Said: "I Have a Favor to Ask" (*Memphis Press-Scimitar*)

One Associated Press wirephoto showed Phil and Chug jumping with the lead-in to the caption reading, "Two Veterans Take Hurdles." Another API wirephoto showed Phil looking up to Chug with the lead-in: "Crippled Vet Gets Pet Horse."

Of course, my father would have recoiled at the term "crippled." He also hated the term "disability." Pop would say, "I will never allow a 'dis' to hamper *my* ability."

After purchasing Chug, Phil, like many soldiers, utilized the GI Bill. He attended the University of Virginia while living on the horse farm belonging to President Truman's benefactor. Based upon my father's 100 percent disability, which brought in just over $200 per month, plus his GI Bill benefits, a stipend for managing the stables, and free room and board, my father meant it when he wrote home and told his parents, "I am a rich student."[329]

From 1947 until 1954, my father lived in a rather posh basement on the Red Acres Estate,[ii] built a few years after the Civil War in 1869. The horse farm was part of the Farmington Hunt Club near Charlottesville. Chug was stabled at Red Acres, and the two of them competed in equestrian events up and down the East Coast and were actively involved in the local foxhunting club.

So, whatever happened to Marilyn Fountain after they called off the engagement?

My father never mentioned her name before his death in 2003 at the age of seventy-eight. We only learned bits and pieces about her from my grandmother.

In 1973, after Barb and I got engaged, and four years after grandfather's death, we drove to Memphis so she could meet my dad's mom, Ethyl, who fell in love with Barb. During the visit, she presented us with a box containing eight place settings of Wallace Stradivari sterling silverware. She said she and Granddad had purchased them as a wedding gift for Phil and his then-fiancée, Marilyn Fountain. She offered the expensive silverware to my mother upon her engagement to my father, but Mom flatly turned it down.

Grandmom also showed me, for the first time, the boxes of letters and memorabilia that she had saved. I didn't see them again until 2003, after Dad's death.

Records showed that Marilyn graduated from Gulf Park College in 1944 and from the Drake University Law School in August 1950. She took the bar

---

ii   Dad's letters to his mother from 1947 to 1952 were all addressed from "Lone Acre, Route #2, Charlottesville, Va." Researchers at the Albemarle Charlottesville Historical Society believe this was actually the "Red Acres Estate." William Faulkner, an avid equestrian and a Nobel Prize- and Pulitzer Prizewinning author, came to Charlottesville, Virginia, from Oxford, Mississippi, in the last decade of his life. He nearly purchased Red Acres Estate in 1962, a property he had looked at covetously several times. Faulkner foxhunted with the Farmington Hunt, and his daughter, Jill, would become Master in 1968, a role Phil briefly held while in school.

examination and was admitted to law practice in October. On Christmas Day in 1950, Marilyn married Dr. Warren Ashton McCrary of Lake City, Iowa. Marilyn had always told my father that she wanted to marry a doctor, and she did. They had four children.

So, who's my mother? I'm glad you asked.

During a trip home to Memphis in early 1949, my father met a young nursing student—a brunette, of course—named Maxine Wilson. She hailed from the tiny hamlet of Clay City, Illinois, about a hundred miles due east of St. Louis, Missouri. One of Dad's childhood best friends, Billy O'Bannon, was dating Maxine's nursing school roommate—her sister, Martha—and suggested Maxine as a blind date for Phil.

Before the first date, however, Maxine had emergency brain surgery to remove a benign growth and relieve pressure. Phil met her at the hospital, her head completely bandaged, including her eyes. She later said she immediately liked his voice. They dated during her recovery, and the attraction was sizzling and instantaneous. They were an interesting pair since he was an only child, and she was the ninth of eleven children.

Phil and Maxine quickly fell in love and were married on June 21, 1949, after her graduation. Following their honeymoon, they lived at Red Acres while my father continued his schooling at the University of Virginia.

By this time, my father had decided that he didn't want to become a doctor or study international law after all, but his love for the outdoors and extraordinary ability to read maps led him to earn bachelor's and master's degrees in geography from the University of Virginia.

Upon Phil's graduation, they moved to Baton Rouge in 1954 with their two sons—30-month-old me and my one-year-old brother Billy. My father began his doctoral studies at Louisiana State University (or what I jokingly call "Harvard on the Bayou"). He decided to make cartography—mapmaking— the focus of his teaching, research, and publishing career as a college instructor and Director of the Cartographic Information Center, which was part of LSU's Department of Geography and Anthropology.

As a professional cartographer, my father published several books, co-founded the Louisiana State Geography Alliance, and founded and oversaw the Louisiana Geography Bee for years. Since he was a former Eagle Scout,[iii] he made sure that my brothers and I were active in Boy Scouting. We all achieved the rank of Eagle Scout. Dad served as a long-time scoutmaster and received Scouting's prestigious Silver Beaver Award.[iv] He and Mom were also active members of St. Alban's Chapel and enthusiastically involved in student ministry at the LSU Episcopal Student Center.

---

iii   Phil was awarded his Eagle Scout two weeks after being commissioned as a 2nd Lieutenant, just after he turned eighteen. His mother had to accept for him.

iv   The Silver Beaver Award recognizes Scouters of exceptional character who have provided long and distinguished service within a council.

I remember asking him one time whether he felt he had a personal relationship with God. He thought for a moment and told me, "In World War II, there was a popular phrase: 'There are no atheists in foxholes.'ᵛ That was sure true for me."

He reached into his wallet and pulled out an unfolded a piece of paper. "This is what I came to believe in combat," he said.

> *No shell or bomb can on me burst,*
>
> *Except my God permit it first.*
>
> *Then let my heart be kept in peace;*
>
> *His watchful care will never cease.*
>
> *No bomb above, nor mine below*
>
> *Need cause my heart one pang of woe.*
>
> *The Lord of Hosts encircles me,*
>
> *He is the Lord of earth and sea.*[330]

During a trip to visit his parents' home in Memphis when I was in elementary school, Dad took me and my brother, Billy, to the Peabody Hotel to see the March of the Peabody Ducks. He never mentioned his history with those mallards. We were amazed when he made some unusual sounds and they walked right over to him. But he never talked about his equestrian history, his military exploits, or the horses he saved during the war throughout my childhood.

Although Mom was an avid bridge player, as I was in college, Dad never joined either one of us—or even offered advice on bidding—in a game of bridge. This feels strange after learning about his bridge-playing exploits during his training years and with General Eisenhower after the war. I also find it curious that Dad taught us how to shoot .22 rifles on an ROTC range but never took us hunting. I don't remember ever seeing him shoot a gun or ride a horse.

I was an excellent competitive swimmer in high school, but I never came close to winning against a father who swam with one leg the few times I raced him. At my physical peak, while playing rugby at LSU, I had no chance of defeating him in arm wrestling.

In researching this book, I communicated several times with Ross Calvert's oldest son, Ross Calvert III, who goes by "Topper." He says that he also never knew his father was an equestrian or played bridge.

---

v   Department of Defense (DoD) data show that "atheist" is selected as a religious preference by about one-half of one percent of the total DoD force. In the heat of World War II, men who experienced intense combat were more than twice as likely to turn to prayer as those who did not.

After the war, Phil and Ross didn't see each other very much, although Topper met my father once when Dad visited their home near Washington, D.C., in the early 1960s. Topper's sister sat on my dad's lap and noticed the different textures of his two legs. To her mother's severe consternation, she asked Dad about it. He told her a German sniper had shot off his leg during the war.

Her father, Ross Calvert, interjected, "That's not true, Lucy. He was trying to shoot a fly off his knee with a pistol and missed!"

The two men howled in laughter.

Topper said, "It was obvious this was a long-standing joke with them."

After Lucy hopped off Dad's lap, Ross' brother, Harry, asked my dad which leg was wooden. As his mother gasped at her children's ill-mannered questions, Dad exclaimed, "Let's find out!" He pulled out a pocketknife, opened it dramatically, and then stabbed himself through his pants and into his artificial leg.

"It's *not* that one!" he screamed.

Once again, he and Ross roared in laughter. Topper said that his father later told him and his siblings the real story.

Dad would often tell his Scouts that he was Superman and repeat the stunt to their amazement. At other times, he would bet a rookie Scout, who had been egged on by the older ones, that he could pull his leg backward, behind his back, and over his shoulder to tie his shoe. They'd always take the bet—and lose. One morning, while on a Scout camping trip, Dad awoke to find his leg hoisted to the top of the flagpole. The boys said he couldn't stop laughing about the prank and that he said, "This proves I have a leg up!"

Like boys of my vintage, who grew up in the 1950s and early 1960s with World War II epics on TV and at the movies, I wanted to believe that my daddy had been brave and courageous, maybe an unknown or forgotten Audie Murphy, someone I could boast about to my friends. But my questions about the war were never answered by my father or my mom. "He doesn't like to talk about it," she would say.

At one point, I wondered if he had ever seen any action at all. But the pictures and medals in his office hinted at a hidden story. There was a picture of him being awarded the Distinguished Service Cross by Colonel John Albright, a picture from then Brigadier General Robert N. Young[vi] inscribed, "To Capt Phil Larimore with great admiration as one of the outstanding combat soldiers in World War II," and by far his favorite, a picture from then Major General John W. "Iron Mike" O'Daniel signed, "To a fighting man," a phrase O'Daniel had repeated each time he presented Phil with a medal.

---

vi General Young had been the XO of Phil's 3rd Infantry Division in Europe and then the Commandant of the Military District of Washington when Phil served there.

These founded my hopefulness that Dad *had* been a hero. But since I didn't know what he did during the war, I couldn't match the stories the other boys told when they bragged about their fathers' adventures on the battlefield.

One time, when acting out an imaginary war scene, one of my friends, playing a "Kraut" who had imprisoned me in a treehouse cell, yelled at me to halt as I bravely led my fellow prisoners on a dash to safety.

Of course, I kept running. He threw his unsheathed knife at me, which pierced the skin between my Achille's tendon and tibia, dropping me to the ground. I began hemorrhaging with blood spurting everywhere. I went into shock as my friends hurriedly carried me home, leaving a trail of blood behind. They lay me on our back patio, where my parents were hosting a fancy cocktail party. My mom—the nurse—and my dad—the war hero—instantly jumped into their respective roles and stopped the hemorrhaging.

I remember in my groggy, hypotensive state, saying, "Mom, just take me to my bed and let me die there."

Dad smiled and carried me to his car for the trip to the emergency room, saying, "Nope. No son of mine's dying on the battlefield!"

I tried to get him to tell me war stories while the surgeon numbed, cleaned, and sutured my battle wounds. "I've seen a lot worse," was all he said. "Just a minor flesh wound."

As far as the real war, he had moved on, with one exception—his enduring admiration of the world-famous Lipizzaner horses that he had helped save. The year of my twelfth birthday, in 1964, he took me to see the Lipizzaners in Washington, D.C., in what would be their last U.S. tour for another eighteen years. I remember his silent admiration of these stunning horses as we toured the paddock. He was strangely quiet, and I wonder if his eyes weren't misty, but he didn't brag a bit of his role in saving them.

We were able to tour the paddock because he knew one of the tour leaders—an officer with a thick Austrian accent. I now wonder if it wasn't the director of the Spanish Riding School, Colonel Alois Podhajsky,[vii] who had been involved in saving the Lipizzaners and was accompanying the tour—but perhaps that's wishful thinking. After all, no official records were kept of my father's role in his daring flight behind enemy lines to meet Captain Rudolph Lessing—not a whisper of a hint in the thousands of documents I looked at in the National Archives. As far as is known, Captain Lessing never came to the U.S. to see those involved, and he and my father never had any post-war contact that I can find.

---

vii   Alois Podhajsky was the director of the Spanish Riding School in Vienna, Austria, as well as an Olympic medal winner in dressage, a riding instructor, and a writer. He competed at the 1936 and 1948 Summer Olympics. During World War II, worried for the safety of the school and the horses due to bombing raids on Vienna, he evacuated most of the stallions out of the city to Sankt Martin im Innkreis in Upper Austria. He also evacuated the mares from the Piber Federal Stud, the breeding farm that supplied horses for the school.

A second Lipizzaner event occurred on June 9, 1981, when ten Lipizzaner horses were donated to the caisson platoon at Fort Myer. Dad and Mom were invited to attend as the team of magnificent stallions was accepted on behalf of the Army by the Secretary of the Army John O. Marsh, Jr. The Lipizzaners became the "White Horse Team" for use in military funerals at Arlington National Cemetery. The baroque mounts would later lead the inaugural parade for President Ronald Reagan and Vice President George H. W. Bush. My father never would say who invited him or how they knew of his involvement.

I don't remember him ever talking about or taking us to Fort Myer, Arlington, or the Riding Hall where he purchased Chug. But I recall a family trip to Charlottesville to visit the estate where he and Mom first lived. I remember him walking off by himself, and I asked Mom where he was going. She said Dad wanted to visit the grave of an old friend, a horse named Chug, but he wouldn't allow her or us to accompany him.

It wasn't until his 50th wedding anniversary that my father was finally comfortable sharing the remarkable stories he and his men experienced. Once that dam was breached, oh, how the stories flowed.

As he and his warhorse brothers reached their twilight years, people began showing more interest in their incredible stories. Dad took Mom to several reunions before he died, which they both enjoyed far more than they thought they would. She noted that as time went on, the number attending reunions increased each year, and the men began to talk more and more about their experiences.

On a return trip to Memphis for a private reunion with some of the men he had fought with, he met privately with Ross Calvert, who was in the midst of a highly successful military career, at the Lobby Bar at the Peabody Hotel. They shared smokes, scotch, and stories.

Phil reminisced about one of the hospital nurses on Anzio telling him that by being willing to share his stories with others, that he could bear them—even heal from them. She was right—it *was* hard to start, but once he and Ross began to share their stories with each other, recalling their past not only softened the pain, but softened them.

They agreed that the horrible realities of war—and their crucial roles in combat—had forever altered their lives. They had seen and now understood the reality of true good and awful evil, but even more so, developed a deep appreciation of life, liberty, and the pursuit of happiness.

Before the war, Dad, like most of his fellow soldiers, had been a self-centered and immature young man looking for quest and conquest. In battle, he and his men were assigned tasks they never thought themselves capable of accomplishing. They had observed unimaginable horror and indescribable courage. Each had exhibited bravery and strength in the face of overwhelming odds that they could not have imagined they possessed.

These extraordinary men and their brothers in combat faced and conquered fear, heartbreak, dread, chaos, stench, casualties, wounds, opposition, inevitable defeat, and certain death. They learned to sacrifice the daily comforts that many consider essential. Fortitude, perseverance, loyalty, and service were seared into their characters and branded their souls. Decades after they returned to the home front, they still savored each new day, each breath, in a new way. They knew their many friends in battle who had left their all on the altar of war—who had sacrificed their tomorrows—had allowed them to live, truly live for their todays.

During the last few years of his life, Dad more frequently shared his stories with family and friends. He answered the questions my brothers and I asked. One of the positive consequences of sharing his stories was that his pain waned, and his sleep became calmer and more tranquil. Dad finally seemed to be at peace with his past, hopeful for the future, and secure in knowing that he had served his country honorably.

Philip Bonham Larimore Jr. died a happy man, in his sleep, on October 31, 2003,[viii] and was buried at Port Hudson National Cemetery just north of Baton Rouge. An Army general from the Pentagon called our home just after Dad died and told me that there was a special plot reserved for him at Arlington, not far from where his friend, Ross Calvert, was buried. The Army would transport his body for burial with full military honors, if that was our wish, and the family could accompany him.

When I told Mom, she just shook her head. "That's very nice, but he wants to lay in rest close to home. And I'd like to have him nearby also."

Despite his distinguished service, the only honor guard the Army could muster for his burial was two elderly volunteers wearing Veterans of Foreign War (VFW) caps who played a cassette tape of "Taps" from a cheap portable boombox. It wasn't that the Army didn't care or didn't want to honor his fantastic feats on the battlefield, but with over four million living World War II veterans at the time, this country was losing more than a thousand soldiers every day. Along with the war losses in Afghanistan and Iraq, there was no way to keep up.

Before my mother's death three years later in 2006 at the age of eighty,[ix] she gave me his old military footlocker, which contained hundreds of his

---

viii My father was admitted to the hospital on the evening of October 30, 2003 with abdominal pain. A nurse found him dead at about 3 a.m. She said he looked peaceful. We didn't ask for an autopsy, but with a history of smoking heavily most of his life, which led to atherosclerosis (hardening of the arteries) and coronary heart disease (he had had a heart attack a year earlier), my guess is that the pain was from a leaking or dissecting abdominal aortic aneurysm that suddenly ruptured.

ix My mother died of a ruptured thoracic aneurysm. She is buried with my father at Port Hudson National Cemetery.

personal letters and the published histories of the 30th Infantry Regiment and 3rd Infantry Division. I also found a half dozen scrapbooks jammed with magazine and newspaper articles saved by my grandmother. These accounts confirmed his amazing stories and the exploits of the brave soldiers he fought with on the "forgotten fronts"[331] of Anzio, the Vosges mountains of France, the Colmar Plain, and thick German forests and well-protected villages.[x]

Dad's stories proved to be enthralling and horrifying—and undoubtedly worthy of recounting. Furthermore, his adventures as a master equestrian before, during, and after the war added to his captivating chronicles. And finally, I felt his struggles of being an amputee fighting to remain on active duty in the Army he dearly loved deserved to be told for future generations.

I began transcribing Dad's letters and recording the stories he told my brothers, his friends, and me. Where the accounts differed in minor ways, I always chose the storyline most consistent with others. I researched historical accounts of his battles and World War II in hundreds of books, memoirs (some unpublished), periodicals, newspaper articles, and websites. I interviewed a few of the remaining men he fought with and the children of others. I traveled to and spent months studying exhibits and documents at archives, museums, posts, forts, redoubts, and stables.[xi] The information I discovered allowed me to fill in holes and add color and detail to an already incredible story.

I began formulating more than a decade's worth of work into what I thought might be an interesting novel, but trusted writing colleagues strongly urged me not to fictionalize the story. Jerry B. Jenkins, a *New York Times* best-selling author and a dear friend, told me, "A novel needs to be believable, and a nonfiction book needs to be unbelievable. Your dad's story is the latter. Make it nonfiction."[332] So it is.

At First Light is the result of more than fifteen years of dogged research and endless writing and rewriting, and I'm proud to honor my father's legacy as well as the men he fought with and the women who aided in his recovery. Plus, it's unbelievable—and all the better for that.

---

x   Dad told me one time, "The Northern Front guys had one D-Day; we had seven. The Northern guys had one Battle of the Bulge and one Battle of the Hürtgen Forest—and so did we. But who knows all that?" My father was referring to the five 3rd Infantry Division amphibious assaults in French Morocco, Sicily, Salerno, Anzio, and southern France as well as two of his 3rd Battalion, 30th Infantry Regiment's amphibious attacks on Sicily. He was also referring to the bulge at the Battle of the Colmar Pocket and the dreadful battles in the forests of the Vosges Mountains.

xi   The research sites include the 3rd Infantry Division Museum at Fort Stewart, Georgia; the American Cemetery at Nettuno, Italy; Arlington National Cemetery in Arlington, Virginia; Beachhead Museum in Anzio, Italy; Caisson Stables in Arlington, Virginia; the Eisenhower Center at the University of New Orleans in New Orleans, Louisiana; Joint Base Myer-Henderson Hall in Arlington, Virginia; Maneuver Center of Excellence at Fort Benning, Georgia; Musée de l'Armée in Paris, France; the National Archives at College Park, Maryland; the National Infantry Museum and Soldier Center at Fort Benning, Georgia; the National WWI Museum and Memorial in Kansas City, Missouri; the National WWII Museum in New Orleans, Louisiana; the Old Guard Museum Caisson Stables at Fort Myer, Virginia; the United States Army Heritage and Education Center in Carlisle, Pennsylvania; and the United States Army War College in Carlisle, Pennsylvania.

Someone gave Dad a copy of Stephen E. Ambrose's *Citizen Soldiers* with the following note inside: "This is a wonderful book that tells a great story about men like you…. It is about you…. I did not fully realize who you were until I saw you through these great stories. Our nation owes you and many others a great debt. I always enjoyed our friendship; now I am honored by it."[333]

I would echo his sentiment.

Dad, I always loved being your son.

Now more than ever, I'm honored by it.

FINAL THOUGHT

"It is the Soldier, not the minister
who has given us freedom of religion.
It is the Soldier, not the reporter
who has given us freedom of the press.
It is the Soldier, not the poet
who has given us freedom of speech.
It is the Soldier, not the campus organizer
who has given us freedom to protest.
It is the Soldier, not the lawyer
who has given us the right to a fair trial.
It is the Soldier, not the politician
who has given us the right to vote.
It is the Soldier
who salutes the flag,
who serves beneath the flag,
and whose coffin is draped by the flag."

—Charles Michael Province, U.S. Army, Ret.[334]

PHOTO GALLERY

The world was a simpler place when Philip B. Larimore, Jr., was born on January 4, 1925, in Memphis, Tennessee, the only child of Philip Sr. and Ethyl Larimore. He was a latchkey kid because his father was a Pullman conductor for the Illinois Central Railroad and his mother (holding Philip aloft) was a legal secretary.

Growing up, Phil was undisciplined and a whirling dervish of energy and mischief. Most schoolwork didn't interest him; he preferred to swim, hunt, fish, and ride horses. His school years became so challenging—to Philip and his teachers—that his parents sent him to Gulf Coast Military Academy (GCMA) in Gulfport, Mississippi, where he boarded during his high school years.

At Gulf Coast Military Academy, Philip excelled at military history, strategy, tactics, and weapons and became adept at competitive shooting, compass work, and close combat. His parents attended his graduation in the spring of 1942 after America went to war following Pearl Harbor. During his senior year of high school, he met Marilyn Fountain (second from the left with her suitemates), a freshman attending nearby Gulf Park College, and would remain close to her during his time in the military.

After becoming the youngest graduate of the Army's Officer Candidate School (OCS) at Fort Benning, three weeks shy of his eighteenth birthday, Phil underwent another year of training before being transported to Naples, Italy, where a military band playing in the streets welcomed him. He first saw action in the Battle of Anzio, where the Germans, who occupied the surrounding mountains, pinned down the GIs in muddy, flat, mosquito-infested farmland for over three months. After a vicious breakout from what they called the "Bitchhead," the Allies liberated the first European capital, Rome, on June 4, 1944 (middle photo).

As a 2nd lieutenant in charge of a frontline platoon at Anzio, Phil was one of the youngest officers in the European Theater of Operation at the age of nineteen and won his first medal—the Silver Star (the Army's third-highest decoration). After liberating Rome, the men trained for and participated in their fifth Divisional Amphibious D-Day of the war—which followed their D-Days at French Morocco, Sicily, Salerno, and Anzio. He wrote home, "Enclose[d] you will find the little U.S. flag I wore the day we made the invasion of Southern France." He added, "Sorry I won't be home for Christmas but going to try like hell to be in Berlin I betcha."

9 Oct 1944
France

Dearest Mom,

Just a hurried note. I haven't gotten any mail from any one in some time so there is no news.

Enclose you will find the little U.S. flag I wore the day we made the invasion of Southern France. I thought it would be nice to put in my scrap book.

Still it keeps on raining. It is almost as if some one turned on the hose and it is all falling in the part of France where I am. Mud is getting bad also.

Sorry I won't be home for Christmas but going to try like hell to be in Berlin I betcha.

Write soon
Phil

Will you send me a package!

Phil is standing behind the door of his military jeep, which he named "Monk," a nod to his girlfriend Marilyn Fountain, whom he nicknamed "Monk" after her hometown of Des Moines, Iowa ("moines" being the French word for "monk"). Fellow officer Lt. Abraham Fitterman is sitting atop a massive German railroad gun used at Anzio that was called "Anzio Annie" by the GIs. The seventy-foot barrel had an eleven-inch diameter and could propel 500-pound projectiles up to forty miles and create a crater large enough to swallow a Sherman tank.

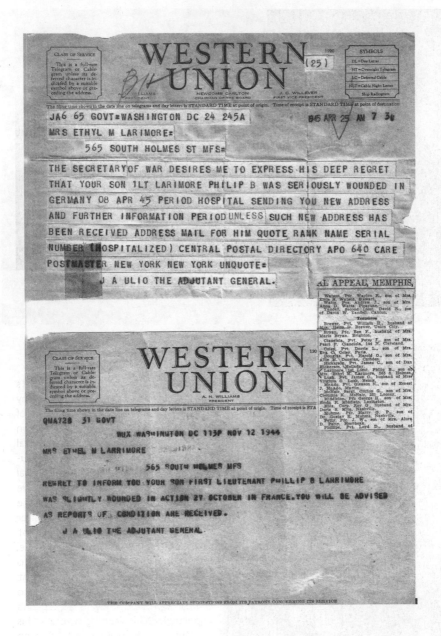

Phil's mother received the upper Western Union telegram after her son was "seriously wounded" in Germany on "08 APR 45." The lower telegram was about Phil being "slightly wounded" on "27 OCTOBER" 1944. Both resulted in battlefield decorations including two Purple Hearts, one Silver Star, and a Distinguished Service Cross. After receiving his second leg wound in 1944, Phil recuperated in a field hospital in a bed next to World War II hero Audie Murphy.

Previewing a bit of postwar "conversion" at The Hermitage Hotel, Capt. P. B. Larimore of Memphis (left) and Capt. Ross Calvert, of 1111 Porter Road, Nashville, help Sgt. A. P. Mays, of Roanoke, Va., into a civilian sport coat. Captain Calvert was two months a German prisoner, and Captain Larimore lost his right leg in action soon after crossing the Rhine.

Photo Credit: Richard Fitterman and
Ruth Fitterman Cazden

Following the amputation of Phil's right leg below the knee in Germany only one month before the end of the war, he spent a year at Lawson General Hospital, an army hospital specializing in the care of amputees in Atlanta, receiving additional surgeries and undergoing intensive rehabilitation. Phil is pictured to the left in a newspaper clipping after reuniting with his army buddy, Capt. Ross Calvert in Nashville, Tennessee. They are helping Sgt. A. P. Mays into a civilian sport coat. At this point, Phil was still on crutches, unable to wear a prosthetic leg. In his captain's portrait, Phil is wearing several of his battle awards. The striped patch on his left shoulder represents the "Blue and White Devils" of the 3rd Infantry Division. Phil was wounded six times in battle but refused three of the six offered Purple Hearts.

Marilyn Fountain and Phil had an off-again, on-again relationship after they met in Gulfport, Mississippi, when Phil was a senior at Gulf Coast Military Academy. Both in school and after being reunited following the war, they shared a love for horses and equestrian activities.

While preparing to appeal the Army policy of automatically discharging Army officers who were amputees after they completed rehabilitation, Phil's former commanders, along with his best friend, Ross Calvert, worked to get him assigned to the Military District of Washington. One of his tasks was attending the visits of dignitaries. Phil is standing next to General Dwight D. Eisenhower (seen just at the right of Eisenhower's shoulder) and British Field Marshal Bernard Montgomery. In the bottom right picture, Phil is seated to the far left, next to Marilyn Fountain. In the foreground is Colonel Lionel C. McGarr, Phil's 30th Infantry Regiment commander. In the bottom left photo, Phil is assisting Brigadier General John "Iron Mike" O'Daniel.

Phil's closest friend in the military was Ross Calvert (left photo, standing to the right). They were together at Officer Candidate School training at Fort Benning and would fight together in epic battles against the Germans. Phil was held in high esteem by his superior officers, including Brigadier General Robert. N. Young, Commander of the Military District of Washington after the war (top right). In the bottom photo, Phil receives the Distinguished Service Cross, the Army's second-highest decoration from Colonel John J. Albright, the Commanding Officer at Fort Myer next to Arlington National Cemetery.

RECEIVING DIST. SERVICE CROSS FROM COL. JOHN. J. ALBRIGHT

Infantry Major, 22, Is Honored With Decoration and Parade

European Veteran, Wounded Five Times, Got Commission at 17

Maj. Philip B. Larimore, youngest man commissioned an infantry officer in World War II, yesterday was awarded the Distinguished Service Cross as all troops in the military district of Washington paraded at Fort Myer in his honor.

The ceremony marked the end of the 22-year-old officer's military career. He was retired yesterday for disability. He has become so proficient in the use of his artificial leg that he plays baseball with the Fort Myer soldiers and is an excellent horseman.

The youthful major lost his right leg above the knee in the fighting at Colmar, France. His latest decoration also came out of that campaign. Though wounded so seriously that his leg had to be amputated, Maj. Larimore destroyed three enemy machine-gun nests, according to his citation.

Commissioned a second lieutenant at 17, when he graduated from the Gulf Coast Military Academy, the officer was so young that he had to remain on inactive duty for three months until his 18th birthday. While still 18, he became a first lieutenant and was promoted to captain at 19.

Maj. Larimore joined the 82d Airborne Division and fought with the division overseas until he broke both ankles in a jump. Then he became an infantry officer with the 30th Regiment of the 3d Division at Anzio. He bears the marks of five wounds, suffered at Anzio and in France.

His other decorations include the Silver Star with Oak Leaf Cluster, the Bronze Star with Oak Leaf Cluster and the Purple Heart with four Oak Leaf Clusters. The DSC was pinned on him by Col. John J. Albright, acting commandant of the Military District of Washington.

Maj. Larimore, a native of Nashville, Tenn., hopes to become an instructor in infantry at one of the nearby military academies.

Maj. Philip B. Larimore gets a smile from his fiancee, Miss Marilyn M. Fountain of Des Moines, at the Fort Myer review yesterday.
—Star Staff Photo.

After Phil received the Distinguished Service Cross in a ceremony at Fort Myer, his story was featured in this newspaper clipping that noted how he was the youngest man commissioned as an infantry officer during World War II. Shortly after this photo of him and "fiancée" Marilyn Fountain was taken, the couple called off their wedding plans. Around the same time, Phil was written up in newspapers around the country after successfully bidding $50 for Chugwater during an army auction of surplus horses.

Auctioneer Byron Brumback made a special request to the audience: "I want to ask a favor right at the start. I want to ask you not to bid on horse number five," referring to Chugwater.

Times-Herald Staff Photo

General View of Horse Auction in Progress at Fort Myer

An attendant parades one of the horses up for auction before part of crowd of 500 who turned out at Fort Myer to bid on surplus saddle horses. Horses once ridden by Gen. Marshall and Eleanor Roosevelt were not shown.

Assets that Government horses would not be sold as surplus after they reached the age of 12. Each horse, it was stated, was in "sound" condition and had been so certified by a veterinarian.

Despite this claim, Mystic came into the ring on "ouchy" legs, displaying a spavin and bad feet. Perkins, Thomas and several others were "sore-going" as they were forced to jump around the corner of the Fort Myer "ring" under the lash of the floor man's whip.

Carlisle Corcoran was the top bidder. When Lady Dan came into the ring he engaged in a duel with Truman Dodson, getting the mare for $260. Later Corcoran topped

Auctioneer in Action

Byron Brumback (microphone in hand) and George L. Wallihan, his assistant, knock down a horse to a bidder. Bids ranged from $50 to $330.

Times-Herald Staff Photo

by Marshall, is a 17-year-old bay mare. She is a polo type and was used by the All American polo team.

Here's How left Front Royal, Va., according to Col. Marion Vorhees, in 1943, under orders to

tested to the fact that Mrs. Roosevelt did ride the horse. It is a chestnut gelding whose mouth indicates he is more than eight years of age. He is leggy, fully 16 hands tall and weighed 1,350 pounds when he left Front Royal. When high in flesh he should be quite showy and a striking looking animal.

But neither he nor the other eight taken for Beltsville yesterday will have to depend on their looks for their livelihood now. Their blood is all that is wanted.

be placed at the disposal of Mrs. Roosevelt. The horse was kept in the White House stables at Ft. Myer until President Roosevelt died.

Two enlisted men, assigned to stable duty at that time, have at

Phil and Chugwater were a match made in heaven, but because Phil had lost his right leg, he had to teach his horse how to respond to his "one-leg lead," meaning his left foot and knee movements. Chugwater, a ten-year-old bay gelding, was quite a jumper. After the war, Phil loved participating with "Chug" in formal foxhunts, where he served as Field Master, being part of horse shows, and engaging in steeplechase competitions.

In the spring of 1949, Phil met a young nursing student, Maxine Wilson, in Memphis, Tennessee. They quickly fell in love and were married on June 21, 1949, after her graduation. Phil continued his studies, earning both a bachelor's and master's degree in geography from the University of Virginia. Two of their four sons were born in Charlottesville, Virginia. After graduation, the family relocated to Baton Rouge, Louisiana.

This is Phil's official photo (top left) while pursuing doctoral studies and later directing the Department of Cartography (map-making) at Louisiana State University. Phil, a former Eagle Scout, loved involving his four sons in the Boy Scouts—all of whom became Eagle Scouts. Maxine places the Silver Beaver Award, the distinguished service award of the Boy Scouts of America, around Phil's neck. In the bottom photo, "Mac" is pictured with her boys (from the left): Walt, Billy, Rick, and Phil. At Phil and Maxine's 50th wedding anniversary celebration in 1999, (left center) Phil began sharing stories about his exploits during World War II—the first time he had done so with his children. Following Phil's death several years later, his son Walt Larimore began going through scrapbooks and spent over fifteen years investigating Phil's movements during the war, which led to the writing of At First Light.

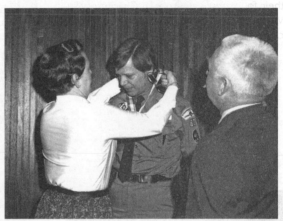

APPENDIX A:

ACKNOWLEDGMENTS

"The way to get things done is not to mind
who gets the credit for doing them."

—Benjamin Jowett, 19ᵗʰ century British theologian[335]

From Walt Larimore:

My father's story was drawn from his letters and the accounts he told family members and friends over the years, nearly all of which were shared with more than one person. From my research, I also used the anecdotes and memoirs of several the men who served with him. I'm very grateful for the records they have left behind. I'm also appreciative to the families of many of these men for granting me permission to use their words. My prayer, hope, and goal are that their stories will not be forgotten.

I'm delighted to have found so many military records that filled in gaps and fleshed out the details of many of Dad's battles before, during, and after the war. I also depended upon hundreds of published sources (books, periodicals, newspaper articles, and trusted internet sources) to provide much-needed detail and background.

As carefully as I could, I matched my father's accounts to the accounts from archives, museums, historians, and those with whom he fought, including several unpublished interviews and memoires. Dialogue, of course, often had to be created or enhanced, but hopefully with accurate context.

I'm thankful to the many who assisted me in the research and writing of this book. First and foremost, I want to acknowledge my wife, Barb, the amazing woman I first met when we were both five years old, who has been my best friend and girlfriend for fifty-three years and my wife for forty-eight years. As a confidant, advisor, and editor par excellence, she gave me countless hours of research and writing. She loved my father, and these were just some of the ways she honored him and his memory.

The Ridgway Hall staff at the U.S. Army War College Library and the U.S. Army Heritage and Education Center (AHEC), both located at Carlisle Barracks in Carlisle, Pennsylvania, provided wonderful assistance during my week-long research visit there in 2016. Thanks to the staff at the U.S. Army War College Library: Rich Baker, Senior Technical Information Specialist; Steve Bye, Archives Technician; Rodney Foytik, Reference Historian; Shannon S. Schwaller, Technical Information Specialist; Thomas E. Buffenbarger, Library Technician; and Ms. Greta Andrusyszyn, Acting Director. Also, a special thank you to the staff of the U.S. Army Heritage and Education Center (AHEC) in Carlisle, Pennsylvania: Jack Leighow, the Director of the Army Heritage Museum, and Colonel Peter D. Crean, AHEC Director. Thanks to Dr. Mike and Pam Gaudiose for their guidance and hospitality during my visit to the Keystone State.

The staff of the Textual and Cartographic Reference Divisions at the National Archives and Records Administration in College Park, MD was wonderfully accommodating during my many days working with them in 2016. In particular, I'm indebted for the assistance of Military Archivist Paul Brown, Archive Specialist Andrew Knight, and Archivist Rebecca Crawford.

In addition, Kirk Heflin, former Museum Curator at the Old Guard Museum in Arlington, Virginia, was a kind host and an extremely informative guide when I visited the Old Guard Museum and Conmy Hall (formerly the Fort Myer Riding Hall) at Joint Base Myer-Henderson Hall (formerly Fort Myer) in 2016. I want to thank Colonel Jason T. Garkey, then the Commander of the U.S. Army 3rd Infantry Regiment (The Old Guard) for his hospitality and also give a special shout-out to Specialist Justin Ekeren of the Caisson Platoon and Honor Guard, who took me on an extended and detailed behind-the-scenes tour through the historic Caisson Stables, also at Joint Base Myer-Henderson Hall and the adjoining Arlington Cemetery. A big thank you to Ken and Jane Daniel for their guidance and hospitality during my visit to Washington.

Toni M. Kiser, Assistant Director for Collections Management at the National WWII Museum, New Orleans, Louisiana, and Z. Frank Hanner,

Director of the National Infantry Museum at Fort Benning, Georgia, provided additional assistance during my visits to their terrific museums in 2017. And special cheers to Ilene B. Kent, Director of Dedications at the National Infantry Foundation at Fort Benning, who spent a day with my son, Scott, and me at the National Infantry Museum.

I appreciate the time and assistance of David S. Stieghan, U.S. Army Infantry Branch Historian at Fort Benning and Ericka Loze-Hudson, Reference Desk Inquiries at the MCoE HQ Donovan Research Library at Fort Benning, as well as the expertise and support of Genoa R. Stanford, the Reference/Systems/Virtual Librarian at the MCoE HQ Donovan Research Library in helping me find difficult-to-locate records and documents.

All of the men with whom Phil fought and who are mentioned in the book have passed away, but it was quite an honor to communicate with some of their family members: LTC Ross Hamilton Calvert, Jr. (sons Ross III [Topper] and Harry); 1LT Abraham Fitterman (son Richard and daughter Ruth Fitterman Cazden); MAJ Russell W. Cloer (daughters Barbara Cloer Moody, Linda Cloer Plyler, and son Jim); SSG Charles O. Beardslee (sons Greg and Brian, and daughter Shirlee Beardslee Baker); SGT Norman Matthew Mohar (his now deceased wife, Maxine, along with daughter, Nancy Mohar Kreuger, and granddaughter Mandy Johnson); and Carl J. Hartstern (son, Steve, and daughter-in-law, Sue) for sharing stories and memoirs (both published and unpublished) of their fathers. Thanks to the late Edward J. P. Drabczyk and Lucy Drabczyk, the son and granddaughter of SGT Edward L. Drabczyk, and Brent K. Miles, the great grandson of MAJ James Lamar Boutwell, who also passed on pictures, stories of, and interviews with their father and great-grandfather, respectively.

Tim Stoy (USA LTC, Ret.), the historian for the Society of the 3rd Infantry Division, was very helpful, not only in carefully reviewing the manuscript for historical accuracy but for providing previously unpublished information on the Maison Rouge battle. William Thomas (USA W-4, Ret.) a staff historian for the Pike's Peak Library District in Colorado Springs, Colorado, assisted me in locating difficult-to-find books and newspaper articles.

Judith F. Brown, PhD, the former historian for the 3rd Infantry Division in Fort Stewart, Georgia, documented Dad's awards and medals. Walter W. Meeks, III, Director of the Fort Stewart Museum at Fort Stewart, Georgia, helped provide additional information. Scott Healy of the History Department at the Memphis Public Libraries helped me locate articles from Memphis newspapers during the war years.

A number of men and women with equestrian, historical, legal, medical, military, and weapons experience carefully reviewed the entire manuscript and made numerous and valuable suggestions that improved the final book in incredible ways. My appreciation goes to Fred Brown, MD (USA LTC, Ret.); Dan Brownell (former USMC CPL); John C. Buckley III (USAFR LTC, Ret.), JD; Thomas E. Buffenbarger, BSL; Joseph Aaron Carter (former USA CPT); Stephen Houseworth, MD (former USA officer); and Alexander (Al) Shine (USA COL, Ret.). Aviation expert Robert Rew (former USN) helped hone my language about gliders and planes. I was blessed to have the sharp eyes of equestrians Sherry Compton, Steve Dail, and Tara Stricko, PhD. Author and historian, Flint Whitlock (former USA CPT), the editor of *WWII Quarterly* magazine, provided edits and expertise that were invaluable.

My deepest gratitude goes to two gentlemen who expertly combed through several drafts of the manuscript: Raymond A. Millen (USA LTC, Ret.), PhD, a professor at the U.S. Army War College, whose extraordinary mind and encyclopedic memory offered many critical corrections and clarifications about all things Army, Infantry, and World War II. And much appreciation is due to Dan Brownell, a former Marine, past acquisitions editor for a major publisher, and current editor of *Today's Christian Living*, who provided myriad suggestions and edits. This book would have been far less accurate without their expertise.

Also, credit for editorial expertise in trimming an initial 600,000 words of compiled research into a 250,000-word draft, and then cutting *that* manuscript in half, as well as dramatically improving its readability, goes to professional editors Mandi Mooney Morrin and Lois Johnson Rew, the author of *Editing for Writers*. Katherine Larimore Ritz provided several rounds of excellent proofreading while she and two of my brothers, Billy and Rick, checked and double-checked references and citations.

My friend, author Jerry B. Jenkins, was a fan of this project from its inception. He provided his writing and editing experience to make the initial sample chapters dramatically more readable and appealing to potential agents and publishers. I doubt my meager efforts would have ever seen the light of day without Jerry's expertise. But that said, he certainly now has plenty of material for his writing courses—he can use me as a great example to show young budding authors how *not* to do it! And he will!

Thanks to my brother, Rick, and son-in-law, Charles Ritz, for assistance in scanning and organizing the pictures. I owe a huge debt of gratitude to the LSU Department of Geography & Anthropology. To honor my father's over-forty-year career there, the department provided the maps used for this book. Thanks to John Anderson, the Map Librarian and Director of the Cartographic Information Center. And a very special virtual hug to Mary Lee Eggart, who worked as a cartographer for my dad for nineteen years. She's also an artist (tinyurl.com/w9t7v4wk) and drew the maps in this book as a gift to "Pop."

Greg Johnson, founder and president of WordServe Literary and my agent, has been an enthusiastic supporter as well as a cheerleader since this book was merely a dream. I'm grateful for the way he shepherded *At First Light*. Almost forty publishers rejected early renditions of this book, yet Greg never gave up on the project. After several years of revision and continuing rejections, Greg called one day in the fall of 2020 and said, "Do you know Mike Yorkey?"

Of course, I did. Mike and I collaborated on a book entitled *God's Design for the Highly Healthy Teen* in the 2005 (coincidentally, the year I began researching this book), and I loved working with him. Greg suggested we talk about working together. We took baby steps by having Mike take a few chapters and rework them from a heavily sourced history book into a compelling story.

After reading his rewrites of the first few chapters, Barb and I were convinced that Mike should come on as a co-author, and I believe we formed a great storytelling team. Once Mike worked his "magic," it didn't take long for us to land a publisher—Knox Press. Thanks, Mike, for bringing my father back to life. We also had a great content editor in our corner—Jessica Snell. She did a fantastic job "cleaning up the sawdust," as she would say, and her eagle eye caught many writing miscues.

Speaking of Knox Press, I'm forever indebted to publisher Roger S. Williams for believing in and supporting this book. He and his skilled team put the "icing on the cake" on the final manuscript. Much credit is due to the hard work and expertise of Kate Monahan, Jessica Vandergriff, and Rachel Hoge. Thanks to Mal Windsor and Tara Mandarno for copyediting and proofing. We're also grateful for the graphic artist skills belonging to Emily Morelli of Blue Muse Studio, who designed the cover.

Despite spending many years of meticulous research, I'm not a professional historian and have never served in the military, so I suspect that there will be errors that a person with military experience or a trained historian will find in this work, even though I made diligent efforts to avoid them. For any errors, may I offer a mea culpa and prayers that none of these mistakes will moderate or weaken the expression of my endless admiration for the men and women who joined arms to fight in this terrible, but completely necessary, war in Europe. I hold each of them in the highest esteem—and so should we all.

A final thought: After reading a series of chapters re-written by Mike Yorkey and edited by me, my chief editor and critic—that would be my wife, Barb—said something that left me speechless: "In this book, Walt, you and Mike have nailed it. You are telling the story of an extremely courageous man and his brothers on the battlefield, most in their teens and early twenties, who fought bravely with only months of training, with fierce odds against them in vicious battles, for the cause of freedom. You have honored them, their sacrifices, and their memories. They will be forgotten no more."

I couldn't stop the tears when she told me this. I believe from the bottom of my heart that our wonderful country and the freedoms we all enjoy exist because we sit on the shoulders of these amazing men and women. We can only try to fill their very big boots—to make them proud—and do our best to preserve the freedom and liberty for which they surrendered so much.

From Mike Yorkey:

Walt won't brag on himself, but I will.

When we finished the rewrite of *At First Light*, I casually asked him how many hours he thought he had put into researching and writing this book before we started working together.

Walt, being the super-organized man that he is, had kept a time log. From 2014 through 2021, he spent around 3,500 hours writing, rewriting, and editing the manuscript. And these hourly totals do not include the *weeks* he spent on researching his father's story at Fort Benning, Fort Stewart, the old Fort Myer, our National Archives, several museums in New Orleans, Kansas City, and Paris, France, the U.S. Army War College Library and the U.S. Army Heritage and Education Center in Carlisle, Pennsylvania, along with trips to Europe to visit old battlegrounds and museums.

It was hard for me to get my head around how many hours this is, so I did a little math. Figuring forty-hour work weeks, that meant Walt devoted nearly eighty-eight weeks or over twenty full-time months of his life working hard on his father's story. Plus, all the time, money, and travel to track down where Phil trained, fought on the battlefield, and did his darndest to stay in the Army after coming home with one less leg. What I'm trying to say is that this book wouldn't have happened without Walt's perseverance and Barb's encouragement.

While I was really disappointed that Phil didn't win his appeal to stay in the Army, the tale of him flashing five ten-dollar bills and seeing the auctioneer immediately bang his gavel and announce, "Sold to the soldier for fifty dollars!" brought this amazing story to a satisfying close.

I'm honored that I've got to come alongside Walt and Barb and introduce Philip B. Larimore, Jr. to a new audience. As I told them when I started reshaping the original manuscript, his absolutely incredible story was hidden in plain sight.

Now this hero lives on, and there's nothing more satisfying than that.

APPENDIX B:

ABOUT THE AUTHORS

Walt Larimore has always had an interest in history and is the oldest son of Philip B. Larimore, Jr., the hero in *At First Light*. As a writer, Walt is a prolific author and has published forty books, thirty medical textbook chapters, and over 1,000 articles in various journals and lay magazines. He's authored several best sellers, garnered international and national writing awards, and his books have had sales of more than 750,000 units. In 2019, an early draft of *At First Light* received two international Page Turner Awards—the Finalist and Patron's Awards.

As a doctor for forty-five years, Dr. Larimore has been called "one of America's best-known family physicians." He has been listed in the *Best Doctors in America, Distinguished Physicians of America, Who's Who in Medicine and Healthcare, Who's Who in America,* and the *International Health Professionals of the Year*. In 2019, *Marquis Who's Who* awarded him their distinguished Lifetime Achievement Award, and in 2021 he was listed in *Who's Who in the World*.

Walt's MD degree is from Louisiana State University, with AOA Honors, while his Family Medicine residency, with an emphasis in Sports Medicine, was at the Duke University Medical Center, where he was named one of the top twelve Family Medicine residents in the U.S. He has delivered more than 1,500 babies and still sees patients part time.

As a medical journalist from 1996 to 2001, Dr. Larimore hosted over live 850 episodes of the daily *Ask the Family Doctor* show on Fox's Health

Network and was awarded the prestigious Gracie Award by the American Women in Radio and Television in 2000. From 2002 to 2004, he hosted *Focus on Your Family's Health*—a nationally syndicated radio and TV feature. He currently hosts three television shows for Liftabletv: *Ask Dr. Walt, The Daily Apple: Medical News You Can Use*, and *The Inside Story: Conversations on the Art and Heart of Writing.*

Walt and his wife, Barbara, have been married nearly fifty years and make their home in Colorado Springs, Colorado. They are the parents of two adult children, Kate and Scott, and two beautiful granddaughters. Walt's website is DrWalt.com.

Mike Yorkey, who shares a fascination regarding World War II, is the author, co-author, editor, or collaborator of more than 110 books, including two novels set in Switzerland, Germany, and France in 1944: *The Swiss Courier* and *Chasing Mona Lisa.* Mike previously collaborated with Dr. Larimore on *God's Design for the Highly Healthy Teen.* He is also known for these collaborative efforts:

- *Out of the Wilderness* by Elishaba Doerksen
- *What Belief Can Do* by Ron Archer
- *The Shot Caller* by Casey Diaz
- *After the Cheering Stops* by Cyndy Feasel
- *Every Man's Battle* by Stephen Arterburn and Fred Stoeker
- *The Great Physician's Rx for Health & Wellness* by Jordan Rubin
- *Fit Over 40 for Dummies* by Betsy Nagelsen McCormack
- *My Big Fat Greek Diet* by Nick Yphantides, M.D.
- *Play Ball* by Dave Dravecky
- *Holding Serve* by Michael Chang

Mike Yorkey grew up in La Jolla, California, and graduated from the University of Oregon with a B.S. degree from the School of Journalism. After a stint as a newspaper editor, he was editor of *Focus on the Family* magazine for eleven years and held other titles there, including editorial director and editor-in-chief. He has also written for *The Los Angeles Times Travel Section, Skiing, Tennis Week, World Tennis, City Sports,* and *Racquet.*

Mike and his wife, Nicole, are the parents of two adult children, Andrea and Patrick. The Yorkeys make their home in Encinitas, California. His website is mikeyorkey.com.

APPENDIX C:

THE PIONEER LARIMORES AND THEIR HORSES

Horses have been in the Larimore family for a long time, dating back to 1760, when James Larimore emigrated from Ulster, Ireland, to the United States at the age of twenty with two of his brothers. The Larimore name meant "he who shoes horses" in Irish, and the Larimore family trade was blacksmithing.[336]

Called Jimmy by his friends, he settled in New Jersey with fifty cents in his pocket. He worked odd jobs, saving as much money as possible while drifting through Pennsylvania and Maryland. Jimmy finally settled in Hampshire County, Virginia, on land owned by Lord Fairfax that had been confiscated by the State of Virginia. Jimmy was one of the first to jump at the opportunity to claim land thrown open for settlement.

After purchasing farming supplies and a muscular draft horse that he named Clyde, Jimmy explored the wilderness, where he discovered a cold, rushing, crystal-clear brook fed by a bubbling mountain spring. He pitched his tent on a thick carpet of needles underlying a massive hemlock tree.

Because the French and Indian War was still raging, he kept a loaded pistol and a tomahawk in his belt as he cut his name in the bark of several trees with his jackknife, thus laying claim to 400 acres of Virginia land. This so-called "Tomahawk Right" carried a preemptive right to an additional 1,000 acres of adjoining land, provided a log cabin was built and a crop of corn was raised on the property in a reasonable amount of time. With Clyde's help, Jimmy began clearing and plowing the land while hauling logs to a homesite. He worked hard and managed to do both within the first year, naming his newly claimed 1,400 acres "Jersey Mountain."

Atop Clyde, James would often spend days or weeks exploring the wilderness and hunting for game. On one trip, James and Clyde were investigating unfamiliar territory along an old Indian trail. They moved into a tall, dense rhododendron thicket that would have been impenetrable without a path cut through it.

Suddenly, Clyde began to behave in a jittery, skittish way. He was grunting and pawing at the ground. Jimmy pulled out his loaded musket as he and his nervous horse moved slowly through the dark brush. Despite the coolness of the thicket, sweat poured from his brow and down his neck.

He shared Clyde's apprehension, wondering if some unfriendly natives might be stalking them. If so, they could face a barrage of deadly arrows at any moment. When Clyde stopped to stomp his front hooves in resistance, Jimmy dismounted, and they cautiously shouldered on.

Jimmy was thankful when they finally exited the thick bushes and entered a virgin forest. The massive trunks held a canopy that was at least one hundred feet above their heads. Movement behind him caused him to turn. To his astonishment and horror, a huge cougar darted among the boulders, drawing closer. He had seen bobcats and lynx before, but never a cougar, a dangerous and vicious predator that the Indians called "mountain panthers."

With his musket ready, he approached the area where he'd last seen the cougar. When he didn't find the animal, Jimmy breathed a sigh of relief. "Think we're clear of danger," he told his horse.

They turned around and resumed following the trail. Jimmy was startled by a snarl from behind and spun to face the leaping beast as it released a blood-curdling scream. In shock, the pioneer instinctively fired his rifle from his hip, wounding the shrieking cat and momentarily knocking it to its side, but its claws lacerated Jimmy's left shoulder and spun him to the ground, sending searing pain down his arm.

Jimmy dropped his now-spent weapon to the ground as Clyde whinnied and pranced forward. For an instant, Jimmy thought the cougar was going to bolt. He quickly pulled his tomahawk from his belt and leaped to his feet. He and the enormous cougar faced each other. The cat crouched as Jimmy prepared for a fight to the death—knowing it was likely his.

The massive brute inched forward, snarling, its fangs dripping with saliva. To make himself look larger and more ferocious, Jimmy threw his arms up, puffed out his chest, and jumped up and down as he shouted. The cougar screamed one last time and then launched himself at Jimmy, who swung the tomahawk with all his strength.

At that moment, as if by instinct, Clyde lashed out with his rear legs, thrusting backward. Whether it was the force of the two hooves or the hatchet, the mortally wounded feline flew backward, roaring out its last breath before landing on the forest floor.

Jimmy shook uncontrollably for a few moments. Whether it was the cold or the shock, he couldn't be sure. He bound the bleeding gashes on his shoulder and gave Clyde a thankful hug. "You saved us both, Buddy."

Jimmy had no idea that Clyde was instinctively performing one of the most famous and complex maneuvers a horse could perform in battle, known as the capriole. The thick, velvety coat of the cougar lay on Jimmy's cabin floor for many years.

Jimmy loved his new home, calling it "Heaven on Earth." His large farm was located on a plateau of the richest and largest valley in all the Virginias, the Shenandoah Valley, situated between the Blue Ridge on the east and the Alleghenies on the west. The lush land was densely covered with over one hundred varieties of forest trees, an aviary of songsters, and a forest full of wild animals that provided meat and fur.

His most treasured asset was his pocket Bible. In it, he read, "It is not good that the man should be alone" (Genesis 2:18), so he began searching for a wife. In Berkeley County, one county to the east, he met Susannah, born in the Rhenish Palatinate of Germany, who'd emigrated with her parents at eighteen years of age. Both were deeply religious and had learned biblical lessons on their mother's knee.

Susannah's parents had left their homeland on account of religious persecution. They immediately took to Jimmy and allowed him to court Susannah. He won her heart and hand. They married on August 2, 1776, the same day fifty-six members of the Second Continental Congress, meeting in Philadelphia, signed an enlarged parchment containing the Declaration of Independence.

Jimmy brought his new wife back to his hand-hewn cabin and homestead, where all the perils of a pioneer and wilderness life confronted them. It was here that Susannah gave birth to thirteen children, with eleven surviving past their first year. From their cabin, Jimmy and Susannah heard the guns of the American Revolution until that war ended in 1783.

Like most wilderness pioneers who tilled what soil they could and conducted patch farming, which was primitive hand-planting around the dead stumps of felled trees, they purchased a cow to provide milk and labor. And it was Clyde who pulled their wagon down the slopes of Jersey Mountain to the village of Three Churches for Sunday school and church each week.

The Larimores purchased and bred horses, specializing in a newer breed called Thoroughbreds, while also running a successful blacksmith and livery operation in Jersey Mountain. Their knowledge concerning various breeds was legendary. Equestrians and farmers would travel from nearby counties and even neighboring states to purchase their magnificent steeds.

The Larimores were said to be above-average in height and weight, and always bore a strong family resemblance to and fondness for each other. Two of their sons fought in the War of 1812. On August 24, 1814, from their porch, they saw a light in the night sky of the east—the burning of Washington City by General Ross of the British Army.

သ

After the tragic death of Jimmy in 1817—from a snakebite—and Susannah in 1822, the children sold off the family farm, blacksmith business, and most of the horses. Nine of the eleven children, along with their spouses and offspring, then loaded up their belongings and migrated West by wagon, first to Licking County, Ohio, where five settled. Another four journeyed to Tazewell County, just north of Springfield, Illinois. All continued to be involved in equestrian activities for generations.

Abraham Lincoln, who practiced law in nearby Springfield, met and represented a number of the Larimores, two of whom, Tom and Sam, attended his first inaugural in March 1861. The boys were also in the procession to the White House. While shaking hands with the new President, he stopped them, recognizing the family resemblance.

"See here, do you have family in Tazewell County, Illinois?" he asked.

The boys replied in unison, "We do."

President Lincoln invited them to return later that evening to the White House, where they sat in the basement kitchen exchanging stories. Their connection was enhanced because Lincoln was quite fond of horses and owned several throughout his life. When there was a fire at the White House stables, the President tried to run into the burning stable to save his son's horse and had to be physically restrained.

In 1865, after Lincoln's assassination, the funeral train reached Springfield, Illinois, where the horse Lincoln rode on the circuit as a lawyer, Old Bob, was draped in a black mourning blanket. Mourners followed Old Bob to Lincoln's burial spot.

Less than one hundred years later, Philip B. Larimore, Jr., carrying a similar love of horses in his blood, would sit in the same White House kitchen talking to a U.S. President.

This heritage helps explain the roots of Philip Junior's early and lifelong expertise in adventure and his love affair with horses and his country.

APPENDIX D:

THOSE WHO FOUGHT WITH PHILIP B. LARIMORE, JR.

(In alphabetical order and with their hightest rank)

SSG Charles Beardslee (October 21, 1921–July 17, 2006) was born in Bothell, Washington. He fought for twenty-eight months with the Headquarters Company and led an Anti-Tank Squad with the 1st Battalion, 30th Infantry Regiment. He was awarded a Bronze Star, a Purple Heart, and a Combat Infantry Badge. He was married to Jacqueline for twenty-one years and had three children, and then was married to his second wife, Donna, for thirty-six years. After the war, he completed his college education on the GI Bill. He initially worked for Boeing and Lockheed Aerospace for many years before relocating to the Eastern High Sierra in Central California, where he taught middle school woodshop for many years until retiring in Montana.

LTC Ross Calvert, Jr. (February 6, 1918–August 28, 1997) was born in Nashville, Tennessee. He fought for twenty-two months in World War II, serving with the Headquarters Company and as Commander of Company K, 3rd Battalion, 30th Infantry Regiment. He was awarded a Distinguished Service Cross, a Silver Star, a Bronze Star with Oak Leaf Cluster, a Purple Heart, and a Combat Infantry Badge. He was also held as a prisoner of war for over three months at the end of the war. As a POW, he almost died from pneumonia and suffered problems with his lungs for the rest of his life. He was married to Betsy for fifty-one years and had three children. He retired as a career Army officer in 1973 after thirty-two years of faithful service. Then, along with his wife, he returned to college, and they both graduated summa cum laude.

MAJ Russell W. Cloer (January 4, 1921–July 7, 2008) was born in Jersey City, New Jersey. He fought for fifteen months in World War II, serving as an I&R Unit Commander, 3rd Battalion, 30th Infantry Regiment. He was awarded a Bronze Star with three Oak Leaf Clusters and a Combat Infantry Badge. He married Beverly and had four children. He retired from the Curtiss-Wright Corporation in Livingston, New Jersey, after thirty-five years of faithful service.

SGT Edward L. Drabczyk (October 26, 1925–June 22, 2015) was born in Niagara Falls, New York, and was unable to finish his high school education during the Depression. He fought for eight months in World War II, serving as a machine gunner with Company L, 30th Infantry Regiment. He was awarded a Bronze Star, a Purple Heart with an Oak Leaf Cluster, and a Combat Infantry Badge. He was married to Florence for sixty-one years and had one child. He retired from Goldome Bank and Parkview Pharmacy in Tonawanda, New York.

1st LT Abraham Fitterman (September 4, 1914–April 9, 1992) was born in Bronx, New York. He enlisted in February 1942 and fought for six months in World War II, first with the 276th Infantry, 70th Division and then with the 3rd Battalion, 30th Infantry Regiment, 3rd Infantry Division, where he served as XO and then Commander for Company L. He was awarded a Silver Star, a Purple Heart, and a Combat Infantry Badge. Abe was married to Bernice Steinberg for fifty years and had two children. After the war, he was a restaurant owner and later became a stockbroker at Plymouth Securities.

Major General Lionel Charles McGarr (March 5, 1904–November 3, 1988) was born in Yuma, Arizona, and graduated from the U.S. Military Academy in 1928. He fought for thirty-three months in World War II, serving as Executive Officer (June 1, 1942–August 19, 1943) and Commander (October 20, 1943–December 12, 1944) of the 30th Infantry Regiment, as acting Assistant Division Commander (December 13, 1944–January 6, 1945) of the 3rd Infantry Division, and again Commander (January 7, 1945–May 5, 1945) of the 30th Infantry Regiment. He was awarded a Distinguished Service Cross, an Army Distinguished Service Medal with an Oak Leaf Cluster, a Silver Star with two Oak Leaf Clusters, a Legion of Merit with two Oak Leaf Clusters, a Bronze Star with four Oak Leaf Clusters, and a Purple Heart with six Oak Leaf Clusters. He was married to Harryette, and they had two children. He retired from the military after thirty-four years of faithful service.

MAJ Audie Murphy (June 20, 1925–May 28, 1971) was born in Hunt County, Texas, to sharecroppers, and only had a fifth-grade education. He fought for thirty months in World War II, serving as an enlisted man and then later as the commander of Company B, 1st Battalion, 15th Infantry Regiment. He was awarded every combat award for valor available from the U.S. Army, including the Medal of Honor, a Distinguished Service Cross, a Silver Star with an Oak Leaf Cluster, a Legion of Merit, a Bronze Star with an Oak Leaf Cluster, a Purple Heart with two Oak Leaf Clusters, and a Combat Infantry Badge. He was married to Wanda for two years, and then Pamela for twenty-one years. They had two children.

After the war, he became an actor and television producer for twenty-one years, making forty-four feature films in all. In addition to acting, he wrote poetry and became a successful country music songwriter. He also bred and raced champion quarter horses. Although Murphy was initially reluctant to appear as himself in the movie, *To Hell and Back*, the 1955 adaptation of his national best-selling book, he eventually agreed. The movie became the biggest hit in the history of Universal Studios at the time. Murphy refused to appear in commercials for alcohol and cigarettes, however, mindful of the influence he would have on the youth market, and suffered significantly from post-traumatic stress disorder (PTSD).

LTG John Wilson "Iron Mike" O'Daniel (February 15, 1894–March 27, 1975) was born in Newark, Delaware. He fought for thirty months in World War II, serving as commander of the 3rd Infantry Division and the VI Corps. He was awarded a Distinguished Service Cross, an Army Distinguished Service Medal, a Silver Star, a Legion of Merit with three Oak Leaf Clusters, a Bronze Star, and a Purple Heart. He was married to his first wife, Ruth, until her death. He then married Gretchen and had two children. His only son, John W. O'Daniel Jr., a paratrooper, was killed in action in World War II, near Arnhem, Netherlands, in September 1944. He retired from the military after forty-three years of faithful service.

GEN Lucian King Truscott, Jr. (January 9, 1895–September 12, 1965) was born in Chatfield, Texas. He fought for thirty months in World War II, serving as commander of the 3rd Infantry Division, VI Corps, Fifteenth Army, and Fifth Army. He was among only a few U.S. Army officers to command a division, a corps, and a field army on active service during the war. He was awarded a Distinguished Service Cross, an Army Distinguished Service Medal with Oak Leaf Cluster, a Navy Distinguished Service Medal, a Legion of Merit, and a Purple Heart. He was married to Sarah. He retired from the military after thirty years of faithful service.

APPENDIX E:
TIMELINE FOR PHIL LARIMORE

1/4/25 . . . . **Born in Memphis, Tennessee**

5/30/30 . . . . Graduates from Miss Lee's School of Childhood

5/29/36 . . . . Promoted to the seventh grade

2/6/37 . . . . Joins the Boy Scouts

9/7/38 . . . . Enters Gulf Coast Military Academy in Gulfport, Mississippi

5/17/42 . . . . Graduates from Gulf Coast Military Academy in
Gulfport, Mississippi

9/21/42 . . . . **Enters Infantry Officers' Candidate School at Fort Benning, Georgia**

12/17/42 . . . . Graduates from Infantry Officers' Candidate School at Fort Benning, Georgia

1/4/43 . . . . Phil's 18th birthday

1/20/43 . . . . **Commissioned 2nd Lieutenant at age 18 years, 16 days**

1/22/43 . . . . Sworn into the Army

1/25/43 . . . . Entry into Active Duty at Fort Wheeler, Georgia

2/6/43 . . . . His mother accepts his Eagle Scout award in his absence

2/15/43 . . . . Transfers to Glider Troops of the 82nd Airborne Division at Fort Bragg, North Carolina

2/15–7/1/43 . . . . Platoon Leader, Company C, 1st Battalion, 326th Glider Infantry,
82nd Airborne Division, Fort Bragg, North Carolina

3/1/43 . . . . Leaves Fort Bragg, North Carolina, for Army Air Base,
Alliance, Nebraska, serves as Train Quartermaster

4/19–5/2/43 . . . . Fort Meade, Maryland, for special school in Dehydrated Foods

7/1/–7/19/43 . . . . Battalion S-2, HQ Company, 1st Battalion, 326th Glider Infantry,
82nd Airborne Division, Alliance, Nebraska

7/20/–10/26/43 . . . . .Battalion S-1, HQ Company, 1st Battalion, 326th Glider Infantry, 82nd Airborne Division, Alliance, Nebraska

10/27/–12/31/43 . . . . Platoon O, Company C, 326th Glider Infantry, 82nd Airborne Division, Alliance, Nebraska

11/1–11/20/43 . . . . .Parachute Demolition School at Fort Benning, Georgia

11/25–12/4/43. . . . . Company C, 1st Battalion, 326th Glider Infantry, 82nd Airborne Division, Alliance, Nebraska

12/4/43 . . . . Takes train back to Fort Bragg, North Carolina

1/4/44 . . . .**Phil's 19th birthday**

1/10/44 . . . . Reports to AGF Replacement Depot #1, Fort Meade, Maryland

1/30 or 31/44 . . . . Sails from Fort Meade

2/9/44 . . . . Arrives at Casablanca, French Morocco, North Africa

2/20/44 . . . .**Arrives at Anzio Beachhead, Italy**

3/6–10/15/44. . . . . .Platoon Leader, A&P Platoon, HQ Company, 3rd Battalion, 30th Infantry Regiment, 3rd Division

–3/9/44 . . . . .Hospitalized for malaria, offered and refuses a Purple Heart

3/15–16/44 . . . . Phil and Ross Calvert capture two houses, and Phil earns first Silver Star

4/44 . . . . Begins using mules to deliver ammunition

5/17/44 . . . . Promoted to 1st Lieutenant at age nineteen

5/25/44 . . . . **Breakout from the Anzio Beachhead, Italy**

6/4/43 . . . . Liberation of Rome

6/28–7/14/44. . . . . Intense training for invasion of France

8/12/44 . . . . .Leaves Naples, Italy, by boat

8/15/44 . . . .**D-Day invasion of southern France**

8/18/44 . . . . Wounded in action, first Purple Heart

8/20/44 . . . . .Phil and Ross Calvert liberate small French towns (likely Masaugnes, Tourves, Rougiers, Seillons, Ollières, Pourcieux, St. Zacharie, Pourrierers, Trets, Peynier, Rousset, and Puyloubier)

8/27/44 . . . . Phil and Ross Calvert liberate Taulignan, France

8/29/44 . . . . **Phil and Ross Calvert round up horses around Montélimar, France**

9/8/44 . . . . Phil, Ross Calvert, and Colonel Lionel McGarr in Battle of Besancon

9/9/44 . . . . .Rigs up a ferry and earns first Bronze Star

9/11/44 . . . . .Heads into the Vosges Mountains

9/17/44 . . . . Phil and Robert Pridgen almost battle to the death near Raddon, France

9/23/44 . . . . Defuses TNT on bridge over the Moselle River

10/2/44 . . . . .Coordinates using mules to deliver ammunition

10/27/44 . . . . **Severely wounded, Vosges Mountains near St. Diè, France, earning second Purple Heart**

10/28–12/12/44. . . . . .Hospitalized, 3rd General Hospital, Aix-en-Provence, and recuperates in a cot next to decorated war hero Audie Murphy

11/2/44 . . . . Surgery to close leg wound

12/12/44 . . . . .Released from hospital and works to get back in fighting shape

12/25/44 . . . . Arrives back at 30th Infantry HQ

12/26–12/31/44. . . . . Becomes Executive Officer, Company K, 30th Infantry, 3rd Division

1/4/45 . . . . Phil's 20th birthday

1/6/45–2/1/45 . . . . Platoon Leader, A&P Platoon, HQ Company, 3rd Battalion,
30th Infantry, 3rd Division

1/23/45 . . . . Phil and Ross Calvert separated in Colmar Pocket

2/1/45 . . . . First battle as a Company Commander, earning second Bronze Star with Valor

2/1/45–4/8/45 . . . . Company Commander: Company L, 30th Infantry, 3rd Division

2/20/45 . . . . .Awarded Croix de Guerre with Palm

3/9/45 . . . . Officers' Dance in Nancy, France

3/14/45 . . . . Attack across the Siegfried Line into Germany

3/25/45 . . . . Crossing the Rhine River

3/30/45 . . . . .Crossing the Main River

4/3/45 . . . . .Secret one-day mission into Czechoslovakia to save the Lipizzaners

**4/8/45 . . . . .Severe leg wound, earning third Purple Heart and second Silver Star
(eventually elevated to Distinguished Service Cross)**

4/9/45 . . . . Below-knee amputation at 10th Field Hospital

4/14–29/45 . . . . Patient, DOP 4364 US AHP

4/23/45 . . . . .Promoted to Captain at age twenty

4/29/45 . . . . .Military evacuation to US

5/8/45 . . . . V-E Day

5/9/45 . . . . .Arrives at Mitchell Field, New York

5/11/45 . . . . Arrives at Lawson General Hospital in Atlanta, Georgia

5/11/45–5/10/46 . . . . Rehabilitation, Lawson General Hospital

5/21/45 . . . . Above-knee amputation

6/6/45 . . . . 30th Infantry awarded Presidential Unit Citation

6/6/45 . . . . Company L awarded Distinguished Unit Citation

9/7/44 . . . . Receives his first prosthesis

2/27/46 . . . . .Additional surgery to remove neuroma at Lawson General Hospital

**4/13/46 . . . . .Initial conversation with Ross Calvert and Colonel McGarr
about job at Fort Myer, Virginia**

5/1/46 . . . . .Offered and accepts transfer to Fort Myer

5/2/46 . . . . .Discharged from Lawson General Hospital

5/13/46–5/12/47 . . . . .Executive Officer, 2511th S.C.U., Ceremonial Detachment, Ft. Meyer, Virginia

1/27/47 . . . . Admitted one day to Walter Reed General Hospital for evaluation
after expiration of six months temporary limited duty (TLD);
ordered to permanent limited duty

3/3/47 . . . . .Ordered to appear before Army Retiring Board

4/15/47 . . . . **Proceedings of Army Retiring Board at Walter Reed General Hospital regarding appeal to stay in the Army as an amputee, but found permanently incapacitated for active service**

5/5/47 . . . . Awarded the Distinguished Service Cross

5/13/47 . . . . Promoted to Major at age twenty-two

5/29/47 . . . . Retreat Parade and Review of two battalions honoring Phil by the Military District of Washington

7/10/47 . . . . **Auction of Chug at the Riding Hall of Fort Myer**

7/12/47 . . . . .Date of separation from the U.S. Army; authorized to wear:

- Distinguished Service Cross

- Silver Star with Oak Leaf Cluster

- Bronze Star with Oak Leaf Cluster

- Purple Heart with Two Oak Leaf Clusters

- European Theater of Operations Campaign Medal with Four Bronze Stars & Arrowhead[i]

- Presidential Unit Citation with Two Oak Leaf Clusters

- Fourragère—France

- Croix de Guerre with Palm—France

- American Campaign Medal

- World War II Victory Medal

- Combat Infantryman Badge

Sept 47. . . . . .Begins college at the University of Virginia

6/21/49 . . . . **Marries Maxine Wilson in Memphis**

3/7/52 . . . . **Birth of first child: Walter Lee Larimore**

6/9/52 . . . . Receives Bachelor of Arts, University of Virginia

8/14/54 . . . . Earns Master of Science, Geography, University of Virginia

Aug 54. . . . . Moves family to Baton Rouge, Louisiana

---

i   A soldier would get one bronze service star for each campaign in which he took part. In Phil's case, it was the Italian, Southern France, Northern France, and Central Europe campaigns. The arrowhead signifies that the soldier participated in an invasion in World War II.

APPENDIX F:
GLOSSARY AND ABBREVIATIONS

"The word *abbreviation* sure is long for what it means."

—Zach Galifianakis, American actor, comedian, and writer [337]

1LT	first lieutenant
A&P	ammunition and pioneer
AA	anti-aircraft
AGF	Allied Ground Forces
AP	anti-personnel
API	Associated Press International
AT	anti-tank
AWOL	absent without leave
BAR	Browning automatic rifle
BBC	British Broadcasting Corporation
CIB	Combat Infantry Badge
CO	company
COL	colonel
CP	command post
CPL	corporal
CPT	captain

DoD ....Department of Defense

DSC .... Distinguished Service Cross

DUKW ....two-and-a-half-ton amphibious truck or D (1942), U (amphibian), K (all-wheel drive), W (dual rear axles)

ETO .... European Theater of Operations

FBI .... Federal Bureau of Investigation

FO .... forward observer

G-1 ....personnel officer or section of a major command—Division or above

G-2 .... intelligence officer or section of a major command—Division or above

G-3 .... operations/training officer or section of a major command—Division or above

G-4 .... logistics officer or section of a major command—Division or above

GCMA .... Gulf Coast Military Academy

GI .... American soldier, especially an enlisted man

GR ....Graves Registration Company

HQ .... headquarters

I&R ....intelligence and reconnaissance

ID .... Infantry Division

IR ....Infantry Regiment

IV .... intravenous

JAG .... Judge Advocate General's Corps

KIA .... killed in action

KP .... kitchen patrol

LCI ....Landing Craft, Infantry (or Infantry Landing Craft)

LCT ....Landing Craft, Tank (or Tank Landing Craft)

LCVP ....Landing Craft, Vehicle, Personnel (or Higgins boat)

LOD .... line of departure

LSI ....Landing Ship, Infantry (or Infantry Landing Ship)

LST ....Landing Ship, Tank (or Tank Landing Ship)

Lt. .... lieutenant

LTC .... lieutenant colonel

LTG .... lieutenant general

MAJ .... major

MG .... major general

MIA ....missing in action

MLR .... Main Line of Resistance

mm .... millimeter

MP. .... Military Police

mph ....miles per hour

MWR .... Morale, Welfare, and Recreation

NAZI . . . . Nationalsozialistische Deutsche Arbeiterpartei

NCO . . . . non-commissioned officer

npn . . . . no page number

OCS . . . . Officer Candidate School

OLC . . . . Oak Leaf Cluster

OR. . . . . operating room

PBS . . . . Public Broadcasting Service

PFC . . . . private first class

PM. . . . . Prime Minister

PMS&T. . . . . Professor of Military Science & Tactics

POW . . . . prisoner of war

Ret. . . . . retired

ROTC . . . . Reserve Officers' Training Corps

SGT. . . . . sergeant

SSG . . . . staff sergeant

S-1 . . . . personnel officer or section of smaller units—Brigades or lower, i.e., Regiments, or Battalions

S-2 . . . . . . intelligence officer or section of smaller units—Brigades or lower, i.e., Regiments, or Battalions

S-3 . operations/training officer or section of smaller units—Brigades or lower, i.e., Regiments, or Battalions

S-4 . . . . logistics officer or section of smaller units— Brigades or lower, i.e., Regiments, or Battalions

SP . . . . self-propelled

SS . . . . Schutzstaffel (German elite guard)

TAC. . . . . Teach, Access, and Counsel Officer

TD. . . . . tank destroyer

TNT . . . . 2,4,6-trinitrotoluene explosive

TO. . . . . tactical officer

TOT . . . . time on target

TTP. . . . . Tactics, Techniques, and Procedures

USA. . . . . United States Army

USAF. . . . . United States Air Force

USAFR . . . . United States Air Force Reserve

USMC. . . . . United States Marine Corps

USN. . . . . United States Navy

USS . . . . United States Ship

ÚVOD. Ústřední vedení odboje domácího (Czechoslovakian Resistance Group)

V-E. . . . . Victory in Europe

Wehrmacht . . . . German armed forces

W-4 . . . . chief warrant officer

XO. . . . . executive officer

APPENDIX G:

BIBLIOGRAPHY

"I try to uncover the adventures and personalities behind each character I research. Once my character and I have reached an understanding, then I begin the detective work of reading old books, old letters, old newspapers, and visiting the places where my subject lived. Often, I turn up surprises, and of course, I pass them on."

—Jean Fritz, acclaimed American biographer[338]

All URLs have been converted to TinyURLs and were last accessed October 15, 2021, unless otherwise indicated.

BOOKS:

1.   Allen, Max. *Medicine Under Canvas: A War Journal of the 77th Evacuation Hospital.*
2.   Kansas City: Sosland Press, 1949.
3.   Ambrose, Stephen E. *Band of Brothers: E Company, 506th Regiment, 101st Airborne. From Normandy to Hitler's Eagle's Nest.* New York: Simon & Schuster, 1992.
4.   Ambrose, Stephen E. *Citizen Soldiers: The U.S. Army from Normandy Beaches to the Bulge to the Surrender of Germany. June 7, 1944–May 7, 1945.* New York: Simon & Schuster, 1997.
5.   *Anzio Beachhead: 22 January–25 May 1944. American Forces in Action Series.* Nashville: Battery Press, 1986.
6.   Atkinson, Rick. *The Day of Battle: The War in Sicily and Italy, 1943–1944. Volume 2 of the Liberation Trilogy.* New York: Henry Holt and Company, 2007.

7.   Atkinson, Rick. *The Guns at Last Light: The War in Western Europe, 1944–1945. Volume 3 in the Liberation Trilogy*. New York: Henry Holt and Company, 2013.

8.   Atkinson, Rick, James Balog, and Bruce Dale. *Where Valor Rests: Arlington National Cemetery*. Washington: National Geographic, 2009.

9.   Baime, A. J. *The Accidental President: Harry S. Truman and the Four Months That Changed the World*. New York: Houghton Mifflin Harcourt, 2017.

10. Barger, Melvin D. *Large Slow Target: A History of the LST*. Columbia, SC: U.S. LST Association, 1986.

11. Batzli, Samuel A. *Fort Myer, Virginia: Historic Landscape Inventory*. Champaign, IL: Department of the Army. Construction Engineering Research Laboratories, 1998.

12. Bearse, Ray. "The Thompson Submachine Gun: Weapon of War and Peace." *Gun Digest Treasury: The Best from 45 Years of Gun Digest*, edited by Harold A. Murtz. Cincinnati: DBI Books, 1994.

13. Beschloss, Michael R. *The Conquerors: Roosevelt, Truman and the Destruction of Hitler's Germany, 1941–1945*. New York: Simon & Schuster, 2002.

14. Bishop, Eleanor C. *Prints in the Sand: The U.S. Coast Guard Beach Patrol During World War 2*. Missoula, MT: Pictorial Histories Publishing Company, 1989.

15. Blythe, Lt. Col. William J. (ed). *Thirteenth Airborne Division: History of the 326th Glider Infantry Regt*. Doraville, GA: Albert Love Publishers, 1946.

16. Bolté, Betty. *Dressage*. Philadelphia: Chelsea House Publishers, 2002.

17. Bongianni, Maurizio. *Simon & Schuster's Guide to Horses and Ponies*. New York: Simon & Schuster, 1988.

18. Bonn, Keith E. *When the Odds Were Even: The Vosges Mountains Campaign, October 1944–January 1945*. Novato, CA: Presidio Press, 1994.

19. Botula, Mike. *LST 920: Charlie Botula's Long, Slow Target! A ship that made history in World War 2!* Seattle: CreateSpace, 2016.

20. Bradlee, Ben. *A Good Life*. New York: Simon & Schuster, 1995.

21. Bradley, Melvin. *The Missouri Mule: Showing and Showmen*. Columbia, MO: University of Missouri-Columbia, Extension Division, 1993.

22. Bradley, Omar N. *A Soldier's Story*. New York: Henry Holt and Company, 1951.

23. Brown, Al. *My Comrades and Me: Staff Sergeant Al Brown's WWII Memoirs*. Bloomington, IN: Xlibris, 2004.

24. Capps, William, ed. *The Vietnam Reader*. New York: Routledge—Taylor & Francis Group, 1991.

25. Carlson, Lewis H. *We Were Each Other's Prisoners: An Oral History of World War II American and German Prisoners of War*. New York: Basic Books, 1997.

26. Carroll, Andrew, ed. *War Letters: Extraordinary Correspondence from American Wars*. New York: Scribner, 2001.

27. Cartwright, William H. Jr, and Major Louise E. Goedin. *The Military District of Washington in the War Years. 1942–1945*. Abridged by William M. Offutt. Bethesda: Brother's Printing, 1945.

28. Chamberlin, J. Edward. *Horse: How the Horse Has Shaped Civilizations*. New York: BlueBridge, 2006.

29. Chambers, III, John Whiteclay, ed. *The Oxford Guide to American Military History*. New York: Oxford University Press, 1999.

30. Champagne, Daniel R. *Dogface Soldiers: The Story of B Company, 15th Regiment, 3rd Infantry Division: From Fedala to Salzburg: Audie Murphy and His Brothers in Arms*. Bennington, VA: Merriam Press, 2003.

31. Churchill, Winston S. *Closing the Ring. The Second World War, Volume 5*. Boston: Houghton Mifflin Company, 1951.

32. Churchill, Winston S. *Never Give In! Winston Churchill's Speeches*. New York: Bloomsbury Revelations, 2013.

33. Churchill, Winston S. *Triumph and Tragedy. The Second World War, Volume 6*. Boston: Houghton Mifflin Company, 1953.

34. Clarke, Jeffrey J., and Robert Ross Smith. *Riviera to the Rhine: U.S. Army in World War II: The European Theater of Operations (United States Army in World War II: European Theater of Operations)*. Atlanta: Whitman Publishing, 2012.

35. Coates, John Boyd Jr., ed. *Activities of Surgical Consultants. Volume I. Surgery in World War II Series*. Washington: Department of the Army Medical Department, 1962. https://tinyurl.com/d6ut8mvd.

36. Colby, John. *War from the Ground Up: The 90th Division in World WWII*. Austin, TX: Nortex Press, 1991.

37. Collier, Richard. *Fighting Words*. New York: St. Martin's Press, 1989.

38. Cope, Samuel W. *The Story of a Happy Life*. Chillicothe, MO: Johnson & Kiergan, Reliable Printers, 1898.

39. Cosmas, Graham A., and Albert E. Cowdrey. *The Medical Department: Medical Service in the European Theater of Operations*. Washington: Center of Military History, United States Army, 1992. tinyurl.com/jy34qfb.

40. Croll, Mike. *The History of Landmines*. Barnsley, England: Leo Cooper Publisher, 1998.

41. Cowley, Robert, ed. *No End Save Victory: Perspectives on World War II*. New York: Putnam Adult, 2001.

42. Cowdrey, Albert E. *Fighting for Life: American Military Medicine in World War II*. New York: Free Press, 1994.

43. Daiches, David. *Scotch Whisky: Its Past and Present*. London: André Deutsch Limited, 1969.

44. Daniels, Roger. *Franklin D. Roosevelt: The War Years, 1939–1945*. Champaign, IL: University of Illinois Press, 2016.

45. Demarest, Chris. *Arlington: The Story of Our Nation's Cemetery*. New York: Roaring Book Press, 2010.

46. Dietrich, John. *The Morgenthau Plan: Soviet Influence on American Postwar Policy*. New York: Algora Publishing, 2002.

47. Doubler, Michael D. *Closing with the Enemy: How GIs Fought the War in Europe, 1944–1945*. Lawrence, KS: University of Kansas Press, 1994.

48. Egger, Bruce E., and Lee M. Otts. *G Company's War: Two Personal Accounts of the Campaigns in Europe, 1944–1945*. Tuscaloosa, AL: The University of Alabama Press, 1992.

49. Ellis, John. *On the Front Lines: The Experience of War through the Eyes of the Allied Soldiers in World War II*. New York: John Wiley & Sons, 1991.

50. Essin, Emmett M. *Shavetails and Bell Sharps: The History of the U.S. Army Mule*. Lincoln, NE: University of Nebraska Press, 2000.

51. Evans-Hylton, Patrick. *Hampton Roads: The World War II Years*. Mount Pleasant, SC: Arcadia Publishing, 2005. Google Books. tinyurl.com/jcuozlb.

52. Fast, Richard Ellsworth, and Maxwell, Hu. *The History and Government of West Virginia*. Morgantown, WV: Acme Publishing, 1901.

53. Fisher Jr., Ernest. *Cassino to the Alps. The Mediterranean Theater of Operations. United States Army in World War II*. Washington: Government Printing Office, 1977.

54. Fussell, Paul. *Thank God for the Atom Bomb and Other Essays*. Logan, IA: Summit Books, 1988.

55. Fussell, Paul. *The Great War and Modern Memory*. New York: Oxford University Press, 1975.

56. Gieck, Jack. *Lichfield: The U.S. Army on Trial*. Akron, OH: University of Akron Press, 1997.

57. Glasser, Arthur F. *And Some Believed: A Chaplain's Experiences with the Marines in The South Pacific*. Chicago: Moody, 1946.

58. Goethe, J. W. *Italian Journey [1786–1788]*. Translated by W. H. Auden and Elizabeth Mayer. London: Penguin Books, 1970.

59. Gordon, Wallace J. *Soldier: Rifleman by Training, Clerk-Typist by Accident. In North Africa, Italy, and Austria*. Bloomington, IN: AuthorHouse Publishing, 2002.

60. Grafton, John, and James Daley, eds. *28 Great Inaugural Addresses: From Washington to Reagan*. Mineola, NY: Dover Publications, 2006.

61. Grant, Yvette. *The Little Red Book of Horse Wisdom*. New York: Skyhorse Publishing, 2012.

62. Gray, J. Glenn. *The Warriors: Reflections of Men in Battle*. New York: Harper & Row, 1959.

63. Greene, Bob. *Once Upon a Town: The Miracle of the North Platte Canteen*. New York: William Morrow, 2002.

64. Hartstern, Carl J. *World War II: Memoirs of a Dogface Soldier*. Bloomington IN: Xlibris, 2011.

65. Hauer, John. *The Natural Superiority of Mules*. Lyons, NY: Lyons Press, 2006.

66. *History of the Second World War. Volume 6*. London: Purnell and Sons, 1966.

67. Hayes, Karen E.N., and Sue M. Copeland. *Hands-On Senior Horse Care: The Complete Book of Senior Equine Management and First Aid*. North Pomfret, VT: Trafalgar Square Books, 2001.

68. Heefner, Wilson A. *Dogface Soldier: The Life of General K. Truscott, Jr.* Columbia, MO: University of Missouri Press, 2010.

69. Holland, Matthew F. *Eisenhower Between the Wars: The Making of a General and Statesman*. Westport, CT: Praeger Publishers, 2001.

70. *Infantry in Battle*. Washington: The Infantry Journal, 1939. tinyurl.com/j48a9s5.

71. Ingersoll, Ralph. *Top Secret*. New York: Harcourt, Brace & Company, 1946.

72. Jay, G. M. "Chapter 8: Euthanasia as an Equine Welfare Tool." *Equine Welfare* edited by C. Wayne McIlwraith, and E. Berbard E. Hoboken, NJ: Wiley-Blackwell, 2011.

73. Jeffers, H. Paul. *Command of Honor: General Lucian Truscott's Path to Victory in World War II*. New York: New American Library, 2008.

74. Jenkins, Carol Brennan, and Deborah Jean Downs White. *Nonfiction Author Studies in the Elementary Classroom*. Portsmouth, NH: Heinemann, 2007.

75. Jenkins, Ryan. *Saving Horses in WWII: The Untold Story of Operation Cowboy in World War 2*. Raleigh, NC: Success Publishing, 2014. Kindle.

76. Keane, Michael. *George S. Patton: Blood, Guts, and Prayer*. Washington: Regnery Publishing, 2012.

77. Kelly, Fred C., ed. *Miracle at Kitty Hawk: The Letters of Wilbur and Orville Wright*. New York: Farrar, Straus & Young, 1951.

78. Kennedy, David M. *The American People in World War II. Freedom from Fear. Part Two*. New York: Oxford University Press, 1999.

79. Kephart, Horace. *The Book of Camping and Woodcraft: A Guidebook for Those Who Travel in the Wilderness*. New York: Outing Publishing Company, 1906.

80. Kershaw, Alex. *The Liberator: One World War II Soldier's 500-Day Odyssey from the Beaches of Sicily to the Gates of Dachau*. New York: Crown Publishers, 2012.

81. Kershaw, Ian. *Hitler: A Biography*. New York: W. W. Norton & Company, 2008.

82. Keyes, Ralph. *The Quote Verifier: Who Said What, Where, and When*. New York: St. Martin's Griffin, 2006.

83. Larimore, Joseph Herbert. *James and Susannah (Bonheim) Larimore Family History*. Self-Published. The original is held in the library of the Licking County Genealogical Society in Newark, Ohio. The account "is drawn largely from a history of the Larimore family written by Caroline Larimore Williams of Wheeling, W. *Va.*"

84. Letts, Elizabeth. *The Perfect Horse: The Daring U.S. Mission to Rescue the Priceless Stallions Kidnapped by the Nazis*. New York: Ballantine Books, 2016.

85. Lionberger, John. *Renewal in the Wilderness: A Spiritual Guide to Connecting with God in the Natural World*. Nashville: Skylight Paths, 2007.

86. Litoff, Judy Barrett, and David C. Smith. *We're in This War, Too: World War II Letters of U.S. Women in Uniform*. New York: Oxford University Press, 1994.

87. MacDonald, Charles B. *Company Commander*. New York: History Book Club, 2006.

88. Markley, Craig. *The Gatherers*. Bloomington, IN: iUniverse, 2014.

89. Mauldin, Bill. *Up Front*. New York: Henry Holt & Company, 1945.

90. Meagher, Thomas, ed. *The Gigantic Book of Horse Wisdom*. New York: Skyhorse Publishing, 2007.

91. McDonough, James Lee. *William Tecumseh Sherman: In the Service of My Country: A Life*. New York: W. W. Norton & Company, 2016.

92. McPherson, Larry E., and Charles Reagan Wilson. *Memphis*. Jackson, MS: University Press of Mississippi, 2002.

93. Miller, Donald L. *The Story of World War II*. New York: Simon & Schuster, 2001.

94. Miller, Thomas Condit, and Hu Maxwell. *West Virginia and Its People: Volume 1*. New York: Lewis Historical Publishing, 1913.

95. Miller, William Lee. *Two Americans: Truman, Eisenhower and a Dangerous World*. New York, 2012.

96. Mohar, Norman. *Sgt Norman Mohar's Recollections of WWII*. Raleigh, NC: Lulu Press, 2015.

97. Molony, Brigadier C. J. C. *The Mediterranean And Middle East Volume VI: Victory in The Mediterranean. Part I, 1st April to 4th June 1944. History of The Second World War*. London: Naval and Military Press, 2004.

98. Monahan, Evelyn M., and Rosemary Neidel-Greenlee. *And If I Perish: Frontline U.S. Army Nurses in World War II*. New York: Alfred A. Knopf, 2003.

99. Morpurgo, Michael. *War Horse*. London: HarperCollins UK, 2011.

100. Munsell, Warren P. *The Story of a Regiment, A History of the 179th Regimental Combat Team*. World War Regimental Histories. Book 34. New York: Newsphoto, 1946. tinyurl.com/joxq8qk.

101. Murphy, Audie. *To Hell and Back*. New York: Henry Holt, 1946.

102. Newmark, Amy. *Chicken Soup for the Soul: It's Beginning to Look a Lot Like Christmas. 101 Tales of Holiday Love & Wonder*. New York: Simon & Schuster, 2019.

103. Nordholt, Jan Willem Schule. *Wilson: A Life for World Peace*. Originally published as: *Woodrow Wilson: Een Leven Voor de Wereldvrede*. Translated by Herbert H. Rowen. Berkley: University of California Press, 1991.

104. Norwood, David I., ed. *Handbook on German Military Forces. U.S. War Department*. Baton Rouge: Louisiana State University Press, 1990.

105. Palmer, Robert R, Bell I Wiley, and William R. Keast. *The Procurement and Training of Ground Combat Troops (United States Army in World War II)*. Washington: Superintendent of Documents, U.S. G.P.O., 1971.

106. Parker, Ken. *Civilian at War*. Traverse City, MI: Horizon Books, 2002.

107. *The Passing Parade. Graduation Book for AOC No. 5*. Fort Benning, GA: The Infantry School, 1947.

108. Paterson, Michael. *Winston Churchill: Personal Accounts of the Great Leader at War*. Newton Abbot, England: David and Charles Publishers, 2005.

109. Patton, George S., Paul D. Harkins, and Beatrice Banning Ayer Patton. *War as I Knew It*. New York: Houghton Mifflin Company, 1947.

110. Perret, Geoffrey. *There's a War to Be Won: The United States Army in World War II*. New York: Random House, 1991.

111. Podhajsky, Alois. *My Dancing White Horses*. New York: Holt, Rinehart, and Winston, 1965.

112. Polmar, Norman. *The Enola Gay: The B-29 That Dropped the Atomic Bomb on Hiroshima*. Washington: Potomac Books, 2004.

113. Porter, Valeria, Lawrence Alderson, Stephen Hall, et al. eds. *D. Phillip. Mason's World Encyclopedia of Livestock Breeds and Breeding*. Volume 1. Oxfordshire, UK: CABI. 2016.

114. Poyser, Larry, and Bill Brown. *Fighting Fox Company: The Battling Flank of the Band of Brothers*. Havertown, PA: Casemate Publishers, 2013.

115. Prange, Gordon W., with Goldstein, Donald M., and Dillon, Katherine V. *At Dawn We Slept: The Untold Story of Pearl Harbor*. New York: Penguin Books, 1991.

116. Prohme, Robert. *History of 30th Infantry Regiment, World War II*. Washington: Infantry Journal Press, 1947.

117. Province, Charles M., and Hans-Joachim Diesner. *The Unknown Patton*. New York: Hippocrene Books, 1983.

118. Pyle, Ernie. *Brave Men*. New York: Henry Holt and Company, 1944.

119. Reitan, Earl A. *Riflemen: On the cutting edge of World War II*. Bennington, VT: Merriam Press, 2001.

120. St. John, Philip. *History of the 3rd Infantry Division*. 75th Anniversary Edition. Nashville: Turner Publishing, 1994.

121. Santayana, George. *Soliloquies in England and Later Soliloquies*. London: Constable and Company, 1922.

122. Schrijvers, Peter. *The Crash of Ruin: American Combat Soldiers in Europe During World War II*. New York: New York University Press, 1998.

123. Scott, Hugh A. *The Blue and White Devils: A Personal Memoir and History of the Third Infantry Division in World War II*. Nashville: Battery Press, 1984.

124. *The Sea Gull*. Gulfport, MS: The Students of Gulf Park College, 1942. tinyurl.com/jofe79r.

125. Sevareid, Eric. *Not So Wild a Dream*. New York: Alfred A. Knopf, 1946.

126. *The Seventh United States Army: Report of Operations France and Germany 1944–1945*. Heidelberg, Germany: Aloys Graf Publisher, 1946.

127. Shakespeare, William. *Henry V* (Act III, Scene VII). *The Complete Works of William Shakespeare*. Leipzig, Germany: Baumgärtner Publishers, 1854.

128. Shelton, Lt Col Louis H, and Paul Shelton. *No Use Both of Us Getting Killed…You Go! A Quarter Century of Life, Love, and War*. Bloomington, IN: AuthorHouse, 2011.

129. Simpson, Harold B. *Audie Murphy: American Soldier*. Dallas, TX: Alcor Publishing Company, 1982.

130. Sincock, Morgan, John Keliher, and Randy Baumgardner, eds. *Twenty-Fifth Infantry Division: Tropic Lightning, Korea 1950–1954*. Paducah, KY: Turner Publishing Company, 2002.

131. Sloan, C. E. E. *Mine Warfare on Land*. London: Brassey's Defense Publishers, 1986.

132. Soskil, Murray. *From the Bronx to Berchtesgaden: The Combat Memoir of a WWII Hero*. New York: Temurlone Press, 2013.

133. Spitter, Roger J., ed. *Combined Arms in Battle Since 1939*. Fort Leavenworth, KS: U.S. Army Command and General Staff College Press, 1992.

134. Stannard, Richard M. *Infantry: An Oral History of a World War II American Infantry Battalion*. New York: Twayne Publishers, 1993.

135. Starr, Lieutenant Colonel Chester G., ed. *From Salerno to the Alps: A History of the Fifth Army, 1943–1945*. Washington: Infantry Journal Press, 1948.

136. Steinbeck, John. *The Long Valley*. New York: Viking Press, 1938.

137. Swainson, Bill, ed. *The Encarta Book of Quotations*. Bellevue, WA: Encarta, 2000.

138. Swanson, Vernon E., ed. *Upfront with Charlie Company: A Combat History of Company C, 395th Infantry Regiment, 99th Infantry Division*. North Royalton, OH: Red Danube Publishing, 1997.

139. Taggart, Donald G., ed. *History of the Third Infantry Division in World War II*. Washington: Infantry Journal Press, 1947.

140. Talty, Stephan. *Operation Cowboy. The Secret American Mission to Save the World's Most Beautiful Horses in the Last Days of World War II*. 2014. Kindle.

141. *The Sea Gull*. Gulfport, MS: The Students of Gulf Park College, 1942.

142. *The Tammy Howl. Alumnae Register*. Gulfport, MS: Gulf Park College. Vol. 16, No. 5. May 29, 1943. tinyurl.com/hyv7fdv.

143. *The Tammy Howl. Alumnae Register*. Gulfport, MS: Gulf Park College. Vol. 21, No. 4. April 15, 1947, https://tinyurl.com/yc6ussnw.

144. *The Tammy Howl. Alumnae Register*. Gulfport, MS: Gulf Park College. Vol. 24, No. 2. December 1949. tinyurl.com/yb343nc7.

145. *The Tammy Howl. Alumnae Register*. Gulfport, MS: Gulf Park College. Vol. 25. No. 3. February 1951. tinyurl.com/h43ckyq.

146. Hollen, Sharon. "The North Platte WWII Canteen." *Let Us Not Forget: A Tribute to America's 20th Century Veterans*, edited by Vurlee A. Toomey, Helen K. Polaski, and Margaret Marr. Lincoln, NE: Writer's Club Press, 2002.

147. Truscott, Jr., Lt. General L. K. *Command Missions: A Personal Story*. New York: E. P. Dutton and Company, 1954.

148. Turner, John Frayn and Robert Jackson. *Destination Berchtesgaden: The Story of the United States Seventh Army in World War II*. New York: Charles Scribner's Sons, 1975.

149. Turow, Scott. *Ordinary Heroes: A Novel*. New York: Farrar, Straus, and Giroux, 2005.

150. *The U.S. Army Leadership Field Manual. Field Manual No. 22–100*. New York: McGraw Hill, 2004.

151. Underwood, Lamar, ed. *The Quotable Soldier*. Guilford, CT: The Lyons Press, 2000.

152. Vannoy, Allyn R. and Karamales, Jay. *Against the Panzers: United States Infantry Versus German Tanks, 1944–1945*. Jefferson, NC: McFarland Publishers, 2006.

153. Waple, III, George H. *County Boy Gone Soldiering*. Princeton, NJ: Xlibris, 1998.

154. Warlimont, Walter. *Inside Hitler's Headquarters*. Translated by R. H. Barry. Novato, CA: Presidio Press, 1964.

155. Wavell, Field-Marshal Earl. *The Good Soldier*. London: Macmillan & Company, 1948.

156. Weissberg, Michael W. *Honor, Glory, Respect: Conducting Police Funerals*. Miami, FL: White Mountain Publishing Company, 2011.

157. Welch, Bob. *American Nightingale: The Story of Frances Slanger, Forgotten Hero of Normandy*. New York: Atria Books, 2004.

158. Westerman, Frank. *Brother Mendel's Perfect Horse: Man and Beast in an Age of Human Warfare*. London: Vintage Digital, 2012.

159. Whiting, Charles. *America's Forgotten Army: The True Story of the U.S. Seventh Army in WWII—And an Unknown Battle that Changed History*. New York: Sarpedon, 1999.

160. Whitney, Courtney. *MacArthur: His Rendezvous with History*. Santa Barbara, CA: Praeger Publishers, 1977.

161. Whittingham, Richard. *Rites of Autumn: The Story of College Football*. New York: The Free Press, 2001.

162. Wilson, George. *If You Survive: From Normandy to the Battle of the Bulge to the End of World War II— One American Officer's Riveting True Story*. New York: Ballantine Books, 1987.

NEWSPAPER ARTICLES

SB = a newspaper clipping in Ethyl Larimore's scrapbooks
CL = copy sent from Cossitt Library, Memphis Public Library

1. "Amputee Hero Gets Horse at Auction." *Seattle Post Intelligencer*. July 10, 1947. SB.

2. "And the Auctioneer Said: 'I Have Favor to Ask—Please Don't Bid on Horse No. 5': Story Concerns a Memphis Hero." *Memphis Press-Scimitar*, July 10, 1947. SB, CL.

3. "Be-Ribboned Major Larimore Retires with Coveted D.S.C." SB.

4. Bethea, Nathan Bradley. "War Is About More Than Heroes, Martyrs, and Patriots." *The Daily Beast*, November 12, 2014. tinyurl.com/yckb5l73

5. Biggerstaff, Valerie. "Chamblee's Lawson General Hospital." *Dunwood Crier*, August 27, 2019. tinyurl.com/jvh3u838

6. "Blondin, Brolo, Rotundo Are Made Famous by Thirtieth." *The Third Division Front Line* 1, no. 3, November 4, 1944: 6.

7. "Bracken Says Nazis Receiving Thrashing." *The Los Angeles Times*. Wednesday, May 24, 1944.

8. Brown, Craig. "The White Horse with a Dark Secret." *The Daily Mail*. August 11, 2012. tinyurl.com/y6x2xzug

9. "The Chi Omega Festival." May 18, 1929. SB.

10. "The Chi Omega Festival." May 13, 1930. SB.

11. Chinigo, Michael. "Outwitted by Yankee Trick, Nazis Complain at Cisterna." SB.

12. Christmas, Rhonda, and Frank M. Smith. "500 Attend Sale. Horses Formerly Used by Gen. Marshall And Mrs. Roosevelt Auctioned." *Washington Times Herald*. SB.

13. Clemens, Ida. "Memphian Says Life at Anzio Far From 'Beer and Skittles.'" *The Commercial Appeal*, Memphis, Saturday, May 27, 1944.

14. "Daring Tennesseans Give Germans Fright." SB.

15. "David Rayl." Social Column. *Biloxi Daily Herald*, July 14, 1943. Page 5. tinyurl.com/m5seqs4

16. De Luce, Daniel. "H-Hour Came At 6:30 a.m. May 23, 1944." SB.

17. De Luce, Daniel. "'We'll Get to Rome,' Promise of Doughboys." May 24, 1944. SB.

18. "Dirty Fighting Specialists." *The Lincoln Star*, Lincoln, Nebraska, January 24, 1943.

19. "DSC Honors Maj. Larimore, Gallant Hero of Anzio." *Memphis Press-Scimitar*, May 31, 1947. SB, CS.

20. "D. S. Cross Awarded to War Hero Major Larimore in Retreat Parade Here." *The Fort Myer News* 1, no. 14, Fort Myer, Virginia, June 10, 1947.

21. Egnash, Martin. "U.S. cavalry unit commemorates Gen. Patton's order to save hundreds of Lipizzaner Stallions from being eaten by Soviets." *Stars and Stripes*, May 2, 2019. tinyurl.com/y663qldt

22. "Escape up Rhône Valley Smashed at Montélimar." *Beachhead News. Souvenir Edition* 1, no. 100, October 15, 1944: 3. tinyurl.com/hva4wvz

23. "G-2 Report—Perturbed French Woman and Her Chickens." *The Third Division Front Line* 1, no. 3, November 4, 1944: 6.

24. "Germans Blasted Bridge: Memphian Rigs Up a Ferry." September 9, 1944. SB.

25. "Germans Have Wood Bullet." Battle Creek, Mich. March 30. SB.

26. "Germans Lose an Army." SB.

27. "Germans Retreating in Vosges." *The Third Division Front Line* 1, no. 6, November 25, 1944: 1.

28. "Give Thanks for the WWII Generation." *Colorado Springs Gazette.* Colorado Springs, CO, December 7, 2018: A–10. tinyurl.com/yaqpwaf5

29. "Graduated from Gulf Coast Military Academy." May 18, 1942. SB.

30. "Heroic Memphian Decorated." *The Commercial Appeal*, Memphis, June 1, 1947. SB.

31. "Hero's Lone Bid Buys a Pal at Horse Auction." *New York World Telegram*, July 10, 1947. SB.

32. Hopper, Hedda. "Frances Slanger." *Chicago Sunday Tribune*, Graphic Section, Cook County Regional Edition, January 7, 1945: 2,5. tinyurl.com/zqo2zq9

33. "Horse Show Begins Tonight at Paragould. Over 125 Entries from Six States Will Participate." July 27, 1947. SB.

34. "Infantry Enjoys Hot Bath as Germans Abandon Town." *Beachhead News. Souvenir Edition* 1, no. 100, October 15, 1944: 3. SB. tinyurl.com/hva4wvz

35. "Infantry Major, 22, Is Honored with Decoration and Parade." SB.

36. Jernigan, Meg. "The History of Peabody Hotel in Memphis." *USA Today*, March 15, 2008. tinyurl.com/jgjg9cx

37. "Just Jottings." *The Washington Post*, July 13, 1947. SB.

38. Kahn, Sam. "The Ex-Major and His Horse Go to College." *Sunday Mirror*, New York, May 9, 1948. SB.

39. Kaufman, Sarah. "At Tomb of the Unknowns, a ritual of remembrance." *The Washington Post*, May 28, 2011. tinyurl.com/ydx435rb

40. Lane, Dick. "Army Has Another Engineer—With Wooden Leg, Stout Heart." *The Commercial Appeal*, Memphis, Tenn., October 3, 1946.

41. Lane, Dick. "Beribboned Captain Larimore Not Interested in Point Total." (likely *The Memphis Commercial Appeal*, Memphis, Tenn). SB.

42. Lapointe, Joe. "Notre Dame and Army to Wake Up the Echoes." *New York Times*, September 8, 2005. tinyurl.com/y9mfrzt7

43. London, John. "Crowd Keeps Still as Amputee Bids in Pet Horse, Then Cheers." SB.

44. "Looking Back Over Our Shoulder." *Beachhead News, Souvenir Edition* 1, no. 100, October 15, 1944: 2. tinyurl.com/hva4wvz

45. Malone, Andrew. "Stolen by the Nazis: The tragic tale of 12,000 blue-eyed blond children taken by the SS to create an Aryan super-race." *The Daily Mail*, January 9, 2009. tinyurl.com/y4d8dycl

46. "Marksman Stops German Attempt to Blow Bridge." *The Third Division Front Line* 1, no. 3, November 4, 1944: 1.

47. "Mary Lona Hicks Bunton." *The Times and Democrat*, Orangeburg, SC, January 18, 2014. tinyurl.com/mpv35qf

48. McKee, Jim. "Army Airfield at Alliance trained glider pilots, paratroopers." *Lincoln Star Journal*, Lincoln, NE, January 23, 2011. tinyurl.com/h6qjmc5

49. "New Phone Booths at Ft. Benning Prove Popular." *The Bayonet* 2, no. 12, December 2, 1943: 2.

50. "PX Reports Gift Shortages." *The Bayonet* 2, no. 12, December 2, 1943: 1.

51. Pyle, Ernie. "Fate of Anzio Beachhead Rests Heavily on the 'Ducks.'" SB.

52. Pyle, Ernie. "The God-Damned Infantry." May 2, 1943. Indiana University. tinyurl.com/za5qb5x

53. Pyle, Ernie. "Supply Lines at Anzio." About April 18, 1944. SB.

54. Roosevelt, Eleanor. "Pyle Reminds Us of What We Owe the Infantrymen." *The Press-Scimitar*, Memphis, June 14, 1944. SB. See also: tinyurl.com/yypl6m5x

55. "Service Stripe, AMC." Washington, DC, July 19, 1947. SB.

56. "A Soldier Will Be Home Soon with His Understanding Horse." *The Memphis Commercial Appeal*, July 11, 1947. SB CL.

57. Sparrow, Paul M. "How Roosevelt crafted his 'Day of Infamy' speech." *Poughkeepsie Journal*, December 7, 2016. tinyurl.com/hqsnao7

58. "'Stag Night' at Kirven's." *The Bayonet* 2, no. 12, December 2, 1943: 10.

59. Sutherland, Anne, Bill Brownstein, Michelle Richardson, et al. "Bit by bit, the best of Just for Laughs." *Montreal Gazette*, July 24, 2007.

60. "Text of Emperor Hirohito's Declaration of War on U.S." *Chicago Daily Tribune*. December 8, 1941.

61. "Third Overseas Two Years." *The Third Division Front Line* 1, no. 1, October 25, 1944: 1.

62. Tibbetts, Meredith. "Headstones and horses: Caisson Platoon at Arlington adds to solemn traditions." *Stars and Stripes*, June 17, 2014.

63. "Valor of Foot Soldiers." SB.

64. Vermillion, Robert. "Tribute to the Infantryman—Courage His Greatest Armor." SB.

65. "Veterans Hit Riviera Beaches. Mediterranean Vets Wade Ashore D-Day." *Beachhead News. Souvenir Edition* 1, no. 100, October 15, 1944: 1. tinyurl.com/hva4wvz

66. "Vienna's White Stallions to Perform Here in May." *New York Times*, March 9, 1964. tinyurl.com/ybgfnrkb

67. Wavell, Field-Marshal Earl. "In Praise of Infantry." *The Times*, April 19, 1945. tinyurl.com/jcywklu

68. Woodruff, Jim. "What Are the Duties of a Battalion S3?" *Houston Chronicle*, June 27, 2018. tinyurl.com/jmmp99h

69. "'You Did It', General Truscott Says in Tribute to Troops." *Beachhead News, Souvenir Edition* 1, no. 100, October 15, 1944: 1,4. tinyurl.com/hva4wvz

70. "Youngest Officer Benning Graduate." Possibly Macon, GA. February 6, 1943. SB.

PERIODICALS

1. Amelinckx, Andrew. "Dang! Draft Horses are Amazingly Strong. Like, Can-Pull-a-Semi-Truck Strong." *Modern Farmer* (December 17, 2015). tinyurl.com/jd4uh9b

2. Barth, Brian. "The Draft-Horse Gear and Tools You Need." *Modern Farmer* (December 16, 2015). tinyurl.com/p8w27p2

3. Carden, Gary. "Appalachian Bestiary: Wondrous and Fearsome Creatures of the Southern Wild." *North Carolina Folklore Journal* 59, no. 2 (Fall-Winter 2012): 60–89. tinyurl.com/y258f5zc

4. Chamberlain, General Joshua L. "Abraham Lincoln Seen from the Field." *The Magazine of History with Notes and Queries. Extra Number—No. 32. Rare Lincolniana #5*. Pages 311–332. tinyurl.com/mzlgnvc

5. Churchill, Winston. "Alfonso the Unlucky." *Strand Magazine* (July 1931): 15–23.

6. "Disabled Vet Gets Show Horse for $50." *Congressional Record—Senate* (July 10, 1945): 8618.

7. Dougherty, Paul J., and Marlene DeMaio. "Major General Norman T. Kirk and Amputee Care During World War II." *Clincal Orthopaedics and Related Research* 472, no. 10 (October 2014: 3107–3113. tinyurl.com/klsog3f

8. Gareau, Frederick H. "Morgenthau's Plan for Industrial Disarmament in Germany." *The Western Political Quarterly* 14, no. 2 (June 1961): 517–534.

9. Hauer, John. "You Can Learn a Lot from a Mule." *Saturday Evening Post* (November–December 2015):

12–14. tinyurl.com/y23sjn5k

10. "I am the Infantry." *Infantry School Quarterly* (July 1956). In *Infantry* 81, no. 5 (September–October 1991): 53. tinyurl.com/y2szba7c

11. "In Memorium: Congressional Medal of Honor Recipient Sergeant Harold O. Messerschmidt." *Sun Ships Magazine*. Available at the Mahanoy Area Historical Society Website. tinyurl.com/zo55zqf

12. Jensen, Karen. "How General Patton and Some Unlikely Allies Saved the Prized Lipizzaner Stallions.: *World War II Magazine* (November 2009). tinyurl.com/l58nm6a

13. Jones, Major Lloyd E. "Infantry-Artillery Liaison in Combat." *The Field Artillery Journal* 20, no. 5 (September-October 1930): 491–524. tinyurl.com/yy472ocz

14. Jurga, Fran. "Cracking the Lipizzaner ceiling: Hannah Zeitlhofer promoted to first woman 'Reiter' at the Spanish Riding School in Vienna." *Equus Magazine* (updated March 10, 2017). tinyurl.com/y8mqsv53

15. Lale, Max. "My War: 1944–1945." *East Texas Historical Journal* 32, no. 2 (1994): 3–19. tinyurl.com/y674gl77

16. Lang, Will. "Lucian King Truscott, Jr." *LIFE* 17, no. 14 (October 2, 1944): 97–111. tinyurl.com/zvpagvk

17. Loosbrock, Captain John F. "The A&P Platoon in Combat." *Infantry Journal* 56, no. 2 (February 1945).

18. Miller, Henry I. "The Nuking of Japan Was Tactically and Morally Justified." *Forbes Magazine*. August 5, 2014.

19. Monea, Antonio C. "The Beast of Lichfield; Colonel James A. Killian and the Infamous 10th Reinforcement Depot." *Army Lawyer* 2019, no. 3: 20-22. tinyurl.com/y7znpu56

20. Muller, Richard R. "First Mount Vesuvius, Then the Nazis." *World War II Magazine* (September-October 2015). tinyurl.com/jy2d7d4

21. "The Price of Life in the United States: 1946 vs. 2006." *Signal Magazine* (September 2006). tinyurl.com/ybf5ufpq

22. Reed, Charles Hancock. "The Rescue of the Lipizzaner Horses: A Personal Account." Virginia Historical Society (Spring/Summer, 1970). Also at: tinyurl.com/3bbfajmy

23. Small, Collie. "The Third: Tops in Honors." *The Saturday Evening Post* 218, no. 6 (August 11, 1945): 28-29, 86, 88.

24. Vesuvius. Eruption of World's Most Famous Volcano Competes for Attention with War in Italy. *LIFE* 16, no. 16 (April 17, 1944): 96–97. tinyurl.com/zzf8goo

25. Wildenboer, Louis. "Anzio Annie: The story of a gun." *Military History Journal* 13, no. 3 (June 2005). tinyurl.com/gtv7boy

WAR RECORDS

1. Appel, John. "Prevention of Manpower Loss from Psychiatric Disorders (Report of a trip to North African Theater of Operations, 17 May–29 July 1944)." File: 730 (Neuropsychiatry) Manpower, NATO, Prevention of Manpower Loss from Psychiatric Disorders—1944, Box 1343, Office of the Surgeon General World War II Administrative Records, Entry 31 (ZI), RG 112, National Archives, College Park, MD.

2. Armed Services Experiences Questionnaire, Army Heritage and Education Center, Carlisle, PA. Accessed August 22–25, 2016.

1. Ellis, William J. "Jack"

2. Fisk, William F.

3. McDonough, James G.

4. Valenti, Isadore L.

3. Armed Services Experiences Questionnaire and Associated Personal Documents, Army Heritage and Education Center, Carlisle, PA. Accessed August 22–25, 2016.

    1) 7th Infantry Regiment

- Cloer, Russel W. Box 4: survey, memoir, 7 discs.
- Valenti, Isadore. Box 3: survey.

    2) 15th Infantry Regiment

- Ravenscroft, Earl. Box 3: notes concerning theories of Infantry quality and participation.

    3) 30th Infantry Regiment

- Anderson, Henry. CPT, 1st Battalion, Company C. Box 1: survey.
- Andrews, Edward. PFC, 2nd Battalion, Anti-Tank Company. Box 1: survey, discharge document.
- Ellis, William H. T/4, 1st Battalion, Headquarters Company. Box 1: survey.
- Fisk, William F. SGT, 3rd Battalion, Company L. Box 1: survey, V-Mail.
- McDonough, James G. SSGT, 1st Battalion, Company C. Box 1: survey.

    4) Friend, James A.

4. Archives of the 3rd General Hospital Records, 1942–1945. Icahn School of Medicine at Mount Sinai. New York, NY. tinyurl.com/2hdwn8y5

5. Beardslee, Charles Owen, Undated typewritten memoir, provided by his children.

6. A Brief Resume of Lt. Col. Ross H. Calvert, Jr., provided by Ross H. Calvert, III.

7. Calvert, Ross H., Jr. Unpublished typed letter to "Leroy," dated 26 July 1977. Provided by Ross H. Calvert, III.

8. Clark, Lieutenant General Mark W. Conduct of Fifth Army Troops in Rome. Headquarters Fifth Army. APO #464, U.S. Army. 6 June 1945. From the National Archives and Records Administration. tinyurl.com/u3j5fepf

9.   Cloer, Russell W. *Infantry Replacement: The Story of My Three Years as an Infantry Officer in World War II*. Unpublished Memoir. 1998. (3rd Infantry Division. 7th Infantry Regiment. Headquarters Company. Veteran's Survey. Box 4). U.S. Army Heritage and Education Center at Carlisle Barracks, PN. Accessed and photographed August 22–25, 2016.

10.   The Eisenhower Center. University of New Orleans.

      1)   Galdonik, Clair. Oral history.

      2)   Schultz, Arthur, Memoir.

      3)   Shoo, Donald. Memoir.

      4)   Stockell, Charles. Memoir.

      5)   Webster. Memoir.

      6)   Zeihe, Paul-Arthur. Interview by Hugh Ambrose.

11.   Heflin, Kirk. Museum Curator, Old Guard Museum, 3rd U.S. Infantry Regiment. Fort Myer, VA. Personal communication. September 27, 2016.

12.   Interview Transcripts

      1)   Boutwell, James Lamar. Interviewed by phone. May 2016.

      2)   Cloer, Russell. Interviewed by Sandra Holyoak. Rutgers Oral History Archives. tinyurl.com/gwlrdvf

      3)   Drabczyk Edward L. Interviewed by Michael Russek. June 2002.

      4)   McLaurine, Luke Layton. Interviewed by phone. February 2017.

13.   Larimore, Jr., Philip B.

      1)   Army Retiring Board meeting of 15 April 1947.

      2)   Citation for Bronze Star.

      3)   Citation for Distinguished Service Cross. War Department. The Adjutant General's Office. Washington 25, DC.

      4)   Exhibit C of the Army Retiring Board meeting of 15 April 1947.

      5)   Exhibit G of the Army Retiring Board meeting of 15 April 1947.

      6)   Exhibit K of the Army Retiring Board meeting of 15 April 1947.

      7)   Officer's and Warrant Officer's Qualification Card.

      8)   Military Transcript.

      9)   Report for re-boarding after expiration of 6 months TLD. Walter Reed Hospital. 3 March 1947.

      10) Separation Qualification Record.

      11) Special Orders. Number 110. Headquarters, Army Medical Center, Washington 12, DC Contained in the file of the Army Retiring Board meeting of 15 April 1947.

      12) Transcript of Military Record.

14. Lasky, Melvin J. Historical Officer, 7th Army. La Maison Rouge: The Story of an Engagement. 3 March 1945. Report provided by LTC (Ret.) Timothy R. Stoy, Historian, The Society of the 3rd Infantry Division.

15. MCoE HQ Donovan Research Library, Fort Benning, GA.

      1)   Anzio beachhead, 22 Jan–25 May 44 (American forces in action series). U.S. Dept. of the Army. Historical division. Wash, govt. print. off., 1948. D 769.33. A 202. Acc. No. D-34836-41.

      2)   Operations Report or Reports of Operations, 30th Infantry Regiment, Microfilm, for the period(s) of:

            a.   1–31 Aug 1944, SOUTHERN FRANCE. D-280. (Item 1982)

            b.   1–31 Jan 1945. D-289. (Item 3055, Part D).

            c.   1–28 Feb 1945. D-289. (Item 3055, Part C).

            d.   1–31 Mar 1945. D-289. (Item 3055, Part B).

            e.   1–30 Apr 1945. D-289. (Item 3055, Part A).

16. Millen, PhD, Lieutenant Colonel Raymond A. Professor of Security Sector. Peacekeeping and Stability Operations Institute. U.S. Army War College. Carlisle, PA. Multiple personal communications, March 2018 through December 2020.

17. Oppenhimer, Captain John S. Public Relations Release. Department of War. Pentagon. Washington, DC. September 10, 1946.

18. National Archives and Records Administration. College Park, MD. Record Group 407. Records of the Adjuvant General's Office. WWII Operations Reports, 1940–1948. 3rd Infantry Division. Accessed and Photographed September 19_21, 2016.

      1)   Boddy, Captain Robert M. Bn S-3, 3rd Bn. 30th IR. S-3 Periodic Report. From 161200A to 171200A. 17 March 1944. Entry Box 5646, HMFY 2007. 303-INF (30)–3.2 MAR 1944 TO 303-INF (30)–3.2 APR 1944.

      2)   VI Corps G-2 Periodic Reports. 15–19 October 1944. Entry 427. Boxes 3696–3697.

      3)   Journal 30th Infantry. 16 March 1944. Entry Box 5646, HMFY 2007. 303-INF (30)–3.2 MAR 1944 TO 303-INF (30)–3.2 APR 1944.

      4)   Journal of Hq. Co., 3rd Bn 30th Inf. September 1944. Entry Box 5642, HMFY 2007. 303-INF (30)–3.2 FEB 1942 TO 303-INF (30)–1.2.

      5)   Journal Notes. March 1945. Headquarters. Third Battalion Thirtieth Infantry. Entry Box 5655, HMFY 2007. 303-INF (30)–3.2 MAR 1945 TO 303-INF (30)–3.2 APR 1945.

      6)   Journal Notes. April 1945. Headquarters. Third Battalion Thirtieth Infantry. Entry Box 5655, HMFY 2007. 303-INF (30)–3.2 MAR 1945 TO 303-INF (30)–3.2 APR 1945.

      7)   Operations Report. Thirtieth U.S. Infantry. 1–31 January 1945. Entry Box 5630, HMFY 2007. 303-INF (30)–0.3 1944 TO 303-INF (30)–0.3 1945.

      8)   Operations Report. Thirtieth U.S. Infantry. 1–28 February 1945. Entry Box 5630, HMFY 2007. 303-INF (30)–0.3 1944 TO 303-INF (30)–0.3 1945.

      9)   Operations Report. Thirtieth U.S. Infantry. 1–31 March 1945. Entry Box 5630, HMFY 2007. 303-INF (30)–0.3 1944 TO 303-INF (30)–0.3 1945.

10) Operations Report. Thirtieth U.S. Infantry. 1–30 April 1945. Entry Box 5630, HMFY 2007. 303-INF (30)–0.3 1944 TO 303-INF (30)–0.3 1945.

11) S-1 Journal. 30th Infantry. 1–31 Aug 1944. Entry Box 5648, HMFY 2007. 303-INF (30)–0.2.0 JUL 1944 TO 303-INF (30)–3.2 SEP 1944.

12) S-1 Journal. 30th Infantry. 1–30 Sep 1944. Entry Box 5649, HMFY 2007. 303-INF (30)–3.2 SEP 1944 TO 303-INF (30)–3.2 OCT 1944.

13) S-1 Journal. 30th Infantry. 1–31 Oct 1944. Entry Box 5650, HMFY 2007. 303-INF (30)–3.2 OCT 1944 TO 303-INF (30)–3.2 DEC 1944.

14) S-1 Journal. 30th Infantry. 1–31 Dec 1944. Entry Box 5651, HMFY 2007. 303-INF (30)–3.2 DEC 1944 TO 303-INF (30)–3.2 AUG 1944.

15) S-1 Journal. 30th Infantry. 1–31 December 1944. Entry Box 5643, HMFY 2007. 303-INF (30)–1.2 TO 303-INF (30)–1.2.

16) S-1 Journal. 30th Infantry. 1–31 Jan 1945. Entry Box 5653, HMFY 2007. 303-INF (30)–3.2 JAN 1945 TO 303-INF (30)–3.2 FEB 1945.

17) S-1 Journal. 30th Infantry. 1–31 Mar 1945. Entry Box 5655, HMFY 2007. 303-INF (30)–3.2 MAR 1945 TO 303-INF (30)–3.2 APR 1945.

18) S-1 Journal. 30th Infantry. 1–31 March 1945. Entry Box 5643, HMFY 2007. 303-INF (30)–1.2 TO 303-INF (30)–1.2.

19) S-3 Journal. 5 April 1945. From 0015 to 1940. Headquarters Thirtieth Infantry. Entry Box 5655, HMFY 2007. 303-INF (30)–3.2 MAR 1945 TO 303-INF (30)–3.2 APR 1945.

20) S-3 Journal. 6 April 1945. From 0045 to 2340. Headquarters Thirtieth Infantry. Entry Box 5655, HMFY 2007. 303-INF (30)–3.2 MAR 1945 TO 303-INF (30)–3.2 APR 1945.

21) S-3 Journal. 7 April 1945. From 0015 to 1755. Headquarters Thirtieth Infantry. Entry Box 5655, HMFY 2007. 303-INF (30)–3.2 MAR 1945 TO 303-INF (30)–3.2 APR 1945.

22) S-3 Journal. 8 April 1945. From 0015 to 1940. Headquarters Thirtieth Infantry. Entry Box 5655, HMFY 2007. 303-INF (30)–3.2 MAR 1945 TO 303-INF (30)–3.2 APR 1945.

23) S-3 Report. 31 March 45. From 311201 to 011200. Report #76. Headquarters Thirtieth Infantry. Entry Box 5655, HMFY 2007. 303-INF (30)–3.2 MAR 1945 TO 303-INF (30)–3.2 APR 1945.

24) S-3 Report. 4 April 45. From 041201 to 051200. Report #80. Headquarters Thirtieth Infantry. Entry Box 5655, HMFY 2007. 303-INF (30)–3.2 MAR 1945 TO 303-INF (30)–3.2 APR 1945.

25) S-3 Report. 5 April 45. From 051201 to 061200. Report #81. Headquarters Thirtieth Infantry. Entry Box 5655, HMFY 2007. 303-INF (30)–3.2 MAR 1945 TO 303-INF (30)–3.2 APR 1945.

26) S-3 Report. 6 April 45. From 061201 to 071200. Report #82. Headquarters Thirtieth Infantry. Entry Box 5655, HMFY 2007. 303-INF (30)–3.2 MAR 1945 TO 303-INF (30)–3.2 APR 1945.

27) S-3 Report. 7 April 45. From 071201 to 081200. Report #83. Headquarters Thirtieth Infantry. Entry Box 5655, HMFY 2007. 303-INF (30)–3.2 MAR 1945 TO 303-INF (30)–3.2 APR 1945.

28) S-3 Report. 8 April 45. From 081201 to 091200. Report #84. Headquarters Thirtieth Infantry. Entry Box 5655, HMFY 2007. 303-INF (30)–3.2 MAR 1945 TO 303-INF (30)–3.2 APR 1945.

29) S-3 Report. Headquarters Thirtieth Infantry. 081200B April 1945. 303-INF (30)–3.2.

30) Unit Journal (S-1). Headquarters 30th U.S. Infantry. 1–29 February 1944. Entry 427, Box 5642, HMFY 2007. 303-INF (30)–0.2.0 FEB 42 TO 303-INF (30)–1.2.

WEBSITES

1. "3rd U.S. Infantry Regiment (The Old Guard)." Wikipedia. tinyurl.com/yaysgn5c

2. *10th Field Hospital.* Unit History. WW2 U.S. Medical Research Centre. tinyurl.com/km4ffa9

3. "326th Glider Infantry Regiment. Unit History." WW2 Airborne. tinyurl.com/z2n9a8d

4. "189th General Hospital. Unit History." WW2 US Medical Research Centre. tinyurl.com/kag3kga

5. "1941: Japanese planes bomb Pearl Harbor." BBC News. tinyurl.com/aduq6

6. "1946 Army vs. Notre Dame football game." Wikipedia. tinyurl.com/ydhcrqq6

7. "About the Service Flag." Blue Star Mothers of America. tinyurl.com/mfxqd6x

8. "Abraham Fitterman." Military Times. tinyurl.com/ks4xl8e

9. "Airs above the ground." Wikipedia. tinyurl.com/ycfzu5ud

10. "American Forces in Action. Anzio Beachhead (22 January–25 May 1944)." iBiblio. tinyurl.com/y5ylzmcz

11. "AM-Lira." Wikipedia. tinyurl.com/y488h5q4

12. "Ammo bearer." WW2 Forum. tinyurl.com/hs2mbsf

13. "Arabian-Berber Horse." The Equinest. tinyurl.com/yckdsxa8

14. "Army Reserve to Honor Medal of Honor Recipient—Again." Arlington Cemetery. tinyurl.com/yy65agc6

15. "'Artificial Moonlight.' Allies Illuminate Night Battlefields." Lone Sentry. tinyurl.com/y5obpv8s

16. "Audie Murphy." Wikipedia. http://tinyurl.com/zoz62ej

17. "Auschwitz concentration camp." Wikipedia. tinyurl.com/ouq9bja

18. Bagley, Mary. "Mount Vesuvius & Pompeii: Facts & History." LiveScience. tinyurl.com/y89e4g86

19. "Barrage Balloons." World War Two. tinyurl.com/zu6l5gr

20. "Battle of Anzio." Wikipedia. tinyurl.com/zdxn4wh

21. "Beauford Theodore Anderson." Find a Grave. tinyurl.com/y7mymahg

22. Bernard, Suzanne. "Did Plato write 'Only the dead have seen the end of war'?" Plato Dialogues. tinyurl.com/yaa4ghaw

23. "Bill Piper and the Piper Cubs." HistoryNet. tinyurl.com/yy9pwd5j

24. "Biography, Audie Leon Murphy." Audie Murphy. tinyurl.com/ctm3rg9

25. "Blue and White Devils: The Story of the 3rd Infantry Division." Lone Sentry. tinyurl.com/zbczvaf

26. "Bungalow Restaurant and Lounge." Card Cow. tinyurl.com/zawvysf

27. "Caisson Platoon." Old Guard. tinyurl.com/y4dbpcfk

28. "Camp Wheeler." Wikipedia. tinyurl.com/zaj4vkd

29. Carey, Norman C. "The Crossing of the Rhine." 35th Infantry Division Association. tinyurl.com/hknpce4.

30. "The Changing of the Guard." Arlington National Cemetery. tinyurl.com/y2yssysx

31. Cloer, Russ. "Biography of Russ Cloer." Justin Museum. tinyurl.com/jxqfgbs

32. Cloer, Russ. "Infantry OCS." 6th Corps Combat Engineers. tinyurl.com/ybmjl9cq

33. "The counties of Maryland and Baltimore City: their origin, growth, and development, 1634–1963." tinyurl.com/yc6jqnav

34. "A Date Which Will Live in Infamy. The First Typed Draft of Franklin D. Roosevelt's War Address." National Archives. tinyurl.com/juegock

35. D'Este, Carlos. "A Lingering Controversy: Eisenhower's 'Broad Front' Strategy." ArmChair General. tinyurl.com/yyqlzynu

36. DiMarco, Lou. "Army Fox Hunting." A Horse Soldier's Thoughts. tinyurl.com/z7p8kt8

37. "Don McCullin Quotes." Brainy Quote. tinyurl.com/yxuj352m

38. Dopheide, Deb. "History of Alliance." City of Alliance. tinyurl.com/zlyv74l

39. "Dragon's teeth (fortification)." Wikipedia. tinyurl.com/9jswhpj

40. Dresbach, Jim. "Eisenhower Lore Centers Around Fort Myer Flag Pole." U.S. Army. tinyurl.com/ycpb7llq

41. "Dressage." University of Florida Equestrian Club. tinyurl.com/y56n2wp7

42. Dunigan, James. "History of the U.S. 30th Infantry Regiment." 6th Corps Combat Engineers. tinyurl.com/y4n9hbv5

43. "Eagle Scout (Boy Scouts of America)." Wikipedia. tinyurl.com/nv7wzc6

44. "The First Americans." 2 June 2003 letter from Lieutenant Byke. Eaglehorse. tinyurl.com/y4w9h5e7

45. "Fort Myer Virginia." Army History. tinyurl.com/y2jz7zbp

46. "Friendship Oak." University of Southern Mississippi. tinyurl.com/y2h8dm42

47. Gaspa-Ward, Claudia. "The Napoletano." Dressage Today. tinyurl.com/jdy5y5f

48. Griffis, Vicki Ellis. "Nursing a Broken Heart. Charlie Company." tinyurl.com/y3b3kwq9

49. "Has Scotland Taken Over the Presidency?" Rakemucker. tinyurl.com/hyuvpsf

50. "Hear the breaking news report from Pearl Harbor, 75 years later." PBS News Hour. tinyurl.com/hohgo7u

51. "High Flows and Flood History on the Lower Mississippi River." National Weather Service. tinyurl.com/y4dr6e4w

52. Holyoak, Sandra Stewart. "Interview of Russell Cloer." Rutgers Oral History Archives. tinyurl.com/gwlrdvf

53. "Horses in the Middle Ages." Wikipedia. tinyurl.com/y84muh64

54. "How to Do Basic Dressage Successfully." WikiHow. tinyurl.com/gwt2wwc

55. Hullinger, Pam, and Carolyn Stull. "The Emergency Euthanasia of Horses: Consideration for Owners, Equine Facility Managers, Auction Market Operators, Horse Transporters, and Law Enforcement Officers." School of Veterinary Medicine. University of California, Davis. tinyurl.com/yyr9humq

56. Hyatt, C.P. "The Old Guard." U.S. Army Military History Institute. April 2, 2009. tinyurl.com/y8bq5trl

57. "I'll be home for Christmas." Wikipedia. tinyurl.com/y8pkvoul

58. Jacobson, Tyler. "The History of Equine Therapy." Of Horse. July 19, 2018. tinyurl.com/hz8392p9

59. "Japan declares war, 1941. A Spotlight on a Primary source by Hirohito, Emperor of Japan." Gilder Lehrman Institute of American History. tinyurl.com/gm3ftoq

60. "Japan surrenders, bringing an end to WWII." History.com. tinyurl.com/33soljk

61. Jenkins, Jerry B. "Precious Memories: Billy Graham (1918–2018)." Jerry B. Jenkins. tinyurl.com/ychjhptw

62. Kamson, Matt. "Why did the Germans tend to use green tracers during WWII, while the Allies used red? Who decided on a color first?" Quora. tinyurl.com/y36comp5

63. Kern, Michael. Dogfaces: The Infantry in Normandy. Carlisle Schools. tinyurl.com/y53f7oa4

64. Krause, Joshua. "See How You Stack Up Against the WW2 Fitness Test." Ready Nutrition. tinyurl.com/jrb23nz.

65. Krause, Joshua. "See How You Stack Up Against the WW2 Fitness Test." Ready Nutrition. tinyurl.com/jrb23nz

66. Kugler, Jason. "Infantry Leads the Way!" December 8, 2015. LinkedIn. tinyurl.com/y9b7v99j

67. "Krupp K5." Wikipedia. tinyurl.com/hu56f9h

68. Larimore, Kelly. "Larimore name origination." Genealogy. September 18, 2004. tinyurl.com/zsuystd

69. Laurie, Clayton D. "Anzio 1944." U.S. Army Center of Military History. tinyurl.com/yclpprms

70. "Lester Ball...Quiet Hero." Lester Ball. tinyurl.com/m44pe28

71. "Letter from Harry to Bess Truman. July 4, 1947." Harry S. Truman Library. tinyurl.com/a8dbfbfb

72. MacRae, Michael. "The Flying Coffins of World War II." AMSE. February 2012. tinyurl.com/j243jd9

73. Marks, Oliver. "The WWII German Army was 80% Horse Drawn; Business Lessons from History." ZDNet. tinyurl.com/thl8m3q

74. "The Maryland Hunt Cup Programme." Maryland Hunt Cup. tinyurl.com/yczbk2bl

75. "Maximilian von und zu Trauttmansdorff." Wikipedia. tinyurl.com/yyqlhe2n

76. McClure, David. "Rider to Carolyn P. Ryan Statement." October 12, 1973. Audie Murphy. tinyurl.com/lu55zu2

77. Miskimon, Christopher. "Allied Storm in Southern France." Warfare History . tinyurl.com/yyyk76jz

78. Miskimon, Christopher. "Army Mules: The Beast of Burden in War." Warfare History. tinyurl.com/jar2jh9

79. "Mitchel Air Force Base." Wikipedia. tinyurl.com/m7959xb

80. Moloshok, Ralph. "History 3rd General Hospital." Mount Sinai Digital Repository. Volume 2. 1945. Page 4. tinyurl.com/yxd2x56a

81. Morgenthau, Jr., Henry. "Suggested Post-Surrender Program for Germany." FDR Presidential Library. tinyurl.com/m6p26uk and tinyurl.com/mspug7f

82. "Morgenthau Plan." Wikipedia. tinyurl.com/mspug7f

83. Morris, R. "World War Two Glider Pilots—A Rare Breed." August 8, 2007. Untold Valor. tinyurl.com/gvesugc

84. "Mount Bethel Church (Three Churches, West Virginia)." Wikipedia. tinyurl.com/zvu29rm

85. Mustermann, Erik. "Before Paris, There was Rome: The Forgotten Front." War History Online. tinyurl.com/y3gcwkqk.

86. "Neapolitan Horse." Wikipedia. tinyurl.com/h4cgkac

87. "The Neapolitan Horse." Elite Warhorse. tinyurl.com/hs64bxp

88. "The North Platte Canteen." Lincoln County Museum. tinyurl.com/y4mpqfy7

89. Officer Candidate School (United States Army). Wikipedia. tinyurl.com/za2pxxs

90. "Operation Cowboy: How American GIs & German Soldiers Joined Forces to Save the Legendary Lipizzaner Horses in the Final Hours of WW2." Military History Now. tinyurl.com/ycw2o3sr

91. "Order of Battle of the US Army – WWII – ETO. 30th Infantry Division." U.S. Army Center of Military History. tinyurl.com/42eaptzx.

92. "Pam Brown Quotes." AZ Quotes. tinyurl.com/ycaxv2xy

93. "Peabody Ducks." Peabody. tinyurl.com/z2jtngg

94. "A Pearl Harbor Fact Sheet." National World War 2 Museum. tinyurl.com/ltxmqkx

95. "Percheron." Wikipedia. tinyurl.com/gnhk93f

96. Pratt, Sara E. "Benchmarks: March 17, 1944: The most recent eruption of Mount Vesuvius." Earth. tinyurl.com/y38zx3hw

97. "Presidential Planes." Truman Little White House. tinyurl.com/y57js6x3

98. "Presidents and Horses/Abraham Lincoln." Horse Hints. tinyurl.com/y2vge5r9

99. "President Harry S. Truman Places Wreath at Tomb of the Unknowns." Truman Library. tinyurl.com/y3hlhaum

100. "The Presidio." Presidio. tinyurl.com/y6ru7pcp

101. Province, Charles M. "Northeast Kansas Korean War Memorial." tinyurl.com/hwqjy7l

102. "Robert Baden-Powell Quotes." BrainyQuote. tinyurl.com/y4bejn9k

103. Raia, Pat. "Meet the U.S. Army Caisson Horses." The Horse. tinyurl.com/y93lbl2o

104. "Recollections of Carolyn Price Ryan." 12 February 1973. Audie Murphy. tinyurl.com/y2smjnv7. See also: Rider to Carolyn P. Ryan Statement. Audie Murphy. tinyurl.com/y5zq4vwk

105. "Robert Nicholas Young." Wikipedia. tinyurl.com/y8s8t383

106. Roosevelt, Franklin D. "On the Fall of Rome." Address of the President, June 5, 1944. FDR Library. tinyurl.com/y9cpd2tl

107. "Sapper." Wikipedia. tinyurl.com/y6ubuxpt

108. Sarember, Sophia. "Communicating with Your Mule." Rural Heritage. tinyurl.com/gu52gt5

109. "Saving the Lipizzaners: American Cowboys Ride to the Rescue." May-June 1998. Benning https://tinyurl.com/ycmmfjr9

110. Schultz, Duane. "Combat Fatigue: How Stress in Battle was Felt (and Treated) in WWII." Warfare History Network. tinyurl.com/y6suu8oq

111. "SCR-300." Wikipedia. http://tinyurl.com/zx2tbh6

112. "SCR-300." Olive-Drab. tinyurl.com/hkrqugb

113. Sewell, Abby. "These dreamy photos transport you to 8th-century Morocco. This centuries-old tradition is a celebration of the bond between horse and rider." National Geographic. July 10, 2018. tinyurl.com/y72mxwza

114. "The Shakerag Hounds Hunt Club." Shakerag Hounds. tinyurl.com/y8ew3was

115. Shearer, J. K., and Paul Nicoletti. "Procedures for Humane Euthanasia: Humane Euthanasia of Sick, Injured, and/or Debilitated Livestock." University of Florida College of Veterinary Medicine. 2002. tinyurl.com/z4yfx98

116. "A Short History of Foxhunting in Virginia." Freedom Fields Farm. tinyurl.com/hn6wr9y

117. "Spanish Riding School." Austria Information. tinyurl.com/ycgzjzp3

118. "Taulignan en 1939–1945." AJPN. tinyurl.com/hsv7z99

119. "This Is No Joke: This Is War." History Matters. tinyurl.com/2b9cks4

120. "Thoroughbred." Wikipedia. tinyurl.com/lfo2mbw

121. "Time on Target (TOT)." Wikipedia. tinyurl.com/y6vox4jf

122. "Thomas Selfridge." Wikipedia. tinyurl.com/y8789njl

123. "The Thompson submachine gun." Wikipedia. tinyurl.com/na37hga

124. Thompson, Clinton W. "Hell in the Snow: The U.S. Army in the Colmar Pocket, January 22–February 9, 1945." 2017. History Theses. Paper 9. tinyurl.com/y285kdm2

125. "Tom Brokaw Quotes." GoodReads. tinyurl.com/y42cv75j

126. "Tomb of the Unknown Soldier (Arlington)." Wikipedia. tinyurl.com/hocbhyb

127. "Tracer ammunition." Wikipedia. tinyurl.com/ca9kgyt

128. Truman, Harry S. "Independence Day Address Delivered at the Home of Thomas Jefferson." July 4, 1947. Truman Library. tinyurl.com/yy6uewhx

129. "Truman laying a wreath at the Tomb of the Unknown Soldier." Truman Library Photographs. November 11, 1946. Truman Library. tinyurl.com/y3a7dast

130. "Ulster-Scots and the United States Presidents." Ulster-Scots Ancestry. tinyurl.com/h2doe85

131. "The USS Arizona Sinks During the Attack on Pearl Harbor: December 7, 1941." Fold 3. tinyurl.com/gqonz3p

132. Vannoy, Allyn. "Saving Operation Grand Slam." Warfare History Network. tinyurl.com/mgecvpn

133. Walker, Karen. "D-Day Memories of the Bridge Player in Chief." District 8 American Contact Bridge. tinyurl.com/ycrkhnby

134. "War Letters." Program Transcript. PBS' American Experience. PBS. tinyurl.com/yygc48al

135. Watters, Eldon. "Peeking into Lake City's Past. McCrary Clan is Practicing Today. Calhoun County." The IAGenWeb Project. tinyurl.com/yauwdllx

136. Weather History for KBIX (Keesler Air Force Base in Biloxi, MS), May 17, 1942. Weather Underground. https://tinyurl.com/3w7ete7r

137. Weather History for KDCA (National Airport in Washington, DC), May 30, 1947. Weather Underground. https://tinyurl.com/zznj93ub

138. Westerfield, Jim. "Intelligence and Reconnaissance Platoon." Flames of War. tinyurl.com/ycqtr6e6

139. White, David, and Daniel P. Murphy. "Battlefield Injuries and Medicine." Military Blood. tinyurl.com/y989oplo

140. "I often get asked why I ride mules or Why are mules better than horses?" Saito's Dojo. tinyurl.com/hwzwd47

141. "Wonder horses." Wikipedia. tinyurl.com/y7tqs4vu

142. "World War II Experiences of Staff Sergeant Albert R. Panebianco." 45th Infantry Division. tinyurl.com/j5e4teu

143. "World War II Statistics." Shmoop. tinyurl.com/mfbtqm2

144. "World War II Veterans by the Numbers." VA Fact Sheet. Department of Veterans Affairs. tinyurl.com/z2cthjz

145. "WW2 History of the 3rd 'Marne' Infantry Division." Custermen. tinyurl.com/zs2s3t7

146. "WW2 Military Hospitals—Zone of Interior (United States)." WW2 U.S. Medical Research Centre. tinyurl.com/kqaw96o

APPENDIX H:

CITATIONS

1 Websites, Dunigan.

PROLOGUE

2 Books, Wavell, 92; and Newspaper Articles, Wavell.
3 This chapter was augmented from Books, Champagne, 25, Prohme, 341, Murphy, 262–263; War Records, Larimore, Citation; and Websites, Blue and White, and Millen.
4 Books, Murphy, 262–263.

PART 1: PREPARING FOR WAR

5 Books, Whitney, 547.

CHAPTER 1: THE LITTLE STINK

6 Websites, Tom Brokaw.
7 This chapter was augmented from Books, Cope, and Kephart; Newspaper Articles, Jernigan, and The Chi Omega Festival; War Records, Interview, McLaurine; Websites, Thoroughbred, and Wonder Horses; and "Chi Omega program, May 13, 1930," an undated newspaper clipping of the Lee School of Childhood graduation, and a Sunday Morning, March 25, 1934, newspaper clipping from Ethyl Larimore's scrapbooks.
8 Handwritten letter, January 21, 1925.

CHAPTER 2: THE BIG MUDDY

9 Websites, Robert.
10 This chapter was augmented from Books, McPherson, 13, and The Sea Gull, 66; Periodicals, Jurga; War Records, Interview, McLaurine; Websites Airs, Friendship Oak, High Flows, The Sea Gull, Spanish Riding, and Thoroughbred; an undated newspaper clipping found in Ethyl Larimore's scrapbooks; and a 26 July 1938 letter to Ethyl from Gulf Coast Military Academy.

CHAPTER 3: A DAY OF INFAMY

11 Periodicals, Chamberlain, 311.
12 This section was augmented from Books, Prange, and The Tammy, 1943: 22, 24–27, 40; and Websites, Bungalow, and Weather History for KBIX.
13 Websites, Hear the, and This Is.

14 Ibid.

15 Websites, 1941.

16 Ibid.

17 Newspaper Articles, Text of: 12; and Websites, This just, and Japan declares.

18 This section was augmented from Newspaper Articles, Sparrow; and Websites, A Date, A Pearl, The USS Arizona, and Weather History for KBIX; and GCMA Commencement Invitation found in Ethyl Larimore's scrapbooks.

19 Handwritten note in Ethyl Larimore's scrapbooks.

20 Websites, A Date.

21 Ibid.

CHAPTER 4: ON TO BENNING

22 Newspaper Articles, Pyle, *The God*.

23 This chapter was augmented from Newspaper Articles, New Phone; Websites, Cloer, *Biography*, Cloer, *Infantry, A Short*, The Shakerag, and DiMarco; War Records, Armed, 7th, Cloer, *Infantry*, and Interview, Cloer; and Ethyl Larimore's typed and handwritten timeline.

24 Websites, Cloer, *Infantry*; and War Records, Armed, 7th, Cloer, *Infantry*, and Interview, Cloer.

25 Books, Paterson, 73.

26 Books, Grant, 78.

CHAPTER 5: CAPTURE THE FLAG

27 War Records, Armed, 7th, Cloer.

28 This chapter was augmented from Books, *The Passing*, 22–23, and Perrett, 115; and War Records, Armed, 7th, Cloer, and Cloer, *Infantry*; and Websites, Cloer, *Biography*, and Cloer, *Infantry*.

29 War Records, Armed, 7th, Cloer, and Cloer, *Infantry*; and Websites, Cloer, *Biography*, and Cloer, *Infantry*.

CHAPTER 6: THE SCHOOL SOLUTION

30 Quote at the entrance to "The Last Hundred Yards" exhibit at the National Infantry Museum at Fort Benning, GA.

31 This chapter was augmented from Books, Colby, 235, 237–238, 265, 294, and *The Passing*, 22–23; and War Records, Armed, 7th, Cloer, and Cloer, *Infantry*, and Cloer Interview; Websites, Cloer, *Biography*, and Cloer, *Infantry* and Larimore, Certificate of Completion.

32 Books, Colby, 265.

33 Books, *The Passing*, 32.

34 Certificate of Completion.

35 War Records, Armed, 7th, Cloer, *Infantry*, and Interview, Cloer.

CHAPTER 7: FLYING COFFINS

36 Books, Kelly, 22.

37 This chapter was augmented from Books, Blythe, Chapter, "History of the 326th", and Kennedy, 287; War Records, Larimore, Officer's, and Larimore, Separation; Websites, 326th, Camp Wheeler, Dopheide, MacRae, McKee, and Morris; an undated newspaper clipping from Ethyl Larimore's scrapbook; and Ethyl Larimore's typed and handwritten timeline.

38 Handwritten letter. Post marked 12 Feb 1943. Camp Wheeler, GA.

39 Ibid.

CHAPTER 8: PLATFORM GIRLS

40 War Records, Armed Services, 15th, Ravenscroft, 14–16; and Websites, Reitan, 115.

41 This section and speech were augmented from Books, Bonn, 62; and a handwritten letter, March 6, 1943. No envelope.

42 This section was augmented from Books, Hollen, 113–120, and Greene, npn; and Websites, The North Platte.

43 Handwritten letter. March 6, 1943. No envelope.

44 This speech was adapted from: Newspaper Articles, "Dirty Fighting."

CHAPTER 9: DRAFTS AND SCOTCH

45 Books, Morpurgo, 112.

46 This chapter was augmented from Books, Amelinckx. Barth, Blythe, 3 and Chapter, "History of the 326th", and Daiches; Websites, Krause, Percheron, and The Presidio; Handwritten letters postmarked 7 Apr 1943, 13 Apr 1943, 9 May 1943, and 18 May 1943, Alliance, Nebr, and Handwritten letter, postmarked May 1943, Baltimore, MD; and Certificate of Completion found in Ethyl Larimore's scrapbooks.

47 Handwritten letter. Postmarked 9 May 1943, Alliance, Nebr.

48 Handwritten letter. Postmarked 13 Apr 1943, Alliance, Nebr.

CHAPTER 10: FÜHRERVILLE

49 Newspaper Articles, Roosevelt.

50 This section was augmented from Books, Blythe, Chapter, "History of the 326th"; Websites, Krause; and handwritten letters postmarked 28 May 1943, 9 June 1943, 15 Jun 1943, and 19 Jul 1943, Alliance, Nebr; and War Records, Millen, and Larimore, Officer's.

51 Handwritten Letter postmarked 28 Jun 1943, Alliance, Nebr.

52 Books, Blythe, Chapter, "History of the 326th; and Newspaper Articles, McKee.

53 Handwritten letter. Postmarked 15 Jun 1943, Alliance, Nebr.

54 This section was augmented from War Records, Larimore, Officer's, and Millen; and Handwritten letter postmarked 19 Jul 1943, Alliance, Nebr

55 Handwritten letter. Postmarked 25 Aug 1943, Alliance, Nebr.

56 Handwritten letter. Postmarked 28 Jun 1943, Alliance, Nebr.

CHAPTER 11: FINAL PREPARATIONS

57 Websites, Kugler.

58 This section was augmented from Typed letters postmarked 6 Sep 1943, 9 Sep 1943, and 14 Oct 1943, Alliance, Nebr.

59 Handwritten letter postmarked 6 Sep 1943, Alliance, Nebr.

60 Typed letter postmarked 14 Oct 1943, Alliance, Nebr.

61 This section was augmented from Books, Poyser, 25; Ethyl Larimore's typed and handwritten timeline; Larimore's Graduation Certificate; and War Records, Larimore, Officer's.

62 Handwritten letter postmarked 6 Nov 1943, Fort Benning, Ga.

63 This section was augmented from Books, Palmer, 187; Newspaper Articles, First War Bonds, New Phone Booths, PX Reports, and Stag Night; War Records, Larimore, Officer's; Websites, I'll be home; Handwritten letter postmarked 14 Dec 1943, Fort Bragg, N.C.; and Ethyl Larimore's typed and handwritten timeline.

64 Handwritten letter postmarked 3 Jan 1944, Fort Bragg, N.C.

65 Handwritten letter postmarked 14 Dec 1943, Fort Bragg, N.C.

66 This section was augmented from Books, Bishop, 56–59, Evans-Hylton, 26–27, Gordon, npn, and Palmer, 187.

PART II: ITALIAN CAMPAIGN

67 Books, Grafton, 88.

CHAPTER 12: SHIPPING OUT

68 Newspaper Articles, Valor.

69 This section was augmented from War Records, Cloer, *Armed Services*, 7th Infantry, and Cloer, *Infantry*, Chapter V; and Websites, Moloshok.

70 This section was augmented from Websites, Arabian-Berber, Horses, and Sewell; and War Records, Armed, 7th, Cloer, and Cloer, Infantry, Chapter V. A typewritten timeline in Ethyl Larimore's scrap books says, "January 24, 1944, sailed from Fort Meade." However, Phil's Officer's and Warrant Officer's Qualification Card says, "30 Jan 44, Depart USA for Foreign Service Outside Continental U.S.," and his "Transcript of Military Record" says, "30 Jan 44, Date of Departure, Destination Europe." The Card also says, "9 Feb 44. Arrived in NATO USA." Various sources indicate the trip was nine days, so they likely docked on February 8, 1944, in Casablanca, but it may have been late and he may not have been processed in until February 9, 1944.

71 Handwritten letter postmarked "Passed by Examiner, Base 0416, Army" and "U.S. Army Postal Service, A.P.O., 15 Feb 1944."

72 This section was augmented from Books, Hartstern, 15–18, and Pratt; Periodicals, Muller, and Vesuvius; and War Records, Armed, 7th, Cloer, and Cloer, *Infantry*, Chapter V; and Websites, Bagley, Cloer, *Infantry*, and Holyoak.

CHAPTER 13: MEETING MAGELLAN

73 This section was augmented from Books, Atkinson, *The Day*, 507, Hartstern, 18, and Porter, 489; War Records, Cloer, *Infantry*, Chapter V, 32; and Websites, Arabian-Berber, Battle of Anzio, Gaspa-Ward, Horses, Neapolitan, The Neapolitan, and WW2 History.

74 Books, Atkinson, *The Day of Battle*, 507.

75 This section was augmented from Books: Bolté, 8–9, and Porter, 489; Websites, Dressage, Gaspa-Ward, and How to Do.

CHAPTER 14: GETTING PREPPED FOR HELL

76 Book: Murphy, 125. (Kerrigan's full name, possibly fictitious, found here: tinyurl.com/l63wcw5. Wikipedia says, Audie Murphy's "poem 'The Crosses Grow on Anzio' appeared in his book *To Hell and Back* but was attributed to the fictitious character Kerrigan).

77 This chapter was augmented from Books, Atkinson, *The Day*, 379, 485; Barger, title page, Botula, title, and Taggart, 123–124; War Records, Cloer, Armed, 7th, Cloer, Chapter V, 23, 38, and Chapter VI, Larimore, Transcript, and National Archives, Unit Journal (S–1); and Websites, Barrage Balloons, Krupp, and Order.

78 War Records, Cloer, Armed, 7th, Cloer, Chapter V, 23.

79 This speech was adapted from Books, Taggart, 124, and Soskil, 35–36; Periodicals, Small. *You're now part of the __th Infantry* is the actual quote. Taggart indicated an unnamed "regimental commander" in the 3rd Division, while Soskil seems to implicate the commander of the 7th Infantry Regiment as giving this speech. We've made it Colonel McGarr for the purpose of this story.

80 Adapted from: Books, Markley, 122.

CHAPTER 15: INTO NO MAN'S LAND

81 Books, Bradlee, 65.

82 Books, Champagne, 58, Mohar, 98–99, and Prohme, 136–137, 383; Periodicals, Small; War Records, Armed, 7th, Cloer, 30th, Anderson, Cloer, *Infantry*; and Websites, Websites, Cloer, *Biography*, Cloer, *Infantry*, Holyoak, Sapper, and Westerfield.

83 This section was augmented from Books, Mohar, 98–99.

CHAPTER 16: OPENING SALVO

84 Books, Parker, *Monte*, 275.

85 This section was augmented from Books, Allen, 140, Ambrose, *Citizen*, 45–46, 321–322, Heefner, 168, Litoff, 9, Prohme, 140–143, Sincock, 93, Soskil, 41, and Stannard, 187; Websites, American Forces, Blue and White, Laurie, and Vannoy.

86 This section was augmented from Books, Champagne, 65, Kennedy, 284, and Prohme, 143; War Records, Larimore, Officer's, and Millen; and Websites, American Forces, and Laurie.

87 Books, Churchill, *Closing*, 481.

88 Websites, Cloer, *Biography*.

89 Undated, handwritten letter from Anzio Beach.

90 Undated, handwritten letter (V-Mail copy).

91 This section was augmented from Books, Ambrose, *Citizen Soldiers*, 261, and Monahan, 221; Newspaper Articles, Germans Have; and War Records, The Eisenhower, Schultz.

92 Undated, handwritten letter (V-Mail copy).

93 Handwritten letter dated 16 Mar 44.

CHAPTER 17: BAPTISM BY FIRE

94 Quote at the entrance to "The Last Hundred Yards" exhibit at the National Infantry Museum at Fort Benning, GA.

95 This section was augmented from Books, Atkinson, *The Day*, 492, Prohme, 146–147, Pyle, *Brave Men*, 163, and Taggart, 140, 142; and War Records, Millen, National Archives, Boddy, and Journal 30th Infantry.

96 Handwritten letter. Postmarked "U.S. Army Postal Service, A. P. O., 306, 17 Apr 1944."

97 Books, Taggart, 140.

98 This section was augmented from Books, Atkinson, *The Day*, 494, and Prohme, 152; Periodicals, Muller, and Vesuvius, 96; War Records, Armed, Friend; and Websites, Bagley, and Pratt.

99 Atkinson, *The Day*, 494.

CHAPTER 18: MULES TO THE RESCUE

100 Newspaper Articles, Vermillion.

101 This section was augmented from Books: Ambrose. *Citizen*, 47, Champagne, 65–66, Mohar, 53, and Taggart, 143; Newspaper Articles, Vermillion; and Websites, Bill. The mule information in this section was adapted from: Books, Bradley, Melvin, 385–387, Essin, 147, Heefner, 105, 118, 123; Periodicals, Hauer, 2, 12, and Loosbrock, 24–26; War Records, Millen; and Websites, Miskimon, Sarember, and Why.

102 This section was augmented from Books, Mohar, 54, Prohme, 165, and Taggart, 147.

103 This section was augmented from Books, Champagne, 98, and Prohme, 165; War Records, Beardslee, 79; and Websites, American Forces, and Laurie.

104 Handwritten letter. 30 Apr 44.

105 This section was augmented from Books, *Anzio Beachhead*, and Prohme, 165–167; Periodicals, Jones; and Websites, American Forces.

106 This section was augmented from Books, Atkinson, *The Day*, 537, MacDonald, ix–x, Murphy, 150, Prohme, 167–168, Starr, 228–232, and Taggart, 153; War Records, Millen; and a quote from an exhibit at the National Infantry Museum at Fort Benning, GA.

107 Handwritten letter. 30 Apr 44.

CHAPTER 19: BREAKING OUT

108 Books, Brown, 214.

109 This section was augmented from Books, Atkinson, *The Day*, 538, Champagne, 66, Fisher, 130, 133; Heefner, 174, Murphy, 150, Prohme, 167–173, Starr, 233–236, and Taggart, 149–150, 156–157; Newspaper Articles, Chinigo, and De Luce, *We'll get* and *H-Hour*; Periodicals, Small; War Records, Beardslee, and Websites, American Forces.

110 Books, Atkinson, *The Day*, 538.

111 Books, Atkinson, *The Day*, 541, and Fisher, 130, 133.

112 Books, Atkinson, *The Day*, 541.

113 This section was augmented from Books, Atkinson, *The Day*, 542–543, Champagne, 69, Heefner, 175, Prohme, 171,178–179, and Taggart, 149, 164; Websites, American Forces; and Newspaper Articles, Bracken.

114 Taggart, 149.

115 Newspaper Articles, Bracken.

CHAPTER 20: ALL ROADS LEAD TO ROME

116 Books, Bradley, 321.

117 This chapter was augmented from Books: Atkinson, *The Day*, 509, 571–573, 575, Collier, 157, Molony, 235, 281–282, Murphy, 161–162, Prohme, 182–187, 189–192, 194, Reitan, npn, Sevareid, 418, and Starr, 267; and Websites, American Forces, Dunigan, and Roosevelt; and Typed letter (V-Mail copy). Postmarked 29 May 44; and Handwritten letter. Postmarked 14 Jun 1944.

118 Typed letter (V-Mail copy). Postmarked 29 May 44, and Handwritten letter. Postmarked 14 Jun 1944.

119 Books, Atkinson, *The Day*, 575, and Collier, 157.

CHAPTER 21: ROMAN HOLIDAY

120 Book: Goethe, 128, 129, 133.

121 Books, Champagne, 117, Hartstern, 32, Mohar 89–90, Soskil, 38, Taggart, 189–193, and Spitter, 277; Periodicals, Lang; War Records, Beardslee; Websites, AM-lira; and Handwritten letter (V-Mail). Postmarked 7 Jun 1944. I have the handwritten letter from Phil, and his mother's typed copy. It's interesting that she corrects all his spelling and punctuation errors.

122 Handwritten letter (V-Mail). Postmarked 7 June 1944. Phil's handwritten letter was typed by his mother. She corrects all his spelling and punctuation errors.

123 Books, Mohar, 90.

124 This section was augmented from Books, Champagne, 118,120, Heefner, 190, Prohme, 206, Truscott, 408, Taggart, 201–202, and Turner, 31; War Records, Armed Services, Valenti; and Websites, Dunigan.

PART III: THE FRENCH CAMPAIGN

125 Books, Daniels, 312.

CHAPTER 22: CÔTE D'AZUR'S D-DAY

126 Newspaper Articles, Vermillion.

127 This chapter was augmented from Books, Atkinson, *The Guns*, 190, 196, Champagne, 129, Clarke, 110–111,

Heefner, 191, Mohar, 104–111, Morrison, 291, Murphy, 169–170, Prohme, 210–213, Soskil, 33, Taggart, 208–212, and Turner, 39–43; Newspaper Articles, Veterans; War Records, Armed Services, Cloer, Mohar, and Beardslee, 88–90; and Websites, Allied, Cloer, *Biography*, Cloer, *Infantry*, Miskimon, and Sgt.; and Handwritten letter, 30 Apr 44.

128 Books, Kershaw, Hitler, 145, and Warlimont, 451.

CHAPTER 23: HEROES AND LIBERATORS

129 Newspaper Articles, Vermillion.

130 Books, Whiting, 58.

131 This section was augmented from Books, Clarke, 211, and Murphy, 184; Newspaper Articles, Looking Back; and War Records, Larimore, Officer's.

132 This section was augmented from Books, Bearse, 201, Champagne, 84, Hartstern, 52, Mauldin, 204, Murphy 183, Parker, *Civilian*, 44, Prohme, 215, 221–223, and Taggart 215; Newspaper Articles, Veterans; Periodicals, Small; War Records, Beardslee, 90–92, MCoE, Operations Report, 1–31 Aug 1944, and National Archives, S-1 Journal, 30th Infantry, 1–31 Aug 1944; and Websites, Taulignan, The Thompson.

133 Newspaper Articles, Daring.

134 Handwritten letter. 22 Aug 1944.

CHAPTER 24: THE HORROR OF MONTÉLIMAR

135 Websites, Don.

136 This section was augmented from Books, Colby, 241, Champagne, 133, Hartstern, 52, Heefner, 193, 203, Murphy, 187, Prohme, 223, 225, Taggart 221–222, Truscott, 432, Turner, 62, and Whiting, 61–63; Periodicals Wildenboer; Newspaper Articles, Escape, and Third Overseas; and War Records, Beardslee, 94; and Websites, 3rd Division.

137 This section was augmented from Books: Ambrose, *Band*, 103, 260–261, Heefner, 203, Murphy, 186–187, Taggart 221–222, and Wilson, 70; and War Records, Armed Services, 7th Infantry, Cloer, Beardslee, 94, and McDonough; and Websites, Cloer, Biography, and Marks.

CHAPTER 25: A THRILLING ROUNDUP

138 Books, Grant, 156.

139 This chapter was augmented from Books: Champagne, 133, Clarke, 166, Colby, 232, Heefner, 203, Jay, npn, and Truscott, 433; Websites, Hayes, 399, Hullinger, 3–4, and Shearer, 3, 7; and Personal Communication, Striko.

140 Called "longtime male equestrian wisdom" with no source, although often credited to Ronald Reagan, Winston Churchill, Henry Ward Beecher, Oliver Wendell Holmes, and Lord Palmerston. Books, Keyes, 91.

CHAPTER 26: THE CHAMPAGNE CAMPAIGN

141 Books, Munsell, X.

142 This section was augmented from Books, Ambrose, *Citizen*, 107, Clarke, 171, Ellis, 92, Prohme, 225–226, Truscott, 437–438, and Turner, 67,70; War Records, Armed Services, 7th; Cloer, National Archives, Journal of Hq., and S-1 Journal, 30th Infantry, 1–30 Sep 1944; and Websites, Holyoak.

143 This section was augmented from Books, Champagne, 89, Clarke, 189, Prohme, 228, 233, Taggart, 224, and Turner, 72.

144 This section was augmented from Books, Champagne, 89, Hartstern, 57, Heefner, 208; and Prohme, 235; Newspaper Articles, Germans Blasted; War Records, National Archives, Journal of Hq. Larimore, Citation for Bronze Star; and Handwritten V-Mail dated 16 Sep 44.

145 This section was augmented from Books, Bonn, 4, Chambers, 94, History, 2347, Prohme, 235–237; and Websites, D'Este, and Vosges Mountains.

146 Handwritten V-Mail. 7 Sep 44.

CHAPTER 27: CRUEL COMBAT

147 Books, Wavell, 92; Wavell, Newspaper Articles, 5.

148 This section was augmented from Books, Ambrose, *Citizen*, 365, Bonn, 5, Champagne, 136; Clarke, 198, 242, Taggart, 237–238, and Whiting, 66, 68; and War Records, S-1 Journal. 30th Infantry. 1–30 Sep 1944.

149 This section was augmented from Books, Doubler, 251, *Infantry*, 1, 223, Prohme, 240–244, and Taggart, 241, 434; Periodicals, *In Memoriam*; and War Records, S-1 Journal. 30th Infantry. 1–30 Sep 1944.

CHAPTER 28: AN EXPLOSIVE WAR

150 Books, Carroll, 233; and Websites, War Letters.

151 This section was augmented from Books, Turner, 80, 83–84; and Newspaper Articles, Marksman. The newspaper report does not name Phil but describes the shooter as "one unknown Third Division soldier." However, the published report perfectly parallels Phil's stories about that night.
152 This section was augmented from Books, Clarke, 292, Hartstern, 67, Murphy, 196, Prohme, 253, 261, The Seventh, 549, Taggart, 244, Truscott, 445–446, and Turner, 87; War Records, Millen, and National Archives, S-1 Journal, 30th Infantry, 1–30 Sep 1944, and 1-31 Oct 1944; and Websites, Dunigan.
153 This letter was reconstructed by Phil. There is a record, however, of who the young man may have been. See: Newspaper Articles, David Rayl.
154 Handwritten V-Mail dated 4 Oct 44.
155 Handwritten V-Mail. 27 Sep 44.
156 Newspaper Articles, You Did It.
157 Handwritten V-Mail. 16 Oct 44.

CHAPTER 29: THE VICIOUS VOSGES

158 Books, Egger, 114.
159 This chapter was augmented from Books, Cosmas, 360–361, Prohme, 263–265, and Taggart, 258; and War Records, National Archives, VI Corps.

CHAPTER 30: POINT-BLANK RANGE

160 Websites, Kugler.
161 This chapter was augmented from Books, Ambrose, *Citizen*, 311, Colby, 73, Perret, 488, Prohme, 265, and Shelton, 350.

CHAPTER 31: RECOVERY WITH MURPH

162 Books, Stannard, 71.
163 This section was augmented from Books, Ambrose, *Citizen*, 321, Hartstern, 69; and handwritten letters.
164 Handwritten letter. 29 Oct 44.
165 Handwritten letter. Postmarked, "U.S. Army Postal Service, A.P.O. #3, 30 Oct 1944." Also stamped, "Memphis, Tenn. (De Soto Sta.) 11 Nov 1944."
166 Telegraph in Ethyl Larimore's scrapbooks.
167 Handwritten V-Mail. Undated.
168 Handwritten V-Mail. 7 Nov 44.
169 This section was augmented from Books, Mohar, 192; Newspaper Articles, Hopper; War Records, Archives, and Larimore, Officer's; Websites, Audie, Biography, and McClure; and Handwritten V-Mail. 26 Nov 44.
170 Ambrose, *Citizen*, 326, Litoff, 169, and Welch, 1–3; Hopper. Newspaper Article.

CHAPTER 32: BACK TO THE FRONT

171 Books, Egger, 114.
172 Phil's records and letters don't record what happened from 30 November until Christmas, when he returned to his battalion. This section was augmented from Books, Hartstern, 71, MacDonald, 137 (MacDonald followed a similar course), and Turow, 213; and War Records, National Archives, S-1 Journal.
173 Books, Truscott, 555.
174 Handwritten V-Mail. 12 Dec 44.
175 This section was augmented from Books, Prohme, 297, and Swanson, 11; War Records, National Archives, S-1 Journal, 30th Infantry, 1–31 December 1944; and Handwritten letter—V-mail. 26 Dec 44.
176 Handwritten letter—V-mail. 26 Dec 44.

CHAPTER 33: COLD MISERY

177 Books, Clarke, 565.
178 This section was augmented from Books, Soskil, 111–112; and War Records, The Eisenhower, Zeihe.
179 This section was augmented from Books, Colby, 243–244, MacDonald, 150, Prohme, 299, 383, and Taggart 295–296.
180 Handwritten letter. 4 Jan 45.
181 This section was augmented from Books, Ambrose, *Citizen*, 258, 372, Cowdrey, 267, Ingersoll, 111, MacDonald, 137, Prohme, 297–298, Pyle, 165, Stannard, 65–66, and Soskil, 60, 111; and War Records, Beardslee, 124, The Eisenhower, Shoo; and Millen.
182 This section was augmented from Books, MacDonald, 68, Soskil, 114–115, Poyser, 254, Soskil, 111–113, and Taggart 299–301; Newspaper Articles, G-2 Report; and War Records, Armed Services, Beardslee, 125, and MCoE, Operations, 1–31 Jan 1945, National Archives, Operations, 1–31 Jan 1945, and S-1 Journal, 1–31 Jan 1945.
183 This section was augmented from Books, Prohme, 306; and War Records, Larimore, Officer's.

CHAPTER 34: THE MAISON ROUGE BRIDGE

184   Websites, War Letters, 18.
185   This section was augmented from Books, Beschloss, 144, 160, 172–173, Dietrich, 4–7, and Schrijvers, 127; Periodicals, Gareau, 530; and Websites, Morgenthau, Jr, and Morgenthau Plan.
186   Handwritten Letter—V-Mail. 9 Jan 45.
187   This section was augmented from Books, Clarke, 537, Prohme, 326, Taggart, 302, and Turner 119; and War Records, Lasky.
188   This section was augmented from War Records, Beardslee, 126, Calvert, Lasky, and MCoE, Operations, 1–31 Jan 1945, National Archives, Operations, 1–31 Jan 1945, and S-1 Journal, 1–31 Jan 1945.
189   This section was augmented from Books, Clarke, 543, Murphy, 229, Prohme, 326, and Taggart, 302; and War Records, Lasky, and Calvert.

CHAPTER 35: A DISASTROUS RECEPTION

190   Books, Underwood, 3.
191   This chapter was augmented from Books, Clarke 544–545, Murphy, 229, Prohme, 315, and Taggart, 308–309, 322; War Records, Interview, Drabczyk, Lasky 16–17, MCoE, Operations, 1–31 Jan 1945, Millen, National Archives, Operations, 1–31 Jan 1945, and S-1 Journal, 1–31 Jan 1945; and Websites, 3rd Infantry, and Artificial.
192   War Records, Lasky, V.

CHAPTER 36: TAKING A LICKING

193   Newspaper Articles, Valor.
194   This section was augmented from Books, Clarke, 546, Turner, 120, Prohme, 315–316, and Taggart, 308, 322–324; War Records, Beardslee, 127, and Lasky, 5, 8, 13–15, 20, 26–28; and Websites, 3rd Infantry.
195   Handwritten letter—V-mail. 27 Jan 45.
196   This section was augmented from Books, Clarke, 547, Murphy, 256, Prohme, 316–317, 319, 338–339, Taggart, 316–319; and Reitan, 80; and War Records, Beardslee, 128, MCoE, Operations, 1–28 Feb 1945, and Thompson.
197   This section was augmented from Books, MacDonald, 150, Prohme, 319–320, and Soskil, 81; War Records, Armed Services, 7th Infantry, Cloer, Cloer, Drabczyk, Interview, Larimore, Officer's, Larimore, Military; Websites, Lester; and Action resulting in Bronze Star, undated stationary from "Headquarters, Fort Myer, VA" found in Ethyl Larimore's scrapbooks.
198   Handwritten Letter. 4 Feb 45.
199   Websites, Lone Sentry.

CHAPTER 37: THE BIG DANCE

200   War Records, Cloer, *Infantry,* vi.
201   This section was augmented from Books, Clarke, 559, Champagne, 145, 207, Mohar, 205–207, Prohme, 326, Taggart, 327, and Soskil, 48.
202   Handwritten Letter—V-Mail. 11 Feb 45.
203   This section was augmented from Books, Clark, 553–554, Mohar, 205, Murphy, 262, and Prohme, 323–327, Scott, 158, Taggart, 324–327, and Turner, 121; Newspaper Articles, Germans Lose; and Websites, Blue and White.
204   Books, Prohme, 323–324, and Taggart, 324.
205   Websites, 254th.
206   This section was augmented from Program found in one of Ethyl's scrapbooks
207   Program found in one of Ethyl's scrapbooks.
208   This section was augmented from Books, Champagne, 208, Prohme, 328, Mohar 206, Soskil, 82, and Taggart, 328; and War Records, MCoE, Operations, 1–31 Mar 1945, Millen, and National Archives, S-1, 1–31 Mar 1945.

PART IV: THE GERMAN CAMPAIGN

209   Books, Nordholt, 223.

CHAPTER 38: DRAGON'S TEETH

210   War Records, Beardslee, 62.
211   This section augmented from Books, Ambrose, *Citizen,* 144, Champagne, 209–211, Croll, 53, MacDonald, 305, Mohar, 208, Norwood, 486, Prohme, 328, Sloan, npn, Soskil, 38, Taggart, 329–330, 337, Turner, 135, 143, Wilson, 112, and Whiting, 89; War Records, Millen; and Websites, Beardslee, 136–138, Blue and White,

Dragon's, Dunigan, Lone Sentry, and Sapper.
212 This section augmented from Books, Champagne, 224, Prohme, 221, 332, Soskil, 95, Taggart, 336, 338–339, Turner 145–149, 148, and Whiting, 156–157; War Records, National, S-1 Journal, 1–31 Mar 1945; and Websites, Blue and White.

CHAPTER 39: CROSSING THE RHINE

213 Newspaper Articles, Valor.
214 This section was augmented from Books, Champagne, 215, Prohme, 332–333, Taggart, 338–339, Turner, 151–154, and Whiting, 161; War Records, National, S-1 Journal, 1–31 Mar 1945, and MCoE, Operations, 1–31 Mar 1945; and Websites, Carey.
215 This section was augmented from Books, Prohme, 334–338, Taggart, 343, and Turner, 154; and War Records, MCoE, Operations, 1–31 Mar 1945.
216 This section was augmented from Books, Champagne, 224, MacDonald, 165–166, Scott, 168–169, and Swanson, 28; and War Records, National, S-3 Report, 31 March 1945.
217 Handwritten Letter—V-Mail. 03 Apr 45.
218 This section was augmented from War Records, National, S-3 Report, 31 March 1945.

CHAPTER 40: A SECRET MISSION

219 Periodicals, Churchill.
220 This chapter was augmented from Books, Jenkins, chapter 1, Letts, 31, 33, 50–53, 59–61, 148–150, 152–153, and Talty, Locations 13–22, 31–35, 40–45, and 112–118; and War Records, National, S-3 Report, 4 Apr 45.

CHAPTER 41: OPERATION LIPIZZANER

221 Books, Morpurgo, 112.
222 This chapter was augmented from Books, Bongianni. Entry 37, Jenkins, chapters 1–2, Letts, 36–37, 40–42, 53–54, 83, Podhajsky, 88–89; Newspaper Articles, A Soldier; and Websites, Marks.

CHAPTER 42: RIDE OF A LIFETIME

223 Books, Shakespeare, 447.
224 This chapter was augmented from Books, Jenkins, npn, Keane, 139–140, Letts, 36, 41, 53–54, 59, 71–73, 242, Podhajsky, 88–89, Talty, npn, Westerman, loc. 2445; Newspaper Articles, Brown, and Malone; Periodicals, Jensen, and Reed; War Records, National, Journal, April 1945, and Operations, Thirtieth, 1–30 April 1945; and Websites, Maximilian, and Saving.

CHAPTER 43: HELMET TRICK

225 War Records, Cloer, *Infantry*, vi.
226 This section was augmented from Books, Champagne, 225, MacDonald, 200–201, Prohme, 340, and Taggart, 348; War Records, National, S-3 Report, 5 Apr 45; and Websites, Abraham.
227 War Records, S-3 Journal, 5 April 1945.
228 This section was augmented from Books, Doubler, 250, Prohme, 152, 161, 340, and Taggart, 348; War Records, National, S-3 Journal, 6 Ap 45, and S-3 Report, 6 Apr 45, and Operations, Thirtieth, 1–30 Apr 1945.
229 Books, Mauldin, 5.

CHAPTER 44: PERFECT TIMING

230 This section was augmented from Books, Champagne, 148, and Taggart, 348; War Records, National, S-3 Journal, 6 April 1945, and S-3 Report, 6 April 45, and Operations, Thirtieth, 1–30 April 1945; and Websites, Blue and White.
231 This section was augmented from Books, Prohme, 340, and Taggart, 349; and War Records, S-3 Report, 6 Apr 45 and 7 Apr 45, and Operations, Thirtieth, 1–30 April 1945.

CHAPTER 45: NO SPA DAY

232 Books, Truscott, 9–10.
233 This section was augmented from Books, Prohme, 340–341, Mohar, 162, Soskil, 132–133, and Taggart, 349; War Records, National, S-3 Journal, 7 April 1945, and S-3 Report, 7 Apr 45, and Operations, Thirtieth, 1–30 Apr 1945.
234 This section was augmented from Books, Taggart, 350–351; and War Records, National, Journal Notes. March 1945–April 1945.

CHAPTER 46: NOWHERE TO GO

235   Books, Bradley, 321.
236   This chapter was augmented from Books, Ambrose, *Citizen*, 62–63, Prohme, 341, MacDonald, 44, 132, 292, and Stannard, 281; Newspaper Articles, Lane; War Records, Larimore, Citation, National, Journal Notes, April 1945, National, S-3 Journal, 8 April 1945, and S-3 Report, 8 April 45; Websites, Tracer; and an undated letter from "Headquarters, Fort Myer, VA" in Ethel Larimore's scrapbooks.
237   Books, *Infantry*, 205.
238   Books, *Infantry*, 195.

CHAPTER 47: THE SOUND OF A GUNSHOT

239   Books, Churchill, *Never*, 56.
240   This chapter was augmented from War Records, National, S-1 Journal, 30th Infantry, 1–30 Apr 1945.
241   Books, *Infantry*, 390.

CHAPTER 48: HOMEWARD BOUND

242   Books, Miller, *The Story*, 359.
243   This section was augmented from Books, Ambrose, *Band*, 254–255, Poyser, 255, and Prohme, 342; War Records, Larimore, Officer's, and Report; and Websites, 10th, 189th (14 Apr 45 to 29 Apr 45, Patient, DOP 4364 U.S. AHP [the 195th General Hospital operated Hospital Plant # 4364]), and Mary.
244   War Records, Larimore, Report.
245   Handwritten letter. 13 Apr 45.
246   Handwritten letter. 24 Apr 45.
247   This section was augmented from Books, Prohme, 357–358, Kershaw, *Hitler*, 956 and Taggart, xiii, 373; War Records, Larimore, Military; and Websites, Bitterstaff, Dunigan, and Mitchel.
248   Books, Prohme, 358.
249   Handwritten letter and envelope in Ethyl Larimore's scrapbooks.

PART V: AFTERMATH

250   Quote from a film at the National World War II Museum in New Orleans, LA.

CHAPTER 49: BITTER OR BETTER?

251   Books, Santayana, 99 (in *Soliloquy #25 Tipperary* [see: tinyurl.com/k3and37]. This line was later used by General Douglas MacArthur at his Farewell Speech to the Corps of Cadets at West Point, May 12, 1962. He attributed the line to Plato [see: tinyurl.com/pgyayf]. However, there is no evidence that this quote is from Plato [see: Websites, Bernard]).
252   This section was augmented from Books, Coates, 212; Newspaper Articles, Biggerstaff; Periodicals, Dougherty, 3107; War Records, Larimore, and Report; Websites, WW2 Military; and an undated telegram in Ethyl Larimore's scrapbooks.
253   War Records, Larimore, Report.
254   War Records, Larimore, Army.
255   This section was augmented from War Records, Calvert.
256   Handwritten letter. Postmarked, "Atlanta, GA. 26 July 1945."
257   Typed letter. 24 Jul 45.
258   This section was augmented from Newspaper Articles, Lane; and War Records, Calvert.
259   . Newspaper Articles, Lane.
260   Typed Letter. 2 Aug 45.
261   Handwritten letter. 24 Jul 45.
262   This section was augmented from Books, Baime, 340, Fussell, *Thank*, 14, Polmar, npn, and Stannard, 289–290; Newspaper Articles, Give Thanks; Periodicals, Miller; and Websites, Japan surrenders, and World War II Statistics.

CHAPTER 50: BACK IN THE SADDLE AGAIN

263   Books, Meagher, 67.
264   This chapter was augmented from Books, Meagher, 67; War Records, Larimore, Exhibit G; and Websites, The Shakerag, and A Short (the foxhunting information was adapted from this website in consultation with Dr. Tara Stricko Myers).

CHAPTER 51: IN THE HUNT

265 Books, Steinbeck, 153.
266 This chapter was augmented from Websites, The History, A Short, and The Shakerag in consultation with Dr. Tara Stricko Myers.

CHAPTER 52: A CHRISTMAS REUNION

267 Books, Newmark, 27.

CHAPTER 53: A HOPEFUL FUTURE

268 Books, McDonough, 692.
269 This section was augmented from Books, Atkinson, *The Guns*, 192, 196, Cartwright, 7, 46, Churchill, *Triumph*, 70–71, Demarest, 1919–1921, *The Tammy*, 1947, 24, Weissberg, 78–79; Newspaper Articles, Egnash; War Records, Heflin, and Larimore, Report; Websites, 3rd U.S., Dresbach, Hyatt, Tomb, and Robert; and handwritten letters, 4 Feb 46, and 20 Feb 46.
270 Handwritten letter. 20 Feb 46.
271 War Records, Larimore, Report.
272 This section was augmented from War Records, Larimore, Exhibit G; and Handwritten letter. 7 Apr 46. In Ethyl Larimore's scrapbooks.
273 War Records, Larimore, Army, and Special Orders.

CHAPTER 54: BURYING HEROES

274 Websites, Raia.
275 This and the next section were augmented from Books, Atkinson, *Where*, 35–36, Batzli, 4–6, 47, and Waple, 108; Newspaper Articles, Tibbetts; and Websites, Caisson Platoon, and The Changing; and a personal tour of the Caisson Platoon and stables by and interviews with specialist Justin Ekeren, Caisson Platoon/Honor Guard and Kirk Heflin, Director, The Old Guard Museum at Joint Base Henderson-Myer in 2016.
276 This section was augmented from Books, Waple, 110; and Newspaper Articles, Kaufman.

CHAPTER 55: A FOUNTAIN OF HOPE

277 Books, McDonough, 692.
278 This section was augmented from Books, Carlson, 109–111; and War Records, Calvert.
279 This section was augmented from Books, Jenkins, Chapters 2 and 3, and Letts; Periodicals, Jensen, and Reed; and Websites, Davis, Operation Cowboy, and Saving.

CHAPTER 56: ONE-LEG LEAD

280 Newspaper Articles, Bethea; and Quote at the National Infantry Museum, Columbus, GA.
281 This section was augmented from Books, Holland, 61–62, and Miller, William, 18; Websites, Army Reserve, Beauford, President, Truman Library Photographs, and Walker; handwritten letter. 4 Jun 46, and typed letter. 26 Aug 46; and Newspaper picture in Ethyl Larimore's scrapbooks.
282 Handwritten letter. 4 Jun 46.
283 Typed letter. 17 Jul 46.
284 Books, Holland, 61.
285 This section was augmented from Books, *The Tammy*, 1949, 23, and 1951, 21; handwritten letter. 4 Jun 46, and typed letters, 17 Jul 46, and 26 Aug 46; and Application found in Ethel Larimore's scrapbooks.
286 This section was augmented from Books, Baime, 142, 145, 199–200, and Waple, 110; Newspaper articles, Press release and pictures in Ethyl Larimore's scrapbooks; Websites, Truman; and Typed letter, 26 Aug 46, and 19 Sep 46.
287 Press release in Ethyl Larimore's scrapbooks.
288 Press release in Ethyl Larimore's scrapbooks.

CHAPTER 57: GAME OF THE CENTURY

289 Books, The U.S., 2.
290 This section was augmented from Books, Whittingham, 158; Newspaper Articles, Lapointe; Periodicals, The Price; Websites, 1946; and Typed letter. 12 Nov 46.
291 Typed letter, 12 Nov 46.
292 This section was augmented from Books, Baime, 202, and Waple, 115; and Typed letters, 8 Nov 46, and 12 Nov 46.
293 Typed letter. 8 Nov 46.

294   This section was augmented from War Records, Larimore, Exhibit G, and Exhibit K; and Handwritten letter, 9 Mar 47, and Typed Letter, 14 Apr 47.
295   War Records, Larimore, Exhibit G.
296   Handwritten letter. 9 Mar 47.
297   Handwritten letter. 9 Mar 47.
298   Handwritten letter. 9 Mar 47.
299   Ibid.
300   Typed Letter. 14 Apr 47.
301   Typed Letter. 17 Apr 47.
302   Ibid.

CHAPTER 58: THE APPEAL

303   Books, Brown, 214.
304   This entire chapter was adapted from Exhibit C of the Army Retiring Board meeting of 15 April 1947, the hearing transcript concerning Captain Philip B. Larimore, 0511609, Infantry, Army of the United States, found in Ethyl Larimore's scrapbooks. It should be noted that Phil's account included some demeaning language that—not surprisingly—was not recorded in the official transcript.
305   This chapter was augmented from Books, Gieck, 152; Periodicals, Monea; and War Records, Exhibit C of the Army Retiring Board meeting of 15 April 1947.

CHAPTER 59: THE GREAT DEBATE

306   Books, Egger, 114.
307   As a reminder, this chapter was adapted from the official transcript of the Army Retiring Board meeting held on April 15, 1947.
308   This chapter was augmented from War Records, Larimore, Exhibit C (the hearing transcript concerning Captain Philip B. Larimore, 0511609, Infantry, Army of the United States) found in Ethyl Larimore's scrapbooks.

CHAPTER 60: DECISION TIME

309   Books, Taggart, 373.
310   These two sections are augmented from Larimore, Exhibit C.
311   War Records, Larimore, Exhibit C.
312   This section was augmented from War Records, Larimore, Special Orders, and Transcript ; Websites, The Counties, and Maryland Hunt; and Handwritten card, 2 May 47, and Typed letter,14 May 47.
313   Ibid.
314   Typed letter. 14 May 47.
315   This section was augmented from Websites, Weather History for KDCA.
316   Newspaper Articles, Be-ribboned Major, DSC Awarded, D.S.Cross, Infantry Major, and Heroic Memphian.
317   Newspaper Articles, Infantry Major.
318   This section was augmented from Newspaper Articles, Just Jottings; and Websites, Letter from, Presidential, and Truman.
319   Websites, Truman.
320   Newspaper Articles, Just Jottings.
321   This section was augmented from Newspaper Articles, Horse Show, Kahn, and Raia; and Handwritten card, 30 Nov 47.
322   Newspaper Articles, Horse Show; and Handwritten card, 30 Nov 47.
323   Newspaper Articles, Kahn.

CHAPTER 61: THE AUCTION

324   Books, Soskil, 130.
325   This chapter was augmented from Newspaper Articles: Amputee, Amputee Hero, And the Auctioneer, Christmas, Hero's Lone, London, Service, A Soldier, and Just Jottings.

EPILOGUE

326   Books, Ambrose, *Band*, 293.
327   The Epilogue was augmented by Books, Ambrose, *Band*, 294, Glasser, 109, *The Tammy*, 1951, 21, Taggart, 189, Truscott, 464, and Whiting, inside of the front cover, 5; Periodicals, Disabled Vet; Personal Communication, Stoy; War Records, Calvert, Websites, Caisson Platoon, Mustermann, Vienna's, Watters, and World War II Veterans, along with a video of Phil's office mementos taken by Rick Larimore in 1999.
328   Senate. July 10, 1945: 8618.

329 Undated handwritten letter.
330 Books, Glasser, 109.
331 Books, Taggart, 189, Truscott, 464, and Whiting, inside of the front cover, 5; and Websites, Mustermann.
332 Jerry B. Jenkins, personal communication.
333 A handwritten note from "Bill."

FINAL THOUGHT

334 Websites, Province, Northeast.

ACKNOWLEDGMENTS

335 Books, Swainson, 496.

APPENDIX A: THE PIONEER LARIMORES AND THEIR HORSES

336 This chapter is augmented from Books, Fast, 11, Larimore 1–3, and Miller, Thomas, 51; Periodicals, Carden; and Websites Airs, Has Scotland, Larimore, Mount, Presidents, and Ulster-Scots.

APPENDIX D: GLOSSARY AND ABBREVIATIONS

337 Newspaper Articles, Sutherland.

BIBLIOGRAPHY

338 Books, Jenkins, Carol, 103.

APPENDIX I:

INDEX

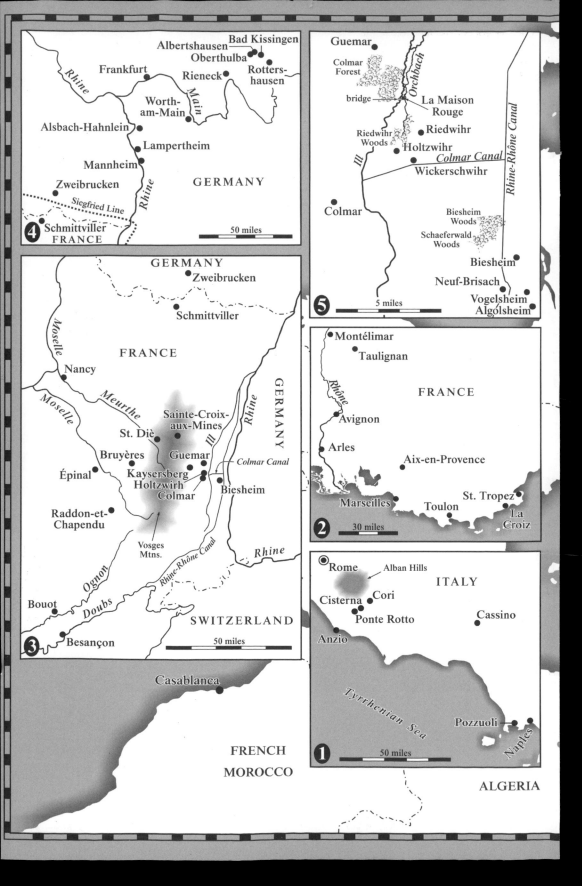

④

Albertshausen
Bad Kissingen
Oberthulba
Frankfurt
Rieneck
Rotters-
hausen
Rhine
Main
Worth-
am-Main
Alsbach-Hahnlein
Lampertheim
Mannheim
GERMANY
Zweibrucken
Rhine
Siegfried Line
Schmittviller
FRANCE

50 miles

⑤

Guemar
Orchbach
Colmar
Forest
bridge
La Maison
Rouge
Riedwihr
Woods
Riedwihr
Holtzwihr
Rhine-Rhône Canal
Colmar Canal
Wickerschwihr
Colmar
Biesheim
Woods
Schaeferwald
Woods
Biesheim
Neuf-Brisach
Vogelsheim
Algolsheim

5 miles

③

GERMANY
Zweibrucken
Schmittviller
Moselle
FRANCE
Nancy
Meurthe
Moselle
Sainte-Croix-
aux-Mines
St. Diè
Ill
GERMANY
Bruyères
Guemar
Colmar Canal
Épinal
Kaysersberg
Holtzwirh
Colmar
Biesheim
Rhine
Raddon-et-
Chapendu
Vosges
Mtns.
Rhine-Rhône Canal
Rhine
Ognon
Bouot
Doubs
SWITZERLAND
Besançon

50 miles

②

Montélimar
Taulignan
Rhône
FRANCE
Avignon
Arles
Aix-en-Provence
St. Tropez
Marseilles
Toulon
La
Croix

30 miles

①

Rome
Alban Hills
ITALY
Cisterna
Cori
Ponte Rotto
Cassino
Anzio
Tyrrhenian Sea
Pozzuoli
Naples

50 miles

Casablanca

FRENCH
MOROCCO

ALGERIA